Tunesmith

INSIDE THE ART OF SONGWRITING

Jimmy Webb

HYPERION

New York

Library of Congress Cataloging-in-Publication Data
Webb, Jimmy.
Tunesmith : inside the art of songwriting / Jimmy Webb.—1st ed.
    p.   cm.
Includes index.
    1. Popular music—Writing and publishing.   I. Title.
MT67.W32   1998   97-32584
782.42164′ 13—dc21   CIP
        ISBN 0-7868-6131-2

Book design by Christine Weathersbee

First Paperback Edition
Paperback ISBN 0-7868-8488-6

5 7 9 10 8 6 4

Talking about music is like
dancing about architecture.
—Martin Mull

HOW TO WRITE A SONG

by Harry Nilsson

If you write it on guitar
Place your guitar upon your knee
If you write it on piano
Don't do that
Place your fingers on the strings
Of your guitar, not your piano
If you write it on piano
Don't do that
Now strum or press to get a feeling
This might take a little time
Now think of something sad or something funny
Which inevitably brings us to the rhyme
Let's assume you're just an asshole
And there's nothing in your brain
It might help if you remember
These helpful little hints
Don't try to rhyme silver with anything
That goes for orange as well
Now notice how cleverly I just used them both
And all I have to do is rhyme well
You've got to be tricky
To avoid these words takes talent
So never ever trap yourself like that
Or you'll end up saying words like
Ballant, phallant, gallant, wallant
Callant, ballant...well

I'm sure you'll catch on fast
Now some tips on tempo and
Some subjects to avoid
Like the use of the word "baby"
Unless you really have to say it
As to tempo, or as we say "time"
That's strictly up to you because
That depends on how to play it
Now let's do one
Now think of a rhyme
That's it, you're doing fine
Now think of the good time we just had together
If you practice these instructions
On the boat of song you'll sail
And if you listen very carefully
I'm sure you shalln't fail
I said shalln't, yeah shalln't
That rhymes with talent, that takes talent
That is talent
Oh my God, I've done it again
Shalln't rhymes with talent
That takes talent
That is talent
Oh, I can't stand it
Oh my God, I've done it again

Without my friend, manager, earliest editor,
research coordinator, computer-operator
and confidante, Robin Siegel,
this writing would have been abandoned
a thousand times over.

acknowledgments

I would like to thank everyone who went out of their way to help make *Tunesmith* a reality:

The Hyperion Team Editor David Cashion, Publisher Bob Miller, David Z. Cohen (cover designer), Tracey George (publicist), David Lott (production editor) and Christine Weathersbee (interior designer).

Interviews Lynn Ahrens, Jane Arginteanu, Burt Bacharach, Alan and Marilyn Bergman, Stephen Bishop, Felice Bryant, John Bucchino, Lynn Crystal, Hal David, Frank Di Minno, Michael Feinstein, Irwin Fisch, Stephen Flaherty, Nanci Griffith, Henry Gross, Adam Guettel, Bobby Hart, Billy Joel, Jay Landers, Robert Lantz, Jerry Leiber, Barry Mann, Linda Newmark, Mac Pirkle, Frances Preston, Joyce Rice, Tommy Riggs, Lindy Robbins, Norman Rothstein, Stephen Schwartz, Carly Simon, J.D. Souther, Michael Stipe, Mike Stoller, John Titta, Diane Warren, Cynthia Weil, Peyton Wimmer and Peter Yarrow.

Research Bill Zimmerman

Invaluable Assistance ASCAP's Michael Kerker, ASCAP's Karen Sherry, BMG Music Publishing, BMI's Pat Baird, Bug, Pat Collins, EMI Music Publishing, The Ezra Pound Estate, Famous Music, Gelfand, Rennert & Feldman, Melani Gold, Gold Mountain Management, Hal Leonard Publishing, The Harry Fox Agency, House of Bryant Publications, L.L.C., Jobete Music Co., Inc., Jonico Music, The National Academy of Popular Music's Songwriter's Hall of Fame, No Soap Productions, P.A.M. Management, Maritime Music, Inc., Robin Mathiesen, Music Sales Corporation's Yolanda Blum, Lisa Phelps, PolyGram Music Publishing's Joan Schulman, Razor & Tie Music, Georgiana Regalbuto, R.E.M./Athens, L.L.C., The Richmond Organization, Rodgers & Hammerstein Music, Nancy Roof, Michon Stanco, Warner Bros. Publications' Rosemarie Gawelko, Warner Bros. Publications' David Olsen, Meredith Williams, Williamson Music's Kathy McCullough and Graham Woolwine.

Special Thanks Lloyd Biggles, Montana Dodel, George Fearon, Danny Ferguson, Art Garfunkel, Janis Ian, Marc Jacobson, Photographer Carolyn Jones & Staff, Mick Jones, Carole King, Jim Legg, Ron McGowan, Joni Mitchell, Pat Mulcahy, Randy Newman, Donald Oliver, Paul Simon, Jim Steinblatt, Fred Tackett, Mary Tiegreen, Ed Weisel, John Wilk and Paul Zollo.

preface

The word "Tunesmith" is on one hand the trivial and offhand diminutive with which gossip columnists have been known to refer to creators of such gravity as Johnny Mercer, a *lyricist*, and on the other, a self-demeaning affectation employed by many composers to camouflage egos larger than the Death Star (as in "I am but an humble tunesmith."). In any case, it was not my definitive choice for the title of this book even though it has always been the *working title* and I would like to explain how that came to be.

When I was a somewhat strange and lonely child even while growing up among four siblings in West Texas and Southwestern Oklahoma, my secret yet true educators were not the like of Mrs. Wise—God bless her—whose fourth grade field trip consisted of the discovery of a roiling sand storm in the middle of a bone-dry Red River. Instead, science fiction writers like Ray Bradbury, Issac Asimov, and Arthur C. Clarke informed me as to the shape of things to come. From Bradbury I learned *expression*, from Asimov *form*, from Robert A. Heinlein *sexual politics*, and from Lloyd Biggles *aesthetics*. In Biggles's novelette, "Orphan of the Void," (1960) a n'er-do-well alcoholic songwriter named Marty Worrel writes a "homing song" that inexplicably sends abductees from all over the galaxy on a search for their planets of origin. In "Spare the Rod," (1958) Biggles predicted computer-composing formats like Finale and Performer (he called them "music writers") and outpaced today's computers with a "word selector" for poets in his ironic tale about a robot that teaches violin. In "Tunesmith" (1957), a long story with every bit of scope and pro-fundity called for in a great novel, he foresaw a nightmarish culture where "songs" as we know them had vanished from the public's consciousness, replaced by the "coms" or singing commercials. Not only had all other music, including classical, disappeared, but rigorous standards of mediocrity were enforced to ensure that even "the coms" were bland and uninspired. In this aes-thetically destitute world there were no concerts or dances, no art, literature, or poetry. Biggles's hero, Erlin Baque, held his considerable talent in check while searching vainly for a single surviving pianist, bassoonist, or piccolo player. In Biggles's story the ending is a happy one. Baque reinvents songwriting and saves culture by sacrificing himself to the media moguls as a kind of Techno-Christ. All of Earth becomes a vast conservatory.

When I spoke to Biggles on the telephone and told him I was thinking of calling my book "Tunesmith," he seemed happy that one of his early disciples had gone on to be a songwriter, but cautioned me that "it's a lot harder to write a book!" In the four years that have elapsed since, his warning has sounded many times in my imagination as I have wrestled with my book's propensity to annoyingly redefine itself, change its mission, and yes, even its title. At the heart of the struggle has been the fact that logic, instinct and experience indicate that much of the material presented is useless for the following reasons:

1. Inspiration comes from the guts.

2. Technique is a personal and very private conceit.

3. Creativity as a concept is perhaps not well understood
   by the people who practice it most successfully.

And fourth, communicating and describing the complex abstractions represented in a genuine and moving work of art is in all likelihood a contradictory exercise. Like a sodden Bronze-age wood carving upon excavation from the sea bed which—under water—displays the most delicate nuance of light, shadow and craftsmanship, but when brought into the dry light of day crumbles into meaningless pulp even as the archeologist tries to touch it, photograph it, analyze and then *preserve* it?

Oscar Hammerstein II wrote of his kindly and brilliant *Notes On Craft*, "I am discontented with what I have written here," and my God, so am I! But I have done it out of love for songwriting and songwriters whose company I prefer above all others, though to be truthful, we are not by nature a particularly jolly crew. Mostly I have done it for those who still believe in the great power of songs and who may be attempting the delicate transition from amateur to professional like my sons, Chris, Justin and James. (Corey, Charles and Camila are songwriters as well though they may not know it yet.) There are others who may benefit from a candid portrayal of the way one songwriter works. Keep the faith.

Jimmy L. Webb
Heald Pond, Maine
April 20, 1998

contents

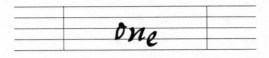

OUT OF THIN AIR

You might wake up some morning,
To the sound of something moving past your window in the wind,
And if you're quick enough to rise,
You'll catch the fleeting glimpse of someone's fading shadow . . .
—BOB LIND,
"ELUSIVE BUTTERFLY"

"So what have we got on the Housewife Tapes?" she asked her producer. "She" is one of the most successful and talented singers in the history of America's recorded music. There was an unpromising silence as he tended the recording console for a moment. Then he swiveled his chair around to face her.

"The truth?"

She just smiled.

"Notha," he said, and went back to his faders and pots and VU meters.

Let us put an end to the myth that amateur songwriters do not have the slimmest chance of being heard by anyone of importance. Every living soul in the record business, bar none, is looking for The Great Song. Oscar Hammerstein once said, "The people who claim that the publishing and songwriting game is a tight ring into which beginners are not permitted are usually people with carelessly written manuscripts in their brief-cases. The men who write the good songs haven't time for all this kind of talk. They are too busy writing and loving what they write before they show it to anybody else." The Housewife Tapes? That is the great singer's name for the flood of unsolicited material from amateurs that rises ceiling high whenever word goes out that she's making another album. It is her claim that never in over two decades in the record business has she recorded a song from one of these. But still she asks, "So what have we got on the Housewife Tapes?"

There is no recording artist, manager, producer or publisher who would not experience a transcendent thrill should they happen to discover some perfect gem on such an unlikely tape. So what is the primary factor that separates the rejected amateur songwriter from the accepted profes-sional? Probably this: Most amateurs do not regard the writing of songs as serious hard work. Indeed, there are members of my family who believe that worrisome character flaws and much moral ruin have evolved from the fact that I've never had a real job. In reality, however, songwriting is Hell on Earth. If it isn't, then you're doing it wrong.

Are you still with me? Then let's take the following concept and eradicate it from our minds forever: "Songwriting might be a fun way to make some easy money if I get lucky." "Lucky" would seem to be the operational word in this sentence, in which case it would be wiser for the gambler to embark on a career as a film actor. Oscar Hammerstein also said, "My reservation about amateurs is that they are money-mad. The professional loves songs and loves songwriting. The amateurs want some quick money and think that songwrit-ing is an easy way to get it." Movie stars make a hundred or a thousand times more money than songwriting stars, and besides, everyone knows what they look like. Let's consider some goals that are more specific: "I would like to make a living as a songwriter," or "I have my heart set on writing The Great American Musical," or "I want to write those clever country tunes," or "I'm a good singer but I want to write my own material and write it extremely well." A writer's ultimate purpose is in many ways irrelevant because a good song-writer can do all of these things and even do them all at the same time (within reason). The paramount joy of the craft is that however simply it is begun it can take the writer on a lifelong voyage across many wondrous and diverse musical seas. Versatility is the hallmark of the great professional songwriters. Consider Lennon and McCartney together and separately. "I Want to Hold

Your Hand," "Norwegian Wood," "Penny Lane," "I Am the Walrus," "Here, There and Everywhere." Such stunning facility is not necessarily a birthright, though some are born with quicker minds and nimbler fingers than others. It could easily be said of one who has "talent" that he or she knows *how* to do what they *want* to do. A good songwriter should be able to write a song in any genre for virtually any purpose.

Countless times by people from other vocations I have been asked: "Where do you get your ideas?" I would worry somewhat about such a person's potential development into a professional songwriter. Let me give you an example. I was sitting at home the other night watching a Public Service announcement on TV and heard the announcer say in voice-over, "At the place where good and evil meet, the victim of crime is alone." Immediately I started thinking about a song, fascinated by a place where good and evil might possibly meet. Song ideas are the most intense long-ings of the soul and its deepest regrets. For the sake of argument, let me propose that they arrange themselves in these nine categories:

1. People, places or events in our memory that make us happy, sad or angry: "Last Night When We Were Young"—Harold Arlen & E. Y. Harburg

2. People, places or events that are affecting us at the present time by the same criteria: "You've Lost That Lovin' Feelin' "—Spector, Weil & Mann

3. People, places or events that are likely to affect us in the future by the same criteria: "Any Day Now"—Burt Bacharach & Bob Hilliard

4. Satire; sarcasm and humor of a personal or political nature, usu-ally exercised at the expense of others but sometimes aimed at ourselves: "A Simple Desultory Philippic"—Paul Simon

5. Songs emanating from fictional characters (untrustworthy narra-tors) whose identities we assume in order to make our point—serious or humorous: "Rednecks"—Randy Newman

6. The recounting of events in story form—the true ballad: "El Paso"—Marty Robbins

7. Silly music. Comedic and/or novelty numbers that teach dances: "Ahab the Arab"—Ray Stevens

8. Abstract surrealism: "Strawberry Fields"—Lennon & McCartney

9. The allegorical tale: "The Day the Music Died"—Don McLean

Are you buying that? Perhaps you can think of other "kinds" of songs. Let's just say that if a man or woman doesn't feel strongly enough about something or someone to write about the issue, helpful hints will not suffice. I have never heard a great song wherein the writer proclaims that he or she is not upset or excited about anything in particular. Where do ideas come from? From caring (or loathing). One of Carly Simon's recent albums (*Letters Never Sent*) was inspired entirely by actual letters that she had chosen not to mail and subsequently found in a forgotten cache in her house. (I wrote a song—"Simile"—for Joni Mitchell about a letter I had sent her that ended up behind her couch, resulting in the fact that she didn't answer it until quite a few years later when she was in the process of moving.)

To be more specific about ideas, it is hard to prove where songwriting is concerned that "idea" and "title" are not virtually synonymous. For instance, that one might hear professional writers or other insiders say that Paul Simon's title "Still Crazy After All These Years" is a great "idea" for a song is important to remember. The following is not an "idea":

I want to write a song about someone who goes through acute mood swings—from euphoria to emotional exhaustion. I love this person and want to address the song to him.

If, however, you add the following sentence: "I want to call the song 'Problem Child,' " *then* you have an "idea," even though the song may not end up being called "Problem Child." While writing the lyric and melody a completely different fulcrum may manifest itself, but you will have begun to write with a specific idea tied to a title. You have announced a destination and all your efforts from then on will be dedicated to arriving at that destination (though when you arrive at your anchorage it may be known by a different name). This is what a truly great artist does when he decides who or what he is going to paint. (He must already know *how* to paint; do not confuse the "how to" with "the manner in which" he will paint.)

It is quite common for someone to have a great idea for a song. Many people do. I have heard a plethora of these ideas discussed in social situations and as quickly forgotten. Sadly, I have seen many half-finished songs based on a perfectly valid and interesting premise. I have been asked by others to execute their song ideas for them, some of them excellent. T. S. Eliot wrote in "We Are the Hollow Men": "between the idea and the reality, between the motion and the act, falls the shadow." I've always suspected he might have been speaking to his colleagues—other writers. How do we get through Eliot's shadow zone and bring our songs into the light of day? Almost without exception every great songwriter whom I know personally or that I've heard of or read about, uses a specific technique. Some free-associate on legal pads for hours and then pare lists of cross-referenced words or phrases down to related components that can be used in lyric lines. Many write draft after draft—as many as twenty—of a whole lyric in composition notebooks, lining out their less fortunate efforts as they go. Some sit at a piano or hold a guitar and chain-of-consciousness sing-any-old-thing-that-comes-into-their-heads at the outset—getting a "sound" first and working out the intricacies of meaning later. Another well-known writer stands in front of huge speakers and "word jams" to tracks that are already finished. Some write lyrics. Some only music. Some write both and among those, many write the words first. Others write a catchy tune and add words that fit. Many move the lyrics and melody along simultaneously in careful steps. All these techniques are valid. It is almost a certainty that before a writer achieves full-fledged professional status they will have developed a unique method of working their tail off. But there is one thing that these gentlemen and ladies have in common—whatever their style. Virtually all of them keep a rhyming dictionary and a thesaurus close by. No shame here. In fact it is not a very lucid act to attempt the writing of verse in any form without these unless one happens to be a Mensa. And even then . . .

I find that other reference materials can be invaluable: *Bartlett's Familiar Quotations* for either avoiding or searching for clichés (sometimes a cliché can be a valuable component of a lyric if recognized for what it is); specific research material when writing about an unfamiliar subject; but mostly the work of other writers of song, prose and poetry. Writers must read. One corollary being that composers must listen. There are some very superficial and obvious reasons for this. Writers may benefit from the influence of like minds, particularly the brightest and most successful. One might be more aware of "the fashion" if one's desire is to emulate those who are successful (not a very good reason). I am more concerned with a reasonably comprehensive knowledge of the history of the art form and here we have a good reason indeed for reading and listening. In his splendid book on craft for prose writers, *The Art of Fiction*, John Gardner states, "No ignoramus—no writer who has kept himself innocent of education—has ever produced great art. One trouble with having read nothing worth reading is that one never fully understands the other side of one's argument, never understands that the argument is an old one (all great arguments are) . . ." To bring this fine and probably old argument into the area of our concern: How can one write an original song if one hasn't heard and "read" at least a few of the most famous and best examples that have ever been written?

In the distant past composers were most often very learned men who not only read but wrote, were critics, poets and autobiographers. In a precursor to the "singer/songwriter" phenomenon of the late sixties, many wrote the text, or "libretto," to their own operas. Whatever their level of scholarly enlightenment, songwriters and composers are and always have been somewhat notorious in their unwillingness to subject themselves to the horror of listening to someone else's work, particularly a contemporary who might be perceived as a competitor, especially to a "work in progress."

A songwriter whom I idolize came to see me at the Troubadour a few years ago and visited backstage after the show. I invited him to my house in Encino, California, for a game of billiards and a couple of beers. He waffled noticeably and I found myself wondering if for some reason he had reason to dislike me or if it was just a matter of indifference. Finally, he spit it out, so to speak. "I'd really like to come over for a beer, Jimmy, as long as nobody plays any *music*," he said. It was not that he was anathematic toward *my* music—or so he claimed—he was terrified of hearing *any* music.

On another occasion I was seated at a banquet table at the BMI awards in Nashville next to the reigning Southern Icon of Nashville Songwriters. This man was to famous songs what Colonel Sanders was to fried chicken. We struck up a conversation and he was warm and kindly toward me. After a while he offered me an invitation.

"Would y'all like to come out and see my Southern mansion?" he drawled. I replied that I would consider it a great privilege.

"Good," he said and then paused. "Only thing," he continued, "y'all don't play no songs, y'all hear?"

Without doubt some of this reluctance has a valid foundation exclusive of petty egotism. Songwriters are usually working on something and may fear being overtly influenced by a strong outing from a respected colleague. I don't like to listen to radio—sometimes for three or four days at a time when I'm writing. Often it causes me to forget something I'm trying to remember and at other times I have found myself subliminally "borrowing" something I did not intend to appropriate.

So when an amateur songwriter submits a tape of songs to a professional songwriter in hope of assistance he is committing what is essentially an unnatural act for the following reasons:

1. The professional songwriter is usually not equipped logistically for the promotion of someone else's music.
2. He is preoccupied with his own endeavors and unlikely—except in very rarefied circumstances—to diminish his own chances of placing a song with an important artist by taking on an amateur song as a cause célèbre.
3. He is letting himself in for serious legal trouble by even *accepting* a tape from an amateur. (It is sad that a few greedy individuals have spoiled the 1960s spirit of free and easy camaraderie by harassing brilliant men like Billy Joel with long and costly nuisance suits.)

In reference to the latter and most pressing concern I spoke with good friend and angelic chanteuse, Nanci Griffith.

I was introduced to Julie Gold and a week later she gave me "From a Distance." Otherwise I don't know how Julie would have ever been discovered as a writer. In 1986 Christine Lavin introduced me to her and Julie asked, "Can I send you some things?" And I said, "Sure!" This must have been at Folk City or the Bottom Line, and a week after she sent me "From a Distance" we recorded it. At the time I was open to listening to people's tapes, but since then I've been sued by someone I never heard of or had access to, and because of that I've been very, very hesitant to take tapes from someone I don't know.

It is a paradox. It is possible to get into trouble by listening—both legally and creatively. On the other hand—and this is my view—we run a much higher risk when we go through life wearing earplugs. I was speaking to a young writer and member of a very successful band who was standing at the bar in the Bottom Line, in New York City. His band was enjoying a runaway hit and I was engaging him on the subject of the abysmal ignorance that young writers exhibited toward even fairly recent material like that of the Beatles. "You know," I said, "there's a record on the charts right now that has a line verbatim from 'Blackbird.'" "What a shame," he replied—fervently sympathetic. "Yeah," I blundered on. " 'Take these broken wings and learn to fly,'" I sang in sarcastic imitation. My companion's face turned white. "I wrote that," he said. "That's our record."

I am sure that he didn't mean to plagiarize McCartney, but it is also my certain knowledge that he was not a hairsbreadth from a trouncing by an eight-hundred-pound lawyer. Is there any excuse for this? Sadly I write that I am hard pressed to think of one.

In 1971 when Harry Nilsson and I were chumming around London together and he was recording the *Nilsson Schmilsson* album produced by Richard Perry (one of the best albums ever made), he came to me as a pal over a snifter of brandy. He asked me, almost contritely, if he could borrow the phrase "up, up and away" for a delightful send-up song called "Gotta Get Up."

> *Down by the sea she knew a sailor who had been to war*
> *She never even knew a sailor before*
> *She never even knew his name*
> *He'd come to town and he would pound her for a couple of days*
> *And then he'd sail across the bubbly waves*
> *And those were happier days*
> *But now . . .*
>
> *Gotta Get Up*
> *Gotta get out*
> *Gotta get home before the morning comes*
>
> *What if I'm late*
> *Gotta big day*
> *Gotta get home before the sun comes up*
> *Up and away*

Gotta big day
Sorry can't stay gotta run yeah

Gotta get home
Pick up the phone
Gotta let some people know I'm gonna be late.
                    —Harry Nilsson,
                    "Gotta Get Up"

I was impressed by his thoughtfulness in "checking" with me even though the phrase "up, up and away" had first appeared in a 1941 radio show about Superman. (He was asking to borrow something that had already been borrowed.) Knowledge of and respect for the work of others is the first essential ingredient in the development of a truly effective technique if for no other reason than because, as John Gardner states, "All great writing is—in a sense—imitation of great writing." That is the way my career started, imitating the writers of songs that I heard on the radio in my early teens. As new songwriters we walk in the footsteps of colossi. Whatever our field—country, rock, pop, blues or Broadway—it is from their influence that we will ultimately derive our chances at "genius" and "originality."

So what about before the Beatles? Those same Beatles who, like Paul Simon and Art Garfunkel, were heavily influenced by the graceful and crystalline harmonies of Don and Phil Everly? Who wrote those Everly Brothers songs? Many of the great ones—"All I Have to Do Is Dream" and "Take a Message to Mary" come to mind—were written by Felice and Boudleaux Bryant. (How many songwriters in the twenty- to thirty-year-old bracket know who wrote "Wake Up Little Susie"?) And before the Bryants (who were they influenced by?) there was Hank Williams. And before that what about Noel Coward, Larry Hart and Harry Warren? Charlie Chaplin? "Now wait a minute!" I can hear you saying. "You don't mean to say that Hank Williams was influenced by Charlie Chaplin?" There is a unilateral quality to influence and emulation that transcends "styles" of music. "Smile," Chaplin's heartrending and ironic masterpiece, would seem to be the mirror image of Williams's "I'm So Lonesome I Could Cry." (Arthur Fieldler, who achieved near deific status conducting the Boston Pops Orchestra for over thirty-six years, said there were only two kinds of music—good and bad.)

Recently a friend of mine was talking music with his thirty-year-old daughter, a journalism major at university who wants to specialize in covering the entertainment field. "Well, probably the greatest was Cole," he said. "Oh yeah, Nat King Cole . . . right," she replied.

"No, darling," he said. "I mean Cole Porter." She gave him a blank look. "Dad, who's Cole Porter?" (Sammy Cahn was right about the Songwriters Hall of Fame Museum. We needed one desperately.)

Of course (so they say in America) it all goes back to Stephen Foster. There are irritations associated with many musicologists and their blind acceptance of Foster's position as the father of all American musical things—one being that it is commonly supposed that he invented the "form of the American popular song." Specifically it is stated that he originated the so-called A/B structure (which we will hereafter refer to as verse/chorus). Consider this verse and chorus from the ancient Irish lament "Kerrick Fergus":

Verse: *If I could go over to Kerrick Fergus*
          Or else to Antrim or to Ballingrave
          Then the deep sea ocean I would swim over
          The deepest ocean my love to find

Chorus: *But the seas are deep and I can't swim over*
          Nor do I have light wings to fly
          But if I had me a Kerry boatsman
          Then I would row my love, my love and I.*

In England and America this song more than likely metamorphosed into "The River Is Wide" (also known as "There Is a Ship") a verse/verse/verse form, the last of which goes:

The water is wide
I cannot get o'er
Neither have I
The wings to fly
Give me a boat
That can carry two
And boat shall row
My love and I

*The exact technical description of a "chorus" is included in a subsequent chapter.

Perhaps Foster only reinvented or *imitated* the verse/chorus structure of the Irish folk song. What he was, without embellishment, was the first famous American songwriter and creator of the first truly "native" American songs. (He was also a bit of a political agitator, becoming a writer of antiseparatist propaganda ditties as tensions between the North and South increased.) It is widely accepted that his "native" quality—which presumably owed a great deal to the work songs, chants and spirituals of Negro laborers—all but disappeared with Foster's death (January 13, 1864, in New York City) and did not reappear in American musical culture until the 1880s.

Another major irritation regarding Foster's preeminence as the Father of American Pop Music is that such hero worship for the most part ignores the contributions of the great numbers of black poets and country singers who either preceded or paralleled his heyday and without doubt put their stamp on him: "Gwine to run all night, gwine to run all day." During the late 1800s black performers began to copy white minstrel shows which were, in themselves, copies of black minstrel shows. It is said many a white person probably got their first taste of real black music in whorehouses, but the breakthrough into the white world of music publishing was first accomplished by a northern Negro named James A. Bland, who composed more than seven hundred songs for black minstrel shows. Another African American forerunner, Ben Harney, was always assumed by blacks and whites alike to be a white man.

To return to Foster's work, it suffers somewhat in comparison with the generic folk music that predates him, those seamless masterpieces that someone once said had been "worn smooth by millions of voices like pebbles in the bottom of a stream" and benefited from being fitted together in a vivid New World mosaic. Such songwriting entailed collaboration through time and space. No single human being lives long enough to write a song in this way. It is in the Scots, Irish and English ballads and reels transplanted to the Deep South, subtly altered by African and Christian laments, pounding rhythms and "field hollers," that the roots of modern American songwriting reside. Am I stating the obvious? There are perhaps two generations of young American writers, most of whom do not know this and might not care if they did.

Is rap music "new"? It seems obvious that its American roots lie in the "talking blues" tradition of the Delta country . . . and even so unlikely a composer as Schoenberg introduced "Sprechstimme," a kind of classical rap where the singer lets the note immediately fall or rise as in speaking, producing something between the two. There is probably no literal discernable difference between the emotional content, convention and stylistic application of a modern rap song and a fifteen-hundred-year-old Maori war chant. Part of any contemporary musical attitude is a tendency to ignore or minimize the musical engenderments of the past. Our generation did:

> *Why don't y'all fade away? Don't try to dig what we all say . . .*
>
> —Pete Townsend,
>
> "My Generation"

I still remember the exasperation I would feel on a Sunday afternoon when my father brought forth his collection of "Mugsy" Spaniard and "Fats" Waller records. When he started spinning the "Big Bands," I left the house, a little closer to being one of John Gardner's "ignoramuses." But this book is not about the history of American popular songs. Such material is readily available though none is likely to eclipse the seminal work by Alec Wilder (*American Popular Song: The Great Innovators, 1900–1950*).

There is another even more practical reason to read and listen. It is from the poetry of Dylan Thomas, Patrick Cavanaugh, Pablo Neruda, William Carlos Williams and other mad and gentle spirits that we learn the use of words. We learn that hard words can describe delicate things and soft words unspeakably horrible things. We make friends with new words and perhaps we decide that there are some with which we would rather not be acquainted. We discern the way in which these words can be rhymed or not rhymed. We see the way they can be jammed together in unlikely alliances that delight and entertain and describe in a way that no word can when standing alone. We learn that words create the colors that poets use to paint images on the mind itself. We come to understand that not all great poetry is lyrical but that all great lyrics are poetic. As Richard Rodgers said of collaborator Oscar Hammerstein, "The work of my collaborator and friend has been called poetry; it has been called light verse; it has even been called song-writing."

Which is to say that all great lyrics use the devices of poetry—*metaphor, simile, imagery, alliteration* and *meter*, among others. There are those who would have you believe that as a songwriter you are somehow exempt from the literary standards of true poets, novelists or other intellectuals. This is what I call the Least Common Denominator Syndrome and a spiritual dead end. There is no intrinsic virtue in ignorance.

In a similar vein when we listen to the violin concerto of Samuel Barber or the choral and orchestral works of John Corigliano or any of the sweeping symphonies of Ralph Vaughn Williams we learn that chords are living things; powerful engines that carry melody from one place to another. We learn how effortlessly melody can soar and that a chord can have a different bass than its root. We learn that we can *substitute* one chord for another and that dissonance is pleasing and essential. In just one of the Vaughn Williams symphonies we find enough inspiration and raw harmonic material to underpin a thousand songs. Many of the great composers set folk songs and other lyrics to their music, among them Purcell, Beethoven, Vaughn Williams, Britten, Mendelssohn, Haydn and Copland. The legacy of the great composers is to have shown us the far boundaries of musical expression. It is our responsibility to pay attention.

Not to say that I advocate borrowing piecemeal from classical composers or any other source. The story is told about Arthur Schwartz explaining to friends that he had taken on a particularly stringent series of professional obligations, and that the friends wondered aloud, "My God, isn't that going to take an awful lot out of you?" "Yes," he replied. "But not as much as it will take out of Bach, Beethoven, and Brahms." There is nothing more humbling than to proudly play a new song for a couple of friends and have them say, "Oh yes, but isn't that 'Come Back to Sorrento'?" Then, of course, they can't resist humming the offending notes to point out obvious similarities. (That one has never heard "Come Back to Sorrento" is little consolation and less of an excuse, as already noted.)

Sometimes these benignly malicious observations can be taken with a grain of salt. A dear friend of mine from London and an ace publisher— on a well-lubricated evening about five years ago—proudly produced a book at the end of our dinner. "This book," he said with much emphasis, "has every melody ever written inside." (Shades of Johnny Carson and Ed McMahon.) "Therefore," he continued, "it also contains every melody that ever will be written." "Not," I said even as I opened this marvelous creation and looked wide-eyed at the neat columns of musical phrases in notation, organized in every conceivable category by all composers back to and including the first caveman. "You're on!" I shouted. "Fifty pounds!" (Who is ignorant of the fact that a Cockney is unable to refuse a wager?)

"'By the Time I Get to Phoenix,'" I challenged, concealing a deep insecurity that I was not only a charlatan but fifty pounds poorer. It was an hour later. The table was cleared—when Terry (for that was his name) pounced. "Aha!" he said, "I've got you, mate!" He proudly pointed out a phrase by Puccini that—excepting one semi-quaver—was note for note the first line of "By the Time I Get to Phoenix." I refused to pay. (After all, this was the same man who had once bet me a hundred pounds on the outcome of a heavyweight fight he had previously taped off the telly.)

In the pop music field begging, borrowing and stealing is so prevalent as not to even cause the proverbial eyebrow to be raised. "The guy who wrote 'Handy Man' [Jimmy Jones]," Boy George chortled, "tried to sue us over 'Karma Chameleon.' I might have heard it once, but it certainly wasn't something I sat down and said, 'Yeah, I want to copy this.' We gave him ten pence and an apple." I must risk observing that on this particular occasion Mr. George would have done well to steal more and gloat less. "Artists everywhere steal mercilessly all the time and I think this is healthy." So says Peter Gabriel, even though one must wonder if Mr. Gabriel would be so sanguine about an interloper collecting monies on a copyright that was obviously derived from one of his songs. R.E.M.'s Michael Stipe concurred during a recent conversation with me when he stated, "There's going to be some emulation and there's going to be some blatant stealing—that's pop music at its best!—and that's good and fine." In my view part of rock 'n' roll's roguish image of itself is tied up in this outlaw "it's only rock 'n' roll" mentality. Of course this is augmented with some considerable justification by the hand-me-down traditions of blues and country players in that long-lost era of provincial tutelage, but at *that* stage of the game the stakes were not so high as to induce a nosebleed. Ry Cooder maintains to this day that during some friendly jams with the Rolling Stones in London in the early '70s that Mick Jagger and company purloined virtually all the licks, motifs and rhythmic patterns for their humongous *Sticky Fingers*.

If we carried such concerns to extremes we would never get a melody written but would become full-time researchers instead, perhaps letting our computers devise complicated and never-before-heard combinations. It is a mathematical fact that only twelve notes can be arranged in multiples of millions of unique sequences. Surely all the melodies have *not* been written.

In this light it would seem foolhardy for a composer to imitate too closely the well-known melodic lines of a Puccini or Gershwin, even though inspired imitation can sometimes be raised to the level of an art form. In his book *Nice Work If You Can Get It* (Hyperion), Michael Feinstein reports that Gershwin was rumored to have stolen themes for his concertos from works by Rachmaninoff, who was said to have been quite outraged. Andrew Lloyd Webber, in spite of his megalamoney, has been constantly assailed by detractors and musicologists who claim that he owes way too much to Puccini and others, though I must say that in my own view Puccini has been least damaged in the exchange. He's not the only one! Jerome Kern, according to reputable sources, also pilfered a duet from a Puccini opera. These stories go on and on. One of the most memorable contemporary examples is the stunning *Glass Houses* album (1980) by Billy Joel. Here is a sometimes tongue-in-cheek then deadly serious pastiche that is akin to fine art forgery. Joel demonstrates that like a virtuoso stand-up impressionist he can run the gamut of imitating pop's most sacred cows: the Stones, Sam Cooke, the Four Seasons, just to name a few. One song in particular, "Through the Long Night with You," sounds so much like Lennon and McCartney circa 1965 that the first time I heard it I was sure that it was a Beatles record I had overlooked. (It has become one of my favorite songs.) Many critics seem to have missed Joel's point entirely, not realizing that this kind of imitation was deliberate, and obviously so. The writer was not at a loss to create songs of his own but was paying a fascinating and deft homage. How does an artist get to the point where they can imitate another at this level of perfection?

Linda Ronstadt, on being asked what a young person should do if they wanted a career in the music business, replied, "Learn to read music. Learn to play an instrument." While the untrained take great delight in pointing out examples of musically illiterate geniuses there is profound truth in Linda's deceptively simple answer. Of course if one intends to be a lyricist and nothing but a lyricist then it becomes a moot point. But pure lyricists labor under one serious handicap: they have to find somebody to write with. Many people who collaborate in the contemporary field write both music and lyrics, and so these encounters become what might be called *double collaborations*. Each of the partners could write a complete song in a pinch.

The songwriter does not need to be a virtuoso pianist or guitarist. It suffices to have a repertoire of interesting chords—not just simple tri-ads—and to know how to fit them together and write them down. (To be able to quickly jot down a chord pattern over a printed lyric line is to save hundreds of hours "backtracking" in order to remember what has just been written especially when there is no recording equipment readily avail-able. The muse surprises capriciously.)

At the outset I played almost exclusively by ear but fortunately I had a God-fearing spare-the-rod-and-spoil-the-child Southern Baptist mother who insisted that I learn to read music, at least well enough to be church pianist, which I accomplished by age twelve. When I became a profes-sional songwriter at seventeen I quickly realized the benefits of knowing how to read music. To know how to read music is, in a sense, to automati-cally know how to "write" music. I found myself supplementing my mea-ger income by transcribing other people's songs off a tape and onto a lead sheet at five dollars a copy. I could put my own songs onto lead sheets. I could write simple chord charts for demo sessions and insure that the chords were played exactly the way I wanted them. (What songwriter hasn't winced on hearing an oversimplified version of his or her subtle chord progression?)

Eventually I would write parts for full orchestra, and indeed in 1968 at the age of twenty-one I was fortunate enough to receive a Grammy Award for orchestration. All because Mama made me practice at least thirty minutes every afternoon.

In recent years I have had occasion to regret the fact that I did not complete a full course of study at a conservatory but it is clear that even a basic musical knowledge, particularly of chordal theory and notation (sight singing, musicianship, etc.) goes a long way in the songwriting racket. It is never too early or too late to start. (I recommend highly some of the software programs available for computers such as Performer or Finale which enable a keyboard player to see at a glance the notation of any chord played on the keyboard and just as easily print out such notation in hard copy.)

The ambitious songwriter cannot learn all from books, computers or well-meant advice. There is a popular cliché that the artist must suffer, preferably over a long period of time, as much emotional trauma, poverty and self-loathing as possible, up to and including death if necessary in order to create. Certainly we know of great artists who have lived unhappy lives. Conversely we are led to believe that the callow, carefree youth has nothing of import to offer. His observations may seem to have weight but they are to be mistrusted and such precocious seriousness may often be ridiculed. Among other things financier Otto Kahn said in the presence of George Gershwin, according to author Frederick Nolan (*Lorenz Hart: A Poet on Broadway*, Oxford University Press): "He declared that although George expressed the genius of young America, Gershwin—like America—had not yet experienced 'the ordeal of deep anguish, besetting care and heart-searching tribulations' necessary for true genius."

When I was twenty years old I found myself wandering aimlessly and awkwardly through a swank Beverly Hills pleasure dome surrounded by cinema stars and movie moguls—as well as a few out of work film composers who were feeling not much pain. A bejeweled, matronly ex–cabaret singer homed in on me like a great white shark on an injured flounder. "So, you must tell me!" she ordered. "How do you write music that sounds so grown up?"

At the same affair I bestirred myself from my usual shyness and was talking with a small but amiable group about the future of rock music on Broadway. It was in those days that *Hair* was breaking all records at the Aquarius Theatre and *Jesus Christ Superstar* was in the offing—as well as a very interesting "album/opera" called *Tommy*. "I think" (at this point, it was like the famous E. F. Hutton commercial—the room went silent) "we'll see a lot more rock musicals on Broadway." After a moment of dubious silence a famous film composer lurking nearby blew his nose and said loudly, "You sound like you almost know what you're talking about."

But what if, in fact, the exact opposite of his aggressive and embarrassing prejudice is true? Isn't it possible that in our younger years—not excluding childhood—human beings are like fresh rolls of film taken from sealed canisters, unfogged and unexposed? And if that is true then surely it is the intensity of experience that marks us with knowledge and intuition, not longevity and repetition. Much like a frame of film when it becomes overexposed, it seems to me that one of the battles of aging is to maintain a passion, a sensitivity to our own feelings as well as to the vulnerability of the world around us. Without being able to expose ourselves to pain—to break down and cry if need be—we don't have what we need to be songwriters or even human beings. The reverse is true. Without recognizing the good things life has to offer—the priceless gift of the distant laughter of children—we become sour pedants. It matters little the grave importance of what we have to say. No one wants to hear our dreary self-pitying voice.

When I am stale—and every songwriter has awakened on some god-forsaken morning feeling like a bag of potato chips mistakenly left overnight in the sauna—I find that "experience" is exactly what I need. Then it is time for a change of venue. It is out in the world that I find the means to reload with a fresh roll of film.

A pilgrimage does not have to entail an expensive air ticket to the Greek Isles. It can be a visit of a few days to that small town or neighborhood where we grew up—perhaps for a talk with that special teacher who got us thinking about music in the first place. It can be time spent completely alone—like a friend of mine who walked completely across the United States. It could be playing with another medium—watercolor, perhaps, or a sport like rock climbing or learning to fly an airplane. I have always found that—given a rest—the muse will return. Miraculously she returns with gifts—the subliminal impressions of people, places and situations that can become the raw stuff of those precious ideas. Leonard Bernstein said that the most important thing he had learned from Harvard Philosophy Professor David Prall was a sense of interdisciplinary values— that the best way to "know" a thing is in the context of another discipline. This is as close as the Western mentality can approach describing the attitudes of Zen, the "watercourse way" of Eastern philosophy that teaches that the best way to conquer a problem may not be to attack it head on.

Given, "experience" is important. But that is not necessarily related to how many years one has lived. It is important because, as writers, we need to "experience" as much of the texture of living as humanly possible. We also need to absorb it through the senses of as many others as practicable. Almost by definition a songwriter is reflective, self-obsessive, brooding and apart from others, but there is danger in this loner mentality—both to his craft and to his emotional well-being.

One afternoon my six-year-old son Charles brought a little playmate to my worktable and proudly explained that his daddy was writing a book about songwriting. "My dad does songs," he crowed. "Every single song he's made has been a great success!" Would that this were true! But then again consider for a moment that it is eminently possible for a song to be a success without being a hit. "Didn't We"—while internationally well-known—was never a "hit." "The Moon Is a Harsh Mistress," recorded by

Glen Campbell, Joe Cocker, Joan Baez, Linda Ronstadt, Judy Collins—never a single, never a "hit"—yet it recently found its way onto a respected list of the "Ten Most Perfect Songs Ever Written." (I add in the same breath that "MacArthur Park" recently appeared in a book about the worst songs of all time. My friend Gerry Beckley, whose recording with Dewey Bunell's "Horse with No Name" also appeared, is busily at work on a book called *The Worst Books About Songs of All Time.*)

The implication is that we might be in error when we set out to write "a hit song." The ramifications are disturbing. The worst one being that we may tend to model our efforts on the current rage. The next worst: We may believe that such a thing is possible when it is not. (The factors affecting the successful outcome of the release of any given song on any single record are so diverse and unpredictable as to represent a perfect model for the Chaos Theory.) Sometimes great songs are written. Sometimes they also become "hits." Sometimes mediocre ones do as well.

What we can do and what will give us the most joy and the best chance for success in the long run is to write a *good* song. Everyone has one good novel in them, it has been said. I'm not sure that this is fact but let's assume that every soul also harbors one great song. It is from such a singular beginning that the careers of Randy Newman, Tim Hardin and Joni Mitchell blossomed.

The songwriter's lot is not necessarily a carefree one. I have watched in the last few years with severe misgivings the inexorable progress each of my three oldest sons has made toward becoming one of those creatures and I would not want to be in their shoes for all the tea in China. But their hearts are set on it as was mine. It is an honorable profession—if only the world's second oldest. I would hope they remember that in a best-case scenario ninety percent of what is written never receives the slightest notice. The sensitive, expressive songwriter has to be as tough as an old boot, a paradox that is irreconcilable.

But let us set out anyway with a reasonably complete knowledge of what has gone before. (If we would be Toads let us be aware wherewith we Croak.) By studying some examples of word writing we should eventually come to an understanding of form. With a knowledge of form we can learn more about chord structure and melody in order to develop a technique. Together we will write a good song.

two

IN THIS ROOM YOU'LL NEVER
MAKE A MISTAKE

I'm fixing a hole where the rain gets in
And stops my mind from wandering . . .
—LENNON & MCCARTNEY,
"FIXING A HOLE"

In 1980 I uprooted my family from the relative comfort of Southern California and moved to New York State smack in the middle of the worst blizzard of the decade. While in college, I had written my first musical—a sophomoric attempt called *Dancing Girl*—which contained a passable ballad entitled "Didn't We?" The theatre arts department at the small college I had attended declined to produce the musical—a disaster for me since I had written the show instead of taking my midterms. In spite of my disappointment I found myself infected by a theatre bug which will forever live in my blood. At the end of the '70s I had come to New York to try something new. I wanted to write a real musical.

Within months, due to the influence of my powerful friend, David Geffen, I had the undivided attention of Michael Bennett—creator of *A Chorus Line, Dreamgirls, Ballroom, Coco,* and so many others—who ruled "The Street" (an insider's term for Broadway) from the seventh floor of a beautiful old building on lower Broadway. I quickly learned from my new friend and mentor important truths about songwriting that had eluded me until that time.

The first one he pointed out to me in typically dramatic fashion when for the first time he presented me with my office space on the seventh floor of his building, a small skyscraper completely devoted to the theatrical arts: costuming, dance, and set design. I realized with some nervousness that I was to become what amounted to a "composer in residence." We walked into the room, a small dance studio with large windows facing the street and full-length mirrors on the walls, unforgiving mirrors, real optical ones, not polystyrene, reflecting us—imperfections and all—as we stood there. He looked at me—Michael had a way of easily commanding complete attention—and said with a smile, "In this room, you can never make a mistake." At first I was surprised, not knowing quite what to make of the remark. I had written songs beside the undulating surf on the south shore of Kauai. I had written one song at an Italian villa in Varese—an estate slightly past its prime—on a piano barely in tune. Another I had written in my scarred and rusting Volkswagen on the way to a fraternity party in Newport Beach. Many I had written in my father's garage in San Bernardino. "Up, Up and Away" I wrote in a practice room at college while skipping a theory class. "Wichita Lineman," in the former Philippine Embassy on Camino Palmero in Hollywood on a green baby grand. (How it came to be green I will never know.) I wrote "MacArthur Park" in Laurel Canyon on a nine-foot Yamaha Grand that I had purchased with the royalties from "Up, Up and Away." I was sleeping under it at the time. It and a dozen decorative pillows were my only furniture. (It resides today in decaying serenity in my living room.)

Now this small, handsome, intensely energetic man with all-encompassing dark eyes was proposing something I had never before considered possible: "In this room you can never make a mistake." Let me try to be clear about what he intended with that assurance. He wasn't referring to moral mistakes. He wasn't saying: "You will never be rude needlessly to someone here or fail to fulfill an obligation that you will have promised to fulfill," or, "You will never have too much to drink here and write a piece of shit." What he was saying was this: "Here I am establishing, arbitrarily, a magic perimeter. As far as your creativity is concerned this is a charmed circle." I'm sure you understand the obvious implications of this concept but let's explore it further—not as physical space but as a state of consciousness. What

Michael really meant was that there is no crossed-out, blotted word on paper or half-croaked note or stumbling, tripping step toward the songwriter's goal that is unseemly or shameful. He meant to say—as I understood him—that creativity is a blameless process. That to exist at all it must function unself-consciously and without guilt, that it is a poetic license to kill, and that any other attitude is negative, self-defeating and constipatory. He meant in the tongue-in-cheek ceremony of that moment to set me free from training wheels, to give me wings and extend pardon and forgiveness to our future collaborations no matter how fatuous, pompous, amateurish or downright stupid they might prove to be in the name of *believing in the serendipity of possibility*. He also meant to say: "*I* will not blame you for failure or keep a scorecard on your efforts as long as they are earnest, as long as you are sincerely dedicated to the things we will try to create here."

As I tried out a few exploratory chords on my new Yamaha baby grand and supervised the installation of some recording equipment he explained to me that he had never commenced the development of a Broadway project as director or choreographer without immense self-doubt, wondering to himself: "This time am I going to be able to do this?" Again I understood. When we, as artists, try to imagine perfection in the work we intend to do then we are inhuman if we are not daunted. We are intimidated by the abstract quality of the task and the potential for failure. It is stage fright without the audience.

That is why it is so important to draw an imaginary protective circle around ourselves and step inside. The *place* where we write is important whether it is a physical room or a spacious loft in the heart and mind. We must clear a safe space around us. There are nerveless creatures on this earth who could probably perform brain surgery in a rivet factory but most of us can all too easily lose that tenuous thread woven of concentration and inspiration when interrupted. There is a perverse part of many of us that welcomes that kind of distraction. It is that part of us that is subliminally delighted with being completely snowed in and unable to go to school. It is indolence without guilt. So for those of us who have a nervous system and still want to get some work done, tranquillity is in order. The primary ingredient in that tranquillity might be to pardon ourselves in advance for any real or imagined inadequacies and approach the work with the attitude that we will see what happens, make the best of it and enjoy the journey. Paradise is the road to Paradise.

There are many pragmatic reasons for having a completely dedicated workplace, whether it is a small room in the home or a separate office/studio or even a favorite boulder in a quiet part of the woods. One of the most important is *continuity*. We need to be able to leave a work in progress for hours or days at a time and return to find it completely undisturbed. This afternoon when I came back to the coffee table where I've been working at home, I found this very manuscript glued to the table with a healthy portion of coagulating strawberry jam—courtesy of my young daughter. There is also continuity of thought in a given work period to consider. Rampaging bands of eleven-year-old Civil War reenactors do not make for concentration. Some may find this kind of advice trivial but a surprising number of people will attempt to do creative work in conditions bordering on chaos. I suffer from intense loneliness while I'm writing and crave human companionship. My assistant bringing me a cup of tea is akin to an angel visiting a doomed man on a desert island with a magical elixir. On the other hand it is virtually impossible for me to abandon self-consciousness and write anything meaningful (particularly a lyric) with another person in the room. I have found it better to think of songwriting as *work*—to set up specific hours when this work is to be done and tough out the feelings of isolation, even to *use* those feelings as raw material. Do I mean that songwriters should work an eight-hour day, five days a week? There is a well-known songwriter in Los Angeles with a string of Top-40 smashes nothing short of spectacular. She claims to work *twelve hours* a day. Most writers are going to find after four or five hours of intense concentration that they are ready for an Advil and a B movie. What seems to work best for me is a period of intense focus—say, thirty-five minutes and then a stretch, an unfocused stare out the window (since I'm lucky enough to have one) for five minutes or so before returning to the anvil. The right side of the brain goes into rigor mortis if it's pinioned in the same attitude for too long, resulting in frustration, angst and lack of progress. It is amazing sometimes how tenaciously and blindly we can pursue an artistic goal—feeding on anger or stubborn will—achieving nothing, only to return the next day and in a more relaxed state see the answer immediately and effortlessly. When working indoors it is important if not completely essential to have a sensory escape—a window with a view or a porch or patio with access to the outside world. (Important works have been written in prison but they're not important necessarily *because* they were written in prison.)

I use a tape recorder, nothing elaborate. (It is a cassette model Sony Professional.) I will explain exactly how and why I use it. (If you are making a demo at the piano make sure you place a folded towel or kitchen sponge under the tape machine and remove all loose objects—cigarette lighters, pens, cups and saucers—from the top of the piano. It also pays to play the piano a bit softer than usual and to place the microphone squarely in front of the vocalist.) From the very first tentative chord of the writing session I have my machine running and locked in "record" because even though I am going to be jotting down notes on paper and keeping a reasonable pace with my own thoughts there are going to be times when my brain darts ahead, instinctively doing something impulsively and so quickly that my *conscious mind* will not be able to follow. It may even be something no more mysterious than a *mistake*. (Even though many times these so-called *mistakes* are no such thing. They are the *subconscious* traveling at light speed a few nanoseconds in front of the conscious mind.) In such a case I will not (except on the very rarest of occasions) be able to remember exactly how I did *what* I did because in the strictest sense *I* didn't do it. No worry. I have every note on the tape recorder. If I want to seize that lovely mistake and make it useful I simply rewind the tape and listen to it repeatedly until I learn it well or else write it down on the pad in front of me.

The tape recorder also enables me to consolidate my gains and minimize my losses. Let's say I'm twenty-five percent into the cassette reel and I've managed to rough out a complete verse with a melody. I don't want to risk losing even a nuance of what I've already accomplished but I don't really give a damn about the trial-and-error rubbish that sits on the first quarter of the tape. I immediately rewind to the top of the reel, and while the verse is fresh in my mind I record it again right at the "top" (or beginning) of the tape. If I make a mistake or forget something while recording I have the original "pass" (or performance) at the *end* of the tape that I can refer to. Now I have my verse safely in storage at the top of the tape. I continue writing—perhaps embarking on a chorus section by trial and error. I will continue in this way, storing valuable sections at the top of the tape— being careful not to erase anything previously *stored*—and recording over the detritus. If for some reason I decide to abandon the song temporarily or indefinitely in an unfinished state I throw my work tape in the trunk; nothing lost, no harm done. (I might review it six months later and find that it's not as bad as I thought.) I can work this way on a song at intervals of weeks or even months and never lose my train of thought, never forget a word or note. (One frustration is that sometimes the performances on these low-tech recordings are better than the ones that I do later in a professional recording studio.) Near the end of the process I record the nearly finished song at the top of the tape and then I have the whole remaining cassette for any changes or rewrites. It works.

I keep a legal pad on the piano in front of me and use it in conjunction with my tape machine and in much the same way though sometimes separately and independently. The first page might be consumed with tedious trial-and-error chicken scratches, forging a lyric for the first verse. I am stopping occasionally and matching what I've written with what I'm singing and playing on the tape machine. By and by I develop what might pass as a serviceable verse. It might not be perfect—in fact I know that it will get better—but its *intent* is what I'm concerned with at this early stage. So I flip over a leaf on my legal pad and I copy it out carefully—warts and all—at the top of the page. Perhaps I'm bored with word writing at that moment and I go back to my tape to try to write that soaring chorus melody. I probably already know what the *content* of that chorus is going to be. I may be sure of a hook line or title that I intend to incorporate in that chorus (fulfilling the *intent* of my half-finished verse). I dink around with my chorus line, singing along with the piano and getting a feel for it. My trusty tape machine—my guardian angel—is purring steadily. "Okay," I say to myself, "this could work." (I have been known to talk to myself.) Below my crude verse on the legal pad, I begin to sketch in the lyric to the chorus and to doodle in some rough chord symbols above the lyrics, reminders that are going to help me *learn* my own song and save me rewinding the machine every time I misplace a chord. Let's say I've used up my second page roughing out the verse and chorus. I flip over the leaf and have a beautiful blank page for my first rewrite. The whole evolution of the song is on that legal pad. I usually don't cross anything out because I may want to go back to a previous state of evolution and use something that wasn't as bad as I might have thought it was. So it goes, for page after page of development and improvement with nothing lost or forgotten. If the tape is stored for any reason the notes are stored with it.

Another thing: The workplace needs some magical symbols. Hanging at eye level over the piano in my studio is a magnificently detailed drawing of Gaudi's Sagrada Familia that I brought back from Barcelona after a tour of the cathedral. To me it represents the frozen architecture of music and the depth of feeling and commitment one man can bring to a work of art. The *selflessness* of it, the *sacrifice* of it, the *authority* of it, open a window in my soul. Many artists have come to call this feeling *inspiration* though there are skeptics who insist that there ain't no such animal. On the wall close by is a picture of Michael Bennett and me together on a porch swing in happier days. It's only a Polaroid but it never lets me forget what he expected of me in my workroom or the profound truth that in the pursuit of art there are no mistakes. (Hopefully I will not be deliberately misunderstood on this point. In the *performance* of art there are mistakes aplenty.)

The sharpest memory is fallible. It is not such a difficult thing to keep a small, spiral-bound notebook in a briefcase, wallet or purse. Now we come out of a movie house and a couple is having a knock-down, drag-out, bare-all at curbside while waiting for a cab. He says to her in a loud voice just as we step out on the street: "Someday you'll know how big a mistake this is!" He's yelling. She's very upset. We empathize but not overly so. We are groping for our notebook. "SOMEDAY YOU'LL KNOW HOW BIG A MISTAKE THIS IS." We see the top of the charts. We're song-writers first and human beings second. We really should use a notebook for this. It beats Ballantine's cocktail napkins (so hard to iron out after they've been through a wash and dry cycle) or car parking stubs (you give them back to the attendant forgetting that you've got a Top-10 title writ-ten there) or trusting in your wife or boyfriend ("What do you mean you *forgot* it? It was something about a *mistake.* 'YOU'RE MAKING A BIG MISTAKE'—was that it? Oh, *merde* . . . !").

Larry Hart was infamous for writing some fabulous lyric on nothing more than a scrap of paper and then mislaying it, among these "A Ship Without a Sail," according to biographer Frederick Nolan. One story which may or may not be apocryphal has Richard Rodgers, Hart and a female companion in a Parisian taxi after a near automobile accident that could have proven fatal. "Oh my goodness, my heart stood still!" gasped the woman. "Hey, great title for a song," said Larry (as so many of us do) while Richard Rodgers calmly wrote the title down in his notebook. Weeks later during a songwriting session, Rodgers remarked to Hart, "I've got a tune for that great title of yours." "What title is that?" came the reply. "My Heart Stood Still," said Dick as he thumbed through his note-book. "Never heard of it," Larry replied. (In hope of preventing automobile accidents involving title-stricken songwriters attempting to drive and make notes simultaneously, the author recommends small "Voice-It"–type electronic note-taking devices, some current models of which record as much as thirty minutes of audio in a keyring-sized format.)

There's another way to use a notebook that provides a richer source of raw material than a list of promising titles. Let's say you're relaxing in an old pub just across the Hammersmith Bridge on the outskirts of London and an elderly couple walk in. He's tender with her, making sure her coat is properly checked and that she has a seat by the window. She's beautiful in spite of her years and yet there is a sadness about her. You get the distinct impression that this meeting is more than routine. It is a confrontation that has been delayed for years. His body language, every word that he says, though indistinct, is apologetic. He isn't telling her that he's sorry for running down her poodle with his bicycle, you decide. There is some long-unfinished business between these two. Perhaps they were in love once and he threw her over for someone else during the war—all those years ago. She married well but never forgave him for destroying the special relationship they once had. You get out your notebook and start writing. Giving your imagination and curiosity complete rein you write down a few rough lyric lines about what might be going on between these two strangers. What do their facial expressions convey? What are they wearing? Is that a lavender corsage she wears? Look for detail.

Okay, enough of that. What I am attempting to illustrate is that the whole world, every waking and dreaming moment of it, is grist for the notebook's mill. Try this experiment: Read a book—any book—but to make it interesting, begin to read one that you've *read before*. With a pencil underline every situation or statement in the first chapter that suggests a song idea—*entering them all in your notebook.* Go out on a Saturday and aimlessly wander the town you live in, observing people, animals and structures, intently searching for hidden insights that suggest song ideas. *Put them all in your notebook.* With a little effort you will soon have dozens if not hundreds of ideas and observations recorded. Get in the habit of doing this every time you read or watch a movie, talk to a friend or travel. At least in an observational sense try to become a novelist. Look for deeper meanings behind the seemingly trivial and write them down. You may find that your notebook begins to take on the character of a journal. All the better—you're not only compiling hundreds of song ideas but writing your memoirs, which will be worth a bundle when they induct you into the Songwriters Hall of Fame.

Now let's say you are in songwriting mode: your tape recorder is whirring, your legal pad is leafing; you're writing a song about regret—deep regret—and stuck for a line. Not just a *rhyme*. You're struggling for a way of describing the emotion—the body language, the subdued tone of remorse. Maybe it's time to talk with Mr. Notebook. Hmmm. When I was over in England two years ago—remember the elderly couple at the Sun Inn? Remember that tangible aura of regret that hovered between them? I was on the front lines then. I was right in the thick of it, and—more often than one might think—Mr. Notebook has the answer.

Think of your workplace as the Mother Ship—a laboratory where you provide yourself with time and tools and techniques. You go out on a scouting mission: a vacation, or a date, or a solitary walk in the country, and you collect specimens of all kinds for temporary storage in your notebook. It's not necessary to make any particular sense of them—you're collecting and it's an absorbing, joyful experience. It beats bird-watching and for a songwriter it's a lot more fun. Bring your treasures home to the lab. Work with some of them. Save the others for a rainy day.

After a lyric- or music-writing session, it's important to spend generous amounts of time thinking about what you've done and what you intend to do next—in the current vernacular, "visualizing." Fully half of my songwriting is done as a mental exercise that has nothing to do with proximity to piano or pen and paper. The most important aspects of songwriting, the planning and plotting of story line as well as the inception of images, approaches and various strategies and changes of direction, etc., and even the never-ending search for a proper rhyme—the vital tasks of steering a song in a likely direction—can be done while riding across town in the back of a taxicab.

Sometimes we half-hear music through a closed door and the *feel* of the performance augmented by our own muse suggests a completely new *other thing.* We write down a note or a title in shorthand convinced that we can remember the details later—the whole context of the idea is so brilliantly clear in that moment. But the next day—our euphoria having fled to where emotions hibernate—we look at our shorthand and discover this: *Ask someone who knows.* Now what we have here is a fair title for a song (one is reminded of "It's Not for Me to Say") but where is our cogent, fully fleshed-out, chart-ripping *concept* for an original, interesting record or song? It has gone where our euphoria has gone. The lesson is to always take an extra forty seconds and attempt to write down, even briefly, the *context* of the idea, perhaps even the original record or "feel" that set you off in the first place. Either that or when you get that burst of creative lust drop everything and head for the nearest Mother Ship. Obviously to live even a semblance of a normal life songwriters cannot do this. That is why God made graphite and trees.

Now after all this talk about a permanent base and a stable songwriting environment I must point out that a songwriter is one of the most fortunate professionals in the world precisely because he or she is *not* tied down to a particular room or instrument or array of equipment. Our offices are between our ears. With a notebook, a small tape recorder and a guitar slung over our backs we are completely mobile. In this era of fax machines and fiber optic communications and recording (via satellite dish if need be) it is conceivable that one could function effortlessly as a songwriter en route from a sojourn on the island of Bora Bora to the Marquesas to visit the burial place of Gauguin. (The pianist is at a disadvantage in such conditions though small, lightweight keyboard instruments have brought even this within the realm of possibility.) Ultimately it is important to remember what our "charmed circle" symbolizes—the work habits, discipline and peace of mind that we can take anywhere once we begin to dedicate space and time.

The danger is that we begin to think of writing songs as an elusive, metaphysical process connected in some obtuse fashion to exotic locales or situations. As in: "I can't seem to write anything so I've rented a house on Martha's Vineyard for a month." Such fantasizing has a way of backfiring. We end up with a fat portfolio of gauzy numbers about seagulls and ferry boats or worse—on arriving in paradise we discover that life is so seamless and serene that we begin to wave-watch as our fine ambition dissolves into the local social scene.

Arguably one of the worst things a writer can do is talk too much—or at all—about an idea before finishing it in the workplace. "I'm writing a song about . . . ," the writer begins, dicing with the truth. Yes he's got an idea, yes he's kicking it around in his head—no he hasn't written a note. This is the red "A" on the forehead that brands the "amateur." Something insidious happens when we engage in this kind of verbal free association in the company of others or play half-formed verses at cocktail parties. It would seem that our ambition is often eroded. In some inscrutable fashion the creative genie at the center of our being seems to have a finite capacity and will become recalcitrant as though to say, "Well, if you want to rub the lamp and waste magic at a cocktail party, fine—but don't try to wake me up at one o'clock in the morning."

The sexual metaphor is not too distant. Here we are not discussing the serious "workshop" atmosphere of give-and-take between colleagues (the value of which can also be debated) but a careless venting of emotional enthusiasm for a delicate task, the outcome of which may be in doubt even if all energy is conserved. It's only another reason for a self-enforced artistic isolation that was once taken for granted—a concept that has been eroded by contemporary society's compulsion to share everything, tell all, and its conviction that an enlightened, happy committee of verbose lamebrains is infinitely superior to one struggling, vulnerable and merely dedicated human mind.

This is not to unilaterally criticize group discussion, and since our consideration of the working environment seems to have led inevitably to within striking distance of the "workshop," it might be helpful to evaluate what is out there (for those who have forty or fifty dollars burning a hole in their pocket). These days it is not particularly difficult—or even avoidable—to find four or five songwriters of legendary status sitting together on a stage or dais somewhere, playing their chartbusters in turn and then fielding questions from an audience sometimes numbering in the hundreds. Eclectic New York DJ Vin Scelsa seems to have pioneered this format—at least in terms of selling it to the general public—with his In Their Own Words series at the Bottom Line in New York City, which routinely played to enthusiastic, standing-room-only crowds. After his initial successes, Scelsa took his show on the road and played it successfully all over the country. Who would have thought it?

Such entertainments have even caught on with the Platinum Card set—witness the tony 1994 Songmasters Inside/Out series at the Algonquin Hotel in New York where tickets sold for the price of a nice television set and a portion of the proceeds was diverted to charity. Unfortunately these entertainment events rarely differ in content and form from most of the "learning" encounters arranged by the major performing arts societies and academies across the country.

As a pleasant evening out I don't suppose there could be a better value for a buff or dilettante (I mean no disrespect to dilettantes—some of my best friends are dilettantes) but for the "man or woman on a mission," the person who shows up with their notebook in hand wanting some substantial help, the "panel/performance/discussion" format often proves to be a disappointment. I'll try not to belabor the point. These gatherings are usually supervised by a moderator so that access to the guests is carefully, if randomly, controlled. There is usually a spirit of lighthearted banter prevalent as opposed to a careful, instructive spirit. The punter may go away feeling as though he has had more than his share of cotton candy with his notebook and wallet empty.

In the more professional version of this kind of "class," which usually meets at a regular interval at a specific time over a period of weeks, the acolyte may encounter other disappointments. The panel—starting out I'm sure with the highest possible motives—may become acerbic in their relentless criticism of works in progress. (In spite of themselves they may end up strangling some babies in their cribs.) Panels of experts are only human beings. They may find it difficult to resist the impulse to bounce off each other's egos—to impress each other and forget about the poor student scrabbling to keep up. Their fervent pronouncements of great songwriting dictums might even divert some incipient genius from his or her own true path. A student should not attend such a course hoping for some chrysalis-like transformation into the complete songwriter or even expecting any noticeable improvement. More than likely what the supplicant will take away will be in direct proportion to what has been brought in the first place. Students would be wise to do their homework and have ready a couple of good examples of their best songs and a list of questions to which they really want to know the answers. Professionals are unsympathetic toward complete tin horns. John Thompson's first grade reader questions tire the rest of the class as well. Everyone gets grumpy.

On a university level is found the next best form of commercially available interaction: the "some-on-one" lecture or lecture series. A prime example is the Learning Annex in New York City (variations abound in many college communities). Here, a group of students—say forty or fifty—pay two sawbucks to spend a hefty two and a half hours with the expert of their choice. (Courses are offered in everything from television journalism to salmon fishing.) The advantages in the "one-expert seminar" may not be obvious but are substantial: access to the guest is dramatically increased. The teacher (or guest) may actually be able to mount a coherent lesson, uninterrupted by a moderator or other guests and pursue live performance examples in a logical sequence, unfettered by the necessity of performing the "greatest hits" medley. The student may actually come away with some cogent notebook entries and perhaps return to work with a new angle on a recurring problem.

Said to be the closest thing to Songwriter's Heaven on Earth and also, many believe, the single most beneficial experience for young songwriters currently available is the legendary Kerrville Folk Festival, an annual affair that takes place down in Kerrville, Texas, on the Quiet Valley Ranch. Founded by Rod Kennedy twenty-seven years ago, the festival has grown from a 1,200-seat, three-day event to a week-long camp-out with as many as 6,000 people gathered on some nights in the facility's large outdoor theatre. For three days between festival weekends (usually at the end of May) aspiring songwriters investigate, analyze and experience the craft, business and process of songwriting with industry professionals at the Music Foundation Songwriting School. For eighteen hours of classes, three meals and a free camp-out on the ranch, the $110 fee seems more than reasonable, especially since it is paid to the nonprofit Kerrville Music Foundation. But according to insiders who have been involved since the beginning, like early supporters Peter Yarrow and Nanci Griffith, the real action takes place around the campfires, on the tailgates of pickup trucks and in campers or tents where songwriters immediately get down to the personal business of writing songs, discussing techniques, and interacting with other songwriters and freelance "teachers" like Yarrow who roam the site in an ongoing spirit of give-and-take with the young pilgrims. One of the most important aspects of this get-together is the selection of thirty-two songwriting finalists gleaned from as many as 689 entries from Texas, forty-five other states and Canada. All these talented people are invited to perform their selected songs, and from them six award winners are picked to appear on the "big stage" and are allowed to perform twenty-minute sets of their repertoire, receive $150 each from the ASCAP fund and come to the attention of scores of record company executives, publishers and famous recording artists. (For more information call 1-800-435-8429.)

There is no sequential course of study available for someone who wants to be a songwriter. Hopefuls must put their education together piecemeal—there is no follow-up, no monitor to guide their progress, no emergency line when the going gets tough. There is only the little room with a view and the siege mentality.

If we start with our workroom, notebook, small tape recorder, and legal pad and begin to add accoutrement—microphones, bigger recorders, a mixing board and perhaps a synthesizer or other additional instruments—then eventually we come up with what the bomb shelter was to the '50s: the home recording studio. This can range from a self-contained mixing board and four-track cassette machine to a complete digital layout encompassing sixteen-track recording, multi-buss professional mixing desk, racks of outboard echo, delay and compression modules used in conjunction with sophisticated "samplers" and "sequencers," all of which are often tied into a master computer.

The wonder of it all sometimes threatens to overwhelm me. When I began my career at Bob Ross Recording Studio in 1964, the state-of-the-art professional recorder was the temperamental three-track Ampex. We worked with spring echo units that sounded no better than the cardboard tubes your kids purchase at Toys "R" Us. If you really wanted nice echo you had to dig a pit the size of a swimming pool in the parking lot and put a microphone at one end and a speaker at the other. One famous Hollywood engineer used a toilet bowl. Phil Spector, it is said, once used an elevator shaft. Sometimes the sheer volume of glittering, dazzling toys that are now so readily and inexpensively available tend to become an end in themselves. If you have a kid that plays the guitar you know that rarely does his or her expertise keep pace with the bewildering array of gadgets and amplifiers that are constantly demanded. Which brings me at last to the point: Do home studios really help songwriters?

Let's dispense with the most obvious misconception first. On the face of it no amount of fancy equipment is going to write a great song for a novice who doesn't know a bridge from a fade. On the contrary, to the extent that an amateur is preoccupied with the reading of operations manuals and the self-deluding preoccupation of gilding mediocre work with hi-tech echo cocktails and such, so is the subject less and less likely to conquer the fundamental and vexing problems of brain, voice and finger/ear/eye coordination.

Assuming that there is a songwriter somewhere with a surplus of decent material and working in his house, the home studio suddenly looms in importance, perhaps on a parallel with the invention of electric guitars. It was common in my early days in the industry to witness wet-behind-the-ears writers rushing with pathetic enthusiasm to trade their precious publishing—entire copyrights—for a few barely productive hours in a recording studio, that holy and seemingly unreachable tabernacle of success. Publishing empires were built on this lemminglike compulsion to gain access to the whirring, blinking devices at any cost. Imagine for a moment that to even *see* a studio, a kid from Oklahoma, say, had to go to a major city: New York, Nashville, Los Angeles, etc. (except perhaps producer Norman Petty's spread in Clovis, New Mexico). Keeping all this in mind, understand that it is vital for a songwriter, particularly an amateur, to be able to produce a professional-sounding demo at little or preferably *no* cost. Disregarding for a moment the initial expense of some basic equipment (probably in the range of twelve hundred to five thousand dollars without going completely chip-crazy) the songwriter's dreams of a demo with bass, drums, horns, strings, piano (to be honest everything *except* convincing electric guitars and saxes) is now a reality. There are probably many readers who do not recall the days of "SEND US $5.00! We will evaluate your tape," or "YOUR SONG WITH A REAL STUDIO BACKUP! ONLY $25!" Those were the Mellotron Mills. The age of brazen fraud and exploitation. Thank God and the Japanese those days are pretty much over.

I would like to reiterate that silicon chips are no substitute for gray cells and that there was a time not long ago in our great industry when the fancy demo was looked upon with wary suspicion. Prevailing wisdom dictated that what producers and A&R men wanted to hear was a piano/voice or guitar/voice demo—all the better to pin the unfortunate submission under their harsh, glaring electron microscope of criticism in naked honesty. *They* would decide how to best arrange (meddle with) a man's song. Hell, they might even do it *twice* as fast. Why spend money on a demo at $40=.1$ when they would most likely record it at $80=.1$? (These are metronomic settings.) Not only that—the wisdom continued—but the *artist* preferred the minimalist and rough-edged portrayal for psychological reasons. It made the artist feel insecure for instance if the singer on the fully realized demo was a teeny-mite stronger in the high register. One did not wish to intimidate the delicate artist. Thus was born the "wood-shed" demo and a lot of music that in the unmerciful ear of history will sound sweeter than its finished and overpolished progeny.

Where was I? Oh yes. In my zeal to discredit the fancy demo I almost forgot one very important thing—an ancient certitude actually, one known to any twelve-year-old who ever sneaked into the Baptist church on a Saturday afternoon to pick the lock on the Hammond organ: inspiration.

There is an unaccountable, delicious phenomenon that occurs when any player experiments with another instrument—a strange sound or unfamiliar musical texture. Something wonderful and sensual happens. When I was a boy I first noticed this inexplicable, primeval sensation when I would abandon the relative paucity of my mother's upright Story & Clark, creaking and detuning in the exile and desolation of my father's unheated garage, and travel to the home of an upscale neighbor who possessed a modest but impeccably tuned mini-grand of Asian heritage. From the very first note, the first pianissimo triad (so as not to disturb the prayer meeting in the parlor) my soul was filled with the most profound reverberations. The same, often repeated, tired old chord progressions took on overtones of unexpected brilliance. As I was egged on by this psychic slap-echo from the backside of the universe—tiny fronds of spring green genius began to tenderly uncurl . . .

Now I'm beginning to make myself quite ill. This is an intangible. That's what they call it, isn't it? An *intangible*? I'm foaming at the mouth here about playing on *a different instrument*? Maybe I could just travel around the country writing songs at a logarithmic rate by just PLAYING A DIFFERENT DAMN INSTRUMENT EVERY DAY? I guess I could just go up to people's houses—"Excuse me, ma'am, I'm passing through Omaha. I know y'all probably just got back from church but I sure would like to write a lovely song on that old Knabe upright!"

That is just the point. The incredible variety of sounds and echoes, effects, etc., that a writer can achieve in a modern home studio make it unnecessary to go to Omaha or anywhere else.

On the other hand, what about all those cables and wires and patch cords—what about planned obsolescence? Maintenance, for God's sake! What about buying a DX-7 and then finding out about a week later that there's a DX-8? What about buying a Kurzweil 250 for twenty thousand dollars and finding out five years later you can get a brand new one out of the crate for thirty-five hundred? What about when musicians—undesirable types—start hanging around your *home* studio asking for free recording time? Smoking cigarettes? Blocking your driveway with some big, ugly-looking van?

It is a debate that will never end. Having owned an elaborate home studio for many years I eventually came to the conclusion that writing and recording are as oil is to water. Church and state. I could go further and say mutually destructive—but short of that I choose to think of them as a bicameral legislature, a system of checks and balances. Each area of expertise influences the other but for each to function perfectly perhaps the left hand should *not* know what the right hand is doing. Simple demos of beautifully crafted songs will always suffice with perhaps one exception: Some writers and publishers with a particularly well-honed commercial sense will always want to custom manufacture a "record" for a specific recording artist, sometimes to the extent of actually trying to imitate the singer's sound and vocal style. I would give this practice a fifty-fifty shot of influencing the artist or producer for better or worse. If it doesn't go your way you're stuck with an expensive demo that sounds exactly like Johnny Cash and you've already found out that Johnny wouldn't touch it with a sterilized cattle prod. It's going to be rough going to try that demo out on Trisha Yearwood. Investments of this kind are gambles at worst—calculated risks at best.

So we are back to the charmed circle. It is your circle and you can put anything inside it that will help you tilt at your own private windmills. I once made the mistake of thinking that a little companionship around the old piano might make the hours pass more amiably—"greasing the muse," as it were. I purchased a young mynah bird and installed him in a cage, keyboard-side. All went well until he learned to imitate my early morning hacking cough, the creaking spring on the back screen door and finally mastered *"Shit!"* in an exact imitation of a frustrated songwriter making a mistake. In one of my less noble moments I drop-kicked him—cage and all—across the living room. (No animals were harmed during the writing of this book!)

My best advice? A quiet place. A simple tape recorder. A legal pad. A notebook—and a full heart.

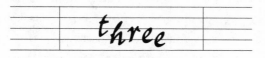

IT'S ONLY WORDS

Talk in everlasting words and dedicate them all to me
And I will give you all my life, I'm here if you should call to me . . .
—BARRY, ROBIN & MAURICE GIBB,
"IT'S ONLY WORDS"

The reason we keep notebooks is to help us remember our ideas, but as I suggested in a previous chapter an "idea" means something entirely different to a songwriter than it might to a novelist, journalist or screenwriter. Songwriters work for the most part in a milieu that might be described as "technological haiku"—for reasons far beyond our understanding or control, parameters dictated and established by complicated machines and economic fact. We must accomplish our aims and tell our entire story in a time frame of about three minutes (plus or minus). Every word, every note must count. This means among other things that we are not vouchsafed the luxury that some of our literary cousins have—the meandering and descriptive setting of scene, the leisurely development of a myriad of colorful characters and the exploration of plot in counterpoint throughout a seamless and climactic story line that culminates in every pesky loose end being tied off in a bowline.

Usually there is only room for one or two characters in our little radio plays and perhaps fifty seconds for each act. We have to get while the getting's good. Does this mean that our efforts are any less valid than those of our privileged colleagues? Hardly. What it means is that we have been challenged with accomplishing an almost impossible task *exquisitely*. We are the Swiss watchmakers of music and literature. It is our complete understanding of what constitutes a song "idea" that enables us to do this at all.

> *When I come home feeling tired and beat,*
> *I go up where the air is fresh and sweet . . .*
> *I get away from the bustling crowd,*
> *And all that rat race noise down in the street . . .*
> > —G. Goffin & C. King,
> > "Up On the Roof"

What could be more descriptive than "*all that rat race noise down in the street*"? Carole and Gerry make us hear it! But most important, they know where they are going.

> *Right smack dab in the middle of town*
> *I found a paradise that's troubleproof,*
> *And if this world starts getting you down*
> *There's room enough for two Up On the Roof . . .*
> > —G. Goffin & C. King,
> > "Up On the Roof"

Carole and Gerry's is a wonderful "idea" for a song. Here, on the other hand, is a song about a roof that isn't much of an idea:

> *I like it on the roof*
> *It's really nice up there—*
> *With pigeons, bugs and airplanes,*
> *I just don't have a care . . .*

What's missing? *Story.* The writer has missed the point by throwing away the title/idea in the first line: "I like it on the roof." Let's always ask the questions or establish the ambiguities first whether in a song like:

> *Why does the sun keep on shining?*
> *Why do the waves rush to shore?*

Don't they know it's The End of the World
'Cause you don't love me anymore . . .
　　　　—Sylvia Dee & Arthur Kent,
　　　　　"The End of the World"

Or to return to Carole and Gerry's masterpiece:

When I come home feeling tired and beat,
I go up where the air is fresh and sweet . . .
　　　　—G. Goffin & C. King,
　　　　　"Up On the Roof"

Where is she going? There is an implied mystery. Perhaps it is essentially sexual. We are all curious about where we're going—but we really don't want to know until we get there. It spoils the fun. Let's pursue this for a moment:

By the Time I Get to Phoenix she'll be rising . . .
　　　　—Jimmy Webb,
　　　　　"By the Time I Get to Phoenix"

The first line of a song. We don't know who is speaking and we don't know about whom he's speaking, but we do know that he's on his way to Phoenix, presumably in the early hours of the morning since by the time he arrives there another person—a woman—will have awakened and will be leaving her bed. It is a situation that is meant to pique our curiosity. Who is this man? Who is the woman? Why is he on his way to Phoenix? This is the songwriter's counterpart of the first lines of a three-act play in miniature. Eventually during the course of this three-minute song in three verses after passing through Albuquerque and discovering that our ultimate destination is Oklahoma, we come finally to these lines:

. . . and she will cry to think that I would really leave her,
Though time and time again I've tried to tell her so . . .
She just didn't know that I would really go . . .
　　　　—Jimmy Webb,
　　　　　"By the Time I Get to Phoenix"

What if we had started the song with the last line? There would have been no story to tell. In the early stages of a song ambiguity is essential as in:

> *There's a light, a certain kind of light*
> *That's never shone on me . . .*
> > —Barry, Robin & Maurice Gibb,
> > "To Love Somebody"

Which takes us eventually to:

> *You don't know what it's like To Love Somebody,*
> *To Love Somebody, the way I love you . . .*
> > —Barry, Robin & Maurice Gibb,
> > "To Love Somebody"

Or beginning with:

> *Oh I can't forget this evening*
> *Or your face as you were leaving . . .*
> > —Peter Ham & Tom Evans,
> > "Without You"

Don't we want to know *more* about this man and the person to whom he is singing? And don't we explode emotionally with the writer and the singer when they admit finally:

> *I can't live if livin' is Without You . . .*
> > —Peter Ham & Tom Evans,
> > "Without You"

It would have been such a waste if the first line of the song had been "I can't live, if livin' is without you." So the placement of the title/idea is of great importance and consequently we usually find it at the end of a verse or in the first strong expository lines of the chorus, or perhaps as a conclusive statement at the last line of the chorus. Sometimes, particularly in the case of two-verse forms, we will only hear it once at the very end of the song.

A great song idea usually utilizes an interesting hook line or title and incorporates it into a fully realized scenario that reveals in careful, logical stages the true goal or intent of the writer. This is the "developmental" component of a verse. For instance, in "By the Time I Get to Phoenix" it is composed of the lines after the "teaser":

By the Time I Get to Phoenix she'll be rising
She'll find the note that I left hanging on her door
And she will laugh to read the part that says I'm leavin'
'Cause I've left that girl too many times before.

—Jimmy Webb,
"By the Time I Get to Phoenix"

Well, if this isn't a soap opera in the making then I've never heard one! We find out some interesting things very quickly: that he's left a note on her door, that it's a farewell note that will cause her some amusement and that as a note-leaver our hero is perhaps a repeat offender. Now this is the way we build up the story, the meat and muscle of the inner lines of verses . . . the strong tissue that connects the sometimes deceptively nondescript opening line with the "hammer," or at Motown in the old days, the "message," the hook, line and sinker, what have you. In the case of "By the Time I Get to Phoenix," the hammer doesn't land until the very end of the last verse when we find out that as smug as she may be, the one who has been left behind is in for a rude surprise, *"And she will cry to think that I would really leave her . . ."* This time he means it. This is the O'Henry-esque twist or surprise ending that is common to the true ballad and is probably descended from the storyteller by the hearthside.

Yes, Paul Simon's "The Boy in the Bubble" is a surreal, chain-of-consciousness epic that fires idea after idea at us machine-gun style so that in the end the effect is almost pointillist. Cumulatively, it is not unlike being bowled over by a tsunami. However, years earlier Simon wrote the gorgeous standard "Bridge Over Troubled Water," which begins simply, "When you're weary . . . ," and ends "Like a Bridge Over Troubled Water I will ease your mind." Amateur songwriters should learn the art of clarity before attempting a pell-mell dash in Mr. Simon's adventurous footsteps.

Try working backward. If my authority is not sufficient on the subject then listen to Stephen Sondheim: "I find it useful to write backwards, and I think most lyric writers probably do too when they have a climax, a twist, a punch, a joke."

Look at that big chorus line like "You've Lost that Lovin' Feelin'" and ask yourself where that story begins. You could find yourself beginning a verse as brilliantly as this:

You never close your eyes anymore
When I kiss your lips . . .
    —Mann, Weil & Spector,
"You've Lost that Lovin' Feelin'"

In this instance there is obvious evidence of the writers' extremely well-honed observational techniques. The fact that she no longer closes her eyes is a small thing but the protagonist has noticed it and it has immediately put us (the listeners) on extremely intimate footing with both the singer and the object of his desire. It is also interesting to note that we are eavesdroppers on this conversation, which we could assume is taking place in a hotel room, on a beach or in the backseat of an automobile. This will be the songwriters' primary communicatory device: they are going to let us overhear one side of a conversation that under normal circumstances we would not even consider auditing.

In another instance consider Foreigner's powerhouse rock ballad "I Want to Know What Love Is" with lyric by Mick Jones, which begins:

I've got to take a little time—
A little time to think things over . . .

Again we are "dropping in" on someone else's reality, their chain of consciousness, so to speak, and we can't help but be intrigued. Why does he need to take some time? What needs to be thought over? The rather unsettled musical accompaniment with its minor chord is suggesting what? An approaching storm? That the singer is troubled? We find that our concerns are well founded as the lyricist cranks up the tension by admitting in a subsequent line, *"in my life there's been heartache and pain,"* this confession leading eventually to the explosive and almost transcendental cry of anguish, *"I Want to Know What Love Is."* Why do I find this simple line so evocative? Because of everything that it *doesn't* say. Because of the lifetime of loneliness that it implies in the existence of someone who tragically has missed out on the meaning of life's fundamental purpose.

Hank Williams's great standard begins:

Today I passed you on the street . . .
    —Hank Williams

Who did he pass? And in this case the writer will eventually indicate that we are not—this time—eavesdropping on a real conversation at all, but rather on his innermost thoughts, a conversation that he would perhaps like to have, words he wishes he could say. Though the opening line may seem mundane at first glance, it serves well in contrast to the mighty killer payoff:

I Can't Help It if I'm Still in Love With You . . .
                    —Hank Williams

at the end of the elegantly brief verse.

Everyday expressions flower and thrive under the pens of writers like Cole Porter ("Well, Did You Evah!" © 1939), Johnny Mercer and Rube Bloom ("Fools Rush in Where Angels Fear to Tread" © 1940) or Ernest Tubbs ("Walkin' the Floor Over You" © 1941). The writer should remember that this kind of title/idea admits to being a cliché at the outset. In fact, the more of a cliché it is, the more desirable, since the cliché title has come to be accepted as a genre of American song. Country songs ("I've Forgotten More Than You'll Ever Know About Him" by Cecil Null) are almost exclusively devoted to these familiar colloquialisms (way down South they call 'em "sayins"); indeed it is hard to imagine country music without them or, for that matter, a good part of the Motown phenomenon: "I Heard It Through the Grapevine," (© 1966 N. Whitfield and B. Strong), "I'll Be Doggone" (© 1965 W. Robinson Jr., W. Moore, M. Tarplin), "My World Is Empty Without You" (© 1968 Holland/Dozier/Holland), "Love Child" (© 1968 P. Sawyer, R.D. Taylor, F. Wilson, D. Richards), "Ain't That Peculiar" (© 1965 W. Robinson, W. Moore, M. Tarplin, R. Rogers), etc.

What will ruin the effect is to include any or too many additional clichés in the lyric proper. The body of the lyric should balance off with great skill the relative triteness of the title by avoiding cuteness. This may require even more effort than other kinds of lyric writing. If the generic colloquialism is the free lunch, it will probably have to be worked off over a hot sink full of cleverly wrought metaphors, similes and images.

To elaborate, the writer will want to work hard to set up a situation or relationship in the main body of the song that will cause the trite title to land with unexpected force, as I tried to do in "Didn't We?"

This time we almost made our poem rhyme
This time we almost made that long hard climb
Didn't We almost make it this time?

—Jimmy Webb,
"Didn't We?"

Berlin's "What'll I Do" is a perfect example. Other kinds of song title/ideas? Country music is also famous for its puns ("Don't It Make My Brown Eyes Blue" by Richard Leigh) and its paragrams ("Love In the First Degree" by Jim Hurt and James Dubois). Of course there are the geographic ones: "I Left My Heart in San Francisco" (Douglass Cross and George Cory); "Penny Lane" (Lennon and McCartney); "Last Train to Clarkesville" (Tommy Boyce and Bobby Hart); "Bowling Green" (Jay Ertel and Terry Slater); "New York State of Mind" (Billy Joel); and so on. The imperatives: "Be My Love" (Sammy Cahn and Nicholas Brodszky); "Take a Message to Mary" (Felice Bryant and Boudleaux Bryant); "Walk Away Renee" (Mike Brown, Tony Sansome & Bob Calilli); or "Love, Love Me Do" (Lennon and McCartney). The temporal ones: "When Sunny Gets Blue" (Jack Segal and Marvin Fisher); "When the Moon Comes over the Mountain" (Kate Smith, Harry Woods and Harold Johnson); "When I Fall in Love" (E. Heyman, V. Young); "June Is Bustin' Out All Over" (Rodgers and Hammerstein); "Where or When?" (Rodgers and Hart); "I'll Be Seeing You" (I. Kahal, S. Fain); and "Tomorrow" (C. Strouse, M. Charnin)— all the way to the completely "abstract": "For Emily Wherever I May Find Her" (Paul Simon); "Judgment of the Moon and Stars (Ludwig's Theme)" (Joni Mitchell); "Texas Girl at the Funeral of Her Father" (Randy Newman); and "Eli and the Thirteenth Confession" (Laura Nyro). There are the "traveling" songs, like "Walkin' In Memphis" (Marc Cohn); "Route 66" (Bob Troup); "Travelin' Man" (Jerry Fuller); "Ramblin' Man" (Richard Betts); "Homeward Bound" (Paul Simon); "This Flight Tonight" (Joni Mitchell); and "Leavin' On a Jet Plane" (John Denver); and the "interrogatories," like: "How Long Has This Been Going On?" (G. Gershwin/I. Gershwin); "What Are You Doing the Rest of Your Life?" (M. LeGrand, M. and A. Bergman); "Do You Know the Way to San Jose?" (B. Bacharach and H. David); "Where

Are You?" (J. McHugh and W. H. Adamson); "When Will I See You Again?" (K. Gamble and L. Hugg); "What Kind of Fool Am I?" (L. Bricusse and A. Newley); and "Is That All There Is?" (Leiber & Stoller).

There are the "dance instruction" songs, starting with "The Turkey Trot" (E. Smith and T. Kelly); "The Bunny Hop" (R. Anthont and L. Auletti); and "The Grizzly Bear" (traditional) and continuing in subsequent years with "Charleston" (C. Mack and J. P. Johnson); "Bambalina" (M. V. Youmans, H. Stothart, O. Harbach, O. Hammerstein II); "The Varsity Drag" (B. G. DeSylva, L. Brown, R. Henderson); "Carioca" (V. Youmans, G. Kahn, E. Eliscu); "The Continental" (C. Conrad and H. Magidson); "Jersey Bounce" (B. Plater, T. Bradshaw, E. Johnson, R. B. Wright); and "The Huckle Buck" (A. Gibson & R. Alfred)—a genre which survived well into the '60s with "Mashed Potato Time" (G. Dobbins, R. Bateman, W. E. Garrett, K. Mann, B. Holland, and F. C. Gorman); "Baby, Hully Gully" (Fred Smith & Cliff Goldsmith); "The Twist" (H. Ballard); "The Loco-motion" (G. Goffin & C. King); "The Stroll" (C. Otis & N. Lee); "The Monkey Time" (C. Mayfield); "The Swim" (Larry Tamblyn); "Do the Freddie" (D. Lampert & Lou Pegues)—(pant, pant, pant) and so on.

And then of course there is the whole vast firmament of sacred and religious ("gospel") songs that require little if any illustration here, though an interesting phenomenon has surfaced in the late '80s and '90s, and that is the love/gospel song in which the listener is given the option of mentally applying the lyric to a physical love interest or alternatively, You Know Who ("Arms of Love" by M. Smith, G. Chapman and A. Grant). There is the Unitarian "I Believe" (E. Drake, I. Graham, J. Shirl and A. Stillman) and Norman Greenbaum's "Spirit In the Sky," as well as Hank Williams's "I Saw the Light." The pop charts are always ready for a good God song.

The overtly humorous song is legion: "Shall We Join the Ladies?" (Marshall Baerer); "Letter to Jesus" (Mimi Farina); "You're My Favorite Waste of Time" (M. Crenshaw); "Dang Me" (Roger Miller); "Your Bulldog Drinks Champagne" (Jim Stafford); "It's Not Easy Being Green" (Joe Raposo); and the political satires: Tom Lehrer's "Send in the Marines" and "The Folk Song Army"; Tom Paxton's "Sold a Hammer to the Pentagon" and "I Read It in the *Daily News*"; Sylvia Fine's brilliant staccato lyrics for her late husband Danny Kaye's musical films, for example, "Anatole (of Paris)" from *Walter Mitty*, and "Happy Times" from *The Inspector General*; "Bad, Bad Leroy Brown" (Jim Croce); "Charlie Brown" (Leiber and Stoller); "Ahab the Arab" (Ray Stevens); "Does Your Chewing Gum Lose Its Flavor on the Bedpost Overnight?" (B. Rose, M. Bloom, E. Breuer); "Walk Like an Egyptian" (L. Sternberg); and so forth.

In addition, the "novelty," or special interest song (which may not be necessarily humorous by nature), has been around since before the turn of the century. Research indicates that there were probably 150 songs about the telephone by 1900. Before Rudolph Valentino had a chance to cool off in his coffin there was a song on sale in New York called "There's a New Star in Heaven Tonight" (J. K. Brennan, J. McHugh, I. Mills) laying the groundwork for a "necro" genre that flourished during my generation's teen years—"Teen Angel" (J. Surey and R. Surrey); "Leader of the Pack" (G. Morton, J. Barry and E. Greenwich); "Honey" (B. Russell); and "Wild Fire" (Michael Murphey and Larry Cansler)—culminating in the carbine-carrying "Ballad of the Green Berets" in 1966, recorded by a real army man, Sergeant Barry Sadler (written with Robin Moore). In counterpoint to Sadler there was Barry McGuire singing "Eve of Destruction" (P. F. Sloan), with its corpses floating in the Jordan River, and lots of other political and antiwar sloganism—"Blowin' In the Wind" (Bob Dylan); "The Times They Are a'Changin' " (Bob Dylan); "The Great Mandella" (Peter Yarrow, Mary Travers, and Albert Grossman); "For What It's Worth" (Stephen Stills); "Ohio" (Neil Young); "I-Feel-Like-I'm-Fixin'-to-Die Rag" (Joe McDonald); "Give Ireland Back to the Irish" (Paul McCartney); "Ballad of a Thin Man" (Bob Dylan); "Positively Fourth Street" (Bob Dylan); and among thousands of other protests, "Give Peace a Chance" by John Lennon.

There are the deliberately "bad" songs, that is to say songs written on the thinnest spring ice by courageous guys like Paul Williams, who wrote "Dangerous Business," "Wardrobe of Love" and "Hello Ishtar" for 1987's *Ishtar*, a movie about a couple of mediocre songsmiths. The same trick was also attempted by Harry Nilsson in the movie *Popeye*, with universally misunderstood results, and by myself in a song for a film (*How Sweet It is*) starring James Garner and Debbie Reynolds in which I repeated the phrase *"I knew that you knew that I knew that you knew that I knew,"* ad nauseam and incorporated the memorable strophe, *"the pimple on my neck began to hurt, suddenly I wished I changed my shirt."* ("Montage from How Sweet It Is," © 1968), though not even in the same class with the brilliantly inept "Fowl Al," written by Quincy Jones with lyrics by Marilyn and Alan Bergman, which the creepy little murdering counterman at the diner listened to with such gusto in *In the Heat of the Night* (1967). On Warner Bros. weekly NBC television series "Friends," the character Phoebe played by actress Lisa Kudrow sings songs of awe-inspiring mediocrity (e.g., about smelly cats), which the actress herself composes (the individual writers of a particular episode do the lyrics). The discerning songwriter will be required to cock a clever ear at most music to judge whether it is a deliberate miscarriage of good taste or just slovenly work. It is enough to say that a contemplative, mature songwriter will probably not relish being hired to write some deliberately odoriferous undercrafted song. It happens.

Finally the oldest of all these songwriting forms, the ballad: "Battle of New Orleans" (Jimmy Driftwood); "Sink the Bismarck" (T. Franks and J. Horton); "El Paso" (Marty Robbins); "Lonesome Valley" (traditional song arranged by Woody Guthrie); "John Henry" (traditional song); "The Highwayman" (Jimmy Webb); and "Ode to Billie Joe" (Bobbie Gentry).

I recommend highly the *Songwriter's Idea Book* by Sheila Davis (Writer's Digest Books), which analyzes songwriting strategies in relation to type/genre in much finer detail, including song ideas based on antonyms, oxymorons, synecdoches, idioms, axioms and what have you. The writer can make a mental habit of analyzing the songs that he or she hears to determine what genre of title/idea is being utilized as this will lead to a clarity of thinking in regard to the writer's own. (As an exercise, write down and classify song title/ideas in your notebook as you hear them.)

The ancient sawhorse of the ambitious-journalist-without-a-clue-seeking-insight-into-the-songwriting-ethos-question is the numbing: "Which comes first, the words or the music?" The professional songwriter knows that this is a red herring but there are few of us with the temerity to respond: "Ask me a better question." The interviewer might as well ask: "Which comes first, the chicken or the egg?"

The songwriter can't answer the question in a tidy little sound bite. The interviewer has not the time or inclination to pursue the real answer, even if there is an audience who gives a damn about it. The respondent usually mutters an evasive or comical response, perhaps something about a snake swallowing its tail. The question persists in the ether unanswered so that it can be asked again and again of artists who won't respond seriously because they have more important things to think about.

In fact the songwriting fraternity has a range of very concrete opinions on the subject, though rarely has one of its members stated unequivocally that "the words should come first," or vice versa. Gene Lees is emphatic in his contention that the melody should come first. The simple truth is that anyone who has had "hands-on" songwriting experience knows that the process is fluid and that to be successful it must be mutable and words and music mutually adaptable.

Is it preferable to write the melody first as some scholars have said? This is an arbitrary statement and a personal opinion at best. It assumes that a lyric is carved first in stone and that the composer is then required to painstakingly and awkwardly fit the music to it in a two-step process. What is more likely is that if a lyric is written first the composer tries a melody and if it doesn't sing, if there are problems with scansion or conflicts between the form of the lyric and the composer's chord structure or melodic intervals, etc., then he will work with the lyricist to change the melody around—sometimes even drastically. The collaborators may pass it back and forth several times in an ongoing process of revision.

"But if the song is to have a truly melodic nature the music should come first," many composers have complained. I would respond: "That depends." Depends on the song, depends on the lyricist, depends on the composer. We have convincing refutations of this traditional dogma readily at hand and many of these contradictions originate in the same ranks. For instance, Oscar Hammerstein acknowledged that once he started working with Richard Rodgers he mostly wrote lyrics first and then his collaborator set them to music. To quote Hammerstein:

> There is, as a matter of fact, no invariable or inevitable method for writing songs . . . It would seem to most people—and I am one of them—that writing the words first would be a more logical procedure, music being the more flexible and less specific of the two mediums.

Why then, did it become accepted practice among the composers and lyricists of the early twentieth century to "saddle" the lyricist with accommodating the whims of the composer? According to Hammerstein,

Feinstein, Bernstein and virtually any other "stein" one would wish to consult, it all derived from the fact that foreign (European) composers who settled in the States found it extremely difficult to adjust to the English language. Lyric writers were the first to be put upon, and reacted with horror to the strange accents and idiosyncratic and confusing rhythmic gyrations to which their precious lyrics were subjected. The initial battle was lost by default. English-speaking lyricists simply gave up and began writing for the tunes that were available.

That the music should come first is not an uncommon position taken by many pure lyricists—traditionalists like as not—who did not come of age in the modern era of the singer/songwriter, which in spite of howls of protest I choose to date from the advent of John Lennon and Paul McCartney. (Before the Beatles singer/songwriters abounded among the minstrels, songsters and bluesmen of the deep South, and certainly Hank Williams and Woody Guthrie were singer/songwriters, as were John Lee Hooker and Muddy Waters and so many others. Harold Arlen earned his living as a singer before he began to write songs, and who could deny that Hoagy Carmichael was among the great singer/songwriters? Bob Dylan, who was a prototypical singer/songwriter himself, predated the Beatles, but the Beatles were the catalyst or infusion in the inauguration of the modern performer/songwriter epoch.)

The actual dynamics and many basic assumptions about technique have been forever altered by the current preeminence of the artist who writes both words and music and frequently also records his or her song once it is finished. A surprising number draft at least a partially completed lyric first. There is nothing about beginning with a lyric that prohibits the careful development of a beautiful chord structure, and chord structure directs melody into areas of grace and originality at least as much as the form and meter of a lyric. In any case, all the components can be changed as a part of an ongoing fluid process.

Gene Lees complains in his foreword to *The Modern Rhyming Dictionary* that the layman holds a somewhat dim view of the lyricist as a craftsman. "The tone of voice conveys unmistakably that melody writing is a strange and wonderful gift while just about anybody can toss off a lyric. After all, it's only words."

Much folklore supports this almost universal complaint of disrespect by lyricists, including this little gem from Michael Feinstein:

After testifying before the California Fact-Finding Committee on Un-American Activities, Ira Gershwin was excused by Jack Tenney, who said, "Thank you very much for being here, Mr. Gershwin. I'm a great admirer of your brother George, who wrote all those wonderful tunes." (*Nice Work If You Can Get It,* Hyperion.)

Indeed many times the efforts of the lyricist are probably overlooked and it does require inordinate *skill* to craft an effective lyric to an existing tune. It does not follow that in every case the music should come first. A composer who deigns to fit music to an existing lyric is *not* doomed to failure.

I propose that much of this debate is irrelevant for the following reason: Whether or not the music comes first, whether the song is being written by the single entity singer/songwriter or by two people ensconced in a small room together or divided by a long-distance wire on separate coasts, a lyric writer still needs to know how to write a good lyric. How will a bad lyric writer succeed in any writing format? Johnny Mercer once said about the much touted lyricist of a trendy East End musical: "I could eat alphabet soup and shit better lyrics." Let's assume that before Mercer wrote "Moon River" to Hank Mancini's wistful tune that he had learned something about the way the written word stands on its own. In any case we need to learn to construct a good lyric by itself before we attempt the more difficult task of setting words to a relatively unchangeable melody.

I am now going to commit myself to a grand analogy, a risky venture at best—especially if the writer doesn't have the goods. To put it to you briefly and mercifully: A song is a structure—a house like any other. I impose on you to give me the benefit of the doubt and stand with me for a moment in the charmed circle where we propose to build. What will we need—standing here bare-handed as we are—with only a vision of a dwelling vaguely formed somewhere in our imagination? (For the moment we will take for granted that we have a workplace and that we have prepared ourselves within reason for the task ahead and that we have an "idea.")

The next logical step would be to provide ourselves with some raw materials. We might be thinking in an abstract sense of the *shape* or *function* of our proposed structure but like the builders of old New England houses we will probably adapt a floor plan as we go along—in the same way succeeding generations add or demolish rooms until the place suits them.

As for materials: There are two simple exercises, either of which will help the writer define his or her purpose and provide lots of raw "stuff" with which to build. A third alternative is to rely on "chain" or "stream" of consciousness. Let's look at the first two.

The first way is simply to isolate the "idea" or the feelings you wish to convey in a sincere letter to yourself or to someone else. In Chapter One I describe a song "idea" called "Problem Child"—a song I want to write about someone close to me who is subject to debilitating mood swings ranging from euphoria to deep depression. Opening the door to every emotion and observation concerning this matter I recently sat down and wrote a "letter" to this person. I did not think of rhyme or any other kind of organization. I simply poured out my feelings (good title, by the way). This is the letter without any alteration.

Dear Problem Child:

When you cross the line between brilliance and madness then you're out there on your own. You might be overjoyed but find yourself destroyed like Icarus flying toward the sun. You put yourself beyond the reach of anyone who can help you but it's up there where you see those dazzling visions of the way the world should be— or could be. It's up there that just for a second your song is clear in your mind. And freedom seems possible, plausible. But it makes me sad when I see you come down and the light goes out of your eyes like a falcon hooded and caged, bewildered by the confines of reality. There has to be a middle ground. There has to be a sane, quiet space where you can live for a while without pain. That place used to be home—but now you're a man—and home is where you hang your heart. That's the problem. A problem you must solve before you tear your beautiful wings to tatters on some cage of your own making.

The letter could be shorter or longer, as long as the object is to completely air out your feelings on the subject. If you're not inclined to write letters there's a second way:

On a legal pad write down at length every word, phrase, comment, cliché, historical reference, literary reference, poetic reference, feeling, instinct, remembrance of actual fact, image, dream, fantasy or observation that can be made or connected with the "idea" you wish to express. Devote at least an entire work period or more to the collection of these materials.

Whichever of these methods you have chosen (or both) put the research materials aside in a safe place for the time being. (You may want to think about what you've written and make some additions or alterations.) Meditate on the observations you have made in an effort to permeate your consciousness with your "idea." You can do this in the car on the way to work. You may find yourself doing it when your attention is rightfully demanded elsewhere. Don't worry. Most songwriters wear a rather permanently glazed expression. Spouses and friends learn to recognize quickly the signs of out-of-body experience and to adjust their behavior accordingly. We will get back to our lists and letters presently but what we should really be trying to do with this exercise is to teach ourselves to think in a certain way. Experienced songwriters can probably accomplish something very similar on a purely instinctive plane and in seconds with a minimum of handwritten notes. Perhaps two or three brief lines will be enough to set the songwriting consciousness off on a true course as the mind offers, considers and discards thousands of possibilities of rhyme, subject matter, descriptive words, analogies, images, etc., then almost instantly seizes on a turn of phrase that can be utilized, finds it serviceable and incorporates it in a line good enough to be jotted down. This is the "chain" or "stream" of consciousness that we have heard so much about but we need to strip it of its intrinsic random and undisciplined quality and put it to work for us in a *certain specific direction.*

The amateur songwriter's greatest single failing and one that is immediately obvious to the listener is that the writer does not know exactly where the song is going. Often the point of the song is circumnavigated brilliantly. Sometimes there are two or even three pretty good ideas in the song but the listener is left unsatisfied. (The hors d'oeuvres were tasty but the waiter never served the main course.) So all of our background materials—letters, lists, "chains" or "streams" of consciousness—must be appraised carefully to make sure the words we have chosen make a meaningful contribution to the story or "idea." The most fabulous metaphor or double entendre ever conceived or the niftiest color-word or rhyme imaginable is expendable if it is not on target—if the meaning of the lyric could be clearer without it.

Now those are just some of the materials we intend to use, but what *form* will they take? Perhaps some will say at this juncture, "A barn doesn't suit my fancy just now. I have in mind a nice, sturdy cathedral." Fine. You build a cathedral, I'll build a barn or log cabin. The same rules will apply. Understanding those rules of construction calls now for a study of the *conventions* of form. That is to say the traditional, generic songwriting forms with which we are all subliminally familiar; the ones that will not leave our listeners confused about whether we have constructed a gymnasium or a motor lodge. Frank Lloyd Wright no doubt began with a modest three-bedroom family home before tackling the Guggenheim.

The first element of "form" is its smallest subdivision: the individual word and its close relative, the rhyme. These will be our timbers and nails. With them we can build an endoskeleton or frame for our edifice. Alan Jay Lerner purportedly said (and I paraphrase) that one word and *one word only* was suitable for each function in a lyric line, a passionate belief said to have been shared by James Joyce. With all due respect, it seems to me to believe that would be to invite failure against odds beyond comprehension.

Without subjecting ourselves to such a strenuous and unrealistic criteria it is fair to say that some words will be more useful than others for our purpose and that one of the writer's most effective tools in the construction of a lyric is the plain old dictionary. We already have a kind of rhyming dictionary stored in our own brains and it is this ever-present and handy list of rhymes to which we will most often refer. Indeed, some songwriters believe strongly that writers should resort only to those words that are already contained in their heads. There is a rationale for this belief, but I prefer to ignore it and regard the rhyming dictionary as an enormous resource. We could think of it as a list of inventory for the different materials stored in the lumberyard.

The architect imagines the kind of building he wants to construct and his mind plays with the wide variety of materials available. In the dictionary he finds oaken words, words of stone and paper, plywood words and words like steel beams, words of ironwood and ash, rich resonant words of mahogany and cherry, rococo words that swirl like burled walnut, simple pungent pine words, heavy words of dark ebony, ephemeral, silly words of balsa, everlasting words of marble and granite, and translucent words like colored glass along with blunt, pragmatic words made of lead and cement.

My adventurous friend—the one who walks across entire countries for sport—likes to read dictionaries. That's right, he reads them from cover to cover. When he runs across a word like *quoin* (a solid exterior angle) and it melts like butterscotch taffy in his mouth, he writes it down on a master list of cherished, descriptive and meaningful words.

Few of us are naturally inclined to sit and read an entire dictionary (like *Merriam-Webster's Collegiate* for example, at fourteen hundred pages) but I will advance the argument that a writer who attempts to write prose, poetry, song lyrics or automobile advertising without a vocabulary of suitable depth is entering a tournament of wits unarmed. I will go one step further and say that if there is any intrinsic merit in curiosity then we *should* read at least one dictionary from *aardvark* to *Zwolle* (a city in the Netherlands). At the very least we should be on the lookout in our reading and conversation for that unfamiliar word with an intriguing sound, the one whose meaning we have always guessed at but about which we are not certain. A few pages in the back of the songwriter's notebook can be set aside for scribbling these meanings down, particularly words of a descriptive or evocative nature.

Is there any advantage in seeking out unusual, interesting words and in using them in preference to the mundane and commonplace? Let's look at the prevailing point of view first. It goes something like this: "Song lyrics should be as simple-minded as possible. Multisyllables or any hint of subtlety or nuance should be avoided. Assume that your listener has the equivalent of a sixth-grade education and you won't be far wrong."

From a commercial standpoint—whether or not his assumption about the mental capabilities of his listener is accurate—the writer would appear to be on safe ground by adhering to this commonly held, preemptive doctrine. In practice, however, there is at least one major pitfall.

The consistent use of overly familiar language in line after line nudges the writer inexorably toward cliché. Why so? Because generations of industrious *rhymers* have already applied themselves to wringing out the possibilities of such standbys as "love" (above, dove) and "heart" (start, apart) and "eyes" (cries, tries). The cliché is waiting in the tired rhyme with a Cheshire cat grin.

A general rule would be: When deciding on a title or a hook line for a proposed song try to include a key word that offers the greatest numbers of rhyming possibilities. I have been recently working on a song called "Just for Now." Let's look for a moment at Clement Wood's list from *The Complete Rhyming Dictionary* of possible rhymes for the word "now":

Allow (usable but brings to mind "all that heaven will allow"
　　—a bit sappy)
Anyhow (usable but not a very attractive word and definitely overused)
Avow (archaic and probably unusable)
Bough (ditto)
Bow (takes me in the "take my final bow" direction—don't like)

Bow-wow (really!)

Brow (nobody really says "brow" anymore—they say "forehead")

Chow (I wasn't really thinking of writing a comical song)

Cow (she's ugly, but not that ugly)

Dhow (arcane, perhaps might find a home in special material)

Disallow (smacks of the IRS)

Disavow (legalese)

Endow (more legalese)

Foo Chow (?)

Frau (she's not German)

Frow (a variation on "froe"—a cleaving tool)

Hankow (in China?)

Hoosegow (it's not a Western either)

How (usable)

Howe (her name isn't Howe)

Kowtow (no comment)

Kwangchow (definitely in China)

Landau (she's not a car)

Mow (a piled-up stack or the sound a Chinese cow makes)

Now (identical)

Overbrow (hmm?)

Plough, Plow (a rough word, distinctly out of place in a romantic song)

Pow-wow (unusable)

Prow (arcane and unusable)

Row (comedic)

Scow (ugly)

Slough (a mass of dead tissue separating from an ulcer)

Snow-plough (they've already listed plough—why list "snow-plough?")

Somehow (usable but eliminates "anyhow")

Soochow (somehow I don't think it looks much like Nashville)

Sow (what I call her when she calls me a pig)

Swatow (Poland?)

Thou (distinctly archaic with religious overtones)

Upplow (not even defined in Webster's)

Vow (Dudley Do-Right—smells moldy)

Wenchow (a buxom Chinese barmaid of easy virtue)

Wow (!)

So, out of this impressive-looking list of forty-four rhymes I have five entire words with which to work. Depending on the direction the song takes as it develops this might be cut down to three. Which shows that perhaps I either need another song title or that I might write the song in such a way that I do not repeatedly need to rhyme the word "now" or that I go to a thesaurus, the second most important songwriting tool, and find a word that means the same as "now" or a similar phrase ending in a different word that essentially means the same thing (syn.: present, today, at once, directly, forthwith, immediately, instantly, right away, promptly, expeditiously, quickly, speedily, swiftly).

Let's say that after perusing this list of possibilities from the thesaurus I decide that it would do just as well to call the song "Just for Today." Now according to Clement Wood I suddenly have a list of 258 rhyming possibilities.

The almighty thesaurus gives us a higher court of appeals to resort to when the going gets tough. If the word which we have chosen doesn't make a true rhyme—or any kind of rhyme for that matter—or offers few, if any, useful alternatives, we can refer to the thesaurus, very quickly find a *synonym* for that troublesome word and go back to the rhyming dictionary searching for a new rhyme that may succeed in completing the same thought. For instance, in the same work-in-progress I have written a line "while the rain falls and the (*blank*)(*blank*) -*alls*." The music fairly cries out for this rhythmic resolution. I have experimented with "and the siren calls" but find it unsatisfactory, suggesting Greek mythology or cop cars. So I change "falls" to "comes," and arrive at "*when* the rain *comes* and the *thunder drums*." This process should go on constantly during the construction of the lyric in a fluid give-and-take of trial and error.

When I wrote my song "Adios" about leaving California to move East I suppose I could have come up with some "title/idea" incorporating the word "good-bye." Other lines in the song would almost inevitably have ended with "cry" or "try"—perhaps the dreaded "I feel like I could *die*"— or the equally noxious "and now it's time to *fly*." Because of my "adopted" mother's Hispanic heritage I decided on "adios," an alternative that gave me both a moody, mariachi-flavored musical framework and access to some unusual rhymes. I actually rhymed the word "morose" (whose inclusion seems to have amazed a great many folks). I was also led to the little-used "close" which is a fuzzy-warm word that fit perfectly. I was safeguarded to some extent from cliché by my decision to shy away from "good-bye" as my premier rhyming choice. (Linda Ronstadt subsequently recorded "Adios" on her platinum-selling *Cry Like a Rainstorm Howl Like the Wind*. It was a Top-10 single.)

In a recent effort called "Time Flies," a somewhat fatalistic view of the way human beings perceive or fail to perceive the passage of time, I observed that "picnics on warm Julys" become strangely—almost without our noticing—"deep *umber* autumns and winter good-byes." There is an extensive palette of names for colors almost as diverse as the colors themselves. Skies do not have to be either "blue" or "gray." Sunsets are not by definition "golden." (There is a sunset in "Adios" that is "blood-red," 'nuff said.)

Even if writers are successful in using commonplace words and rhymes—that is, managing to utilize them without indulging in innocuous clichés—they may deprive themselves of an enormous source of inspiration and opportunity in doing so. The interesting choice of word leads to the unique rhyme. The unique rhyme to an extraordinary line. The extraordinary line to an original perspective that makes a song stand out from the rest. By varying our word choices and being biased slightly in favor of the unusual, by giving our listener the benefit of the doubt in our assumptions of his or her intelligence we grant ourselves the potential to create original and significant works, songs that will make a reputation for the writer as an innovator—someone to be taken seriously. It is such a writer that producers and recording artists listen to almost without question if for no other reason than curiosity.

It is dreadful the way the same mistakes are perpetuated over and over again in songwriting, particularly the same careless false rhymes (*identities*)—"time" with "mine," for example, "self" with "else," "girl" with "world." It would seem that if a sinner will only recommit the same wrong enough times God himself will desensitize and eventually mistake assonance for a good deed. Have *I* ever sinned? Over and over again. Sometimes unconsciously, sometimes deliberately because I could think of no better way to accomplish my aims and sometimes out of simple frustration. (I got tired and gave up.) However in the latter half of my career I have put increasing pressure on myself to avoid these kinds of errors and I believe it has forced me to write better lyrics.

And I need you more than want you
And I want you for all <u>time</u>,
And the Wichita Lineman is still on the <u>line</u> . . .

—Jimmy Webb,
"Wichita Lineman"

The false rhyme is with us so much on a daily basis that we simply don't hear it anymore (I didn't notice this mistake in "Wichita Lineman" until years later). Is this distinction important? Well, yes and no. In popular music it comes down to a stubborn personal integrity: Do I want my lyrics to rhyme like bona fide poetry? And then this: If it comes down to a decision between using a false rhyme or losing the message in this song what will I do? Unfortunately in the latter case often the false rhyme is an excuse. To be idealistic the function of the lyricist is to change prose (or prose-based concepts) into authentically rhymed, emotionally affecting verse. False rhyme is to be frowned upon, especially when you've decided you're going to do it anyway.

Some writers on this subject have referred to the "usable false rhyme" or "imperfect rhyme" meaning two words that while not proper rhymes are close enough in vowel sound to create a passable rhyming effect (assonance). Some examples would be smile/wild, again/friend, or town/around. Another kind of "usable" false rhyme consists of two words with different vowel sounds but similar or identical closing consonants like black/dreck, peel/bell, able/feeble, etc. This is properly referred to as *consonance*. There are others: *unstressed, para rhyme, augmented,* etc. The writer would be wise to note that using these false rhymes even though they may admirably serve a purpose will inevitably weaken the effect of a given line. The listener will be offended on a subliminal level even if he or she doesn't know the *difference* between a false and proper rhyme.

Be aware also that when a word *contains* its rhyming partner as *proof* contains *roof* or *share* contains *hair* that there is a subtle diminishing of its effect on the ear. Using one of these quasi-rhymes is a bit like choosing a dull knife over the sharp-edged dagger with a proper blade. At least one well-respected Broadway lyricist of my acquaintance will not give these *double consonant* rhymes the high sign. This kind of "cheating" should be confined to the least conspicuous parts of the song, the interior rhyme scheme, for example, not paraded out proudly at the end of important lines that close off verses. Consider my song "Highwayman," where I bellow at the end of a verse *"and when the yards broke off they say that I got <u>killed</u>, but I am living <u>still</u>."* (Do as I say, not as I do.) It is common for the amateur to believe that "spit" rhymes with "fits." It doesn't. Pluralities (cats) do not rhyme with singularities (that). The present tense—always ending in an "s" (flies, cries)—will not rhyme with the singular "sky." This will sometimes cause a writer a severe cramp upon committing his syntax to the present tense as I did in a recent song when film producers insisted on the title "Where Love Resides."

> *A heart that's young has to try its wings*
> *It leaves the nest and carelessly glides*
> *Into the clouds where confusion hides*
> *And when it's lost forgets the place*
> *Where Love Resides . . . "*
>
> —Jimmy Webb,
> "Where Love Resides"

An entire category of potential rhymes—virtually half of those available—are eliminated by the insistence of the present tense that it will rhyme only with pluralities. The present tense, though one of the loveliest modes of lyric writing, presents a special challenge.

While the use of false rhymes is implicitly if wrongly condoned in most of popular music, there is one arena where such carelessness is bound to bring fire and brimstone down in bulk on the brow (forehead?) of the offender: In the musical theatre critics have an ear out for such sloppiness and will make a point of calling attention to it. Just a few oversights of this nature could sway a critic to write a distinctly unfavorable review. The theatre buff is likely to be well-educated and inclined to a high literary standard, comparing the work of new lyricists to that of demigods like Lerner, Hammerstein, Sondheim, Hart—well, you get the picture.

When with very high hopes I submitted my first New York written musical, *Tuxedo*, to successful producers, I was chagrined when the score was returned with the comment, "It's no *Sound of Music*." I can assure you there were few if any false rhymes in the libretto. If there had been a preponderance of false rhymes included, the score would have been returned with no comment whatsoever, if not thrown in the shredder. Writers of lyrics for

Broadway musicals are specialists in the most precise sense of the word. Their genre has its own discrete and highly complex rules, mores and customs. Intricate "three-rhymes," amusing mental tricks made infamous by Larry Hart, have been a regular fixture in the lyrics of Broadway shows, though they rarely—if ever—are found in a pop song. Hart regaled some of his audience and permanently offended the rest by rhyming "Syria" and "Siberia," "Virginia," and "Abyssinia," "court you, gal" and "Portugal," "Corner ya," and "California," and finally, "go to hell for ya," and "Philadelphia." Young writers particularly interested in writing for the theatre should obtain copies of Oscar Hammerstein's *Notes On Lyrics*, 1949, Simon & Schuster, as well as Stephen Sondheim's *Talk On Lyrics*, 1973. There is a whole category of rhyme that is found almost exclusively in the Broadway genre known as *minor accent*, consisting of *contiguous, internal (rhyme scheme) trailing*, etc., valid or "perfect rhyme," but definitely off the beaten path in the context of the lowly pop song.

All this having been said it is undeniable that the false rhyme has carved its niche in America's musical heritage. The most famous and memorable false rhyme in history is found in "Red River Valley."

> *Do not hasten to bid me <u>adieu</u>*
> *But remember the Red River Valley*
> *And the cowboy who loved you so <u>true</u>.*
>   —Traditional

To understand without question the nature of a false rhyme it is necessary to consult a rhyming dictionary, which is the most important tool in the shaping of basic materials. I have always used *The Complete Rhyming Dictionary* by Clement Wood for a number of reasons, the most important being facility and ease of operation. In the heat of battle the most significant factor is probably speed. I readily admit that it is more likely the years I have spent using Clement Wood that inspire this favoritism. My copy is well-thumbed. There are grooves in the disintegrating pages that I can read like Braille along with an occasional phone number that will fetch an authentic New York pie or notes that remind me to fix plumbing difficulties in houses in which I no longer live.

I owe it to you to give this rhyming dictionary business the once-over, but first a small digression. A universally esteemed colleague of mine was holding forth a few years ago on the subject of rhyming dictionaries in this way: "Well, you can't really use them (Foo Phaw) because it always *sounds* like you're using them (Huff, Puff) and it doesn't sound *natural* (Sniff, Achoo!) and the listener *knows*, I mean he *knows*, when he's hearing a rhyme that comes from a rhyming dictionary (Yawn). I mean it's a *stilted* thing, you know? and it's just better to sing those words that are common to your own intelligence!" (The speaker had an IQ of at least 180.) Thank you for that! We know now for a fact that guns don't kill people, right? It's rhyming dictionaries that kill people! And it's not incompetence that shoots uninspired hack rhymes into our earlobes with all the finesse of a cannon. Please, if I may: It is bad writing that ruins rhymes—not lists of words that do or do not rhyme. Having taken such a forceful stand on the subject, I must now inform you that Hammerstein fastened a rather jaundiced eye on the rhyming dictionary, feeling in particular that it hampered one's search for sophisticated word play like that of Lorenz Hart. "A rhyming dictionary, however, should be used as a supplement to one's own ingenuity, and not a substitute for it. I do not open mine until I have exhausted my own memory and invention of rhymes for a word." So said Mr. Hammerstein, and it's hard to argue with this perfectly natural description of the way most songwriters work, that is, exhausting their own mental resources first and then falling back on the rhyming dictionary when difficulty sets in.

On a recent trip to Barnes & Noble I found eight rhyming dictionaries on the shelf in a neat row. Store management touted Dell's *Complete Rhyming Dictionary, Revised Edition* as their number-one seller.

The Dell dictionary is a rather undistinguished paperback originally copyrighted in 1936. A representative of the store admitted that its popularity was probably a reflection of its low price because of strenuous mass-marketing on the part of the publisher. Dell sells a lot of dictionaries—mostly to neophytes recently bitten by the rap virus, but if they don't turn up their noses at a rhyming dictionary, then why should those of us who imagine that we are more sophisticated?

What should strike the consumer almost immediately is how venerable some of these dictionaries are. *The New Rhyming Dictionary and Poet's Handbook* (Burge and Johnson) was first published in 1931. Though it is arrayed in a modern-looking soft cover and has been revised in 1957 and most recently in 1991, there is a distinct aura of antiquity about the rhymes listed and the foreword offers little in terms of practical advice for the songwriter.

My own admitted favorite, Clement Wood's *The Complete Rhyming Dictionary*, debuted five years later in 1936, and while songwriting is mentioned briefly in the foreword, Wood's true love is obviously classic poetry. The fact that "Aldebaran" rhymes with "Baconian," "thaumatolatry" with "gyneolatry" and "extra-judicial" with "recrementitial" is of not much interest when one is trying desperately to finish a new song for Meat Loaf.

Jane Shaw Whitfield did not write Victorian novels. Her *Songwriter's Rhyming Dictionary* came on the scene in 1951, with Langford Reed's *The Writer's Rhyming Dictionary* a decade later and, without intending to be deliberately unkind, these are both nondescript.

Finally in 1981 a seminal work appeared, conceived by a recognized professional for use by other songwriters, *The Modern Rhyming Dictionary* by Gene Lees, author of some truly elegant and well-crafted lyrics including "Quiet Nights of Quiet Stars (*Corcovado*)," "Song of the Jet (*Samba Do Aviao*)," and "Waltz for Debbie." The volume holds up well in the present day—particularly the scholarly and extensive foreword in seven chapters, addressing songwriting fundamentals and some finer points even if a bit sternly. Lees has devised a phonetic method of finding words that is quite clear, and has included interesting sub-hyphen groupings according to the consonant that begins the final syllable or syllables of the words in the two and three rhyme sections as well as many *imperfect rhymes*—carefully marked. He pays particular attention to the vernacular, even to differences in speech patterns in various parts of the country—a very nice touch. Cross-referencing is by page number, thank heaven! This dictionary is a no-nonsense tool for the serious songwriter and is highly recommended.

In 1985 the *Penguin Rhyming Dictionary* (Rosalind Fergusson) rolled off the presses completely ignoring Mr. Lees's innovations and one can't help wondering just what exactly *was* the point except that dictionaries are the literary equivalent of pork bellies and most large publishing houses probably feel as though they have to print a few every now and then.

An affable little hardcover volume appeared in 1987, the *Webster's Compact Rhyming Dictionary*, whose primary appeal is its small chunky stature—rather like hefting one's overweight two-year-old brother. Unfortunately cuteness doesn't really count.

To turn to something more useful, Sue Young's *The New Comprehensive American Rhyming Dictionary* is the best new dictionary I have read. What can you say about an author who lists "genitalia" with "never fail ya"? or

"Smokey the Bear" with "ready-to-wear"? or "rouge et noire" with "Hershey bar"? The dictionary is fresh and extremely easy to use, concentrating more on the sound of words than their strict spelling and extensively incorporating American slang. I was impressed with the simple fact that the phonetic sound "ou" (how now brown cow) was listed as "ow"—much more convenient than phonetics and a lot easier to find when a writer is in a hurry. Young submits lists of expressions and ideas that rhyme in addition to individual words. Brilliant!

Random House and Penguin both make a neat little shirt-pocket rhyming dictionary in a durable plastic cover each of which lists over thirty thousand words. Random House would seem to have the edge in ease of operation. (Every writer should have a small dictionary for travel.)

A Zillion Kajillion Rhymes is a program for Macintosh users that lists over six and a half million words. It will rhyme any given syllable in multi-syllable rhymes instantly, always carefully reminding the user of the root word and correct spelling. If it can't find a rhyme for the word you type in, it will attempt to rhyme on a common root word by automatically stripping prefixes and suffixes—usually in less than a second. In fact it will do just about everything (including the dishes) except write the song for you, and one of these days who knows? There may even be a program that will help you to do that as well.

By far the wittiest and most entertaining of the old favorites, *Words to Rhyme With* by Willard Espy (1986) covers heretofore unexplored territory in the discovery and listing of obscure and eccentric rhymes. (As a point of interest Espy maintains that a rhyming "dictionary" is not a dictionary at all since it defines nothing.)

For the writer interested in humorous or comedic creations no work is likely to supplant the drollery of Willard Espy. The monotony of his neat columns is occasionally relieved by a gem like this:

THE MADCHEN AND THE NAZI
A Madchen met a Nazi
And said, "I will not heil.
It isn't hotsy-totsy,
It's going out of style.
Today I'm feeling smoochy;
I'm off to meet Il Duce;

> We'll do the hoochy-koochy,
>
> And snuggle for awhile."

(Try singing that one with "The Addams Family" theme!)

The commonalty of these dictionaries is that all of them will purport to tell you the difference between a false and genuine rhyme. A proper rhyme is simply a word whose terminal (last) sound is exactly like another excepting the consonant which must always be different—provided there *is* a consonant. (In the latter case, for example, *air* rhymes impeccably with *lair*, though the rhyme is not as strong as with *pair* or *fair*.

Usually rhyming dictionaries are divided into three sections—in classical terms semi-iamb, iambic and dactylic. Put simply: one- two- and three-syllable rhymes. Single rhymes ("masculine") always fall on the last syllable:

bird/third, night/invite

Note that in the example even though "*invite*" is a two-syllable word its rhyming with "*night*" is a single rhyme. The same would hold true if "*invite*" were rhymed with "to *fight*."

Double rhymes ("penults," "feminine") or "two-rhymes" are rhymes that fall on the second to last syllable (in two-syllable rhymes, the rhyme must fall on a stressed syllable, otherwise it is called *unstressed* rhyme—shallow/follow, silly/wily):

Action/traction, miasmic/protoplasmic, self-praiser/star-gazer

Note in these examples that regardless of the number of syllables in each they are all double rhymes because of the last two syllables.

Triple rhymes ("antepenults" or "three-rhymes") rhyme on the third to last syllable.

Reference/deference, cheekily/sneakily, beckoning/reckoning.

No word from any one of these three major subdivisions will rhyme legitimately with a word from another. *The number of syllables in a word does not determine whether it is a single, double or triple rhyme*, only the actual placement of the rhymed syllable among the last three syllables.

Three-syllable rhymes rarely occur in most pop songs but, as has been stated, are more likely to turn up in Broadway scores and will almost certainly be heard in the specialty number that precedes the Academy Awards broadcast. One- and two-syllable rhymes, on the other hand, are in constant use. Though it may seem awkward at first the writer will eventually learn to find these quickly.

It is also possible for the fiercely ambitious rhymer with a good supply of diet pills to create "four-rhymes," "quadruple rhymes," or more clearly stated, "four-syllable rhymes."

Slumped on the floor
Dumped on the shore

Compound rhymes of this nature (this amounts to rhyming a complete phrase) are usually not—very rarely *can* be—technically perfect. They are found most often in a comical context where their "busyness" and imperfect nature contribute to a tongue-in-cheek effect. Most rhyming dictionaries will not attempt to list them, as they are an artificial construct distilled by the writer from literally hundreds of thousands of possible combinations.

Here are some things to watch out for when choosing a rhyming dictionary. Most have exclusive systems for searching out rhymes and tend to spell their phonetics differently. As Neil Radisch and David Goldstein ask in their foreword to *A Zillion Kajillion Rhymes*, "Would you find rhymes for the word 'fate' under 'ait' or 'ate'? Or maybe it's listed in the 'ee's' under 'eight.' " Buy one that has a system you can understand.

There is a baker's dozen of types of *near rhymes* that almost always come across as mistakes. Consider *smothered* rhyme: "run*ning*" with "*sing*"—the latter occurring fairly often in amateur songwriting but rarely without achieving an unintentional comic effect. Consider as well *identicals*, words that sound exactly the same with different spellings like "hair" and "hare." Another kind of *identical* is a word having the same consonant and vowel sounds as another word such as acquisitive, inquisitive, uninquisitive. Switching the prefix around does not suffice. Curiously, many dictionaries list these as kosher. "Eye rhymes" are words in which the rhyming syllables are spelled the same and *appear* to rhyme like cow/blow, cough/enough, slough/bough, etc. They don't rhyme, folks. Remember also that many rhyming dictionaries contain errors relating specifically to which words do or do not rhyme. If two words sound like a rhyme in idiomatic or common usage, they can be used no matter what the correct spelling or pronunciation. For instance, some traditional dictionaries would unequivocally condemn the attempt to rhyme "real" with "steal" as clumsy because they are respectively a one- and a two-syllable word. In the trenches this is acceptable.

It is also proper to rhyme two individual words with a two-syllable word as in "miller/kill her," being careful not to attempt "bill sir" (as in "your bill, sir"). To further explain, "Ohio" rhymes with "I owe" as long as the writer is careful not to attempt "I know" or "I go" with "Ohio." Many rhyming dictionaries will provide footnotes pointing out these *mosaic* rhyme schemes to the writer in addition to tricks regarding the rhyming of monosyllables with pluralities as in *mix* with all words ending in "*-ick*" provided that an "s" is added ("mix" with "trick" + "s," etc.).

> *Rhyme is a shelter for mediocrity.*
> —Shelley

Perhaps so. Certainly wonderful songs have been written without rhyme. Gene Lees cites "Moonlight in Vermont" and I agree with him that this exquisite standard does not suffer noticeably for lack of it. Stephen Bishop's gorgeous "Separate Lives" rhymes—it would seem—only in a diffident, unintentional way. John Lennon's "I Am the Walrus" relies for the most part on percussive alliteration and repetition of consonance. Paul Simon's elegant "America" doesn't rhyme one bit, nor does the first verse of "I Got Rhythm" (George and Ira Gershwin).

However, the rhyming tradition so predominates American music that it is interesting to speculate on just what the vast listening public's reaction *would* be if the government of this country were to be suddenly usurped by some mad poetic dictator who would then decree that "all rhyme is a crime" and that all rhyming dictionaries would have to be burned forthwith. Me thinks he would remain in power, not much longer than a hour.

Long ago so-called serious poets abandoned the pretense of rhyme and it is to this development that songwriters probably owe the intelligentsia's perception of us as lying pretty close to the bottom of the cultural food chain. Ezra Pound once wrote in a letter to his mother:

> *Tell me not in mournful wish-wash*
> *Life's a sort of sugared dish-wash*
> *And all that sort of thing.**

A Serious Character: The Life of Ezra Pound by Humphrey Carpenter, ©1988, Houghton Mifflin Co.

This struck home when a writer in *Rolling Stone* referred to my "soapsy, sudsy lyrics" in a review of a Ronstadt album (*The Moon Is a Harsh Mistress*). Jack Nicholson noted in his eulogy to John Huston that one of the only things Huston had truly hated was "maudlin songs." This subject is deserving of a short digression. "Maudlin" songs are said to be songs that are just too "on the nose." Feinstein (in his book *Nice Work If You Can Get It*) points out that Yip Harburg despised maudlin songs and that in his "Brother Can You Spare a Dime" the beggar is portrayed as a man with dignity, not a sap. This is dangerous territory for any writer as the subject resolves itself immediately into a question of judgment. An attack on a writer's lyric is often indistinguishable from an attack on his person. Let's check it out.

What is the difference between a "lyric" and a "poem," between a "poem" and "doggerel," between "doggerel" and "folk art," between a "maudlin song" and one that is merely depressing? First a technical view of an emotional subject: What is the difference between *poetry* and other kinds of writing? A healthy controversy on this subject was still raging when Carl Sandburg wrote, "What can be explained is not poetry." The ear has the answer. Poetry has an audible rhythmic regularity, a *cadence*. Prose or writing that has no deliberate rhythm has a quality of *irregularity*, an undisciplined flow of accented and unaccented syllables. True? Not necessarily. Much serious poetry is written in *blank verse* with only a casual doff of the hat to regularity while the greatest of prose writers agonize over the rise and fall of accents in a given sentence and rewrite endlessly and tirelessly to achieve the correct rhythmic balance, which might as well be defined as a kind of *regularity*. The correct answer is that some writing is arbitrarily divided into lines of a fixed and repetitive regularity and/or rhythmic symmetry or asymmetry, and when deliberately arranged into verses, stanzas, etc., these constructs are called *poems*. Some poetry is divided into irregular or eccentric lines with little or no regard for a fixed syllable count or rhyme, and this is called *blank verse*. Some poetry is simply written out in long elegant strands, sentence following sentence, and sometimes may rightfully be regarded as *prose*. Here I expect some resistance but there is no denying that some prose, that of Pablo Neruda for example, is a kind of poetry. Some have said that the prose of James Joyce is really poetry. Leonard Bernstein has said that Joyce's repetition of elementary sounds gives us "the whole range of poetic assonance." Bernstein said a lot of wonderful things concerning poetry. "We can see poetry born of the repetition of actual words, not just sounds," he said, "that it is repetition, modified in one way or another that gives poetry its musical qualities," he also said, among many other great and wonderful things that cannot be included here. However, the reader is gently nudged in the direction of the composer, who was a more knowledgeable and confident assessor/analyst of the semantic and sub-textual origins and meanings of poetry than many literary men of his generation. "Honesty in this battle of bitterness and justice makes for the musical line in poetry, or for a prosody that can be called accurate, beautiful, free," Bernstein continued, reiterating his consistent and recurring belief in duality at the very core of creativity (*The Unanswered Question, Bernstein's Lectures at Harvard*). Philosopher Eli Siegel seems to have come to the same conclusion. "Poetry is exactitude and value at once. There can be exactitude about the unseen. Poetry gets to the music resulting from authentic, precise, and entire examination," he wrote, and then added, "Poetic music, among other things, is a junction of pride and humility, endeavor and rest" (*The Right of Aesthetic Realism to Be Known*, Letter #170, June 30, 1976, The Aesthetic Realism Foundation).

So we come back to the question: What is the difference between *poetry* and other kinds of writing? The professors will tell you that poetry is *poetry* because it "awakens the higher or nobler emotions." Take a moment to think about that. Such a posture would effectively eliminate Allen Ginsberg's gut-wrenching "Howl" as poetry, not to mention a good deal of what most "serious" poets have written. In truth poetry is a kind of writing that deliberately evokes *any emotional response*. Since especially laughter is an emotional response, a good limerick is unquestionably poetry. Though song lyrics share many of the characteristics of poetry and indeed many times poems have been set to music and used as songs, experienced writers like Stephen Sondheim are aware of many subtle differences. "Lyrics exist in time—as opposed to poetry, for example. You can read a poem at your own speed," he has said. The content of a lyric differs from that of a poem in that storytelling or development must be accomplished more expeditiously within the confines of the song. There are a finite number of "slots" available for syllables of any kind in the format of the popular song. A quick count of the number of notes in many a familiar melody will reveal that there are surprisingly few; therefore, the lyric must contain a relatively large amount of information, content, story, development—call it what you will—in comparison to the poem.

A critic can call any poem "doggerel." That is no more than a slur. "Doggerel" or "maudlin" or "sappy" or "sentimental" is in the ear of the listener. By the by, "sentimental" is okay as it is defined as "marked or governed by feeling, sensibility, or emotional idealism." It is "sentimentality" that is to be avoided, like the fiddleback spider, being as it is "the quality or state of being sentimental to excess or in affectation." Again we are faced with a judgment call and must keep a sharp eye on our outpourings to insure they are not overly gooey.

The intellectual elite probably believe that most of the lyrics that songwriters create are "doggerel" of one kind or another—that is to say "trivial." Even in the early 1700s songwriters appear to have been lodged close to the bottom of the cultural totem pole, as around 1711 Joseph Addison (the famous British essayist) said, "Nothing is capable of being well set to music that is not nonsense." "Mawkish" efforts are even worse, having as they do "an insipid, often unpleasant taste, sickly sentimental." The young songwriter has now been warned about the implacable nature of the enemy. Under a rather large umbrella, preferred twentieth-century taste in art of all kinds has been characterized by a kind of detachment, or sangfroid. It is simply not *chic* to be carried away in one's emotional reaction to a subject. All serious communication or complaint must be carefully wrapped in a protective coating of irony and/or satire.

Believe it or not, one of the classical definitions of a "verse" is that it [a verse] does *not* "awaken the higher or nobler emotions." Curious then, that the first section or division of a popular song has come to be known as a "verse." Even more curious that pure poetry, including elitist blank verse, has lapsed into relative obscurity in the same century while humble popular song has become the universal driving force behind political and social change, not to mention an economic juggernaut whose success is probably eclipsed only by the historical advent of the popular newspaper. Surely these popular songs must be awakening emotions of some kind. Whether they are "higher or nobler" we must leave to the clergy.

My contention is that since song lyrics undoubtedly provoke an emotional response ("Long Tall Texan" by Henry Strzelecki) they *are* poetry. Now we come to the detractors' party trick of reading the lyrics of a given song aloud without benefit of melody. This is roughly akin to viewing the queen of England at her coronation without her gown. I was recently a guest on a popular London radio talk show and my host—as a kind of wicked surprise—launched almost immediately into a reading of the lyrics from "Too Young to Die," a song from my *Suspending Disbelief* album also recorded by David Crosby. He read:

> *I recall my so-called mis-spent youth*
> *It seems more worthwhile every single day*
> *Cruisin' Van Nuys and actin' so uncouth*
> *All the joys of runnin' away . . .*
>
> —Jimmy Webb,
> "Too Young to Die"

"That's really awful, isn't it?" he asked in jocular fashion before proceeding unbidden:

> *No speed limit on Nevada state line*
> *The air was red wine on those top-down nights*
> *Just you and me my old roller skate*
> *And the common sense to know our rights*
> *We knew our rights then . . .*
>
> —Jimmy Webb,
> "Too Young to Die"

He never got to the chorus. If he had, he would have discovered that I wasn't using "roller skate" as a term of endearment for any girlfriend but that I had actually written the song *for an automobile.* Let's not grouse over the fact that most people just don't pay very much attention anymore. Song lyrics are meant to be heard in their entirety and with the music that helped shape them.

A *song* is a magical marriage between a *lyric* (some words) and a *melody* (some notes). It is not a *poem.* It is not *music.* It is in this gray area of synthesis between language, rhythm and sound that some of the most acute of all sensors of human emotion lie.

I would like to hear more experimentation in the area of setting blank verse to music. (There is nothing in this world more stunning than John Corigliano's choral setting for Dylan Thomas's "Fern Hill.") The imaginative and courageous innovator has my blessing for what it's worth, but by and large the world is not apt to pay much attention and airplay will most likely be scarce.

The best most of us can hope for is to continue to "rhyme in time with notes sublime" and to try to do it well. But even if our rhymes are impeccable and reasonably fresh there are other clichés, nonrhyming ones, songwriting "habits" that are rarely scrutinized for the same reason that flies usually attract little notice at a fish fry.

How can one account for the prevalence of the word "fool" in the popular song? Is it just songwriters who are fools or is it a unilateral indictment of the human condition? Either way, hasn't almost enough been written on the subject of clowns, fools, jesters and harlequins of all kinds?

I have a laconic guitar-playing friend from Arkansas who listened patiently while I played him what I supposed to be one of my best new songs. "What do you think?" I asked when I had finished (as songwriters almost inevitably will). "Well, there's only one thing wrong with it," he drawled with a deadpan expression. "What's that?" I wondered aloud. "It doesn't have a 'fool' in it," he grinned.

You will notice that in this book, generally speaking, I am not loath to confess my own guilt in matters such as this. On *Suspending Disbelief* in a song called "It Won't Bring Her Back" a fool sneaked into my bar with a couple of other down-in-the-mouth characters.

> *It Won't Bring Her Back to drive yourself insane*
> *She's already busy with another fool . . .*
>
> —Jimmy Webb,
> "It Won't Bring Her Back"

I wrote it, darn my hide! At least I disproved the theory that it is a magic word that guarantees a hit. I think it would be quite foolish of me to use it again.

And what can be said for "baby"? Well, without "baby" we would have been songless since about 1953. My late friend Harry Nilsson once said, "Never say 'baby' unless you're talking about an infant—a *little* person." The ubiquitous endearment slides by unnoticed for the most part, having become a kind of meaningless buffer or slug in the rhythm and meter of a given line. In pop, rock and R&B, the word will never be displaced even though *it is a word* and should never be just thrown in. (It may seem silly and out of place in some styles of writing; e.g., Broadway scores and most always in gospel songs.)

We are also subjected eternally to the metaphor that someone's poor "heart" is doing this (being broken) or doing that (singing, soaring). This cliché is almost inescapable because we have only one other word to communicate the essence of our emotional being, the equally prevalent "soul," an untranslatable concept, which is in truth a *religious* word. In the English language we have no better word for the essence or distillation of our emotional identity except our poor, overused "heart."

While on a sojourn to Rio de Janeiro in ancient times I repeatedly heard the seductive buzzing murmur of the word *saudade* in the songs of Antonio Carlos Jobim, Milton Naciamento and others. I finally was unable to stifle my curiosity and asked a young female interpreter about the meaning of this most beautiful of Portuguese words. "It has no meaning in English," she said. Still I'm reasonably certain that it has something to do with "heart."

The writer will find it hard to resist ending a song title/idea with the word "love." "This Hopeless Love," "Without Your Love," "When I Had Your Love," and so on and on and on. "Love" is a severely crippled word from a rhyming standpoint. There is "above," "dove," "shove," "glove" (which is a not a strong rhyme). For this reason the stars are always shining "above," a lover is always as gentle as a "dove." God knows what you can do with a "glove," except refer to Paul Francis Webster and Dimitri Tiomkin's beautiful "Thee I Love" in which the writer implores, "So put on your bonnet, your cape and your glove, and come with me, for thee I love." Rhyming "love" with "of" is a false rhyme (the vowels are different) but its worst aspect is that "of" is a preposition so that "love" is something that we're always "dreaming of" or "thinking of."

One reasonable solution is to move the title to the first line of the song as in:

When I Had Your Love
I saw the world through clearer eyes
I felt so strong and young and wise . . .

The writer proceeds through the main body of the song until at the end:

And still they say I'm quite a man
But I don't really give a damn
Cause I was twice the man I am
When I Had Your Love . . .

That's the idea. (Even though the word "man" comes off erroneously as a false rhyme.) Avoid rhyming the word "love" as you would avoid the bubonic plague.

Here's another way of handling the song title as a chorus.

VERSE I: *(We will assume there is a verse of about eight lines here.)*

CHORUS: *When I Had Your Love*
I was the richest man on earth
When I Had Your Love
I knew what life was worth
I've never been a king
I'm not of noble birth
But When I Had Your Love
I was the richest man on earth . . .

In so doing the writer simply takes the vulnerable "love" rhyme out of the line of fire. The same techniques can be used to shield any other vulnerable rhymes that occur when the writer is dead set on using a certain specific title/idea.

One obvious weak spot in the previous impromptu example is the cliché "noble birth." Not only is it rather stuffy-sounding but it is also an *archaism*, which is to say that people just don't talk that way anymore. The writer will wish to avoid Elizabeth Barrett Browningisms such as "this I vow" or "fevered brow." He or she should prefer "I woke up" to "I awoke" and "I won't go home" to "I *will* not go home." (Normally people speak in contractions.) It is an affectation to break these apart for no good reason, particularly when the first half of the contraction is deliberately overaccented in a poor imitation of Bob Dylan. Nilsson caught me in *flagrante delicto* more than once and seemed delighted to gently nag me about it.

A related archaism is the substitution of a forced past tense in order to achieve a proper rhyme as in this line from "Highwayman"—

Along the coach roads I <u>did ride</u>
With sword and pistol by my <u>side</u> . . .
—Jimmy Webb,
"Highwayman"

—instead of the simple and conversational "I rode." Usually the writer does this either to accommodate the melody or to make a rhyme. I support the conceit in this instance by alleging that the character who sings this line in "Highwayman" is a fellow from the eighteenth century—a road agent— *who actually speaks this way*. When the writer's material is specific in its historical context archaisms become more or less permissible. Common sense tells us when we hear a word or phrase that sounds awkward on the tongue of a contemporary character. Of course in the Broadway theatre the writer may find himself making a study of archaisms from a specific period in order to use them accurately. Consider this song from *Camelot* by Alan Jay Lerner:

> *I Wonder What the King Is Doing Tonight?*
> *What merriment is the king pursuing tonight?*
>
> —Alan Jay Lerner,
> "I Wonder What the King Is Doing Tonight"

Merriment is a deliberate archaism.

Sometimes the amateur writer may unwittingly or deliberately usurp a well-known, even classic song title. Some of these are innocuous enough. One would probably not be faulted for writing a new song called "Always." It's only a word after all. And in any case, song titles *are not subject to copyright*. The writer might want to exercise a little more discretion before writing a new song called "Mack the Knife," however. No one is likely to write a "Mack the Knife" that is better than the original by Kurt Weill and Bertolt Brecht. At best the practice indicates that the writer is devoid of imagination, at worse that he is an exploitive sort. Oh hell, it's just dull, stupid behavior that shows little respect for the work of others and perhaps even less for oneself.

Sometimes this inadvertent repetition seems to happen cosmically and simultaneously as though song ideas are adrift in a universal plasma so that on occasion two different writers seem to tune in to the same one at the same time. No experienced songwriter can be completely unaware of this phenomenon. I wrote a song called "Where Have You Been?" just before Kathy Mattea had a number-one country song with the same title ("Where've You Been") written by Jon Vezner and Don Henry, and to be honest the fact that Cole Porter had written a song by the same title in 1930 had unforgivably escaped my attention. What should a writer do in such a case? Tear it up and forget it.

In the same vein we have what I call the "dead-on-its-feet simile." The writer is in trouble if he or she is "crying a river," or if their tears are "falling like rain" or "flowing toward a river" or into a pond or a lake or any other body of water. "Cry Me a River," the immortal standard by Arthur Hamilton, is the most vivid and memorable if not the earliest treatment of exaggerated boo-hooing:

> *So you can Cry Me a River, Cry Me a River*
> *I cried a river over you.*
>
>   —A. Hamilton,
>   "Cry Me a River"

Leave it alone. It's been done already. It's been done *to death* already. The acerbic critic has a word for beating a dead horse with a blunt cliché: *derivative*.

Let's think of another way to describe uncontrolled weeping. To improvise:

> *And when she cried her tears fell like stars*
> *In a meteor shower for hour after hour*
> *And each one glistened in the firelight*
> *Till the unending fall had put the fire out . . .*

I think I could call it "Blubbering on W. B. Yeats's Toes." But seriously, we *must* make an effort to see familiar things in an innovative way. We need not try to "run like the wind." Bob Seger decided to run "against the wind" instead and those of us who have at least half our lives behind us appreciate that metaphor. It is almost *too* close to the truth. When searching for a new way to express the familiar it is always helpful to look at a thing's opposite: The Mafia chieftain who is so angry that he kisses the man he is about to kill. The person who is so overcome by grief that they are laughing hysterically. The woman who is so happy that she can't control her tears. The night that was so pitch black that it "whited-out" on the retina. The explosion that was so loud it couldn't be heard. The room that was so quiet that the clock on the mantel clanked and roared like a steel mill. The fugitive in "Highwayman" who has died three times but still lives. This kind of thinking is father to a whole genre of autonymic song titles such as "Full Moon and Empty Arms" and "I Got It Bad and That Ain't Good."

Try to avoid "this is my song" territory. It's a little corny at this point in time to hear the writer advertising himself by saying "This is my song" about this or "This is my song" about that, especially since this genre has been so brilliantly exploited by the masters.

And you can tell ev'rybody,
This is Your Song,
It may be quite simple but,
Now that it's done,
I hope you don't mind, I hope you don't mind
That I put down in words
How wonderful life is, while you're in the world.
                    —E. John & B. Taupin,
                              "Your Song"

I know it's kind of late
I hope I didn't wake you
But what I've got to say can't wait
I hope you'll understand
Everytime I try to tell you
The words just came out wrong.
So I'll Have to Say I Love You in a Song . . .
                    —Jim Croce,
          "I'll Have to Say I Love You in a Song"

The songwriter is being intimate with the listener about the actual process of writing a song. It is a valid approach and without doubt interesting, but it has been done. Closely related are songs where we find writers and musicians sometimes addressing their own instruments as in Billy Joel's "Baby Grand," or my own "Piano." It is innovative when writers address inanimate objects as opposed to people: buildings, towns, automobiles or even pets. What if the writer sang a song to himself as though he is literally looking in the mirror? "Self Portrait" might be a good title.

An infringement that is no doubt as serious as co-opting song titles or imitating specific approaches is allowing individual lines to overresemble important or significant lines from other famous songs, as briefly mentioned in Chapter One. An example of one of these is playing on the end credits of a movie on my videotape recorder even as I write this. The writer is trumpeting, "We are the power, we are the people." Why not just add, "We are the world, we are the children," and get it over with? Nothing will mark the amateur quite as indelibly as this kind of quasi-cribbing. Please don't do it. At the very least remember that I told you *not* to do it.

What is *two-rhyme hell*? That's when the writer gets stuck on one page of the rhyming dictionary and obsesses in this manner:

> *I've got a strange affliction*
> *That's almost a conviction*
> *Nine-hundred-line prediction*
> *Is now my main addiction.*

Two-rhymes are not as potent as masculine rhymes. The repetition of the suffix *-iction* washes out the effect of the rhyme on the ear. What if we alternate the two-rhyme with a masculine one?

> *I've got a strange affliction*
> *That keeps me on my toes*
> *I'm hung up on prediction*
> *As everybody knows.*
> *And now it's my conviction*
> *That my new concubine*
> *Is now my main addiction*
> *It's my nine-hundred line . . .*

While we're on the subject of these mesmerizing columns of rhyming words it is time to recognize a category of rhymes that might be called *kissing cousins*. These kissing cousins are probably more important to the songwriter than any rules, methods or advisos. These are the words in a given column of proper rhymes that are *related*. We could then refer to them properly as *related rhymes*. How so? And why are they so important to us? Okay. We're writing a song about a sailboat and we declare somewhere in the first couple of lines that "she's a fine trim craft." We want to rhyme "craft" so we go to (in this case) Clement Wood and find:

> abaft
> aft
> craft
> daft

draft
graft
haft
raft
shaft
waft

What are the *related rhymes* in this list? We know we're talking about a sailboat, our "craft," remember? So "aft" (the arse-end of a sailboat), "draft" (the amount of water a sailboat displaces), "haft" (the handle of a captain's sword), "raft" (an inferior form of boat), "shaft" (perhaps we have an engine on our sailboat and the engine has a "shaft"), "waft" (breezes do this and sailboats need a good breeze) and "abaft" (archaic sail talk for something that's further aft than another thing), all of these are *related rhymes* and it is our ability to group them together according to subject matter that enables us to write cogent lyrics, to pick an appropriate rhyme for the word "craft" in the context of a song about a sailboat. As an exercise choose columns of rhyming words at random from your dictionary of choice and (in pencil) underline the *related rhymes*.

She's a fine trim <u>craft</u>
With divine slim <u>draft</u> . . .

The very smallest of words deserve our attention: Conjunctions such as "but," "of," "and," "or," "when," etc., can have a surprisingly potent effect on an entire line.

I loved her but she let me down.

Or:

I loved her and she let me down.

Or:

I loved her when she let me down.

Too often the subtle effect of these tiny words is discounted by the beginning songwriter as unimportant and they are treated as "filler." I have many times on a final rewrite of a lyric changed an "or" to an "and," for instance, and breathed a deep sigh of relief on knowing that everything had finally fallen into perfect order.

So there are our two-by-fours, one-by-sixes, timbers, bricks and some simple tools which we can use to select, shape and connect them. Like all architects and artisans we have rules to create by, building codes and guidelines. We also have arcane knowledge—hints passed down to us by tradition and our colleagues and predecessors. We have instincts and we can emulate the works that inspire us most. We have everyone else's mistakes and their dire warnings not to repeat them. More important than all of these is that once we know how things are usually done we are free to try something else. (When cathedrals became too large to support their own weight some genius broke the rules and erected flying buttresses.)

When we break the rules it is essential to weigh the risk. We must ask ourselves what is to be gained by using unconventional or even substandard materials (false rhymes, blank verse, etc.). Like the architect we may come to the conclusion that we will have to bend the code to create a freestanding arched dome fifteen hundred feet in diameter. Can we make it stand? Can we make it beautiful?

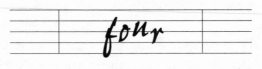

ELEMENTS OF FORM

How delicate the tracery of her fine lines
Like the moonlight lace tops of the evening pines . . .
—JIMMY WEBB,
"WATERMARK"

In this and subsequent chapters, specifically Four through Eight, the casual reader may find him or herself disconnecting from some of the technical information offered relative to song form, composition of melody or chord structure. The reader who is not concerned with some of the finer nuances of songwriting as a craft is invited to simply skip over the weightier passages at will.

Individual words must next be organized into spans of meaning; remember that the basic rules of grammar hold true. Lyrics have no special license to violate sensible guidelines for sentence construction. Regular arrangements of a number of these spans of meaning (*lines*) are analogous to walls that divide a song into different "rooms" with different purposes and names. Generally speaking, the arbitrary arrangement of lines is called *artificial line division*, and before we design our first "room," called a *verse*, we must explore the origins and meanings of artificial line division.

The origins of songwriting form are probably prehistoric. At some point during the Cro-Magnon cave culture's heyday, crude, guttural, most likely monosyllabic communication evolved into the first *line*. There is little doubt that at some location in the ancient past a man similar to us in physiology uttered the first fragmentary sentence. He did this by connecting a series of individual sounds or words representing objects or actions in order to convey meaning. Perhaps the first sentence was: "Holy cow, where did all those cotton-pickin' saber-toothed tigers come from?"

It is not inconceivable that songs, or the Cro-Magnon equivalent, may have been the very first form of complex communication between groups of individuals. If, as is commonly theorized, painting began in those times (or even earlier), who will doubt that aural art began as well? Tribal law, fertility rites and the recounting of great exploits in battle (the first *ballads*) evolved into oral histories of the entire existence of a people. "Primitive chants," these have been called. "Chant" from the Latin *cantus*, meaning "song," or *cantare*, meaning "to sing." Man was "writing" songs before he was making speeches or creating books. To this day poets are romantically said to be "singing" when they are merely reciting the written word.

There is a very real physical problem associated with reciting or singing a lengthy narrative and that is the necessity of breathing. At some point the cantor or narrator must release the thread of the story and take in air. This was the original reason for *artificial line division* and why we see a verse written down like this:

Ug-lug had a little lamb[BREATH]
Its fleece was white as milk [BREATH]
And everywhere that Ug-lug went
The lamb tagged along.

But Ug-lug, the ancient songwriting warrior priest, had another problem as well. After a couple of thousand years how was he supposed to remember all that material? In those days he might have lost portions of his anatomy as a penalty for not remembering a complicated story that his great-grandpa had told him. So he began to use rhyme. He found that words were easier to remember when they sounded similar at the end of phrases and that rhymes also gave clues about what might be coming next. So he changed the words around:

Ug-lug had a little lamb [BREATH]
His fleece was white as snow [BREATH]
And everywhere that Ug-lug went
The lamb was sure to go.

Immediately Ug-lug started looking for a record deal but first he recognized the wisdom of dividing his long, epic poems into subsections in the same way that a concert pianist isolates specific musical movements in order to memorize them more carefully.

After nine or ten thousand years these *mnemonic devices* (or word games that enable us to remember more easily) became formalized, even crystallized into various regimens of expression: the stanza, elegiac, alcaic, sapphic, sonnet, ode, pastoral and ballad forms, etc.

I am not inclined to spend a great deal of time describing and/or analyzing the rules of classical poetry. This information is readily available and not necessarily pertinent to our immediate goals. Doubting that anyone is reading this book in order to learn to create a Shakespearean pastiche, the elements of classical form that will be addressed are the ones that affect us directly as modern songwriters.

What about choosing a clever line in the first place, seeking that "turn of phrase" that is so universally admired and sought? In reference to the previous chapter we will want to keep our minds open and ears tuned for colorful, interesting, descriptive words. When these individual words are organized into a "span of meaning" many terms and definitions from the classical glossary of technique come into play. *Metaphor, simile, imagery, analogy, allegory*, etc. Frequently these terms are not understood with absolute clarity. They may be perceived as synonymous but because they are such important tools, what follows is a precise definition and description of their respective functions.

Metaphor: A semantic device describing one thing by comparing it to another thing and calling attention to their commonality.

Example 1. That tire is *bald as an eagle*.
Example 2. They are *filthy rich*.
Example 3. She's madder than an *old wet hen*.
Example 4. He was *drowning in self-pity*.

All these are metaphoric clichés. The professional songwriter will strive to create original metaphors.

Example 1. The sea *roared with the fury of old age.*

Example 2. She *slalomed through the party.*

Example 3. We were *singing a Masters & Johnson duet.*

Example 4. As lonesome *as a democrat at a victory celebration.*

Obviously the metaphor can be humorous and lends itself to comedy. It can also dramatize profound and serious insights. As an exercise, create some random metaphors on your own, both earnest and tongue-in-cheek.

One of the cardinal sins of writing is to blend or mix one metaphor with another, creating either confusion or unintentional comedy. A momentary lapse of vigilance could result in one of the following:

1. Her *jet-powered mouth* was *flapping like a flag in a Santa Ana.*

2. His *bedside manner waxed and waned* with the tides *of his mercurial humor.*

3. *Between the parted pages* and were pressed *in love's hot fevered iron like a striped pair of pants.*

I rest my case.

Simile: A figure of speech (word game) suggesting a literal relationship between two unlike things, usually beginning with "like" or "as."

Example 1. The plane headed for the runway *like a homesick angel.*

Example 2. She was as uneasy *as a cat on a hot tin roof.*

Example 3. He eats *like a pig.*

These also are clichés. Try to devise fresh and unique similes.

Example 1. The paint brush was *as stiff as an Eskimo's mustache.*

Example 2. Her sigh was *like the last breeze subsiding before a great ship is becalmed.*

Example 3. Wielding his wit *like a chainsaw in a sushi bar.*

Example 4. Her smile faded slowly *like a dying sunset in the Everglades.*

Similes (like metaphors) lend themselves equally to humorous or even grim purposes. As an exercise create similes of your own, quickly and at random.

Imagery: Language that is designed to create mental images in conjunction with the reader's or listener's imagination.

Example 1. *How delicate the tracery of her fine lines.*

Example 2. *A song half heard through a closed door.*

Example 3. *The air was red wine on those top-down nights.*

Example 4. *They buried me in that great tomb that knows no sound.*

Example 5. *The covered bridge gray-shingled and infirm.*

As an exercise think of an object, place or person and then describe same with a single line or phrase. Use colorful, descriptive words to depict the familiar in a fresh, vivid way. Try to differentiate between *imagery* and similes or metaphors.

Analogy: Comparing one thing to another thing in order to suggest that even though the basic nature of these things is different they possess striking similarities.

Example 1. Gambling with someone else's money is *like* (analogous to) *lying on your back to urinate.*

Example 2. Trying to get your video played on MTV is *like* (analogous to) *climbing a flagpole in a sleet storm.*

Example 3. You may as well play Russian Roulette with a speargun *as to pick up a girl in a single's bar.*

Example 4. Mending a broken heart is *harder than* (analogous to) *performing your own triple bypass.*

Analogies are more challenging than metaphors or similes but great fun. Make up some of your own analogies as quickly as you can.

Analogies are not often used in lyric writing but they do occur. The writer should remember that analogies are analogous to jalapeños: One of them can be too many.

Allegory: In essence, *symbolism*. The characters or situations written about—however trivial or obvious they may appear on the surface—represent profound truths about the human condition.

Example 1. *A song about a migrating bird that circumnavigates the globe only to find that happiness lies in the nest where it was a hatchling.*

Example 2. *A song about a frog that joins in with the other animals as they carol beside the manger of Baby Jesus and is ridiculed because he can only croak.*

Example 3. *A song about a wayward marionette who returns after many years, chipped and battered, to the old toy maker who originally fashioned her. He mends her and makes her like new.*

All these are allegories, sometimes referred to as *fables* or *parables*. Think of some symbolic tales or situations of your own and write them down briefly as in the previous examples. Then try writing a simple lyric based on one of them.

I group all the preceding terms in the general category of *imaging devices*. They enable the writer to create vivid pictures quickly (like Picasso's minimalist line drawings) without resorting to reams of merely correct, descriptive language.

Some other effects that might be loosely grouped with these imaging devices are *alliteration*, or the repetition of initial consonants ("he <u>r</u>ocked the <u>r</u>ascal with a <u>r</u>oundhouse <u>r</u>ight"), and *onomatopoeia*, which means using words that actually sound like the things they are describing (the *tinkling* of bells).

The *metric foot* is another term from classic poetic terminology that concerns us directly as modern songwriters. A metric foot is analogous to a single bar of musical notation in the sense that it contains a finite, regular and repeated number of beats. There are traditional names for different kinds of rhythmic subdivisions that will be instructive even though the songwriter usually makes a more informal approach to the construction of lines and their division. Here is the most common metric foot called *iamb* diagrammed as a single *bar* of 2/4 rhythm (2/4 is a common musical *time signature*). The notation over each word is known as *scansion* and signifies the accented and unaccented syllables.

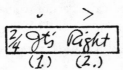

What identifies the example as *iambic* is the fact that the first syllable ("beat") is unaccented and the accent falls hardest on the second "beat" or syllable. When strung together, a number of these metric feet create a regular rhythm or cadence: Music without the notes, a kind of drum beat.

The preceding is a line of iambic verse consisting of four metric feet. With a simple melody it can be sung as four bars of song in 2/4 time.

There is something distinctly unsettling about the previous musical depiction to the experienced songwriter or composer, even though in its particulars it is accurate. When lyrics are combined with music in 2/4 time (iambic) we are accustomed to hearing the *stressed syllable* on the *downbeat* (first beat) of the bar. Unfortunately, in the previous example the natural accent of the lyric in 2/4 time falls on the *second* beat of the bar. So, what the ear wants to hear is this:

Perhaps the conclusion is obvious, but let me explain. The accents become diametrically opposed as the first beat (quarter note) in the first bar of melody is a *rest* (a rest is a beat of rhythm that is *silent*). The remaining note in the bar which falls on the syllable "It's" becomes what is commonly referred to in songwriting as a *pickup*. The stressed syllable then falls on the first beat of the bar where it is most comfortable to the ear. It is necessary then to have at least five bars of regular musical notation to support four metric feet of iambic verse. This illustrates a basic principle of the combining of music and lyrics. *There are almost always more bars of music than there are units of metric feet.*

Here is another kind of 2/4-based metric foot called a *trochee*:

> ⌣	> ⌣	> ⌣	> ⌣
2/4 Take me	down to	Par - is	Tex - as
(1.) (2.)	(1.) (2)	(1-) (2-)	(1-) (2 -)

In this example the pattern of accents is opposite to those of the iambic meter as well as common 2/4 time and sounds perfectly natural to the ear because the stressed syllable is on the downbeat.

It would be possible—but ill-advised—for the lyricist to write endless streams of *trochaic* feet superimposed over bars of 2/4 time and melody.

(For the record all these observations about *iambic, trochaic* and 2/4 time hold true for 4/4 time as well.)

Anapestic and *dactylic* metric feet fall naturally into what amounts to a 3/4 bar or single unit of waltz time. This is *anapestic*:

You will notice that metric feet can be made up of one-, two- or multi-syllable words. If this pattern of accents seems awkward, it is only because it is. The English language contains very few individual words that are naturally *anapestic*. The accents are contrary to the familiar ones of common 3/4 time but notice in the following example how melody has a tendency to overpower if not remove accents of *any* kind, even the natural ones of spoken language. We can give the melody a more *anapestic* feel if we so desire by peaking or cresting the melody on the third beat of the bar.

Quick - ly   she   made   up   her   mind   but   it   wick - ed - ly   changed   (rest)

Dactylic meter falls naturally on the same accents as common 3/4 time.

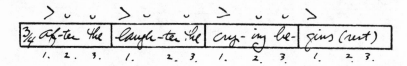

Obviously this rhythm lines up more accurately with the patterns of normal speech because the stressed syllable falls on the downbeat of the bar. We are immediately comfortable with the combination of melody, word and 3/4 time.

Af - ter   the   laugh - ter   the   cry - ing   be - gins

As fascinating as all of this may fail to be, songs are usually not written this way. These musical examples are intended only to make clear some of the most basic rhythms and to illustrate the simplest and most direct method of combining words and music.

Let's look for a moment at the practical differences between this kind of rote composition of iambic, dactylic and trochaic verse and the writing of song lyrics, concentrating especially on the manner in which musical accompaniment alters the conventions of poetic construction. Here is a verse from "She Moves, and Eyes Follow," a song I wrote for a theatrical production:

> *She Moves, and Eyes Follow*
> *Longing to touch*
> *They want her so much*
> *They stare . . .*
> —Jimmy Webb,
> "She Moves, and Eyes Follow"

Except for certain beats on which no syllables fall (*rests*), the example as it will be diagrammed is classical dactylic verse and (as has already been pointed out) *there is a natural relationship between dactylic verse and 3/4 time.* By simply converting the dactylic verse into 3/4 time and adding a melody, we come up with this example:

Easily done but uninspiring. In real life, music breathes and follows its own path. The metronomic cadences of classical rhythm must give way, certain notes must be elongated, space must be allocated for the singer to take air, long musical phrases may call for more metric feet in one line than another, other musical lines will be abrupt and attenuated, etc. In other words there is a *nonregimented* quality to most nonmilitary melody. This calls for a compromise between regular rhythm and anarchy on the part of the lyricist *and* composer. As an example of how this cooperation can be achieved, here is the actual music as written for "She Moves . . . "

Notice that the regular 3/4 rhythm continues uninterrupted underneath "She" for three beats. In fact the entire lyric now "floats" above a 3/4 time signature, sometimes joining it or duplicating it only to once again sustain a note while the rhythm continues underneath.

This illustrates again the underlying principle that there are *almost inevitably more bars of music than there are metric feet in a given song.* It further illustrates that the rhythms of song lyrics are not and should not be constrained by the rules that govern classical construction but can bend themselves to the whim of the musical accompaniment and are validated by the nature of that accompaniment.

Writers will experience immediate difficulty when attempting to combine a dactylic (3/4) based lyric with 2/4 or 4/4 time or vice versa. Not that it can't be done. In the previous example, the word *she* "floats" above the first bar of 3/4. What if we made it "float" above a bar of 4/4 time and adjusted the words and rhythm that follow accordingly? It would look like this:

She   moves and eyes   fol-low   long-ing to

touch   they   want her   so   much   they   stare

The best that can be said about the result is that it doesn't feel quite right. The dactylic-based lyric is being forced into an accommodation with an iambic (4/4) rhythm and even the rhythm-deaf are subliminally aware that something is amiss. There are other ways that these ill-fated marriages can be forced (an iambic-based lyric can be distorted over 3/4 time) but let's leave it. Notwithstanding some exotic situation, on Broadway, perhaps, where the writer would want to reprise a 3/4 song in 4/4 time—say, at the end of the show—or combine it in *counterpoint* with another theme in 4/4 time . . . I've tried it. However frustrating it may be it is not a blood sport and unlikely to cause serious physical harm.

In summary, a *metric foot* greatly resembles a *bar* or single unit of rhythmic notation but it may sustain and take its own shape above the regular rhythm of musical accompaniment. It is one unit of poetic rhythm whether iambic, trochaic, anapestic, whatever. So the length of any given line can be from one metric foot (a *manometer*) to, say, seven metric feet (a *heptameter*) but measuring lyric lines in this manner for the purpose of perfect symmetry is unwise. In songwriting, uniformity in the length of lines creates monotony and works at cross-purposes to the fluidity and diversity that interesting music requires and that the composer will want to achieve. From a songwriting standpoint "nursery rhyme" predictability is not only annoying but debilitating. The best lyrics have an element of asymmetry in the length and positioning of the different lines. When writing a lyric for an existing melody most often asymmetries in the composer's work will be *faits accomplis* that the lyricist will have to accommodate one way or another.

Songwriting styles since the early '70s have incorporated more and more frequently what has come to be called a *conversational tone*. The flowery, sentimental and overwrought lyrics of the traditionalists have been replaced by an almost off-hand "this-is-the-way-people-talk" minimalism, the musical equivalent of *cinema verité*. This has eroded to some extent the cut and dried, formulaic techniques of our predecessors.

In 1972, on her *For the Roses* album, Joni Mitchell wrote "Woman of Heart and Mind":

I'm looking for affection and respect, a little passion
And you want stimulation—nothing more
That's what I think
But you know I'll try to be there for you
When your spirits start to sink
All this talk about holiness now
It must be the start of the latest style
Is it all books and words
Or do you really feel it?
Do you really laugh?
Do you really care?
Do you really smile
When you smile?
You criticize and you flatter
You imitate the best
and the rest you memorize
You know the times you impress me most
Are the times when you don't try
When you don't even try.

—Joni Mitchell,
"Woman of Heart and Mind"

In 1973 she was already well on her way to defining conversational tone when she wrote these lyrics:

Look at those losers glued to that damn hockey game,
Hey honey you've got lots of cash
Bring us 'round a bottle

And we'll have some laughs
Gin's what I'm drinkin'
I was Raised on Robbery . . .
        —Joni Mitchell,
        "Raised on Robbery"

Randy Newman is a master of this "I'll-leave-it-up-to-you-to-figure-out-what's-going-on" genre. We are eavesdropping through a thin apartment wall when we hear:

Vs. I: *What you wanna come back here for?*
          Thought you with your uptown friends
          Don't need none of your junkie business
          Gonna screw us up again
          Get your blackjack off my table
          Get your coat out of my rack
          We don't need you round here jerkoff
          I want you off my back

CHORUS: *We almost made it (repeat three times)*
(Chs.)   *We almost made it to the top*

Vs. II: *Got a gun from Uncle Freddie*
          Got a station all picked out
          Got a plan and now we're ready
          Gonna take that station out
          So you go on 'bout your business
          You just leave us fools alone,
          We don't need no two-bit junkie
          Screwin' up our happy home

Chs.:   *We almost made it (repeat three times)*
          We almost made it to the top . . .
                      —Randy Newman,
                      "Little Criminals"

In "Like a River," Carly Simon's letter to her mother, the conversational tone is more poignant.

Dear Mother the struggle is over now
And your house is up for sale
We divided your railroad watches
Among the four of us
I fought over the pearls
With the other girls
But it was all a metaphor
For what is wrong with us
As the room is emptying out
Your face so young comes into view
And on the back porch is a well-worn step
And a pool of light that you can walk into . . .

—Carly Simon,
"Like a River"

Stephen Bishop transcribes an actual telephone conversation when he writes:

You called me from the room in your hotel
All full of romance for someone that you met
And telling me how sorry you were
Leaving me so soon.
And that you miss me sometimes
When you're alone in your room
Do I feel lonely too?
You have no right to ask me how I feel
You have no right to speak to me so kind
I can't go on holding on to ties
Now that we're living Separate Lives . . .

—Stephen Bishop,
"Separate Lives"

Whereas Bishop's conversation has clearly taken place prior to its recounting, *pure* "conversational tone" always happens in real time as in "It Won't Bring Her Back":

What you doin' sittin' here
With closing time so near?
Looks like you need a friend so I will volunteer
Looks like you're in a world of trouble
Only one thing it could be
You better get a grip on it mister
This is not the remedy . . .

—Jimmy Webb,
"It Won't Bring Her Back"

Or it could be a letter.

Dear friend of mine
The weather's fine
Today I saw some ruins of the Roman world's decline
And I climbed all those Spanish stairs
You've heard of them no doubt
But Rome has lost its glory
I don't know what it's about
And I wish you were here . . .

—Jimmy Webb,
"Postcard from Paris"

So how has conversational tone altered the rules? Well, people don't usually *rhyme* when they talk. Impeccable grammar is not a consideration. The *shape* of speech is much more casual than that of conventional lyric lines. Conversational tone is like frying potato chips at home and leaving the skins on. It is unfinished furniture and we leave it that way on purpose for a more natural effect.

By this time, however, you must have come to your own conclusion that "conversational tone" would not be effective or even possible if it did not fall to some extent within the traditional guidelines of form. Why? Because the music, the *melody*, is always waiting somewhere in the wings with its own demanding sense of order. We expect lyrics to behave in a certain way when combined with music. For instance, we expect rhymes or near rhymes or even false rhymes to fall in certain precise and predetermined locations.

In classical terminology the *couplet* consists of two lines of metric feet rhymed A/A, ("A/A" being a simple notation that indicates that the *exterior rhyme*—"end rhyme"—occurs at the conclusion of each of these two lines).

> *We've got our rout<u>ines</u> (A)*
> *Our friends in faded <u>jeans</u> . . . (A)*
> > —Jimmy Webb,
> > "I Don't Know How to Love You Anymore"

This is the only *rhyme scheme* possible in a couplet. (A rhyme scheme is simply the placement and frequency of rhymes in a given lyric.) When we write four lines, or a *quatrain*, suddenly there are various *rhyme schemes* available. For instance, A/A/B/B or A/B/A/B or A/B/C/B or even A/A/A/A. (There are four additional legitimate rhyming techniques: *random* rhyme, which is pretty much what it sounds like; *initial* rhyme—occurring at the beginning of the line; *interior* rhyme, or *interior rhyme scheme*, which will be explored in great detail; and *cross* rhyme, where a conventional rhyme is married to an *interior rhyme*.)

> *Deep down inside I know I still love him (A)*
> *But he'll never know, 'cause I'll never tell (B)*
> *Or confide that I'm thinkin' of him (A)*
> *And wishin' him well . . . (B)*
> > —Jimmy Webb,
> > "I Keep It Hid"

The possibility also presents itself with four lines or more of introducing a pattern of un-rhymed lines as in "By the Time I Get to Phoenix."

> *By the Time I Get to Phoenix she'll be risin' (A)*
> *She'll find the note that I left hangin' on her door (B)*
> *And she'll laugh when she reads the part that says I'm leavin' (C)*
> *'Cause I've left that girl too many times before . . . (B)*
> > —Jimmy Webb,
> > "By the Time I Get to Phoenix"

As the number of lines in a verse increases, so exponentially does the possible arrangement of rhyme schemes. In the *quintet* five lines can be rhymed A/B/A/A/B, A/B/A/B/A, A/B/C/A/B, etc. A *sextet* could be arranged A/A/B/A/A/B, A/B/A/B/A/B, A/B/C/A/B/C and so on. Particularly in songwriting because it is unconstrained by classical form, the writer can have as many lines as needed in the verse of a song, of any length or meter and rhyme them or *not* rhyme them in any way desired. It is the underlying structure and melodic accompaniment of the lyric that validates songwriting form.

Here is a simple verse from "Highwayman," constructed of seven *lines.* Remember, the placement and frequency of rhymes in a lyric is known as a *rhyme scheme.*

> 1. *I was a Highwayman*
>
> Couplet 2. *Along the coach roads I did <u>ride</u>*
> 3. *With sword and pistol by my <u>side</u>*
>
> Couplet 4. *And many a young maid lost her baubles to my <u>trade</u>*
> 5. *And many a soldier left his lifeblood on my <u>blade</u>*
>
> Couplet 6. *The bastards hung me in the spring of twenty-<u>five</u>*
> 7. *But I am still <u>alive</u>*

> —Jimmy Webb,
> "Highwayman"

The first line does not rhyme. The next two lines (called a *couplet*) have the same length and *meter* (rhythm) and end with a one-syllable masculine rhyme. The same is true of the next *couplet.* The second line of the third and last couplet is much shorter than the first. Its meter is deliberately blunted for more dramatic impact. In essence, it has been shaped *in its length* to match the first line, "I was a Highwayman." The rhyme scheme looks like this: A/BB/CC/DD.

Relentless pounding on the same rhyme for line after line—no matter how cleverly done—is probably to be avoided. It reeks of the rhyming dictionary and one of the finer nuances of professional songwriting is to make use of the dictionary without calling undue attention to it. (The one exception might be a comical theatrical number about a hapless lyricist in bondage to a rhyming dictionary.) Sometimes it can work if carefully handled.

> Vs. I: *Life begins*
> *And spirits rise*
> *And they become memories that vaporize*
> *And the vapor becomes all the dreams we devise*
> *And while we are dreaming,*
> *Time Flies*

Vs. II:	*Night turns to dawn*
	And dreams to sighs
	And sighs change to sweet love that never dies
	And love becomes laughter and lullabies
	And while we are dreaming
	Time Flies
BRIDGE:	*While we are dreaming we meet and exchange*
(Brg.)	*Conversations routinely and nothing seems strange*
	But when we awake there's a sense of unease
	That another night's gone just as quick as you please
Vs. III:	*And night turns to dawn*
	And then bright skies
	And bright skies to picnics on warm Julys
	To deep umber autumns and winter goodbyes
	And while we are dreaming
	Time Flies
	And while we are dreaming
	Time Flies

—Jimmy Webb,
"Time Flies"

"Message" and "story" are the redeeming aesthetic values. If *repetitive rhymes* are helping us get our narrative or emotional plea from point A to point B and make sense naturally, then we can set our teeth and justify them. If we are rhyming "for rhyme's sake" and stretching our line of reasoning like a rubber band on a pegboard from far-fetched rhyme to incomprehensible simile to *false rhyme* and back again, our listener will quickly learn—and rightfully so—to mistrust our expertise and will not venture further into the ramshackle house that we are building.

If we ignore the temptation to rhyme every consecutive line (A/A/A/A), or even every other line (A/B/A/B), we can create a verse that breathes more and can incorporate more expositional language. In other words, be more of a storyteller and less of a rhyming drudge.

The rhyme scheme of a verse form can be quite varied and complex:

Boris wants to meet Juanita
And in broken English he <u>expresses</u> his <u>desire</u> to <u>hire</u> Vanessa
Lately of the Village <u>Voice</u>

She writes love letters of your <u>choice</u>
Famous for her great <u>successes</u>
She <u>impresses</u> him to the <u>degree</u>
That he begins to hope perhaps that <u>she</u>
Can bring him all the romance she <u>revives</u>
In Other People's <u>Lives</u> . . .

—Jimmy Webb,
"Other People's Lives"

The word *expresses* occurs—not at the end of the first line but about two-thirds of the way through the iambic meter. The second line consists of a simple internal rhyme scheme, *voice* with *choice*. Then *expresses* is rhymed twice in the next line—neither time does the rhyme occur at the end of the line—*successes* and *impresses* propel us toward the exterior or end rhyme *degree*. *Degree* and *she* are a simple couplet. The final couplet is cut short as in the earlier "Highwayman" example to bring us more quickly to the point and make the rhythm more interesting. The relationship between *expresses, successes,* and *impresses* in this example is known as an *inner rhyme scheme*—a secondary pattern completely independent of the *exterior rhyme scheme* that occurs at the *ends* of lines.

I may as well tell you outright that I have committed what some regard as a major sin, at least three times in this case, somewhat deliberately in order to explain the dangers of enjambment. You will notice that the syntax of the sentence *"famous for her great successes, she impresses him to the degree that he begins to hope perhaps that she can bring him all the romance she revives in Other People's Lives,"* is broken in three places. After "degree," after "she," and after "revives." These are clear-cut cases of enjambment, or "jammin'," the unethical practice of carrying over the meaning of a sentence from the end of one couplet to another. The effect of discontinuity, only slightly annoying on the printed page, can be amplified to the point of distraction in a singing line. Nevertheless, a beautiful, melodic line properly constructed can gloss over the break in the sentence and a willing singer can make it almost imperceptible. Enjambment occurs in some of the nicest families. "Mountain Greenery," a standard by Larry Hart and Richard Rodgers, has its share. As for internal rhyme schemes, you might be forgiven for assuming that this "fancy rhyming" (which admittedly seems terribly complicated) lies exclusively within the purview of the Broadway lyricist. Not so. For instance, give a listen to "Save the Last Dance for Me" (by D. Pomus & M. Shuman).

This kind of writing is laborious—to say the least—and involves a great deal of trial, error and rewrite. There is, however, a system that can simplify these brain busters.

The most difficult aspect of creating an "inner rhyme scheme" is that each subsequent verse must line up perfectly with the original. Even though the thrust of the lyric may have changed and the rhymes are completely different (in most cases) they must occur at *exactly the same places* in the meter of each line—as though we are substituting different values in the same equation.

What follows is the first verse of "Wasn't There a Moment," first recorded by Michael Feinstein:

> *Wasn't there a <u>smile</u>?*
> *One so remarkable that it's still on <u>file</u>*
> *In my book of dreams,*
> *That <u>pile</u> of memories, all of <u>you</u>*
> *But when I sort them <u>thru</u>*
> *Why do I never find a <u>clue</u>*
> *To why that kissing smile <u>withdrew</u>*
> *Wasn't There a Moment when I <u>knew</u>?*
> —Jimmy Webb,
> "Wasn't There a Moment"

In any subsequent verse, the second syllable of the fourth line (*pile*) <u>must</u> <u>rhyme</u> with the primary rhymes at the ends of lines one and two. Before I write the second verse I make a chart or graph of the syllable count and rhyme scheme, one line for syllables, a double line for rhymes. A fussy way to accomplish this, but a method which is frequently used in the recording studio when keeping a record of vocal tracks, etc., is to draw the graph in ink and then in a notebook format overlay with acetate and write the lyric in nonpermanent inks which can be erased in order to make corrections.

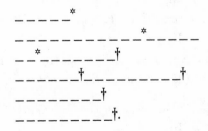

The asterisks and crosses represent syllables that must rhyme with *each other*. By referring to the graph the writer is assured of duplicating the proper rhyme scheme in the second verse with some independence from the need to refer to the music or lyric of the first verse.

> Vs. II: *Wasn't there a <u>time</u>*
> *When life was beautiful like a panto<u>mime</u>*
> *When actors move*
> *Sub<u>lime</u>ly sure of what they <u>do</u>*
> *And my regrets are <u>few</u>*
> *But there's one mystery I still <u>pursue</u>*
> *When life was beautiful and <u>new</u>*
> *Wasn't There a Moment*
> *I can't recall the moment*
> *But Wasn't There a Moment when you loved me <u>too</u>?*
>
> —Jimmy Webb,
> "Wasn't There a Moment"

Yes, the end of the second verse has been altered and extended for dramatic effect. This does not change the basic working principle of the graph. The observant reader may have noticed that in the last five lines the rhyme scheme actually *rhymes between both verses*. Rhyming between verses is possible but it's up to the writer's sense of what is correct for a particular song. (If the first and second verse end with the same title/phrase then the writer may be forced to rhyme from the same list.)

In the song form two or more (usually more) lines that complete one cohesive paragraph of thought is called a *verse*. (A verse rarely exceeds four to eight lines, but nobody really counts or cares.) The most basic *song form* is two verses in a row. Here is "Didn't We?":

> Vs. I: *This time we almost made the pieces fit*
> *Didn't We, girl?*
> *This time we almost made some sense of it*
> *Didn't We, girl?*
> *This time I had the answer right here in my hand*
> *Then I touched it and it had turned to sand*
>
> Vs. II: *This time we almost sang our song in tune*
> *Didn't We, girl?*

This time we almost made it to the moon
Didn't We, girl?
This time we almost made our poem rhyme
This time we almost made that long hard climb
Didn't We almost make it this time?

—Jimmy Webb,
"Didn't We?"

First let me prove that the preceding *is a two-verse form*, as certain traditionalists will already be sharpening their pencils for a rebuttal. It is important for the modern songwriter to understand that the terms used to define the individual components of songwriting form have been in transition for decades, particularly in the last fifty years—not that they were universally agreed upon in the first place. Writers from the era of Richard Rodgers, Burton Lane and the Gershwins would probably refer to "Didn't We?" as a "thirty-two-bar chorus." (The origins of this compound term seem a bit arbitrary. George Gershwin's first published song was not thirty-two bars long, according to Michael Feinstein.) This section was often labeled a "refrain" even though Jerome Kern insisted on calling it a "berthen" indicating that he may have had some misgivings about its popular identity. The synonymous relationship between "refrain" and "chorus" is solidified in the classical context by a shared definition: a section that is repeated *word for word* at intervals during a long poem or song consisting of varied *stanzas*. (Each stanza being completely different from its companions.) In the liturgy of the Protestant church we have clear examples of very early American songs with diverse *stanzas* or *verses* and identical—oft-repeated—*refrains* or *choruses*. (Stanza/refrain seems to have morphed over time to the more informal verse/chorus.) Here is an old Baptist hymn in verse/chorus form:

Vs. I (Stanza): *Would you be free from your burden of sin?*
There's Power in the Blood, Power in the Blood
Pardon for—and cleaning within
There's wonder working Power in the Blood

Chs. (Refrain): *There is Power, Power wonder working power*
In the blood of the Lamb.
There is Power, Power wonder working power
In the precious blood of the Lamb.

There are at least three more verses or stanzas included in the Baptist hymnal. The *chorus* or *refrain* is repeated *exactly* after each verse. How can "Didn't We?" then, possibly be a *chorus*—thirty-two bar or otherwise? It isn't. It is a *two-verse* form, each verse having a different lyric, and to some extent, diverse musical content. (I will stipulate that in a song like Hammerstein and Kern's "The Last Time I Saw Paris," where multiple verses *do* precede the "berthen," it would be technically correct to call this thirty-two-bar section a "chorus" because it is repeated exactly and in its entirety after each verse.) We will return to the debate over what we should actually *call* these various components of the song form, but for now, let's look again at "Didn't We?"

Nothing tricky was involved except that instead of the exterior rhymes occurring at the very end of the couplets they are sneaked in before the title which is repeated at the end of each line—"Didn't We?" It is very common that in this type of slow *two-verse* form the payoff—and a final reprise of the title—will occur in the very last line or two as in this variation.

> *I Wanna Be Around to pick up the pieces*
> *When somebody breaks your heart*
> *Some somebody twice as smart as I*
> *A somebody who will swear to be true*
> *As you used to do with me,*
> *Who'll leave you to learn*
> *That misery loves company, wait and see!*
>
> *I Wanna Be Around to see how he does it*
> *When he breaks your heart to bits*
> *Let's see if the puzzle fits so fine*
> *And that's when I'll discover that revenge is sweet;*
> *As I sit there applauding from a front row seat,*
> *When somebody breaks your heart*
> *Like you broke mine.*

> —Johnny Mercer & Sadie Vimmerstein,
> "I Wanna Be Around"

In fact, this reprise of the opening statement is virtually a defining characteristic of the two-verse form as typified in classics like "What a Difference a Day Makes" (Stanley Adams), or "Here's That Rainy Day"

(Van Heusen). There is considerable flexibility in the way these reprises can be handled. In "Here's That Rainy Day" the last line does not repeat the title exactly, but instead, there is a variation: *Suddenly that rainy day is here.* "It's Not for Me to Say" (Al Stillman and Robert Allen) repeats the title and opening line precisely as the very last line of the song.

Frequently there is an unexpected or ironic twist to the very last or last couple of lines in the two-verse form, a double entendre perhaps, or an O. Henry–esque surprise. In that sense a two-verse song is not dissimilar to a short story. Consider Rodgers and Hammerstein's exquisite "If I Loved You" in which the would-be lover never quite manages to declare himself, or in a similar vein, "When I Fall in Love," Victor Young and Edward Haman's seven-handkerchief number about another wary suitor who just can't seem to say the "L" word (which can't help but surprise us as we assume that is the point of a love song).

In Bricusse and Newley's "What Kind of Fool Am I?" the writer is a man who *can't* fall in love. In the reprise, at the end of the second verse, he proposes a method for answering the question that he poses in the first line of the song:

> *Why can't I fall in love like any other man?*
> *And maybe then I'll know what kind of fool I am.*
> > —Bricusse & Newley,
> > "What Kind of Fool Am I?"

In another permutation the last line is often a study in contrasts, comparing two disparate things in order to suddenly grab the listener's attention. Consider the contrasting elements in the last line of Jerry Herman's moving "It Only Takes a Moment":

> *That it only took a moment*
> *To be loved a whole life long . . .*
> > —Jerry Herman,
> > "It Only Takes a Moment"

What Herman has done is to lull us into expecting a repetition of "It Only Takes a Moment," which is diminutive. But in the last line of the song he surprises and intrigues us by pairing the title/idea with its opposite: "*It only took a moment to be loved a whole life long.*" The words he has chosen deliberately accentuate this reversal of drift: <u>whole</u>, <u>long</u>.

In the Gershwins' "But Not For Me," there are *two* clever endings. (The last verse is repeated.) The first ending substitutes the object of the writer's affection in place of "songs of love" but in the ultimate reprise there is a brilliant and bemused play on words with the spelling *knot* substituted for *not.*

They're writing songs of love, But Not For Me.
A lucky star's above, But Not For Me.
With love to lead the way, I've found more clouds of gray
Than any Russian play could guarantee.

I was a fool to fall and get that way;
Heigh-ho! Alas! and also, Lack-a-day!
First ending: *Although I can't dismiss*
The mem'ry of his kiss,
I guess he's not for me.

He's knocking on a door, But Not For Me
He'll plan a two by four, But Not For Me.
I know that love's a game; I'm puzzled just the same,
Was I the moth or flame? I'm all at sea.

It all began so well, but what an end!
This is the time a feller needs a friend,
Second ending: *When ev'ry happy plot*
Ends with the marriage knot,
And there's no knot for me.

—George & Ira Gershwin,
"But Not For Me"

Get it? You will notice that in the two-verse form, verses tend to be brief and rather elegant. Here are some examples of two-verse forms for you to listen to on your own. You will notice that it was an extremely traditional form common in the '40s, '50s and '60s and a mainstay in film and theatre.

"People"—(Jule Styne & Bob Merrill)
"Suddenly, Here's That Rainy Day"—(Burke & Van Heusen)
"It's Not for Me to Say"—(Stillman & Allen)
"If I Ruled the World"—(Ornadel & Bricusse)
"I Left My Heart in San Francisco"—(Cross & Cory)

"What Kind of Fool Am I?"—(Bricusse & Newley)

"Unforgettable"—(Irving Gordon)

Once we learn to get our message across in two verses we have developed some songwriting muscles and are ready to tackle more difficult forms. First let's learn to diagram the two-verse form.

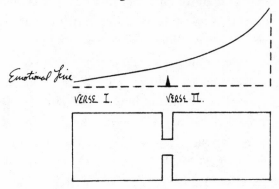

Let the vertical component of the graph represent the level of emotional intensity. Maximum emotional intensity and the "payoff" of the lyric occurs (with very few exceptions) at the end of Vs. II. (It should also be noted that the line on the graph representing emotional intensity tends to mirror the melody line and dramatic musical content itself.)

There are certainly other kinds of two-verse forms—or if you want to think of them as little two-room houses there are some interesting variations with porches, lofts, breezeways or what-have-you, but the reader would be correct in assuming that there are also three-, four- and five-verse forms. Some medieval songs may have had as many as fifty verses. What is the basic nature of these *multi-verse* forms? They are almost without exception long narratives. The balladeers and minstrels of ancient times traveled from town to town recounting current news stories and fictional entertainment in song. The melodies of these *ballads* were identical from verse to verse and were repeated over and over . . . which is another way of saying that they were *strophic*.

This is not an archaic form by any means and there are many examples of hit songs in various country markets during recent years that can only be described as ballads. First we need to differentiate between the slang usage of the term "ballad" (used to refer to any kind of a slow love song) and the true meaning of the word: *a story told in song utilizing multiple verses that are musically identical.* What would seem to define the "form" of the ballad is the story that it tells. The song goes on long enough to tell the tale, so that its length and number of verses is dictated by its plot points and can consist of as many verses as are needed to serve the narrative's beginning, middle and end.

"So give me some examples of this ancient form in a contemporary setting already!" I hear you. A haunting work that comes to mind immediately is Bobbie Gentry's "Ode to Billie Joe." Against a backdrop of ominous low strings that seem to drone like a sweltering summer day in the Delta country, she invokes a mystery of betrayal and obsession. And at the end of the tale, she drops an enigmatic bombshell: What *did* Billie Joe McAllister throw off the Tallahatchee Bridge? As a kind of Tobacco Road Meets the Lindbergh Kidnapping, this song caused a sensation when it entered the charts on August 12, 1967, and stayed on for twelve weeks (including four weeks at number one), also overwhelming the Grammy Awards in 1968 ("Best Female Solo Vocal," "Best Contemporary Female Vocal," "Best New Artist"). The song was also nominated for the Best Song category in the Country Music Awards that same year.

Johnny Horton fashioned a substantial career from historical ballads, craftily releasing his "Sink the Bismarck" in conjunction with the major motion picture of the same name in 1960 (which was based on the book of the same name by C. S. Forester). His "Battle of New Orleans" was a runaway crossover smash before anyone knew what a crossover was. The same could be said for Marty Robbins's "El Paso," a western movie in miniature replete with shoot-out, thrilling chase and love/death scene. Probably the best contemporary ballad in recent memory is John Hartford's wistful "Gentle on My Mind," a paean to the beloved enabler of a compulsive wanderer.

All these songs are true ballads.

Well, what about a multi-verse form that doesn't tell any particular story? Is that a ballad? A good example might be Donovan's "Catch the Wind," or Dylan's "Ballad of a Thin Man," neither of which is a true narrative, but in all other respects—more than two verses, music identical every time around (strophic)—they are balladlike. We don't necessarily have a name for this kind of subtle variant so it must suffice to call these songs "ballads." I include a diagram of a multi-verse ballad form.

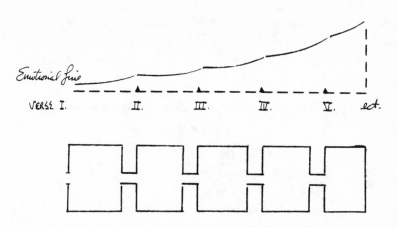

The most popular and well-known multi-verse form in American music is the "blues," which in its most common manifestation is frequently called "twelve-bar blues." It shares some common characteristics with the ballad: it is most often strophic. In terms of length it is, for all practical purposes, open-ended. (It was probably the physical limitation of the recording disc itself that first confined these songs to three or four verses). It boasts a traditional repertoire of dozens of different variations on literally thousands of songs with many different versions of verses for each song. The blues are alive and well, as brand-new blues songs are probably written every day. More significantly there seems to be a cyclic renewal of public interest in this music as succeeding waves of young singers and guitarists pick up the mantles first woven by the likes of Charlie Patton and Robert Johnson.

"The blues" differs from the ballad primarily in that its subject matter is not "narrative" in the true sense but tends to deal with the misogyny of false lovers, oppressive poverty, the wages of sin and substance abuse, cruel and indiscriminate disease, curses, hexes, trouble and grief of all kinds. Rarely does it concern itself with politics. (To get down immediately to the gritty bottom layer give a listen to John Lee Hooker's "T. B. Sheets.") Its depressing palate aside, the blues is based on ironic twists or "punchlines," indicating that the flip side of a tear is a quick grin and that the only way abject sorrow can be endured is to turn it inside out. The prototype "blues" has the title/idea repeated at the *beginning* of the song and the "punchline" or twist occuring on the last line as in Moore's "I'm a King Bee." The verses, to be exact, consist of only *three lines* when written out this way:

> Well I'm a King Bee baby, buzzin' around your hive

"Punchline":   Yeah, I can make honey baby, if you let me come inside . . .

—James Moore,
"I'm a King Bee"

If we apply proper artificial line division to accurately depict the singer's phrasing the song will look like this:

> Well I'm a King Bee
> Buzzin' around your hive
> Well I'm a King Bee baby
> Buzzin' around your hive
> Yeah I can make honey baby

"Punchline":   (If you) <u>let me come inside</u>

> Well I'm a King Bee
> Want you to be my queen
> Well I'm a King Bee baby
> Want you to be my queen
> Together we can make honey

"Punchline":   <u>The world has never seen</u>

"Ad lib":   Well, buzz awhile . . .
Sting it, band . . .

> Well I'm a King Bee
> Can buzz all night long
> Well I'm a King Bee baby
> Can buzz all night long
> Yeah I can buzz better baby

"Punchline":   <u>When your man is gone</u>

—James Moore,
"I'm a King Bee"

Though simplistic on the surface, there are many variations to lyric construction in the blues form. Notice in the following example how the "punchline" occurs at the end of the first four lines while the last two lines are a kind of "wrap-up" incorporating the title/idea.

> Oh, you wore a diamond watch
> Claimed it was from Uncle Joe
> When I looked at the inscription

"Punchline":   *It said, "Love from Daddy-o."*
                Well baby, oh little girl
                I wanna say I've got news for you
                Ah, if you think that that jive will do
"Wrap-up":   *Let me tell you, oh I Got News for You.*
                        —Roy Alfred, "I Got News for You"

Or:

                Let me tell you somethin' funny
                Funny as can be
                If we have a dozen kids, Darlin'
"Punchline":   *You know they're all gonna look like me.*
                I'm gonna move way out on the Outskirts of Town
"Wrap-up":   *See, I don't need no milkman always hangin' round.*
                        —William Weldon,
                        "Outskirts of Town"

The blues is distinct from the ballad in another sense. A blues song has a specific musical form, as rigid in its own way as a Shakespearean sonnet. At its most familiar, a blues verse is precisely twelve bars long and consists of a prescribed pattern of chord changes occurring in a traditional sequence. The arrangement of each line division in the lyric over this twelve-bar pattern is pro forma as are the accompanying melodies or "licks," though there are "eight-bar blues" and in the case of John Lee Hooker "one-chord blues" with little discernible form or even time signature. Most blues songs are distinguished by the originality of their lyric as opposed to chordal and melodic adventurism. In order that the reader may carefully analyze the twelve-bar form the following example is included:

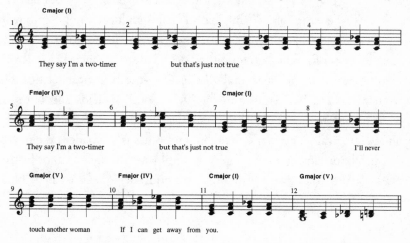

Make up your own melody to the preceding "blues lyric."

If we organize a few of these twelve-bar verses into a complete song we might have something that looks like this:

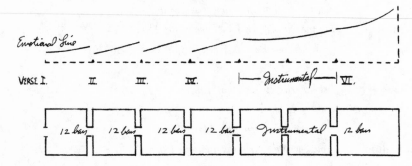

The inclusion of the section marked "instrumental" (Inst.) is not arbitrary by any means. Part of the traditional form of the blues is the custom of reserving two or three twelve-bar patterns in the middle of the song for solo work from various members of the band. The singer has the option of closing out the song with one or two final verses or giving it over to the instrumentalists for a "jam" (improvisation) and a big ending.

Variations on the "pure" form are myriad. "The House of the Rising Sun" (by Alan Price) is a kind of blues even though the chord structure is reminiscent of Scottish-Irish ballads. Berry Gordy and Janie Bradford's "Money (That's What I Want)" is, strictly speaking, a pop song with a strong blues influence, while Mose Allison's "The Snake" is an allegorical ballad with a minor blues feel. Eddie Cochran's "Summertime Blues" ain't. It is a breakthrough rock 'n' roll song with a blues influence or what Francis Davis calls in his comprehensive *The History of the Blues* a "titular" blues which is tantamount to saying, "This is a blues because I say so." There is undoubtedly a "gray zone" where the "blues" and "ballad" rub shoulders if not commingle, owing to the fact that they are both *multi-verse forms* repeating the same melody. More profoundly—as is pointed out vividly by Francis Davis as well as Stanley Booth in his anecdotal *Rhythm Oil*—the historical relationship between white and black music in the Deep South (ballads and blues) is closer if not more downright incestuous than is commonly understood by certain ideological ax-grinders. (Rhythm and Blues is a broader designation indicating almost any kind of a pop song employing the style and/or instrumentation of the blues with little or no attention being paid to strict blues form.)

The ballad and blues forms might be described as two ancient but healthy branches on the song form's evolutionary tree. The *two-verse* and *multi-verse* forms will lead us logically to more complex and modern structures. Accordingly, I would like to return to our little two-bedroom house with a front door and a back door (the first line *title/idea* and the closing *reprise*) with a view to building a nice front porch onto it.

In fact, many two-verse songs *have* what amounts to a "front porch" attached to them and one of the challenges I have faced in the writing of this book is to isolate and identify a universally acceptable term for this "whatever it is." One of my colleagues in New York, a scholar and experienced musical professional, has suggested that I simply call it an "intro." Unfortunately, the most pervasive and colloquial usage of this abbreviation refers specifically to a short *instrumental* preface whose function is primarily to quiet the audience and cue the performer as to the proper pitch. The "porch" I refer to, is a brief *lyrical* construction that precedes the main body of the song and contributes to its meaning. On some vintage sheet music, you will see this referred to as a *verse* and the main body of the song then labeled a *refrain* even though this "refrain" is clearly not a *chorus* or repeated section, but obviously, a two-verse form. (On other sheet music it is simply *not labeled*. It doesn't seem logical that this "front porch" is a *verse* if it is different from yet precedes two obvious *verses*.) On some vintage sheet music this opening section is unaccountably labeled *refrain*. Confused yet? You should be. Because *refrain* means, as previously stated, a section that is repeated at intervals during a long poem. (We have all but dropped *refrain* from the vernacular in favor of *chorus*, the part that everybody "joins in on.") As a last bit of proof that this opening section is no more a "verse" than the two verses following are legitimately called a "chorus" I return to the early church song where proper verses (stanzas) occurred in clusters of at least three and as many as six! This "whatever it is" occurs once only. We never hear it again, let alone with different lyrics. After a lot of thought, I have come to the conclusion that there is need for another term to define this "front porch" or "whatever it is," and I think a dignified term that describes its function is: *prologue* (Pro.).

So the next most complex song form will be the prologue/ verse/verse. What is this *prologue*? A prologue is a traditional, almost antique device—a preparatory statement that is placed in front of the first verse by way of introduction. One of the most famous is the prologue to the *two-verse* form "White Christmas."

> *The sun is shining and the grass is green,*
> *The orange and palm trees sway.*
> *There's never been such a day in Beverly Hills, L.A.*
> *But it's December the twenty-fourth*
> *And I am longing to be up north . . .*
> —Irving Berlin,
"White Christmas"

You know the rest. The prologue's melody is different from that of the main body of the song. Its purpose is to lay the groundwork, to explain just a bit of what the song is to be about, or to set the scene. Frequently it asks a question that the song proceeds to answer. We don't hear many of these anymore—even on the Broadway stage. Scores of classic songs with which we are intimately familiar have lovely prologues which we have never heard, ghosts of another era when nightclub singers carefully created a mood before setting the hook, as in "As Time Goes By"—another *two-verse* form.

> *This day and age we're living in*
> *Gives cause for apprehension,*
> *With speed and new invention*
> *And things like third dimension,*
> *Yet, we get a trifle weary,*
> *With Mister Einstein's the'ry,*
> *So we must get down to earth,*
> *At times relax, relieve the tension.*
> *No matter what the progress,*
> *Or what may yet be proved,*
> *The simple facts of life are such*
> *They cannot be removed . . .*
> —Herman Hupfeld,
"As Time Goes By"

You know the rest. "Wasn't There a Moment" from *Instant Intimacy,* a musical in progress, begins with the following prologue:

Pro.:   *You know I really can't recall the details*
        It's horrific how the memory fails
        As it fades into a blur
        I forget just how things were
        My mind's become a wanderer . . .
                    —Jimmy Webb,
             "Wasn't There a Moment"

The prologue can meander. It is usually sung *rubato* (not in strict tempo) and traditionally is a whimsical or playful moment for the lyricist—an opportunity to pique the curiosity or whet the listener's appetite with four or more intriguing lines. What does it mean to us today? Or as a drummer I used to work with asked, "But how often does it come up?" Not very often. It is, however, part of our musical legacy and it is important for us to understand where it fits in the entire song form. Here's what it looks like when we add it to the two-verse form:

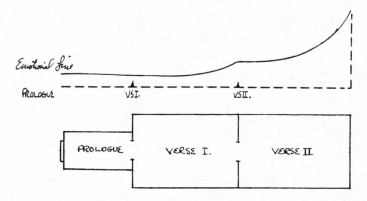

Notice that Verse I is higher on the emotional intensity scale than the prologue and that Verse II goes higher still before climaxing in the last line.

Sometimes the lyric and musical content of the basic verse/verse or ballad/blues form is not enough. The human ear desires some form of relief. "There is not sufficient musical food to satisfy me here!" the brain seems to cry out. No doubt it was that primeval yearning for a song more interesting and engaging that brought about the first departure from verse/verse forms. No matter how beautiful the melody or how clever and moving the lyric, when the same musical pattern is repeated over and over again auditory boredom occurs. Enter the "bridge" (Brg.), a term in common usage which is descended from "release" (in our parents' era) which is, in turn, descended from the venerable "breakstrain."

All three words represent a brief, yet complete musical and lyrical departure from the familiar repeated form of the verse. A perfect example of an early bridge is found in "What'll I Do?" by Irving Berlin. Here is our verse/verse form with a short bridge leading to a final verse:

Vs. I: *What'll I Do when you are far away*
           And I am blue,
           What'll I Do.

Vs. II: *What'll I Do when I am wond'ring who is kissing you*
           What'll I Do.

Brg.:   *What'll I Do with just a photograph*
           To tell my troubles to

Vs. III: *When I'm alone with only dreams of you*
           That won't come true
           What'll I Do?

> —Irving Berlin,
> "What'll I Do?"

We would diagram it like this:

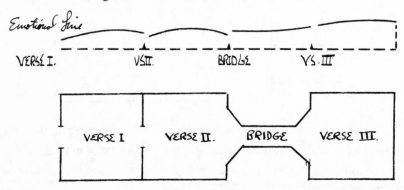

In this immortal song the *bridge* scales the emotional apex (see graph) and the song then subsides poignantly in the final verse.

"Bridge" and "breakstrain" and "release" are supposedly interchangeable words for the same component but are they? "Bridge" implies a continuance. This suggests that it spans an existing gap, that it needs to be there for rhetorical reasons. "Breakstrain" suggests a more brittle—perhaps even arbitrary—change of pace. (I am reminded of John Philip Sousa's thunderous and stirring *breakstrains.*) When considered carefully a *bridge* might be thought to be a completely different animal from a *breakstrain* if not its opposite. "Release" is studio-speak—musicians' slang. The connotation is obvious. We are being "released" from the tyranny of the two-verse form. The songwriter will not be misunderstood if he or she uses the word "bridge" for this midsection. Where does this bridge usually occur? As a rule, it is placed *after a verse* in the two-verse form. At a glance, this would leave us with two possibilities: *It must go between the first and second verse or between the second and third verse.*

Here's another example of bridge placement in a three-verse form:

Vs. I: *They asked me how I knew*
          My true love was true.
          I, of course, replied,
          Something here inside
          Cannot be denied.

Vs. II: *They said someday you'll find*
          All who love are blind
          When your heart's on fire
          You must realize
          Smoke Gets In Your Eyes.

Brg.:   *So I chaffed them and I gayly laughed*
          To think that they could doubt my love,
          Yet today my love has flown away
          I am without my love

Vs. III: *Now laughing friends deride*
          Tears I cannot hide,
          So I smile and say,
          "When a lovely flame dies,
          Smoke Gets In Your Eyes."

—Otto Harbach and Jerome Kern,
"Smoke Gets In Your Eyes"

This is as nearly a perfect demonstration of the lyric function of a bridge as is possible. In the first verse "they" (the writer's immediate circle of friends) ask our hero why he has such unshakable confidence in his love affair. In the second he responds that his faith *"cannot be denied."* In the bridge he laughs to think they *"could doubt my love"* but there is a sudden reversal. By the end of the bridge we know that the relationship has gone sour. This sets up the last verse and his admission that "they" were right all along. Still he manages a sad smile at the end with his wistful and clever explanation of the *reason* that he's been reduced to tears: *"When a lovely flame dies, you must realize Smoke Gets In Your Eyes."* (Harbach and Kern). This is the "surprise twist" so common at the end of the two-verse form as we have already seen. Architecturally speaking, we've added a breezeway between two rooms of our little house, a way of walking from one *state of affairs* to another—or from one *scene* or emotional environment to another.

Required listening on this subject should include the '30s film classic "Isn't It Romantic" (Lorenz Hart and Richard Rodgers), "The Way You Look Tonight" (D. Fields and J. Kern) and "I'll Be Seeing You" (Sammy Fain and Irving Kahal), the latter incorporating our familiar "surprise twist" carried over from the two-verse form: *"I'll be looking at the moon but I'll Be Seeing You"* (©1938 by Williamson Music, Inc.).

The bridge enables us to *expand* the song form due to its salient property of cleansing the musical palate.

Before we explore this any further notice that now we begin to flirt with the potentially cumbersome. There is little need or even room for a prologue in the verse/verse/bridge/verse form even though the elegant "Since I Fell for You" succeeds brilliantly:

> Pro.: *When you just give love and never get love*
> *You'd better let love depart*
> *I know it's so and yet I know*
> *I can't get you out of my heart*
>
> Vs. I: *You made me leave my happy home*
> *You took my love and now you're gone*
> *Since I Fell for You*
>
> Vs. II: *Love brings such misery and pain*
> *I know I'll never be the same*
> *Since I Fell for You*
>
> Brg.: *It's too bad, it's too sad*
> *But I'm in love with you*

You love me then snub me
Oh what can I do I'm still in love with you

Vs. III: *I guess I'll never see the light*
I get the blues most ev'ry night
Since I Fell for You . . .

—Buddy Johnson,
"Since I Fell for You"

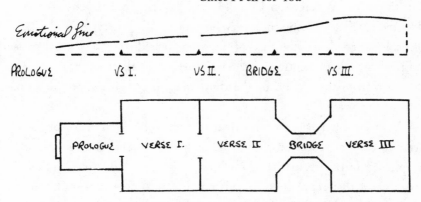

Here is a verse/verse/bridge/verse form written by Boudleaux Bryant decades ago, yet recently rediscovered by several young and voguish bands.

Vs. I: *Love Hurts, love scars, love wounds and mars*
Any heart not tough or strong enough
To take a lot of pain take a lot of pain.
Love is like a cloud, holds a lot of rain,
Love Hurts, Love Hurts.

Vs. II: *I'm young, I know but even so*
I know a thing or two I've learned from you
I've really learned a lot, really learned a lot
Love is like a stove, burns you when it's hot
Love Hurts, Love Hurts.

Brg.:   *Some fools rave of happiness, blissfulness, togetherness.*
Some fools fool themselves I guess, but they're not fooling me.

Vs. III: *I know it isn't true, no, it isn't true,*
Love is just a lie made to make you blue.
Love Hurts, Love Hurts.

—Boudleaux Bryant,
"Love Hurts"

This constitutes a very clever bridge: "*Some fools fool themselves I guess, but they're not fooling me*" which sets up the last verse and its impassioned rejection of the entire concept of "love." (The title itself is fresh and interesting. We might expect to hear "Love Is Great," "Love Is Swell"—but "Love Hurts"?)

Try listening to "It's Almost Like Being in Love" (©1947, Lerner and Loewe), "The Impossible Dream" (©1965, Joe Darien and Mitch Leigh), "On the Street Where You Live" (©1956, Lerner and Loewe), or "For No One" (©1966, Lennon and McCartney), all archetypal V/V/B/V forms. Practice identifying this form when you are listening to other music and pay particular attention to the way the bridge alters or influences the transition from the second to the third verse and then the eventual outcome of the lyric.

We have already determined that the word "refrain"—originally meaning a repeated section with identical words—has in some cases metamorphosed into a term that represents a short introductory passage or even a word that represents, for all practical purposes, a *verse*. The term that has replaced "refrain" in its original definition—the one that is most widely used and easily understood—is "chorus." The most apparent reason for this is that the "chorus" section of a popular song usually calls for vocal augmentation, additional harmony parts, etc., as in "choir" or "chorus." (The "Greek chorus" of Hellenic tragedy.) It contains the key lines, or the "hook," and often, the "title" of the song.

If you decide your song needs a chorus or you want to incorporate one, where does it fit in the overall song form as we know it so far? Here is "Worst That Could Happen," a hit record by Johnny Maestro and the Brooklyn Bridge—reprinted and then diagrammed:

Vs. I:	*Girl, I've heard you're getting married*
	Heard you're getting married
	This time you're really sure
	And this is the end
	They say you really mean it
Lead-in:	*This guy's the one that makes you feel*
	So safe, so sane and so secure and
Chs.:	*Baby, if he loves you more than me*
(repeat)	*Maybe it's the best thing*

> *Maybe it's the best thing for you*
> *But it's the Worst That Could Happen to me*

Vs. II: *I'll never get married*
           Never get married
           You know that's not my scene
           But a girl like you
           Needs to be married

Lead-in: *I've know all along you couldn't live*
           Forever in-between and

Chs.:   *Baby, if he loves you more than me*
(repeat)   *Maybe it's the best thing*
           Maybe it's the best thing for you
           But it's the Worst That Could Happen to me

Brg.:   *Girl, I don't really blame you*
           For having a dream of your own
           Girl, I don't really blame you
           A woman like you needs a house and a home

Chs.:   *Baby, if he really loves you more than me*
(repeat)   *Maybe it's the best thing*
           Baby, it's the best thing for you
           But it's the worst that could happen
           It's the Worst That Could Happen to me

—Jimmy Webb,
"Worst That Could Happen"

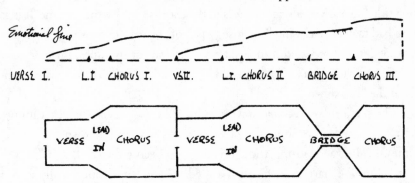

In our songwriting "blueprint" the chorus will represent a larger "room" than does a verse. Think of it as a living room, or maybe even a ballroom. It is more expansive, impressive and easier to remember than a verse. Most often it is repeated without a change of lyric. Its rules of inclusion are simple:

1. It can follow a verse and usually does.

2. It can precede a verse as at the beginning of a song.

3. It can follow a bridge as at the end of a song (illustrated in the previous example).

4. It can precede a verse when it occurs at the end of a first verse and before a second verse.

The verse/chorus now tends to assume a single identity because a chorus almost always appears in tandem with a verse (except as in the previous example, when a chorus follows a bridge at the end of a song and stands alone). It would not be unusual to encounter a verse/chorus/verse form with a *bridge* followed by another unit of verse/chorus. It would almost be unheard of to have a song form consisting of a single verse and chorus.

The basic pattern of alternating verses and choruses is apparent. When a verse/chorus is used as a single unit of form the nature and function of the verse changes dramatically. In the two-verse, verse/bridge/verse or the verse/verse/bridge/verse form we have seen that verses are complete thoughts or paragraphs that usually reach a logical conclusion on or about the last couple of lines with a repetition of the song title/idea or a reprise of an opening statement, etc. When a verse *precedes* a chorus its function is *preparatory*. It begins a story or chain of reasoning that leads to an expository statement (the chorus) much like an elegant foyer prepares the visitor for an entrance into a large and impressive room full of architectural detail and significance. Key lines of the song title/idea are *repeated* at intervals in the chorus to drive them home. It is as if we had taken the closing "surprise twist" of the simple two-verse form and expanded it and repeated it in a statement of four or five lines. Imagine once again if you will "You've Lost that Lovin' Feeling," perhaps the ultimate example of the "big chorus."

The section *"you're trying hard not to show it but Baby, I know it,"* that immediately preceeds the chorus is a separate entity and known by several names. I call it a "lead-in," though it has also been referred to as a "ramp," or a "climb." I have even heard it called a "wind-up." Specifically it is a couplet and some dramatic musical material that sets the stage for the signature chorus lines.

Here is an undisguised attempt by a writer named Webb to imitate this grandiose style:

Vs. I: *I've got to try just one more time to help you believe in me*
        Look into my eyes, check my face for lies and you might see
        My life's never been everything I wanted it to be

Lead-in: *But with you I could change this bad luck*
        With you I could hold my head up Sweet Darlin'

Chs.:   *Just This One Time I really need someone to believe in me*
        Just This One Time I really need someone to leave it with me
        To breathe it with me
        Get beneath it with me Darlin'
        Just This One Time . . .

—Jimmy Webb,
"Just This One Time"

So I am assuming that in spite of the "usable false rhymes" flying all over the place that you are getting the drift of this. The "lead-in" in this case consists of *"but with you I could change this bad luck, with you I could hold my head up."* The verse doesn't give too much away. It holds back deliberately in a process akin to sexual foreplay in order to lambaste the unsuspecting listener with an emotional battering ram (the chorus) as in "The Night They Drove Old Dixie Down" (J. R. Robertson) or "Baby I Need Your Lovin'" (Holland, Dozier and Holland). The emotional catharsis is produced by repeating key lines in a powerful musical setting. Two times in my life I have been forced to pull my automobile to the curb, windshield wipers flailing at top speed, to clear away the tears while listening to the radio. The first time I was blindsided by "You've Lost that Lovin' Feelin'." The next time I narrowly averted a serious multiple-vehicle mishap when Little Anthony and the Imperials sneaked up behind me crooning, *"I know you / don't know what I'm going through / standing here looking at you,"* and then rear-ended me with "Hurt So Bad" (©1964, Teddy Randazzo and Bobby Weinstein).

When I first heard "Without You," sung by Harry Nilsson, I was fortunate enough to have a Cockney gent named Terry Naylor at the wheel. There is no underestimating the emotional impact of the well-crafted verse/lead-in/chorus. It is the nuclear weapon of the modern songwriter.

You might ask, "Well, if this verse/lead-in/chorus thing is so potent, why do we need a *bridge*?" There is the atomic bomb and then there is the *hydrogen* bomb. In a verse/chorus/verse/chorus form an added bridge can be devastating because it *compresses* the first two verse/choruses, lulls us for a moment into believing that the emotional storm has subsided and then with exquisite torture leads us to yet a third and unprecedented cataclysm. You can refer back to "You've Lost that Lovin' Feelin'."

Verse I/Chorus/Verse II/Chorus/Long Bridge/Chorus

Songwriters are quite shamelessly playing with the emotions of human beings when we do this and it is a dirty job, but somebody has to do it.

In "Worst That Could Happen," represented previously, a third and final verse could have been inserted after the bridge, separating it from the chorus like so:

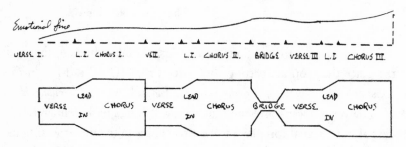

This would approximate (not entirely) what I choose to call a *complete song form*. The problem with these long forms is that they are unwieldy, difficult to write intelligently (you may find yourself "padding" to fill the space) and perilously close to being too lengthy for the marketplace. Another way of putting it: If you can't say what you need or want to say with a verse/chorus/verse/chorus/bridge and *another* chorus, perhaps you should admit to yourself that you are working on an *experimental* song.

What is an experimental song? It is a song wherein a writer has deliberately set out to "break the form." (Carelessly written songs are "accidents," not experiments.) There are some early examples of songwriting that do not seem to fit any repetitive form, German "Liedersong" for instance, where the music was so often *through composed*. (When a song is through composed there is no self-conscious repetition of any particular musical theme or section, rather the melody dictates its own line.) In early twentieth-century songwriting, anomalies often occurred, so-called "patter" sections, which were actually mini-songs or subordinate songs inserted into a traditional form at will, usually to satisfy the exigencies of staging musical numbers in vaudeville shows or on Broadway.

Michael Feinstein suggested I take a look at "Yankee Doodle Blues," music by George Gershwin, lyrics by Irving Caesar and B. G. DeSylva. This song was written in 1922 and makes some unusual detours as it meanders through one hundred and twenty bars. The first twenty-four bars appear to be a kind of vocal fanfare as it is written in imitation of a bugle call and announces *"Hey, here's a word I want to say!"* At this point a deep puzzlement ensues on the part of the analyst due largely to an unwillingness or inability on the part of the publisher to clearly identify subsequent subdivisions of the work. The next section of sixteen bars is clearly labeled "refrain" though it *cannot be a refrain* because it is never repeated. Ignoring the "fanfare" section for the moment, these sixteen bars appear to the author unambiguously to be a "prologue." *"There's no land so grand as my land"* it goes, preparing us for what? A verse or a chorus? Well it turns out to be a proper chorus of sixteen-bars' length that is once repeated, which constitutes what could be called a "thirty-two-bar chorus" even though what we really have is a sixteen-bar chorus sung twice. *"Yankee Doodle, that melody"* it continues, and because it is repeated *word for word* it can be nothing but a chorus. Then what happens? There is a twenty-four-bar segment of complete musical and lyrical disparity that Michael Feinstein has identified for me as a "patter" (Pat.) section. It tells us that the world outside doesn't compare with the good old U.S.A., a sentiment that might have been more valid in Gershwin's day, ending with a cute vignette wherein a U.S. customs officer asks, *"What do you declare?"* and the singer answers, *"I'll declare that"*—now we're back to the chorus and we tell the old customs officer—*"Yankee Doodle that melody,"* etc. Needless to say "Yankee Doodle Blues" is not a blues. (See "titular" blues.) It is an experimental song diagrammed in this way:

*Fanfare (24 bars)/Prologue (16 bars)/Chorus (16 bars)/
Chorus (16 bars)/Patter (24 bars)/Chorus (16 bars)*

In "Swanee" (Caesar and Gershwin, ©1919) there is a long prologue—two verses actually—then a chorus ("refrain" if you insist) that is repeated twice only to enter a "trio" section which is also repeated twice before the song's end.

Verse I/ VerseII/ Chorus I/ Chorus II/ Trio I/ Trio II/ Epilogue

A trio is a critter that all high school band musicians have encountered in march music but to find it in this context indicates that Messrs. Gershwin and Caesar may have been experimenting.

"Cryin' for the Carolinas" (©1930) is another kind of structural free-for-all, courtesy Harry Warren and Lewis and Young, that Michael Feinstein and I unsuccessfully attempted to analyze one afternoon in paroxysms of laughter. It goes something like this:

Verse I/ Chorus/ Bridge/ Chorus/
Verse II/ Chorus/ Bridge/ Chorus/ Patter/ Patter/ Bridge/ Chorus

But not exactly. The publisher does not identify any sections except the "chorus" and the "patter." The delineations of the "verses" and "bridges" are mine and I stand by them.

All of the foregoing indicates that even in the most conservative song-writing circles there have been sporadic attempts to innovate, sometimes driven by the vicissitudes of visual song and dance and on other occasions no doubt simply by the writer's desire to do something unique. The traditional boundaries of the American song create a kind of benign tyranny.

Another example of how writers have sometimes defied convention is the so-called "tag," a slang term for a short additional phrase or two at the end of a traditional form. This postscript might be better described as an "epilogue" since that is wonderfully symmetrical to our "prologue" and in terms of the architectural metaphor constitutes a nice "back porch" for our proposed dwelling. The reader should have little trouble conjuring up a mental performance of "Over the Rainbow" (©1939, Harold Arlen and Yip Harburg).

Verse I/ Verse II/ Bridge/ Verse III/ Tag or Epilogue

What is the tag? It's the bit at the end that goes:

> *If happy little bluebirds fly . . . etc.*
> —H. Arlen & Y. Harburg,
> "Somewhere Over the Rainbow"

Does it come as a surprise that there are differences of opinion in our fraternity as to what constitutes a "tag"? One of my friends believes that the last line of "The Man that Got Away" (©1954, H. Arlen and I. Gershwin) is a "tag" because the line occurs after the "natural" ending of the song—that is to say, subsequent to its final *cadence* (a sequence of resolving chords). Fair enough, but what is its lyrical content? It simply repeats the title: "The Man that Got Away."

And what of its chordal and melodic content? There is no striking or even discernible departure from the harmonic and thematic structure of the song itself. To be identified correctly as an "epilogue" or "tag," this section should differ significantly from the main body of the song in one or both of those elements. Before a "tag" can take place the lyric has to come to a logical conclusion, even if it is a false or misleading conclusion. Therefore, if a conjunction such as "and" or "while" or "because" bridges the lyric to a new melody, lyric and even chordal structure, that material cannot be a tag; rather, it is an *extension*.

In *The Wizard of Oz*, there is a quite extensive epilogue at the end of "If I Only Had a Brain," the song itself being three complete songs, one each for the Scarecrow, Tin Man and Cowardly Lion.

1. Prologue/Verse/Verse/Bridge/Verse (Scarecrow)

2. Prologue/Verse/Verse/Bridge/Verse (Tin Man)

3. Prologue/Verse/Verse/Bridge/Verse (Cowardly Lion)

4. Epilogue (Tag):   *I'd be brave as a blizzard* (Lion)

   I'd be gentle as a lizard (Tin Man)

   I'd be clever as a gizzard (Scarecrow)

   If the wizard is a wizard who will serve

   Then I'm sure to get a brain, a heart, the nerve.
                                    —Yip Harburg,
                                    "If I Only Had a Brain"

The melody becomes a variation on the last line of the verse and then veers in a completely different direction. At the same time the chord structure changes markedly underneath and the lyric is altered accordingly. The last line, *"Then I'm sure to get a brain, a heart, the nerve,"* has a new melody altogether.

"Maria" (L. Bernstein/S. Sondheim) has a legitimate epilogue. Roy Orbison's "Pretty Woman" has a kind of epilogue. "Nights in White Satin" (Justin Hayward), Harry Warren's "Remember Me," "Our House" by Graham Nash, "Some Enchanted Evening" (Rodgers & Hammerstein), "Bye, Bye, Birdie" (Lee Adams and Leslie Strouse) and "If I Ever Say I'm Over You" (John Bucchino) all have epilogues—or close to it.

> *If I Ever Say I'm Over You*
> *The unsentimental things I do*
> *Will have driven out the ghosts somehow*
> *And pulled me through*
>
> *If I tend to disregard your touch*
> *Well, it seems to me it would be*
> *Such a waste of time*
> *To let this poor heart feel that much*
>
> *But sometimes a photograph*
> *Can make me cry, or force a laugh*
> *And somehow the memory*
> *Of how complete we used to be*
> *Is keeping me from you*
>
> *If you ever hear me doubt the past*
> *It's a simple fact we didn't last*
> *Run aground on hard times*
> *While the good times*
> *Flew too fast.*
>
> *I'm not sure if we can make amends*
> *This may be the way our story ends*
> *With too little left for lovers*
> *And too much for friends*
>
> *But sometimes a photograph*
> *Can make me cry, or force a laugh*
> *And somehow the memory*
> *Of how complete we used to be*
> *Is keeping me from you*
>
> Epi.:   *So don't believe it's true*
> *If I Ever Say I'm Over You.*
>
> —John Bucchino,
> *"If I Ever Say I'm Over You"*

It is true that most of these are standards from a golden era and that the authentic tag is an endangered species in today's maelstrom of popular music but it persisted well into the '60s. Hal David and Burt Bacharach's "Alfie" ended with a delicate, enigmatic epilogue.

Verse / Verse / Bridge / Verse / Epilogue (Tag)

Vs. III: *Until you find the love you've missed you're nothing, Alfie . . .*
              —Bacharach & David,
                        "Alfie"

Then this line comes *after* the striking close of the third verse:

When you walk let your heart lead the way
And you'll find love anyday Alfie, Alfie . . .
              —Bacharach & David,
                        "Alfie"

The tag and Bacharach's questioning chords make us wonder: Did Alfie ever get the message?

Listen to "Some Enchanted Evening" and try diagramming it. Find the epilogue (tag).

It has been said that Rodgers and Hammerstein's "It Might as Well Be Spring" is the most beautiful song ever written. If so, then it follows that it ends with the most beautiful *extension* ever written.

Prologue / Verse / Verse / Bridge / Verse / Extension

But I feel so gay in a melancholy way
That It Might as Well be Spring
It might as well, It Might as Well be Spring . . .
              —Rodgers & Hammerstein,
                "It Might as Well Be Spring"

The melody and chords depart simultaneously for "melancholy" territory as does the lyric (a surprising and exquisite shift) and it is almost an epilogue but because the conjunction "but" connects the material to the previous line, it is, in reality, an extension. Some famous extensions are found in "Hello, Young Lovers" (Rodgers and Hammerstein) and "My Funny Valentine" (Rodgers and Hart). In "If I Loved You" (Rodgers and

Hammerstein), we expect the penultimate line to end *"How I loved you so"* but instead we get an exquisite extension which reprises the first line of the song: *"How I loved you, if I loved you."*

In 1968 upon the urging of producer Bones Howe who specifically asked me to alter traditional form, I attempted to incorporate a classical sense of ebb and flow, "movements" if you like, into a long pop song. The result was "MacArthur Park," and a flat-out refusal from the intended artist to record same. Fortunately I knew an Irish actor with a passion for Brendan Behan and James Joyce among other complicated and unusual things, a man who relished the unique and eccentric above all else, the same man who retrieved the music from the bottom of my trunk and demanded that we record it (even though all he really said was, "I'll have that."). Richard Harris's recording of "MacArthur Park" subsequently became number one on the charts in Britain, Ireland, France, Germany, Italy and Australia, and number two in the United States. In 1976 Donna Summer's version was number one on the U.S. charts, but this isn't a press release. Many words have been used to describe "MacArthur Park" ("abomination" comes to mind), but few will deny that it was an "experiment." Let's look at its distinct lack of form:

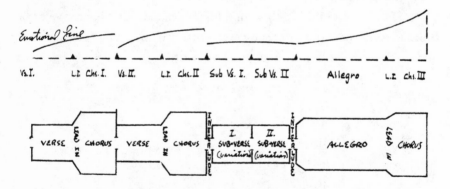

To explain briefly what I mean by a "sub-verse" in the previous example, these are verses with a different lyric and melodic content from the opening verses. They are descended from the "patter" sections that we found in Harry Warren's, Caesar's and Gershwin's songs. In my view they are *subordinate* to Verses I, II and III being as they are preceded if not framed by this initial thematic material, hence subordinate verse or "sub-verse."

Even before "MacArthur Park," I had toyed with *movements* (changes of mood and pace as well as melodic content) in "Rosecrans Boulevard," first recorded by Johnny Rivers on his *Rewind* album and then later by the Fifth Dimension. There was decidedly less controversy over the latter, except from women, some of whom came to the conclusion that I had mistreated the stewardess who stole my virginity.

Verse(4/4)/Chorus(3/4)/Allegro Bridge (7/4)/Half-Chorus (3/4)/
Epilogue (4/4)

With the exception of the fast 7/4 bridge the structure is familiar until the epilogue, where all the previous harmonic and melodic material is abandoned for a minor key and slower tempo. Note the shifting time signatures:

Verse I (4/4):   *I've passed a lot of exit signs in my time*
While driving down this long freeway
To San Diego and points south
But there was a time last summer
When I came down from Manhattan
And though I knew I shouldn't it was just too hard
And I made my move at Rosecrans Boulevard

Chorus (3/4):   *Rosecrans Boulevard stop your callin' me*
You know I never loved her anyway
I just used her over and over

Bridge (7/4):   *But there were times when she'd laugh*
And I'd think I loved her
One night on Manhattan Beach I said things
That moved too fast to suit her
Then I held her close and dried her tears

Half-Chorus (3/4):   *Rosecrans Boulevard who cares what you think?*
Coda I(4/4):   *The girl was half crazy the way she drove that little car*
Down Sunset Boulevard at three in the morning
Doing ninety miles an hour in a thirty mile zone
And blamed me when she got a ticket

Coda 2:   *But then there was that smile*
It was really what made all the airlines go
She was a stewardess you know

Shot down on a non-combatant mission
And though I've hid it
Every time I drive my car past Rosecrans Boulevard
I wonder why I did it

—Jimmy Webb,
"Rosecrans Boulevard"

Probably not one of the great moments in Western literature but an honest attempt to describe a haunting one-sided relationship, the changing time signatures, key centers and melodic content mirroring the lyrics' ambiguities. (We were crazy for experimentation in the late '60s. I suggested to Johnny Rivers that we record the strings for "Rosecrans Boulevard" *backwards*, a technique that had achieved eerie results with electric guitars. After laboriously writing the string parts in *reverse order* and recording them with the audio tape juxtaposed on the machine we could hardly wait to turn the tape over and hear what wonders we had created. When the piece was played in correct order it sounded like violins—very *nice* violins, but ordinary fiddles, nevertheless . . .) Producer and arranger George Martin (who subsequently produced my own album, *El Mirage*, in 1977) had already blazed a trail in experimentation with the Beatles, particularly in his realization of John Lennon's concept of "a sound building up from nothing to the end of the world." Martin stood in front of the orchestra the night "Day in the Life" (©1967) was recorded with no conductor's score, only asking them to play from their lowest possible note to their highest. In between it was "every man for himself," a technique that would have mightily pleased avant-garde composer John Cage (*Shout! The Beatles in Their Generation* by Philip Norman, Warner Books, ©1981 Philip Norman).

"Within You, Without You," George Harrison's contribution to *Sgt. Pepper*, set a lyric to a raga (a rigorously defined Hindu form played on the sitar) under the tutelage of Ravi Shankar. This was more difficult than it may seem, involving the combining of Western syntax with Eastern mode, rhythm and instrumentation. Verses? Choruses? None that we can identify easily. A haunting hybrid resulted that is greater than the sum of its parts.

At the conclusion of the group's *Abbey Road* after three songs in quick succession, which could be described as "movements," the epilogue or "tag" was added: "*And in the end the love you take*," etc., which in its modest way seems to sum up most of life. I would call it an experiment.

Billy Joel felt the same way: "I heard the closing section of *Abbey Road* and immediately I thought 'those are meant to be movements.'" (Joel is classically trained.) When I talked to him about experimental forms he elaborated: "I was fascinated but as I thought about it more I began to think that these were song *fragments* that had been fitted together carefully." Joel maintains that any professional songwriter worth his salt would have recognized this in time (and I can't say I disagree) but it got him to thinking. He likens the process to building a street rod out in the garage from available parts, tinkering with it, reworking it and perhaps creating a brand-new component when necessary.

As we talked further he agreed with me when I suggested that there were arbitrary twists and turns even in the works of the master symphonists. We are inclined to believe, and are even *told*, that their long complex forms sprang from the souls of the immortals fully formed and congruous with some divine template, though in one of his lectures at Harvard, Leonard Bernstein says of Mozart's G Minor Symphony:

> He has established us firmly in B Flat Major; but, no, off he goes on another chromatic adventure which lands us in the impossible key of F Sharp Minor. Now, this was done by absolute whim—*arbitrarily.* [My italics]
>
> —Leonard Bernstein,
> *The Unanswered Question: Six Talks at Harvard*

The door is opened a crack to the idea that even the great classical composers spent time in the woodshed trying new ideas, discarding others, perhaps incorporating an old unfinished one from time to time and occasionally daring to leap into a new key, tempo or mood just for the hell of it.

To my ear, Joel's "Scenes from an Italian Restaurant" (1977) sounds like more than backyard tinkering, having—as it does—a cinematic scope, a story line evocative of Tony Bill's *Five Corners* or George Lucas's *American Graffiti* and a vivid depiction of the passing of many years and the effect that time's erosion has on his characters. (I like to think that this long piece contains its own sequel.) It is constructed like this:

Verse I/ Verse II/ Instrumental/ Allegro/ Piano Solo/ Allegro 2/ Allegro 3/

(sub-verse)   (sub-verse) (sub-verse)

Bridge / Instrumental / Bridge/ Allegro 4 / Instrumental / Verse III / Instrumental (sub-verse)

Way back in 1966 on her album *In My Life* Judy Collins recorded what is essentially a small opera with four movements and a reprise named "Marat/Sade" long before any Broadway composer had dreamed of releasing a score on record prior to a musical's opening.

"Suite: Judy Blue Eyes," the Crosby, Stills and Nash epic from the 1969 album of the same name, consisted of two interconnected songs (movements) followed by an instrumental allegro, itself relieved at intervals by fragmentary statements that are not substantial enough to be diagrammed as true verses and ending with a three-part vocal riff which repeats and fades without lyrics.

Verse/Chorus/Verse/Chorus/Bridge/Chorus/Verse/Chorus/Sub-Verse/Sub-Verse/ Sub-Bridge/Sub-Verse/Sub-Verse/Instrumental (allegro)/ Fragment/Inst./Fragment/Inst./Fragment/Inst./Vocal Fade

Harry Nilsson's "Salmon Falls" (©1975) was an unstructured, rambling recitative in which he seemed to defy analysis while at the same time proselytizing his own wrinkle on reincarnative Eastern philosophy.

For the eclectic among you, the late Laura Nyro's "New York Tendaberry" (©1969) also manages to frustrate dissection or even description.

Carly Simon's "Like A River" has already been quoted as an example of masterful conversational tone but the work's groundbreaking operatic epilogue—a carefully woven contrapuntal trio—stands virtually alone in the songwriting of the '90s as an unabashed yet successful experiment.

Verse/Mini-Bridge/Chorus/Verse/Mini-Bridge/Chorus/Verse/ Mini-Bridge/Chorus/Operatic Epilogue

It was probably "Stand By Me," Ben E. King's version of the Ben E. King, Jerry Leiber and Mike Stoller R&B standard, that got all of this neo-classicism under way in 1961 with its Russian-romantic orchestral midsection that also subtly suggested fugal elements. The recording provoked this striking realization: Rock 'n' roll and the string ensemble are not antithetic after all. To the contrary, the rough, self-taught textures of rock vocalists are ineffably complemented by the silken tones of the orchestra and vice versa. It was only a matter of time until popular recording artists began to co-opt the formalized *shapes* of the classical repertoire as well, resulting inevitably in the songs of the Left Bank, the Moody Blues, the Who, Pink Floyd, Davie Bowie and, more recently, Elvis Costello (*The Juliet Letters* released in 1993).

While listening, pay attention to songwriting that "breaks the form." Try to diagram it and when confused be dogged in your efforts to decode the composer's and lyricist's master plan. If you are uncertain as to the labeling of a particular section, make up your own name for it. As John Lennon wrote: "*There's nothing you can hear that can't be heard*" ("All You Need Is Love," ©1967 Lennon and McCartney)—and may I be so bold as to add: There's nothing you can hear that you can't learn to write for yourself in your own way.

There is one last major element of modern song form that must be included. With the appearance of mass appeal "chorus" songs in the early and mid '50s, a phenomenon occurred, unheard until that time. Loathing to end that catchy "sing-along" section at the ends of records, producers began to "fade" or gradually decrease the gain on the recording, slowly tapering it into silence as the chorus repeated over and over. This provided an ending of sorts, and gave the disc jockey a convenient segue to another record while he identified the title and the artist. At home on the RCA 45 r.p.m. record changer it had—some said—a more sinister effect. It "brainwashed" the teenyboppers. Long after the record was finished and the tonearm was sloughing back and forth in the final groove, the Four Seasons' "Candy Girl" (by Larry Santos) was still playing on a turntable somewhere in the back of little Susie's brain. It was psychological warfare of a profound potency. It was an artificially induced mantra to a generation who did not yet know what that word meant. Fades became part of the modern song form, particularly when producers realized that by augmenting the fade with other instruments and effects, a whole new emotional surge could be generated at the end of a record.

Now what on earth is a "breakdown"? Does that mean the drummer made a mistake? It simply means that between the last chorus and the fade the producer has introduced a segment of perhaps four bars more or less with a distinctly minimalist nature, using only basic instruments or sometimes even silence to falsely lull the audience (they always fall for it) before plastering them with an augmented "fade" that is calculated to blow their socks off. This "fade" will always disappear into the auditory distance at an *apparent maximum volume.* (Rarely if ever does the music actually get softer while being recorded in the studio.)

Very well. Here are some great "chorus" songs with "fades" if you care to listen:

"You've Lost that Lovin' Feelin' "—Mann, Spector & Weil:
    Verse/Chorus/Verse/Chorus/Bridge/Chorus/Fade
"Without You"—Peter Ham:
    Verse/Verse/Chorus/Verse/Chorus/Fade
"I Wanna Know What Love Is"—Mick Jones:
    Verse/Bridge/Chorus/Inst./Verse/Bridge/Chorus/Fade
"To Love Somebody"—Barry, Robin & Maurice Gibb:
    Verse/Chorus/Verse/Chorus/Fade

In closing, let's look at a diagram that will indicate everything that is pertinent to the inclusion of these various components—a master blueprint if you please. It is not meant to be taken literally as a model for a song since such a "song" might easily last fifteen minutes or more.

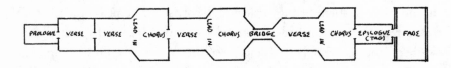

In architectural terms this is indeed a "grand maison" or at the very least a rambling country estate. Obviously impractical, it does show the correct sequence of elements. The prologue precedes the verse. The verse can appear in tandem with another or precede the chorus. The bridge occurs *after* the verse or chorus. Some of the "rooms" can be omitted, but those that remain will be constructed in proper order.

We start with a familiar shape or "model" and alter it to suit us. The Gaudi Sagrada Familia in Barcelona is a church with a nave, a vestibule and a sanctuary. If its form was so distorted as to make worship impossible, then innovation would have nulled purpose.

Perhaps someday there will be a musical Gaudi who will put an end to conventional form and set popular songs free from what remains of formal restraint. There is no sign of such an annihilator on the horizon. "Rap music," the would-be destroyer, is inevitably constructed verse/chorus/verse/chorus/verse/chorus ad infinitum. The innovators of the jazz world as well as the writers of Broadway shows even in the "operetta" style have with few exceptions adhered to the "shapes" that the public recognizes easily and understands. Any attempt to reinvent the popular song has been met by an abject apathy if not open hostility, suggesting that American song form is somehow viscerally imbedded in the human species. Voltaire has said that "if God did not exist, it would be necessary to invent him." If humankind had not invented the American song form, then it would no doubt still exist somewhere on the periphery of our souls as an unrealized architecture of dreams. As Immanuel Kant said in his "Prolem Gamara to Any Future Metaphysics": "It is because it is."

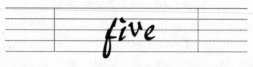

IT CAN'T GET NO VERSE . . .

I search for phrases to sing your praises,
But there aren't any magic adjectives to tell you all you are.
You're just too marvelous, too marvelous for words . . .
—JOHNNY MERCER & RICHARD WHITING,
"TOO MARVELOUS FOR WORDS"

There is a story about Michelangelo which has survived for hundreds of years. An admirer asks the great sculptor to explain just how he manages to create such a living, breathing representation of human flesh out of something so unyielding and difficult to manipulate as stone. "Ah but you see," the painter of the Sistine chapel replies, "the image is already *within* the block of stone. I merely chip away the pieces that are not needed." Something similar happens when we get down to the business of writing a lyric. Much of the process is simply the elimination of less desirable elements in order to expose the more desirable ones.

It's time then to retrieve those research materials from their safe hiding place; the letter to someone else or to oneself, the pages comprising all the thoughts and references the writer has been able to muster on the songwriting subject. There are a thousand ways to write a lyric and the following method is in no way advertised as the best. You are no less welcome to look over my shoulder while I try to pursue this one to a logical conclusion. You will recall that my goal is to write a song called "Problem Child," about someone close to me who goes through uncontrollable mood swings. Take another look at page 51.

—WRITING SESSION 1—

After I look at the "letter" again and think about it for a few moments (I try to imagine the song I want to write—the style, the feel, the nature of it) I turn immediately to the rhyming dictionary to discover what words will rhyme with "child." Right off the bat I can see that the odds are not in my favor (there are only sixteen words total) but I dutifully go through the list and make notes:

Problem child with

aisled	(hard to imagine a line contorted enough to actually make this work)
beguiled	(a good word but hardly conversational)
childe	(antique spelling, why do they bother?)
enfiled	(clearly an obscure word)
foster child	(useless)
love child	(useless)
mild	(good word, unfortunately overused in advertising, etc.)
self-styled	(good)
unreconciled	(good)
wild	(very good)
Wilde	(one of us is gonna have to go . . .)

I hope you've noticed right away that some of the rhymes are logically connected to the subject. They are *related*. Which ones are they?

1. A problem child could conceivably be *wild*.

2. A problem child might end up *beguiled*.

3. He would probably not be *mild* but he might possibly aspire to such a state.

4. A problem child would most probably be *self-styled*.

5. Or *unreconciled* to some degree.

So I find that five of these are eminently usable and should go down on a short list: *wild, beguiled, mild, self-styled, unreconciled.* Is that all I have to work with? My Clement Wood thoughtfully steers me in another direction: "See also IL and add '-ed' where appropriate." Going directly to IL, which is only a couple of columns away on the opposite page, I find immediately the misbegotten *anglophiled*, the much loathed *chamomiled* and the other-worldly *voltaic piled.* Saving you considerable time I made a list of words ending in "-ed" that make a modicum of sense in this universe.

compiled	(has one signal virtue in that to my knowledge it has never appeared in a song lyric)
defiled	(most people still know what this means)
reviled	(a very strong word not often used in songwriting)
riled	(as in "all riled up"?)
smiled	(good)
tiled	(third floor, kitchens, bathrooms)
whiled	(as in "away the hours")

What obvious semantic connections can we establish immediately between which of these rhymes and the subject matter?

1. A problem child might find himself *defiled* or feeling *defiled* or in some cases *defiling* others.

2. He might likewise find himself *reviled* or *reviling* others.

3. *Smiled*—has he ever?

I believe the other rhymes: *tiled, whiled, compiled,* etc. to be well out of the ballpark and so I find myself with three possibilities: *defiled, reviled* and *smiled* in addition to my original five.

1. *defiled*

2. *reviled*

3. *smiled*

4. *wild*

5. *beguiled*

6. *mild*

7. *self-styled (styled)*

8. *unreconciled*

I am now all too aware that there isn't an overabundance of keen rhymes for the word "child," which will inspire me to proceed cautiously. I will use the good rhymes sparingly and wisely. Since I am thinking of a verse/chorus/verse/chorus form I will more than likely reserve them for the chorus or even the very end of the chorus. As an experienced songwriter I am already looking ahead to the chorus and thinking, "If I had more raw rhyming material I might write choruses that would alter slightly each time around." My thinking continues: "With this scarcity of rhymes I may want a chorus that repeats exactly the same material every time it's used." We'll see. (At this point I usually jot the usable rhymes at the top of the first writing page for quick and easy reference.) Next I'll get a rhythm in my head. Is it to be a slow ballad or a rock 'n' roll tune? Is it going to be in common 4/4 time or is it to be a perfect waltz? "Problem Child" I foresee as a medium 4/4 tempo. I usually pat my foot in time while I work on a lyric, to see whether the natural accents of the words fall on the proper beats. This also lays the groundwork for the shape of musical phrases to come. (If you have trouble patting your foot and chewing gum at the same time, how about getting yourself a little metronome or simple drum machine or, better still, play along on your instrument or have your collaborator accompany you.) The point is to give the lyric a consistent rhythm—the way a rapper does.

Every song must begin with a first line, and prosaic as this observation may seem, there is no diminishing the import of the first few words of a lyric. At the beginning of the story the listener will more than likely make a decision to follow along or be diverted elsewhere. Contemplating my "letter" I'm captured immediately by a line at the beginning of the notes: "When you cross the line between brilliance and madness then you're out there on your own." Not only does this express exactly what I want to direct to the person in question, it is also a come-on to the listener. It arouses a certain curiosity regarding what the hell I'm talking about, to whom it is directed and just where the story might be headed. As irrational as it may seem the listener will probably personalize the statement on first hearing and wonder if it applies to him or her. I decide to change the word "the" to "that" because it sounds more emphatic. I count and chant along with each line to give it a definite rhythm.

When you cross that line between brilliance and madness
Then you're out there on your own . . .

(I have inadvertently written a rhyme into my notes and I decide to use it.)

Just when you're overjoyed
You might be destroyed

(For anybody who knows anything about manic-depression there is unintended humor in this couplet but it is pointed in the right direction and I choose to keep it for the present.)

like Icarus <u>too close</u> to the sun.

(The demographics of understanding have just altered dramatically in favor of students with at least a fragmentary knowledge of Greek mythology. I have dropped "<u>flying towards</u>" the sun as unwieldy.)

It's so hard to come down from that dizzying height

(The preceding line will not be found in the notes. I've just had a mental picture of my subject person in a state of intense excitement, hence "the dizzying height" for which I anticipate I will need a rhyme. More importantly, instinct and experience tell me that I'm very near the end of the first verse and it is time to contemplate the beginning of the chorus, perhaps after one more line.)

Descending like a meteorite

(I very much like the image of the "meteorite" but the line is missing some of the drama of a "falling star." What about . . .)

Burning alive <u>just</u> like a meteorite.

(This says more about the pain of the individual involved and the drama of a catastrophic descent. I love the rhyme between *height* and *meteorite*. I add the word "just" for smoother rhythm.)

> Vs. I: *When you cross that line between brilliance and madness*
> *Then you're out there on your own.*
> *Just when you're overjoyed*
> *You might be destroyed*
> *like Icarus, too close to the sun*
> *It's so hard to come down from that dizzying height,*
> *burning alive just like a meteorite*

For clarity's sake, even though it may chop a line or thought into two pieces, I make a practice of dividing lines so that whenever possible the rhyming words occur at the ends of phrases as illustrated. This makes the rhyme scheme readily apparent and later on the lines can be reorganized into complete sentences if the writer so desires.

I now have a rough verse—emphasis on *rough*—but it's important to move along and tell the story. Refinements can wait. In that spirit I plunge directly into a Chorus I.

Oh Problem Child

(I'm thinking of a parental sigh of concern, hence "oh." I'm reminded of Negro spirituals. Believe it or not I'm thinking about "Old Man River," or "Deep River." I go to my notes for words that are related to "problem": *solution, question,* and try to think of others—*enigma?* I get out the thesaurus: *issue, mystery, dilemma, riddle, quandary, obstacle, difficulty, predicament, puzzle.*)

You've got to work this <u>puzzle</u> out

(This is an impulse buy and not very satisfying, what about . . .)

You're a puzzle that you must work out

(Kind of a tongue twister with "your" and "you" in the same sentence but I keep it for now and go to the next line.)

I can't tell you what it's all about

(This is nothing more or less than a blatant '60s cliché. "What it's all about" makes me feel a bit faint so I'll try . . .)

The solution is still in doubt

(It's probably better, certainly more personal to change "the" to "your.")

Chs. I: *Oh Problem Child*
              <u>You're</u> a puzzle that you must work out
              <u>Your</u> solution is still in doubt

(The chorus is most likely destined to end with the words "Problem Child" so I'm going to begin to introduce "-ild" rhymes at the end of some of the lines.)

All these dreams unreconc<u>iled</u>

(The line doesn't make perfect sense but it rhymes and it's the right number of board feet so I'm leaving it in for the time being. I want to move on to another rhymed couplet similar to "work out/in doubt." Remember we're talking about someone who lives on an emotional roller coaster. I'm thinking there has to be a "middle ground" for this person. The word "between" comes to mind, *between* something and something else.)

Between the silence and the sound

(I stumble onward.)

And what you've lost and what you've found
There has to be a middle ground

(I decide to make *ground* an inner rhyme and finish with another "-ild" rhyme.)

There has to be a middle ground where life is not so wild

(Now how to finish the chorus? Inspiration strikes!)

Oh and that's the problem, oh that's the Problem Child

To recapitulate and evaluate:

Vs. I: *When you cross that line between brilliance and madness*
          Then you're out there on your own
          Just when you're overjoyed
          You might be destroyed like Icarus, too close to the sun.
          But it's hard to come down from that dizzying height
          Burning alive just like a meteorite

Chs. I: *Oh Problem Child,*
          You're a puzzle that you must work out
          Your solution is still in doubt
          All these dreams unreconciled
          Between the silence and the sound
          And what you've lost and what you've found
          There has to be a middle ground where life is not so wild
          Oh and that's the problem, oh that's the Problem Child

(I'm not overly pleased. There is a triteness to the "silence/sound" and "lost/found" rhymes. There is a forced quality to the rhythm of the chorus and a "busyness." I like the verse a lot better than the chorus.)

It's good to take a break after writing a verse and chorus to stretch and think about what's been done that's good or what may be disappointing. It's also a good time to consider what form the song is likely to take when it's finished.

In this case "Problem Child" is moving ahead predictably as a verse/chorus/verse/chorus form and it is probably too early to determine if a bridge or other addition will be needed. I decide to try writing another verse (Verse II) and since I like the first one it makes incredibly good sense to create a *template* of Verse I. This can be accomplished easily by counting the syllables in each line and marking the rhyme scheme with letters of the alphabet. "A" must rhyme with "A" and "B" must rhyme with "B," etc.

VERSE I

___ ___ ___ ___ ___ ___ ___ ___ ___ ___ ___(no rhyme)

___ ___ ___ ___ ___ ___ ___(no rhyme)

___ ___ ___ ___ ___ A

___ ___ ___ ___ A

___ ___ ___ ___ ___ ___ ___ ___ ___ ___ ___(no rhyme)

___ ___ ___ ___ ___ ___ ___ ___ ___ B

___ ___ ___ ___ ___ ___ ___ ___ B

If this template is neatly copied onto onionskin or similar transparent material, it can be kept clean and intact while it is used to overlay the lyric in progress. The syllable count and rhyme scheme of any line can be checked quickly and efficiently. The number of syllables in each line of the new verse and their rhyming partners should line up perfectly with this "road map." Why? Because the music of different verses will continue to be for all practical purposes *identical* and if a lyric is written to this template then it will more than likely fit the same music even if there are some minor anomalies. For instance . . .

Problem Child, where do your answers lie?

Compared to:

Problem Child, (we can) work this trouble out

In a case like this it is common for the writer to compress the fourth and fifth syllables of the second example into the same space (beat) normally occupied by only one syllable. Though sticklers for detail will "Tsk! Tsk!" and shake their heads in reproach if the syllable count is not exactly the same from verse to verse and chorus to chorus, most professionals normally give themselves some leeway.

Reviewing the "letter" I try to center on the emotional message. Two lines pop into my head like magic:

I know it's pretty up there in that world of visions
So far away from the hard decisions

(Disastrously, neither one fits the template—count out the syllables for yourself. The first line is only one syllable over but the second one is a yard too long. Equally detrimental is the fact that the rhyme scheme isn't even close to the one on the template. Altering a rhyme scheme or radically changing the number of syllables between verses or choruses is most often considered inelegant and amateurish. Even though I think the lines are super I reluctantly continue my search.)

I know you used to think you knew all the answers

(It's a very close fit and also unfortunately very similar to Bob Dylan's "Like a Rolling Stone," and also a tongue and brain twister of the first order. Basically it sucks. Again, desperation is mother to invention.)

When you cross your fingers and hope for salvation
You're on thin ice in a heat wave

(I have conjured up a would-be provincial witticism or "sayin'" here and I'm liking it. The template tells me that I have a rhyming couplet coming up straight away and I decide to build on the cautionary tone of the opening lines.)

'Cause when you think you've got it made
That's the time to be afraid
Beware when you're having too much fun

(This is just good old-fashioned Baptist guilt working overtime. I decide it would be even spookier to say . . .)

<u>*God knows*</u> *when you're having too much fun*

(Seems okay so far.)

'Cause you're bound to come down, better watch that first step

(Take my word for it, it is going to be impossible to rhyme *step*.)

'Cause you're bound to come down and you're bound to get hurt
And you're bound to be found face-down in the dirt

(I couldn't resist the tendency of the last two lines to rhyme inwardly—
"bound," and "found." I went with it—breaking my own rule about adhering to the rhyme scheme on the template. There is a beat missing between
"found" and "face-down." I interject the word "lying.")

Vs. II: *When you cross your fingers and hope for salvation*
              You're on thin ice in a heat wave
              'Cause when you think you've got it made
              That's the time to be afraid
              God knows when you're having too much fun
              'Cause you're bound to fall down
              And you're bound to get hurt
              And you're bound to be found <u>lying</u> face-down in the dirt.

(I'm thinking about abandoning the catchy inner-rhyme scheme of the last
line because the message is awfully grim. It has a kind of "I won't say I told
you so" fatalism that seems cruel and pointless.)

I'm anticipating trouble with the second chorus because I'm not overly
enthusiastic about Chorus I. I make a template anyway, hoping it will all
fall into place. Maybe I'll write a Chorus II and it will be so good that I
can throw Chorus I away and just use the new one!

CHORUS TEMPLATE

<u>(Oh Prob)</u> <u>lem</u> <u>A</u>

—— —— —— —— —— —— —— <u>B</u>

—— —— —— —— —— —— <u>B</u>

—— —— —— —— —— <u>A</u>

___ ___ ___ ___ ___ ___ ___ __C__

___ ___ ___ ___ ___ ___ ___ __C__

___ ___ ___ ___ ___ ___ ___ __C__

___ ___ ___ ___ ___ __A__

(<u>Oh</u> <u>and</u> <u>that's</u> <u>the</u> <u>prob</u> <u>lem,</u> <u>Oh</u> <u>that's</u> <u>the</u> <u>Prob</u> <u>lem</u> <u>Child</u>) _A_

Concentrating on the first two lines of Chorus II for a while, I demonstrate a technique often used on troublesome couplets utilizing the rhyming dictionary. First by free-associating some beginning lines to this second chorus:

Oh Problem Child,
is there something you don't understand?

The template tells me that *the end of the next line should rhyme* so I go to the rhyming dictionary and find "-and." There are eighty-one words in the basic list. Other rhymes can be found by adding "-ed" to "AN." Tedious as it may seem, the real songwriter will consider each one of these words as a possibility and determine their degree of usefulness by mentally linking each one to the line under consideration.

Oh Problem Child is there something you don't understand?
> with   *aband*
> with   *abby-land*
> with   *ampersand*
> with   *analysand*
> with   *backhand*

. . . Except that these strange rhymes have little or nothing to do with the song I am writing so I need to scan the list of rhymes and find the most likely candidates, the ones that have some logical connection.

hand   *—is the answer close at hand?*
no-man's land   *—are you tired of no-man's land?* or
                              —do you live in no-man's land?

Problem Child, I can see the puzzle in your eyes

From a list of over 440 words I distill the following:

recognize *—there's a look I recognize*
analyze   *—that's so hard to analyze*
visualize *—that I cannot visualize*

I find some other possibilities that do not readily pair themselves with *"there's a puzzle in your eyes."* But I make a list of them because they seem to relate to the overall situation and subject matter:

apologize
compromise
criticize
improvise
fantasize
sacrifice
sympathize
lies

These suggest some other combinations:

Oh Problem Child,
will you ever make a compromise
or become a sacrifice?

Oh Problem Child,
do you ever try to see the lies
in the truths you fantasize?

Oh Problem Child,
do you ever think to sympathize
with the ones you victimize (criticize)?

The related rhymes in a given list represent a huge open-ended mosaic of possibility that can be organized in thousands of different ways. A lot depends on the writer's patience and the strenuous application of intense concentration over long periods of time.

Problem Child,
are you really quite so unconcerned
with the lessons left unlearned?

Oh Problem Child,
tell me of the secrets you have learned
what wisdom have you earned?

Oh Problem Child,
can you hear the questions in the air,
does an answer wait somewhere?

Oh Problem Child,
don't you know that life is hardly fair
are you so devil-may-care?

(and hundreds of others.)

Oh Problem Child,
can you tell me where your answers lie?
What is your alibi?
What principles apply?
Where does your reason fly?
How do you justify?
Why don't you simplify?
Is it hard to qualify?
How can you rectify?
What is your reply?
What does it signify?
When will you testify?
What will you verify?

Another pairing:

Oh Problem Child,
Who, What, Where, How and Why,
Where do your answers lie?

It is obvious that there are potentially countless versions of these first two lines but one of the factors that will cull the more unsuitable is the imminent "-ild" rhyme at the end of the third line (see template). What kind of "-ild" rhymes are left? *Unreconciled* and *wild* have been used in Chorus I which leaves . . . :

1. *defiled*
2. *reviled*
3. *smiled*
4. *wild* (used)
5. *beguiled*
6. *mild*
7. *self-styled* (*styled*)
8. *unreconciled* (used)

Another process of comparison and elimination becomes necessary. I have several pairs of opening lines, some of which I am quite fond, but which of these can I logically connect with one of the remaining "-ild" rhymes?

Oh Problem Child,
can you help me try to understand
is the answer close at hand _____ _____ _____ _____ _____ *-ild?*

For the life of me I can't logically connect this couplet with any of the remaining "-ild" rhymes. You try it.

Oh Problem Child,
will you ever really understand
that you live in no-man's land bewildered and <u>beguiled</u>?

Oh Problem Child,
when I see the puzzle in your eyes
there's no look I recognize in that vision so self-<u>styled</u>

Oh Problem Child,
do you need to find a compromise
and avoid a sacrifice to the gods you have <u>reviled</u>

Oh Problem Child,
do you ever try to see the lies
in the truths you fantasize, do you know that you're <u>beguiled</u>?

Oh Problem Child,
are you really quite so unconcerned
with the lessons left unlearned and the innocence <u>defiled</u>

Oh Problem Child,
tell me of the secrets you have learned
what wisdom have you earned, what life is this you've <u>styled</u>?

Some of these are hopelessly far-fetched but you have to be on tiptoe to reach the cookie jar. (You will not find the perfect solution to such problems without making a fool out of yourself once in a while so don't be afraid of it.) Eventually, by using a process of trial and error while searching for semantic connections between dozens of different rhymes and lines—and always following the template, I come up with Chorus II:

Oh Problem Child
do you ever try to see the lies
in the truth you fantasize?
Do you know that you're beguiled?
Do you live a nightmare of despair
in your game of solitaire?
Don't you care that life could be so sweet and mild
Oh what's the problem, what's the Problem Child?

Before you start I must tell you that I'm decidedly unhappy with both these choruses. They seem complicated and unwieldy. The disproportionate effort that I am investing is not being repaid with any dramatic improvement. What is wrong *mostly*? First, the rhythm of the rhyme scheme is overly complicated and the message is obscure. (I literally don't know what I'm talking about—a sad state of affairs.) Second, I am severely cramped by the lack of available "-ild" rhymes. Conclusion: Retire from the field of battle for the time being, consider going in another direction.

—WRITING SESSION II—

After some reflection I've decided to throw both of these choruses out. I don't have enough "-ild" rhymes for two choruses even if they are only slightly different. Couplets such as this one make me uncomfortable:

Do you ever see the lies
in the truth you fantasize?

The rhythms and rhymes seem forced and I doubt if adding music is going to help very much. (In fact it may even make matters worse.) I desire a simpler chorus; just one version with a smoother rhythm and a clearer message. What do I like about what I have so far? I like the fact that the second chorus is composed of questions, especially the last line—"*what's the Problem Child*," better than the preachier "*that's the Problem Child*" of the first chorus. I believe that putting the second chorus in the interrogatory was a significant breakthrough and will prove to be much more sympathetic. First thing I'm going to do is get rid of the emotional but rather meaningless "oh."

> *Problem Child,*
> *you're running wild*

(Changing it to a question.)

> *Problem Child,*
> *why do you run so wild?*
> *What struggle are you making that's so unreconciled?*

(*Unreconciled* is a rhyme from discarded Chorus I. Doggedly I go to the dictionary to learn its precise meaning: unreconciled—unaccommodated, unattuned, unconformed, unresolved, etc. There is a *struggle* going on inside this person that needs to be *reconciled*.)

> *What struggle deep inside you is so unreconciled?*

(Good.)

> *What are you running from, where are you running to?*

(In spite of the grammatical error—we are not supposed to end sentences with prepositions—these two lines paint a vivid picture of personality in transition, even turmoil. "To" and "from" are opposites and opposites always work aesthetically. I decide I'm going to end the next line with a word that rhymes with "from." *Become, numb, overcome, some, succumb,* all suggest themselves and are related if only distantly to the subject matter. There are a few possibilities that I caution myself to stay away from: *bum, dumb, scum, slum.*)

> *What will you become . . .*

(The next line has to end with a "u" rhyme: *clue, you, do, few, through, pursue,* in order to rhyme with "*where are you running to?*")

—when the running's through?
—whatever will you do?

(or)

—what is to become
of a mixed-up kid like you?

(Okay, let's think about that one. I wish I had a better reference than "mixed-up kid.")

Problem Child,
why do you run so wild?
What struggle deep inside you is so unreconciled?
What are you running from, where are you running to?
What is to become of a <u>clueless twerp</u> like you?

(Just kidding.)

What is to become of a <u>crazy kid</u> like you?

(I would like to think of this line as affectionate and perhaps a little tongue-in-cheek.)

Do you feel exalted or do you feel defiled?

(Opposites working for us—and the line tells us that our subject is out of touch with his real feelings.)

How long since you cried or really smiled?

(There's something unsettling about the grammatical balance of this line. I'm *trying* to ask, "Are you truly involved in the emotions; you seem to feel both positive and negative?" and failing miserably.)

How long since you laughed or even smiled?

(It's natural-sounding language that says, "I'm concerned about the fact that you don't seem very happy.")

You may not give a damn
but Baby here I am
Tell me, what's the Problem Child?

(Okay, a couple of things. The writer/singer is saying, "I'm available, I care, I'm listening," which is an important part of the message. The song is friendlier now and more sympathetic. Phrasing the last line as a question puts on a different twist, a double entendre. Adding the two words "tell me" says, "Confide in me, I'll understand.")

NEW CHORUS
> *Problem Child,* A
> *why do you run so wild?* A
> *What struggle deep inside you is so unreconciled?* A
> *What are you running from* B
> *Where are you running to* C
> *What is to become* B
> *of a crazy kid like you* C
> *Do you feel exalted or do you feel defiled?* A
> *How long since you laughed or even smiled?* A
> *You may not give a damn* D
> *but Baby, here I am* D
> *Tell me what's the Problem Child?* A

This is a good chorus utilizing interesting language. It is true to the original purpose of the song, not overly complicated in its structure and it seems that it will not be so difficult to write the music. It has taken considerable effort to get this far and perhaps the reader is not used to making so much fuss over one lyric but most successful writers are at least this persnickety and perhaps even more so. "True Colors," a mega-hit for Cyndi Lauper (by Tom Kelly and Billy Steinberg), was originally written and rewritten for Kenny Rogers several times before finding its rightful niche on the charts. Indeed, rarely does a lyric arrive in full bloom and neatly arranged on a single page, as a quick perusal of Stephen Bishop's *Songs in the Rough* project (published by St. Martin's Press) will surely confirm. It will reassure the writer who worries too much about messy pages of start-overs and crossed-out lyrics that many of the greatest songs in recent history have graphic beginnings that are not so much humble as inscrutable. Songwriters' notebooks often resemble nothing quite so much as collections of graffiti.

Our architectural metaphor may appear to be in a bit of trouble. We have a blueprint/floor plan (form) and have even begun to erect some walls (lyrics) yet, strictly speaking, the foundation is not in place. This "foundation" is the chord structure, and "building" a song differs from building a house in that our "foundation" can be added after the walls go up or even after the roof (melody) is raised. Remember that writing a song is a fluid process wherein the major components can be freely interchanged almost as though we are working on a zero-gravity construction site in high earth orbit.

Verse I: *When you cross that line between brilliance and madness*
               Then you're out there on your own
               Just when you're overjoyed, you might be destroyed
               Like Icarus, too close to the sun
(Change):   *It's so hard to come down from that dizzying height*
               Burning alive just like a meteorite

Chorus I: *Problem Child, why do you run so wild?*
(Change):   *What struggle are you making that's so unreconciled?*
               What are you running from?
               Where are you running to?
               What is to become of a crazy kid like you?
               Do you feel exalted or do you feel defiled?
               How long since you laughed or even smiled?
               You may not give a damn
(Change):   *But Baby, here I am OR:*   (two alternatives)
                  So tell me what's the deal?
                  How do you really feel?
               Tell me what's the Problem Child?

Verse II: *When you cross your fingers and hope for salvation*
               You're on thin ice in a heatwave
(Change):   *'Cause when you've got it made*
               That's the time to be afraid
               God knows when you're having too much fun
               Cause you're bound to fall down
               And you're bound to get hurt
               And you're bound to be found lying face down in the dirt
     Repeat Chorus

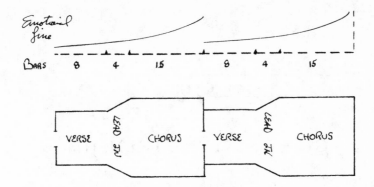

I made a couple of changes. *"It's so hard to come down,"* for one. I've decided to change *"what struggle deep inside you"* in favor of *"what struggle are you making?"* *"You may not give a damn, but Baby, here I am,"* is trite; I'm thinking of perhaps *"So tell me what's the deal, how do you really feel?"* *"'Cause when you think you've got it made"* doesn't nearly fit the template and it is equally effective to say, *"'Cause when you've got it made,"* and then we still face that very wordy and awkward repetition of *"bound to fall down, bound to get hurt, bound to be found . . ."* which I'm going to leave as is for the moment.

The form seems largely complete. The choruses are substantial (they might even be overly long). In my mind another verse and chorus is out of the question, the only possible change being the addition of a short bridge or instrumental before a final chorus. It is time to put the lyric to one side for a while and look ahead to the music.

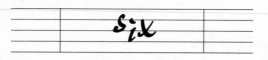

GIVE US A TUNE THEN, JIM

From 1950 on, to a considerable degree words and music became subordinate to the rhythms evolved from blues, Latin and Caribbean music. This increasing emphasis on rhythm is an ongoing process that we might easily perceive to be reaching its zenith in the '90s with the advent of rap and hip-hop. A legendary singer/songwriter whose roots lie deep in the foundations of the Brill Building recently stated in an interview that the next decade would see the complete demise of melody. We can only hope that the outlook is not quite so grim.

What is melody? Technically it is simply *a series of single musical tones*. We have all heard a person, even one completely bereft of musical skill, "pecking out" a rough tune on a keyboard. This series of musical tones is usually of modest duration, then repeats, perhaps with some minor variation, and it is this repetition that serves to familiarize the listener with a "tune" almost immediately. (In classical music the definition of melody broadens considerably to include the most prominent series of tones or "leading part" no matter how lengthy or convoluted.) Imagine melody as a kind of "roof line" above the song form—just picture it graphically like this:

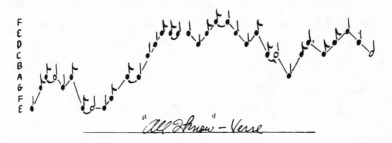

"*All I Know*" – *Verse*

Each time the graph rises, falls or stays put, another syllable of the lyric is usually sung. The notes must do one of three things: they must *ascend, descend* or *repeat*. The changing of the tones is no more significant than is their repetition. Alec Wilder makes much of the fact that repetition of notes was a vital, stylistic trademark of Gershwin, Berlin and many others. In my own song "By the Time I Get to Phoenix" no less than five words are sung to the same repeated note in the first line. It becomes a most delicate matter then whether the composer decides to move a tone upward or downward (and how far) or bravely decides to "let it ride." It could be said that the whole challenge of composing melody is defined by which of these three choices a composer makes plus one other. The fourth is *duration*. The composer must also decide to what degree he or she will elongate or truncate a given tone, depending on the syllable to be sung, the rhythm or meter of the lyric and the number of beats available. We will focus on the question of duration presently, but for the moment, what of this initial problem? How, why and where to direct a succession of tones?

Melodies are, for the most part, rooted in diatonic, minor and chromatic scales, which are common to different and specific keys, these modes sometimes being referred to as *key centers*. Since the beginning of time, melodies have been constructed using specific modes or arrays of notes drawn from these particular scales such as the diatonic, minor, melodic minor, etc., and organized into modes such as the Lydian. This is what a child does when he or she pecks out a melody using only the black notes of the piano. They are utilizing the pentatonic mode. In modern songwriting, notes are chosen from all over the scale, and in all but the simplest nursery rhymes melody usually incorporates chromatic elements, that is to say, both black and white notes.

The "distance" between these tones, indeed the distance between any given note and another, is called an *interval.* If you can count to eight you can easily compute these intervals and speak about them knowledgeably. Using a C-major scale for clarity—and keeping in mind that the number of half steps between intervals is the *same in all keys* and a *mathematical absolute*—here are the names of the intervals in the diatonic scale.

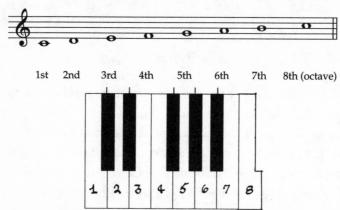

What of the other notes—the so-called "black notes"? (Even though it is only in the key of C major that these notes are actually black and then only on a piano keyboard.) They are either *augmented* (sharped) or *diminished* (flatted) versions of the common intervals, *augmented* meaning that the interval is raised (+) by a half step; *diminished* meaning that the interval is lowered (-) by a half step. (Depending on how they are *approached.* If a melody is *descending,* a modified diatonic interval would be considered diminished and vice versa. If the melody is *ascending* the same interval would be considered augmented.)

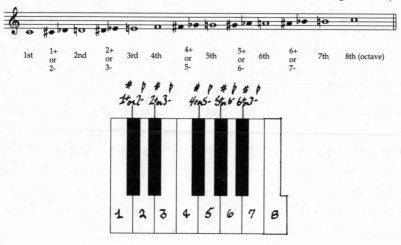

By counting half steps the interval between a given note in a melody and the note that follows can be given a numerical designation regardless of the key signature. Now a brief discussion of what constitutes a *key signature*. A diatonic scale can begin on any one of the twelve notes available. (There are only twelve notes available even though they may be sounded in different *octaves*, lower or higher on the keyboard.) A key signature is a musical notation that has been developed to alert the musician immediately to which of the twelve available diatonic scales is to be used for a particular piece. To the musician who reads music it indicates how the notes should be altered in reference to the C-major diatonic scale which is used in the previous example. Here is an example of a key signature, in this case E-flat. It indicates that the diatonic scale on which the key is based begins on an E-flat, which is simply the third note in the C-major diatonic scale lowered by one half step. (When a note is flatted, it is lowered by one half step. When it is sharped it is raised one half step.) So remembering the C-major diatonic scale, which has no sharps or flats, refer carefully to the following example wherein the E-flat major scale is represented by a key signature which notifies the musician that the first note of the scale (E) is lowered a half step, that the fourth note of the scale (A) is lowered a half step and that the fifth note of the scale (B) is also lowered a half step. This creates another perfect diatonic scale, one that is in the key of E-flat major.

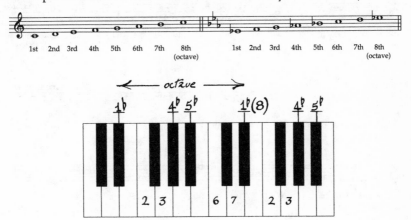

And to continue, here are examples of all the available diatonic scales, the key signatures that indicate to the musician which scale he is to play and the alterations that the key signature imposes on the original "white note" C-major scale.

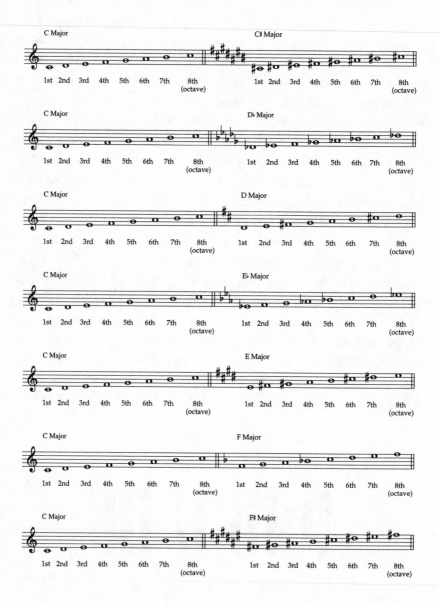

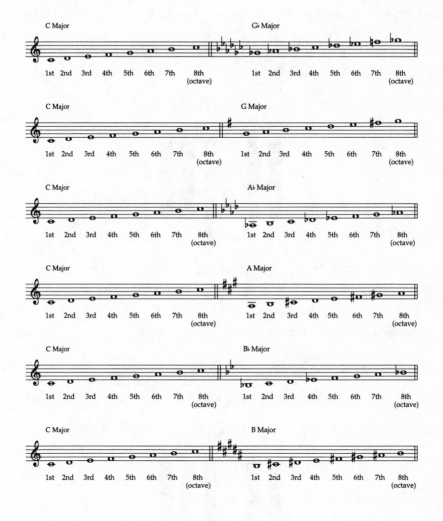

The mathematical principle of counting the distance between different notes in any of these scales and assigning them a numerical value is consistent between the scales and is an inviolate formula. For instance in the key of C major the distance between C and the G above C is an interval of a perfect fifth.

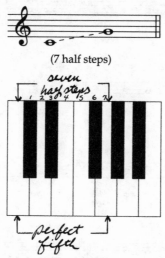

(7 half steps)

In the key of E-flat the distance between E-flat and the B-flat above is an interval of a perfect fifth.

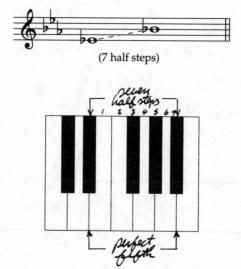

(7 half steps)

To compute a perfect fifth, then, in any key or from any given note in a melody to another note, it is only necessary to count seven half steps from the lower note to the higher note. Expanding this concept to encompass all the intervals available from one note to another, the following chart will indicate precisely how many half steps separate all these possible intervals in the C diatonic scale, which will hold true in any key.

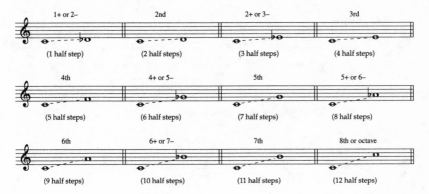

Every major diatonic scale has a relative minor scale. The starting point for this relative minor scale can easily be computed by counting down three half steps. If middle C is used as the starting point and we count down three half steps we arrive at A. *A*, then, is the starting point for the A-minor scale which is the relative minor key of C major and shares the same key signature. At the risk of redundancy this will be true for any starting point of the twelve available. Counting down from E-flat three half steps we arrive at C and therefore we know that C minor is the *relative minor key* to the E-flat major key and shares the same key signature. Now these minor scales have various configurations—harmonic, melodic, etc. These are the sad keys and are distinctly different in tonal color from the major ones but the intervals are computed in exactly the same way. A numerical value can be applied to each interval in a minor scale, in this case A minor.

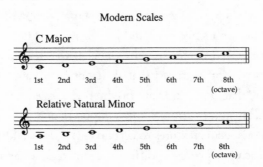

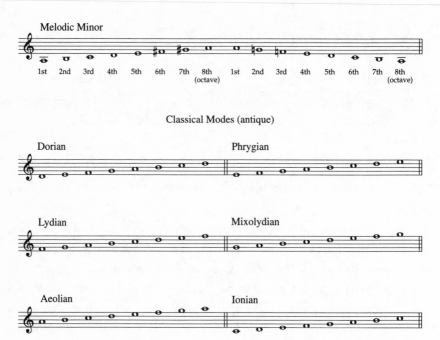

Up until about three hundred years ago, most of melody and/or chord structure was based on one of the illustrated "modes" or some variation thereof. Perhaps you are wondering about the necessity of all these different diatonic scales (keys) and you might ask, "If I can write my song in C major, then why should I bother learning all the rest?" The immediate and obvious answer is that individual singing voices have different capabilities and limitations, especially defined by the differences between male and female, and so a song that can be sung easily in C major by a male songwriter may be unsuitable for a female or a singer with a different range. There are other reasons we experiment with different keys. It is a belief widely held and a theory that has been debated for centuries that different keys have diverse emotional characteristics, that sharp keys are brighter, flat keys warmer and C major rather neutral or nondescript. Some composers and authors have assigned actual colors or specific textures to certain keys. Alec Wilder states unequivocally that "each key possesses different characteristics and enhances either aggressive or passive points of view." He goes on to say that D-flat is "warm and romantic," that D-natural is "forceful," and that E-natural creates a "soft, pavane-like mood." A famous friend—one of the most accomplished singers in the profession—hears different "colors" in different keys: D major is green; F sharp major is purple; E natural, a bright yellow. Others allege to have found that certain instruments in the orchestra perform and sound better in one key than they do another. The key of A major was associated by classical composers with Italy, bright sunny weather and a joyful attitude. "Spring Song" by Felix Mendelssohn is in A major, as well as Beethoven's triumphant "Ode to Joy."

While a working knowledge of all keys contributes immeasurably to an overall comprehension of the purely mathematical nature of music, modern electronic keyboard instruments will immediately transpose any key to another and the writer with limited theoretical knowledge can and should unashamedly adjust the instrument as is convenient. In other words—the amazing truth is—in our contemporary era the writer who uses a keyboard need only know how to play in C major. Guitar players will have always known the magical capabilities of the capo (a device attached to the guitar's neck) in changing the key of the guitar at will. (Irving Berlin only played in C major and had a mechanical piano especially constructed which shifted the action in order to play in other keys.)

"Writing music is easy. What's hard, is knowing which notes to use, and which to let fall to the ground." So said Johannes Brahms, an unforgiving fundamentalist who insisted on dotting all the *i*'s and crossing all the *t*'s. (Brahms seems to be toying with an architectural metaphor of his own. Is he picturing himself high on a scaffold with trowel, mortar and bricks in hand?) His is a negative premise, but given the fact that a composer can sequence notes in an arbitrary or (worse) *obvious* fashion, and that there are literally millions of sequences possible, it seems logical that at least one aesthetic approach could evolve from the *exclusion* of clichéd options.

Prior to the '50s, in the so-called Golden Era of "professional songwriters" we find a great deal of gratuitous *inclusion*. Imagine the whole attitude of the era in this way: "Let's use *all* the notes! All the white ones and all the black ones!" This mind-set made for a rich feast—an orgy of *chromaticism* whose American origins probably lie in the augmented fourth, minor third and dominant seventh tones of the "blues" scale, though Michael Feinstein has pointed out that the same flatted third and seventh are prominent in Jewish folk music, suggesting that Klezmer (an authentic form of Jewish folk music) may have been equally influential.

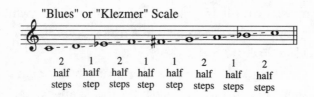

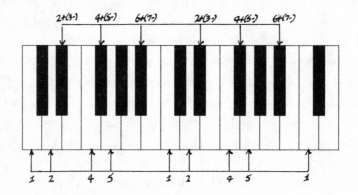

These illustrations are presented in the key of C major for clarity. Mathematically they hold true in any key.

There is something undeniably corny about melody and/or harmony proceeding in increments of successive half steps as when a barbershop quartet sings the last cadence of "How Dry I Am" (traditional song—Anonymous).

I get more than my share of half-step composition in most romantic classical music. It is this kind of whining, which somehow almost always manages to sound out of tune, especially on stringed instruments, that has given classical music a bad name. The use of sequential half steps probably reached its peak in the drawing rooms of the Victorian era, when well-bred ladies fanned their passions with lace-bedecked fans as the half steps cascaded down the keyboards of ill-tuned spinets. Most of this music produces the same effect on my spine as listening to someone with dry, scaly skin rubbing their feet together, which is to say that in my hearing the most beautiful melody is usually developed in intervals of a whole step or more (up or down). Michael Feinstein, in his book, complains that Cole Porter frequently used "step-wise melody" as in the standard "Night and Day." "I find it boring," wrote Feinstein. The word "chromatic" (*chromaticism*) is a somewhat ambiguous one and has a duality of meaning that should remind us of Leonard Bernstein's contention that it is ambiguity and duality which make great art possible. Fittingly there are two distinct definitions of *chromatic tones* according to *Webster's Seventh New Collegiate Dictionary* (G. & C. Merriam Company).

A. Of, relating to, or giving all the tones of the chromatic scale.

This is the definition of chromaticism that makes my skin crawl, implying as it does a consecutive employment of half steps. It is my belief that rarely if ever should three half steps be sounded in sequence in a melody unless the composer wishes to deliberately achieve an antiquated or obvious effect. In support I cite *Webster's* definition of the *chromatic scale*: A musical scale consisting *entirely* (my italics) of half steps.

B. Characterized by frequent use of non-harmonic tones or of harmonies based on non-harmonic tones. (Refers to notes not included in the diatonic scale, diverse from the simple triad.)

This definition is the one that Bernstein has in mind when he refers to the "chromaticism" of late-nineteenth-century composers like Wagner, said to be the inventor of chromaticism, not to mention the leitmotif or interval as a melodic building block. I prefer the term "chordal" in reference to the later music of Ralph Vaughn Williams, Samuel Barber, Benjamin Britten and even Burt Bacharach. "Chordal" composition derives its character from the combining of diverse harmonic and chromatic elements, the emphasis being on the interlocking texture of relatively complex chords in progressions. "Frequent use of non-harmonic tones or of harmonies based on non-harmonic tones" does not imply that the nature of the music is schmaltzy or obvious. Rather, it points out a new direction in twentieth-century music which began with simple dissonance, evolved through the whole-tone scale of Debussy, and was then refined and defined by Stravinsky (only to crash and burn in the serialistic orgy of Schoenberg and his followers), a mathematical dead end that doesn't concern us.

A melodic move from the root to the augmented fourth and then up to the fifth as in Leonard Bernstein's and Stephen Sondheim's "Maria" represents a tasteful use of chromaticism. From the root to the augmented fifth and then down a half step? Good and well. Bernstein used this interval as a unifying device in the whole score of *West Side Story*.

Ma - ri - a   Ma - ri - a

In modern songwriting a lot of diatonic context is needed to support every single half step.

The key to writing interesting—even brilliant—melody is to lead the ear in a path which is both *pleasant* and to some degree *unexpected*. (For the moment those of you who wish to write unpleasant melodies are excused.) Half steps in a series, because of their adjacency, hardly ever come as even a mild surprise. The contemporary composer probably instinctively understands this and makes a mental note: *In a melodic line use half steps sparingly*.

All of these "black and blue notes" were absorbed and thoroughly exploited in ragtime, dance tunes and film and theatre music until the banquet abruptly ended in the late '40s. The guests woke up with slightly sour stomachs craving something with more roughage. The table was set for a fresh course but the five-star chefs, wealthy and aging, lacked the energy or inclination to reinvent an American musical cuisine. (They had completely overlooked the potential of the electric guitar for one thing.) Enter "rock 'n' roll"—home cooking. Pop music suffered greatly. We found ourselves listening to "Itsy Bitsy Teeny Weeny Yellow Polka-Dot Bikini" (Paul Vance and Lee Pockriss), "Flying Purple People Eater" (Sheb Wooley) and other milestones of the decline of Western civilization. But there were also signs of hope: Goffin and King, Bacharach and David, Anka, Leiber and Stoller, Mann and Weil, Doc Pomus and Mort Shuman, and Boudleaux and Felice Bryant to name a few. These new writers of pop tunes differed from their predecessors in two major respects, and as a consequence have sometimes been criticized by the old dragons as well as "blues 'n' roll" purists. First, their lyrics were, well, *lightweight* at first glance. For reasons that are hard to pin down there was a new populism influencing

American taste after World War II. Gene Lees in his foreword to Alec Wilder's book advances this theory: "After World War II the network owners turned their attention to television, more or less abandoning radio, leaving local stations to play records of a constantly declining quality." Culture by default. The taste of sour grapes is ill-concealed in this observation, and though it contains seeds of truth, it completely ignores the fact that when Elvis Presley recorded Arthur Crudup's "That's All Right" in 1956 (the year of my birth) a new American art form was born whole, every bit as valid as the "Jewish/Blues" genre which spawned Tin Pan Alley and the "Golden Age of Songwriting" in the first place. So the New Giants wrote lyrics for adolescents! So what? It is said that Irving Berlin wasn't above writing a song for *money*, and besides, many of these new lyrics were gems of considerable elegance like Gilbert Becaud and Pierre Delanoe's "Let It Be Me" (English translation by Mann Curtis).

Also, the newcomers had all but abandoned *chromaticism*, paying more homage to Palestrina than they did Mendelssohn. Do you think it was because teenagers were too stupid to understand "black notes"? Sorry. It was because of the preceding three decades of chromatic obsession. It was time, then, to cleanse the musical palate. High time to drop some notes to the ground.

The great innovator of popular melody in our generation was Burt Bacharach. The very first notes of "Baby, It's You" (recorded by the Shirelles, 1961), evoke a minimalist virtually *pentatonic* mode. In "Walk on By" (recorded by Dionne Warwick, 1964), Bacharach's melody is forthrightly diatonic in its haunting minor key. His more adventurous skips of fourths and fifths are apparent in such songs as "Are You There (With Another Girl)" (©1965, Hal David and Burt Bacharach), which includes the line "*I hear the music coming out of your radio*," or "My Little Red Book" (©1965, Hal David and Burt Bacharach), introduced in the 1965 film *What's New, Pussycat?*, and 1964's "A House Is Not a Home" (first hitting the charts with Brook Benton's version on July 18, 1964, immediately followed by Dionne Warwick's release on August 1 of the same year). His influence was a breath of fresh air to a public that had tired of schmaltz but could not completely surrender to three-chord rock 'n' roll. Bacharach punctuated his clean, classically influenced melodies with idiosyncratic accents and even introduced *polyrhythms* to the Top 40. ("Anyone Who Had a Heart," which made its *Billboard* debut by Dionne Warwick on

December 7, 1963.) In a nutshell his style is one of unexpected or innovative skips, combined with surprising and uplifting changes of key (modulations) and well-considered *variations* on key phrases. At the moment we are not particularly concerned with changes of key but "skips" and "variations" are important concepts. What is a "skip"? The half step is not a "skip," consisting, as it does, of two adjacent tones, and a whole step doesn't qualify either, as whole steps are also "neighbors" in a diatonic sense. The interval of the third whether major or minor exists in a kind of gray area, i.e., yes it is a skip of sorts, but is so closely related to the root of a chord that it would seem to be living across the street or at least on the same block. Your musical dictionary might tell you that a third is a "skip" but in your conversations with singers a "skip" will more likely be understood to be an interval that *exceeds a major third.*

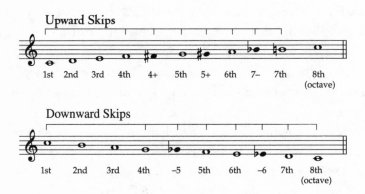

In melody writing "skips" are almost always interesting. The fact that they are sometimes unsingable or awkward to the ear might be perceived as a necessary evil. During one abysmal historic era, the "skip" of one to four plus (augmented fourth), also known as a *tritone,* was thought to be of Satanic origin and was therefore banned from the liturgy of the Roman church. Writers should not be surprised if singers react in a similar fashion when asked to sing an augmented fifth or a major seventh. The careful composer weighs the risks and guards against abuse of this important device.

Even as the writer should be wary—with good cause—of stringing together too many adjacent or near adjacent tones, discretion should also be exercised toward the excessive use of radical "skips."

Too many adjacent tones

Too many sequential skips

Forgetting "sound" for the time being, look at the following example as a two-dimensional representation of graphic art.

Visually weigh the balance between adjacent tones and skips. This aesthetic balance cannot be taught, but the composer should be aware that there are only two kinds of notes in a melody: more or less adjacent notes and more or less separated or "skipping" notes. Neither should predominate to excess. It is a smooth blend of adjacent and "skipping" tones that creates beautiful tunes. As an exercise, noodle out a melody on your guitar or piano (a *front strain* or eight bars). Try to create a nice balance between adjacent tones and the occasional skip. Don't be afraid to sing the melody over and over to determine its facility and ease of motion. Singing is the ultimate test. Most professional songwriters have sung themselves into laryngitis during the course of one or two writing sessions and (while we're on the subject) composers *must* differentiate between what is humanly possible and what is wishful thinking in regard to the vocal range of a soprano, alto, tenor or whatever. A tremendous emotional surge can be generated by beginning a song low and finishing it high while the composer blithely writes the singer out of the picture. Many immortal songs have been written within the span of an octave and indeed a singular professional cachet is attached to the composer who can execute this elegant trick. He will be much beloved by singers of disparate abilities and yea verily he will be covered even unto future generations. (It is advisable to try out songs with experienced singers before carving them in copyrighted stone.)

Now about *variation*. We know that pop songs are *repetitive* in that major elements of the form, verses, choruses, etc., repeat the same musical content—sometimes ad nauseam. In melody writing *variation* refers to the practice of emulating or varying rhythmic and/or tonal materials *within a single verse, chorus, bridge, phrase, or song.* Variation is not the complete opposite of repetition. In order to be effective the variation must remind us of something we've already heard. These are Leonard Bernstein's words from his Harvard lecture: " . . . What is a variation anyway? It's always in one way or another, a manifestation of the mighty dramatic principle known as the Violation of Expectation. What is expected is, of course, repetition— either literal or in the form of an answer, a counterstatement, or whatever, and when those expectations are violated, you've got a variation." He could have said: "When *some* of those expectations are violated"—to violate *all* expectation is to *depart.* "MacArthur Park" will provide some readily accessible examples of *variation.* At the outset the first two lines are identical: same melody, same key (D minor), everything. This is repetition:

When the chorus commences the melody changes to different notes but their relationship to each other remains the same—another way of saying the key has changed.

The melody is reiterated in a different and *major* key for two bars only, and then there is a *departure.* A *departure* is the inclusion of new musical material.

The original phrase is repeated again during the second line of the chorus but this time a fourth higher. In truth it has been transposed (moved) into a new key.

In effect, transposed to C Major

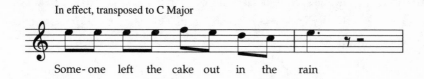

Some- one left the cake out in the rain

The last line consists of mostly new material except that the *rhythm* continues to mimic that of the original *motif* (a fragment or portion of melody that is recalled).

I don't think that I can take it,— 'cause it took so long to bake it,— and I'll

ne - ver have that re - ci - pe a - gain, oh no!

In the middle section of "MacArthur Park" (a new song altogether) this recurring rhythm is used at the beginning of the verse with similar melodic notes, except this time in a *major key,* and also the direction of travel is *reversed* (inverted).

There will be a-noth-er song for me,——— For I will sing it, (orchestra)

There will be a-noth-er dream for me,——— Some-one will bring it.

This principle of variation is common to most pop songs. Once the listener is made aware of its existence the practice becomes obvious and ubiquitous. In the Beatles' "Yesterday" for instance, compare the first word *"yesterday"* to the last two words in the same line, *"far away,"* and then *"here to stay."* Same rhythm, identical descending pattern in the notes but a different position on the scale. Notice how the melody in the first line runs *up* the scale and how that rhythmic pattern is repeated in the second line except that the notes ripple *down* the scale. Think of the first two lines of "Heart and Soul" (Frank Loesser and Hoagy Carmichael) or the first three lines of "Blue Moon" (Lorenz Hart and Richard Rodgers). There is little to be gained by belaboring the point.

Almost any song will contain at least one or even half a dozen instances of variation, and perhaps one of what Bernstein refers to as "transformational operations."

1. Inversion—a melody is inverted when ascending intervals are made to descend by the same degree and vice versa; i.e., the melody is turned upside down.

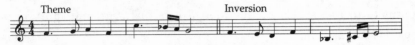

2. Augmentation—increasing the time value of the notes in the melody.

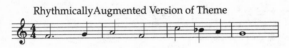

3. Retrograde—playing the melody backwards.

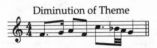

4. Diminution—decreasing the time value of the notes in the melody.

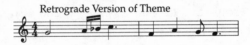

5. Modulation—repeating the melody in another key.

6. Imitation—the repetition of a motive, phrase or theme proposed by one part in another part with or without modification.

7. Harmonic progressions—the advance of one chord to another (while the melody remains the same) or according to the principle of substitution.

8. Dynamic changes—varying the intensity or loudness of musical tones.

9. Deletions—deliberately omitting certain portions of a melodic phrase.

10. Permutations—variations of increasing diversity and/or complexity.

"Plus the infinite interplay of all these with one another," Bernstein adds. It is this "interplay" with its universe of possibility that is both the heaven and hell of the melody writer. (Harmonic progressions are not illustrated, as a subsequent chapter deals exclusively with chord structure.)

Most of the time the placements and durations of these "transformations" are suggested if not dictated by the lyrics *if the lyrics come first*; i.e., if a lyric line is repeated something similar and supportive should probably occur in the melody. On those occasions when the lyric is set to the music the melody's variations will suggest to the lyricist where to repeat or omit rhythms, phrases or even complete lines of the lyric. As an exercise, write or noodle an eight-bar phrase of melody and then vary it in the next eight bars, trying a different key, turning it upside down, playing it backwards or fitting different notes to the same rhythm. Also, try setting a simple lyric to a tune and notice how the lyric pattern will suggest repetition, rhythmic changes or other transformations in the melody.

One factor that anchors a lot of amateur melody in the backwater of the mundane is its predictability and this is caused in the main by the writers' choices of *direction*. To explain: As listeners we are very accustomed to certain pat solutions to melodic problems, lines of least resistance, particularly at the ends of verses or choruses and these clichés are pretty much defined by the *direction*, the up and down motion of the tune.

There is nothing particularly awful about the example except that it's already been written about a half million times. A way to freshen this up is to reverse the direction of travel between one, some or all of the intervals.

OR

This technique of carefully altering the direction of the melody's travel can be applied to any portion of a tune that sounds *derivative* or a bit stale.

We are all capable of grinding along in the well-dredged channels of other composers' passages. It requires a real effort of will and relentless self-criticism to blaze a trail.

Besides fastidious little changes in the inner workings of a melody line there is an overall *emotional direction* involved. When drafted effectively a lyric will usually begin with a question, puzzle or ambiguity and then build to a revelation or declaration, an emotional payoff or high point. When a composer sets such a lyric to music it is only logical to assume that one of the primary functions of the tune will be to enhance the emotional dynamic of the lyric (or vice versa if the melody comes first). How does a melody do this? By changing direction effectively. Let's look at a couple of stupid examples that aren't actually meant to insult your intelligence.

First, when a lyric makes a literal reference in the physical plane—i.e., "My heart soared"—the melody should probably travel in the direction of that physical reference, though not always.

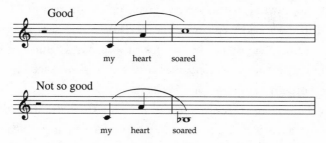

Conversely (bear with me) what if the lyricist has written "The moon descended"?

The point being that the music can help the lyric on its intended path or impede it. What if the lyric says "My heart stopped!" The composer might follow this lyric line with a three-count rest:

my   heart   stopped!   when   our   lips   met (etc.)

Or "My heart waited perfectly still." The inaction or indecision of the heart can be typified by repeating the same note and then resting:

my heart wait-ed per-fect-ly   still   un-til you kissed me

Okay, these are really obvious examples of a correlation between physical direction in the melody and literal references to direction in the lyric. In reality direction is dictated by extremely complex and subtle semantic factors. The composer (and lyricist) will be sculpting a comprehensive emotional line that will extend from the beginning of the song to the end. Each syllable and note should be scrutinized to ensure that the melody and lyric are moving in the same "direction," both in a literal, objective sense and in the broader emotional context. Bernstein said of this: " . . . A composer setting words to music seeks those notes which he considers most condign to the semantic values of the words he is setting." (Or—he probably would have said—"vice versa.")

Now as to *duration*. Melody should mirror the natural rhythm of the language as much as possible. A staccato pattern of multisyllable words, rich with consonants, might call for a lively tune with relatively short time values in each note, and the accented notes would logically fall on the natural accents of the syllables.

com-mun-i- ca-tion is the an-swer to our prob-lem

On the other hand, if each syllable in the big word is elongated to the point where there is difficulty in concentrating on its meaning, we have a problem.

com   -   mu   -   ni   -   ca   -   tion

(Of course this works both ways. The lyricist will have the same concerns as the composer.)

A note of longer duration tends to settle on a single syllable at the end of a line or phrase as in:

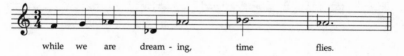

Or at the beginning of a line as in:

"Where Are You?"— (©1937 Harold Adamson and Jimmy McHugh)

Lyricists and composers will want to exercise caution in choosing a vowel sound for an extended note (or vice versa)—especially a high one—as some of these are child's play for a good singer and others can be nightmarish. They are in rough order of diminishing appeal:

Ō Ŏ Ŏ U U Ā Ä I Ĭ Ē Ĕ

The last one, Ē, pinches the glottis and is particularly hard to sustain. Double consonants should also be avoided on elongated notes and are at their most vulnerable when used for a dramatic finale:

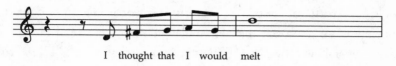

The singer not only has to sustain the relatively difficult vowel on a high note but must close the complicated double consonant at the very last instant. (Alec Wilder believed "the terminal consonants *M, N, L, R*, are sung with ease. *S, z, ch, sh*, as terminals are difficult.")

When a composer writes two or more notes for the same syllable it is called *melisma*.

Predictably this practice is frowned upon in ultraconservative circles though examples can be found subsequent to Francis Scott Key's "Star-Spangled Banner." Jerome Kern and Cole Porter wrote some of these. Referring to a Kern song called "Make Believe" Wilder grouses, " . . . In eleven instances the lyric employs one syllable to fulfill the needs of two notes" and castigates Kern for "flagrant misuse of this license." (Pull over, Mr. Kern. We're going to have to see your Melisma License.) Many traditionalists are horrified by this practice, ignoring the fact that much of what we recognize as a blues vocal style is composed in great part of melisma as are the delicate ornamentations of American folk and country singing in the main. Our national music—rock 'n' roll—would be poorer or perhaps nonexistent without it. Where melisma is most repellent is in a context where it obviously does not belong, that is to say, in the music of the traditionalists. Nothing causes us to cringe more than to hear the "straight" singer gilding an old standard with an awkwardly executed soul riff or—even worse—singing an idiomatic song in a stilted, formalized style, devoid of melisma or any other semblance of feeling. The use or avoidance of melisma is a matter of taste and authenticity. It cannot be denied that an excessive number of notes over too few syllables will create an awkward, sophomoric impression—the word "pompous" comes to mind—and should be a matter of reasonable concern. It is worrisome if not downright annoying as we approach the new millennium to see a tendency among today's Super-Divas toward melismatic one-up-girl-ship, i.e., "I'll bet'cha I can sing more complicated notes than you can!" In regard to such intricacies what *is* "reasonable" concern? I am somewhat notorious among singers for writing "rangy" tunes, difficult intervals and even the odd untidy vowel/consonant at the end of a line. I defend some if not most of my excesses in the name of originality and creativity. If the writer makes no attempt to break the rules on occasion it is doubtful that the end result will ever be distinguished. Many singers welcome a challenge if the temporary stress involved enhances an overall effect, which is to say that a singer should not always be cocooned. I have crossed the line at times. Once, when I was producing a female supergroup and working them pretty hard for several days in a row their lead singer showed up for work one evening with a note from her larynxologist. The tongue-in-cheek message politely requested that she be excused from singing anything above a high C.

There may be a certain cynical sort out there who is thinking that all this blab hasn't really taught anyone how to write a melody. How true. Great melody has an illusive consistency that is unteachable. If the heart is the bow and the soul is the violin and the brain is the musician, then melody is the fragile result of all three in love with the same idea. "Inspiration" this has been called though some say there is no such animal. Oscar Hammerstein was skeptical about pure inspiration but granted that "the legend of inspiration is . . . not a completely silly one if we broaden the base of the word and let it include the stored up memories of the writer's emotional reactions, then inspiration figures very largely in what he puts down on paper." There is no denying the existance of *synaesthesia*, which is the practice of allowing music to influence your nostalgic reveries, remembrances and romantic flights of fantasy. Inspiration, if we regard it as anything other than pure myth, must be linked to this doorway of the subconscious. This writer believes in inspiration and believes that without this indescribable flux melody and lyrics are meaningless rote. There are certain ways to jump-start the heart, soul and mind into a heightened creative mood that can easily be called "inspiration." Got any old demos or other tapes lying around the house? Not cassettes or CDs mind you, but real old-fashioned "reel-to-reels"?

Before continuing you may want to search the garage for that antique tape machine you threw out about ten years back. As an alternative, got any mediocre tunes languishing in sequencer memory? All right. Prepare an herbal tea or other beverage of your choice, settle yourself in a comfortable spot and *play them backwards*.

[A WHILE LATER]

How was it for you? Feel better? Neurons firing? I'm no psychologist but I can propose a very simple explanation for why this works: As songwriters we are used to thinking in a certain specific way. We develop stylistic peccadilloes over time and these become mental traps. Eventually we may be composing inside an invisible cage of habit. But when we hear something we have written in reverse order our songwriting brain is literally turned "wrong side out." Every musical decision, every solution to a problem, is approached 180 degrees out of phase. Reversing the tape brings on a kind of forced originality, pseudo-inspiration if you please, but it gets you to thinking, doesn't it? One of my more well-known songs is from an earlier melody played backwards.

Would it surprise you to know that lots of important melodies have been written to the exact same chord progression? There are the obvious ones of course: "Blue Moon" (Lorenz Hart and Richard Rodgers) and "Heart and Soul" (Frank Loesser and Hoagy Carmichael) are a pair, not to mention "Louie, Louie" (Richard Berry), "Wild Thing" (Chip Taylor) and "La Bamba" (a traditional Mexican folk song). A good jazz musician can *improvise* hundreds of different "tunes" over the same chord progression and the composer in search of ideas need look no further than this time-honored technique of "making up" a melody as he goes along. When Roberta Flack recorded my "Do What You Gotta Do" (©1966 EMP), I couldn't help noticing that her version of the melody bore scant if any resemblance to the original. Lovely as it was, it was not the same. Since I'm not inclined to get overly excited about this sort of thing, I began absent-mindedly to sing the original melody along with her as the record played. My God, what a gorgeous duet it was! A deliberately missing part perhaps? (A young man who had died suddenly without completing the lead vocal in a duet?) The point is that chord progressions are not actually subject to copyright. The writer can gain a lot of experience by improvising; humming or whistling along with instrumental tracks that have already been recorded and changing the notes around. A cautionary note: When we talk about "changing the notes around," we are not talking about co-opting an existing tune and changing it just enough to avoid a copyright infringement suit. According to Michael Feinstein the traditional term for this kind of skullduggery was to "write a melody sideways." Advertising interests commonly indulge in this practice in lieu of paying a reasonable amount of money for use of a well-known song. They will shamelessly copy an artist's writing style, vocal sound, arrangement, whatever serves their purpose. Harry Nilsson and Randy Newman have been notably profaned in this manner.

It has already been mentioned that a turn on an unfamiliar musical instrument focuses musical resolve. It is as though somehow *within the tonal coloration of the instrument itself* are dynamics that stimulate creativity. Bernstein says yes . . . a lot of this spooky, metaphysical stuff like the "sadness" of a minor key is nothing more than a *physiological* response to the overtone series. (Experts attribute this to major and minor dissonances in the harmonic series that create what is called in acoustics "interference" which disturbs the ear.) In support, who can deny that one of the launching pads of melody is the deep-throated drone of bagpipes, sitars, didgeridoo (Australian Aboriginal instrument) and such, and that every note imaginable is lurking in their dreamy drone in varying degrees of prominence. Given such a feast of possibility and the subtle differences in the tonal coloration of an unfamiliar instrument the brain will automatically begin to make choices and it is these unconscious preferences that are most interesting. What are we talking about now? Subliminal composition? Primeval race memory tone selection? Freudian folk singing (the baby was frightened by a boat whistle, etc.)? Whether this is deep insight or shallow speculation I will leave to the people in the white smocks. For my money the brain often responds positively, negatively or emotionally when given a choice of frequencies reflexively and automatically. In the sound of the sea or the wind through the tops of the trees or the city redolent with impossibly long echo at four o'clock in the morning, there is always a musical offering. We prefer some sounds to others and these are music to our ears. Some we reject as nondescript or as noise. Others are so obnoxious that they cause us to interfere with our own hearing by placing obstacles in our ears. My point? *Most if not all of our preferences regarding frequency or texture of sound are involuntary.*

I was completely stricken by a remark that Arthur Garfunkel made in my presence a few years ago while musing aloud. "We [human beings] are either so much alike, so virtually identical in the inner workings of our emotions that we actually feel the same things in the exact same way *or* we are so completely different—even alien to each other—that we have not the slightest inkling of what another feels when he, for instance, pricks himself with a thorn."

Music would seem to offer a means of subjecting this question to a facsimile of scientific analysis. Vast majorities of the population seem to react similarly to a sad song, a happy one or a sexy one. How else can we account for the phenomenon of the "hit" except to say that it strikes a responsive chord in a great many listeners at the same moment in time? Such a reaction indicates that there *is* a part of the subconscious that concerns itself specifically with musical material. It is that part of the brain that tortures us by endlessly repeating a meaningless tune that we have never particularly cared for or indulges in "ear-stalgia," that delicious sense of being transported to another space and time by a fragment of melody from the radio of a passing automobile.

There are a couple of different ways to put this part of the brain to work for us because it not only *remembers* melody but is eminently capable of coining an original phrase without any assistance from the conscious mind. This faculty can also be programmed to solve ongoing musical or lyrical problems with little or no effort of the will. I can *hear* those brakes screeching, people! But—if you get nothing else from this book—understand that the subconscious composer in all of us is a real being, a valid collaborator, and that to ignore his or her existence and not avail ourselves of this immense resource is foolishness. "I write lying down so I can go to sleep easily. I write about ten minutes and sleep for two, on the average," quipped Stephen Sondheim in a lecture, implying a deep connection between creativity and sleep.

One of Victor Herbert's most famous songs was "Kiss Me Again." Michael Feinstein recounts this anecdote: "He woke up in the middle of the night with a melody playing insistently in his head, wrote it down on a piece of paper at the night table, and went back to sleep. When he woke up in the morning, he had no memory of the melody or even of having written it down, but there it was."

Billy Joel's *River of Dreams* album consists predominantly of songs that he discovered—some of them fully realized—in that same subconscious portfolio. As I spoke with him I realized that I too, have found music floating on my own river of dreams and wondered about how many times this may have occurred without my being consciously aware of it. Of course there is the self-aware (lucid) scenario when the dreamer hears a song full-blown.

Recently I dreamed that I was in my dressing room nervously waiting to go onstage when the door suddenly burst open and a bevy of naked chorus girls step-kicked their way into the room singing one of the funniest songs I've ever heard in my life. Unfortunately when I awoke only a vague impression of bosoms remained. In my case it is as though a psychic customs officer searches my luggage for compositional contraband each time I cross that shadowy frontier between the land of dreams and the physical one. Here is a line that recently came to me in a dream: "Tonight will be like a dream and tomorrow we will remember it as a dream." Not devastating, but what I think I meant was: "Tonight will be so beautiful, tomorrow it will seem like a dream." Better. At the optimum, waiting for a song to appear in a dream and then sneaking it into the real world intact is a low-percentage maneuver. It is more likely that the traveler returns with a fragment of melody or a song title or something cribbed from another composer. It is as though the subconscious doesn't make a very fine distinction on the point of plagiarism or even accurate reproduction. Its strong suit would seem to be free association, recombining little chunks of whatever is in the mix into a collage. (Musical jokes are abundant.) Every effort should be made to perceive these happy accidents as significant, to the extent of keeping a pad and pencil or tape recorder on the bedside table because dreams fade quickly but in that shadow land where the two states of being commingle—usually called the alpha state—the conscious mind has a good deal more control. It can remember, direct, program, ask questions, etc. Not only that but with practice the alpha state can be entered with relative ease, and in fact you enter the alpha state at least twice a day (like it or not), when you are falling asleep and when you are regaining consciousness. It is at those times, particularly when falling asleep, that the subconscious is acutely vulnerable to suggestion. Try it. If you have a work in progress go to sleep thinking about it. Concentrate on some specific aspect of the problem as you drift off. Sometimes the answer will come to you before you are fully asleep. Other times you may obtain results on the opposite end of the process as you awaken. Results will vary a great deal according to the individual; you should not be disappointed if *nothing* happens the first time or even the second. Over time however, the subconscious can be trained to automatically enter this mode at nap time and solutions will almost certainly begin to surface.

There are other portals to the alpha state that can be accessed from full consciousness. Transcendental meditation utilizes "mantras," short, autohypnotic phrases that are repeated at length mentally to the exclusion of "background noise" in the brain. "Biofeedback" is a purely physical electronic technique that feeds the subject an audible tone which is then balanced by a kind of controlled relaxation. Recent innovations utilize visual stimuli in helmetlike devices. In my experience none of these is as effective as the mysterious machinery that causes sleep but they are on the market and some may find them effective in varying degrees.

Another subliminal source of melody is a bit more haphazard and a lot harder to explain. Imagine that you are camping out in relative solitude on the shore of a lake. It is that bewitched hour of twilight. The sun has just set and somewhere, across the water, music is playing which can only barely be heard when a gentle breeze blows from the right direction. The melody and chords are indistinct, familiar and strange at the same time. There is not enough musical material available to enable your ear to identify any particular tune. Your brain begins to fill in the spaces automatically, nudged by the physical beauty of the moment and the vague musical stimuli drifting in and out of your consciousness. *Vague* is the operative word here. Once the music is positively identified its catalytic effect ceases and the brain stops inventing. I am at a loss to explain or name this phenomenon except to say that it is undoubtedly some sort of "instant alpha" and that in my experience it most closely approximates what the poets have called "inspiration." Sometimes we hear "phantom melody" in the crossplay between two stations interfering with each other on an old tube-type radio, or in music "half heard through a closed door," in the hum of machinery like large fans, or in the slap of windshield wipers and the roar of rainfall on a convertible top. All we need in order to search out the taproot of creativity is the willingness to surrender our souls to the sounds that surround us.

This kind of environmentally driven inspiration reminds me that often we can take melody directly from our surroundings without meditation of any kind. While scoring a heartrending scene for a film many years ago—*a man has just found out that his wife is dying of cancer and has stepped out of her doctor's office into a street blocked by a massive traffic jam*—I noticed the discordant angry/melancholy din of the automobile horns themselves. I scored the scene with a melody based on those intervals and taking it one step further used actual car horns for instruments. Our respective environments are rich with random tones and rhythms of all kinds, most often generated by technology but also inherent in nature. These can be transferred directly onto the composer's palette.

So far we have discussed naked melody bereft of harmony and by extension modulation, substitution, alternate basses, suspension, dissonance and all the sensual "rubs" that are inherent in a modern chord structure.

Even the unsophisticated music writer can understand all these devices and incorporate them into his or her musical repertoire with no great difficulty. Some of the grainiest, most disturbing progressions in all of music have been spawned in the "open tunings" of folk musicians and blues players where the mechanics of producing a given chord have been reduced to the careful placement of a single finger or perhaps two (at the most three) in the proper position on the neck of the guitar. My one and only songwriting experience with a guitar ("Ocean in His Eyes," ©1973 Canopy Music) resulted from experimentation with a "D tuning" that guitarist and friend Fred Tackett taught me.

From the low *E* string up:
D, A, D, F#, D, D or *D, A, D, A, D, F#* or *D, G, D, G, B, E*

Simply by depressing one, two or three of the strings in random combinations (I used my thumb a lot) interesting, dissonant chords can be created, remembered and possibly even organized into a semblance of a chord progression. The tunings themselves can be altered and many professional musicians have extensive collections of variations on these. Tunings are an introduction to grainier, more sophisticated chords, but there is another way to become acquainted with complex chord structures and to put them to practical use almost immediately. What follows is not misrepresented as being a viable substitute for a proper course in music theory. It is a way to quickly enter a new world of sound, an introduction to what has been called "chordal" composition.

How then to enrich our chordal textures in order to create subtle differences in ambiance? Most writers will no doubt be aware that it is childishly simple to create a major *triad* or chord of three tones from the root, third and fifth tones of any of the twelve diatonic scales. (Do not confuse *root* and *tonic*. The tonic is the first note of the scale in a given key signature. A root is the lowest note of a basic triad wherever it may be on any scale.)

If by any chance you have not done this before, practice by picking any note at random on guitar or piano, locate its third and then its fifth by referring to the interval chart and play each chord. Follow this chart:

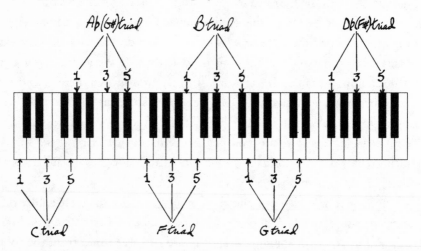

Do this until it's automatic. Then begin to invert the triads like this:

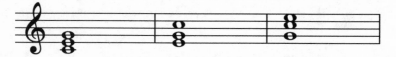

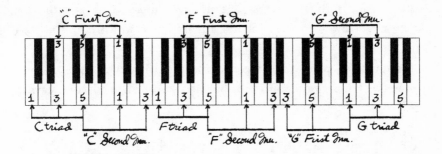

Practice until you can invent and invert any major chord at will.

Now for a simple chord progression: Play a triad on the first note of the C scale, then a triad beginning with the fourth note of the C scale (F) and finally the fifth note (G), back to the fourth note (F) and finish on the first note like this:

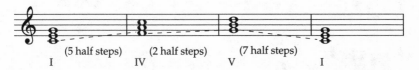

This is what is known in musicians' short speak as a I–IV–V–I progression. Indeed these Roman numerals represent the simplest form of chordal notation as they refer to the relative position of each chord in *any* diatonic scale. (Standard numerals in this text will refer to the positions of individual notes of the scale: 1, 2, 3, 4, 5, 6, 7, 8. Half steps will be designated by pluses or minuses, for instance, C-sharp is 1+ or 2-. A perfect fourth is just 4. G-sharp is 5+, or 6-, etc.)

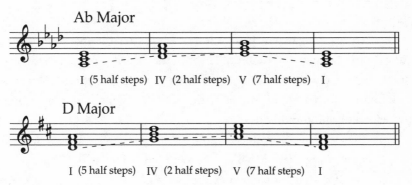

Repeat the above process with each of the twelve diatonic scales or until exhausted. Practice until it is second nature, then put each chord in the progression through its first, second and third inversions with ease. You are now playing in different *keys* depending on which note you start with.

Next, change any or all of these chords into *minor* triads with one simple move: by lowering the third tone one half step. (The fifth tone stays in place.)

Practice again all that you have learned but alter the major chords to minor chords by lowering the middle tone (the "third") one half step and maintaining that interval through the first, second and third inversions. Work until you are comfortable with, and understand, the difference between major and minor chords.

Now that we have introduced minor chords we are ready for what is commonly known as the I–VI–IV–V progression. This is the "Heart and Soul" progression that for some inexplicable reason every child in America can play based on four hands. It begins with a major triad on the tonic, moves to the sixth tone, which is a minor chord, then to a major chord on the fourth tone and ends with a major chord on the fifth tone like this:

Experiment with the sounds of different inversions on these four chords. You will discover that some variations are more pleasing than others as one chord changes to another.

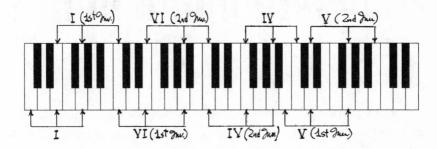

The overall practice of inverting the positions of tones in chords is also known as "voicing." Repeat the preceding progression on different notes of the twelve available. Change the "voicings" by experimenting with different inversions as one chord leads to another, and "doubling" (playing the same note an octave—or eight tones—higher or lower simultaneously).

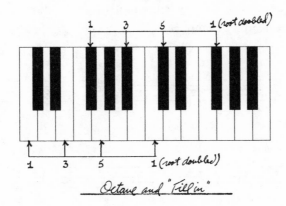

Octave and "Fill in"

Next, let's explore some simple *suspensions*, known informally in the trade as "sus chords." Start with a C-major triad but instead of sounding the third tone, substitute the fourth tone one half step higher than the third tone:

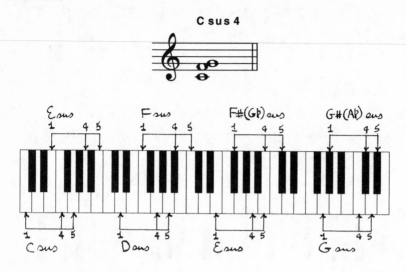

You are playing a "C-sus 4." Practice *resolving* and suspending the "C-sus 4" by moving the fourth tone one half step down to the third and then back up again.

Now, as before, practice the exercise on each of the twelve different keys until you can solve the problem repeatedly and *mathematically*. It is only a simple manipulation of numbers.

A different kind of "sus chord" is a "sus-two." The second tone of the scale is substituted for the third:

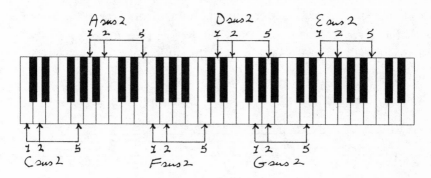

Try to become proficient in devising "sus four" and "sus two" chords in all keys and to understand the practice of "resolving" the suspended tones.

What if we suspend both the second and the fourth tones simultaneously? A very pleasing resolution will result:

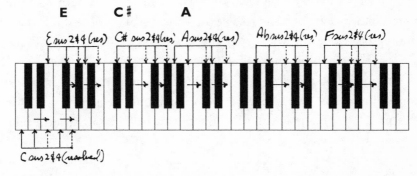

Learn to work out this relationship mathematically for any chord. It may seem like slow going but you will soon be proficient. Both notes are now resolving together and *ascending*. In this previous example, observe that the distance (interval) between the second suspended tone and the fourth suspended tone is what? A minor third (one and one-half steps). Let us *invert* this minor third (revoice it) by placing the second tone (D-natural) at the *top* of the chord and *above* the F.

The interval between the fourth tone and the second tone is now a sixth (eight half steps or four whole steps and a half step).

This mathematical relationship will always hold true. *When a third is inverted it always results in a sixth.* Now resolve the two suspensions back to the major triad in a *descending* direction. Note that now the major triad is inverted as well.

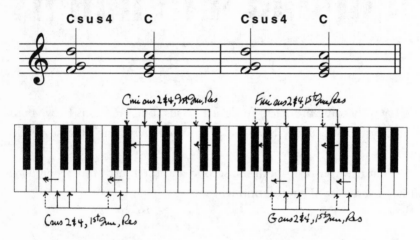

We have *revoiced* the suspensions, and in resolving them have similarly revoiced or inverted the resolution to the major triad. Practice suspending the second and fourth tone in each of the twelve triads and resolving them from their natural position or first inversion. Then invert both suspended notes to the magic sixth and resolve the lower note to a *minor* third (the top note resolves down a whole step, the lower note one half step). Become facile at this and be mathematically precise.

You will find that it is just as easy to suspend the second and fourth tones in minor chords as in major ones. Repeat all the above steps, except this time lower the major third of the triad a half step to create a minor resolution.

You will note that it is of no concern to the suspensions whether they are resolving to a major or minor triad. They don't give a damn as to their final destination. And here is our first opportunity to explore the concept of *substitution*. What if we accustom the listener *by repetition* to the idea that the double suspension will most usually resolve to a major chord? Now let's surprise him! Without warning we resolve the suspension to a *minor chord*. We have circumvented the obvious and have given his ears a little tingle. True, substitution becomes an increasingly complex subject as our knowledge of voicing, suspension and chord progression increases, but the basic principle will always remain the same: *Taking advantage of the ear's propensity to expect a certain result by substituting an unexpected one*, which is to a large extent taking advantage of all the musical literature that has preceded us historically, or repetitive material that we have deliberately "planted" in the listener's mind. (Also known as a "deceptive cadence" or the principle of Violation of Expectation.) If we had time, perhaps we could engage in a lively debate over the aesthetic, moral and philosophical validity of this sort of legerdemain (when to do it or whether to do it at all) but for now my intention is to show you *how* to do it. Returning to H. Carmichael and F. Loesser's "Heart and Soul" we can see the two ways its central progression is most often played.

In and of itself the presence of the "III-minor chord" in the second version is a *substitution*: The E minor for the A minor. What are some other substitutions that could be made with little or no effort? What about major chords for the minor chords. We know that one!

While the effect is not altogether transcendent it is serviceable. How to get to some other, more interesting substitutions with a minimum of effort? (Careful, this is Pandora's box we're tampering with.) The Principle of Substitution: *a chord can always be substituted for another if it contains at least one tone that is shared with that other.*

Let's test it. In the first example we can substitute the A-major for the A-minor because only one note has changed. (The C-natural is replaced by a C-sharp).

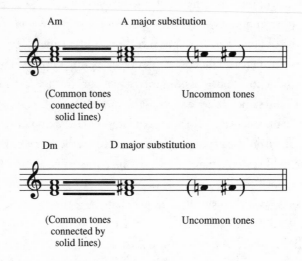

We're on safe ground here. The contending chords share *two* common tones—the E-natural and A-natural. This obviously holds true for substituting the D major for the D minor the second.

Perhaps your concentration may be wavering, but stay with me for a moment and we will open a wonderful golden door. So far we have two substitutions for the second chord in the four-chord progression.

Both subs share the note E-natural, which is the third tone in the C-major scale, the key in which we are playing. This is called in the parlance a *common tone*. So the game is to isolate a tone in any given chord (triad) or scale and find all the other chords (triads) that share that tone. Each of these new discoveries should more or less smoothly substitute for the original chord without creating any noticeable sonic disturbance—i.e., unbearable dissonance, clams, bad notes (provided that the substitution doesn't interfere with an existing melody).

How would this principle work on the second chord of our original progression?

C, A minor, F, G (one, six, four, five) or (I, VI, IV, V)

The A-minor triad has three tones in ascending order: A-natural, C-natural and E-natural. What other chords will contain the A-natural? Easy. We know it's in the A-major triad!

Substitution A major shares common tones
A and E (concert) with original A minor

It also happens to be the third tone (second voice) in the F-major triad. And now can you make a D-major triad?

Substitution D Major shares common tone
A (concert) with original A minor

There it is! The fifth tone (third voice)! So far we have three substitutions, chords that we can sound in place of our original. Take a moment and play the progression using each one, becoming familiar with the different sonorities. Notice how the A-natural changes position (according to the chord substituted) almost as deviously as the little pea hides itself in a shell game.

Substitution F major shares common tones
A and C (concert) with original A minor

Well, we didn't get a lot of bang for substituting the F major instead of the A minor, did we? Regrettably we ended up with a redundancy: Two F majors in a row. We'll drop that. We also find A-natural in the D-minor triad.

Substitution D minor shares common tone
A with original A minor

Something that's a little harder to see is the F sharp minor. Adding that one!

Substitution F# minor shares common tone
A with original A minor

Looks like we're just about at the end of our rope. Nope, there's hope! Remember the A minor triad also contains a C-natural. That should give us three more chords to play with but one of them is a C major which is a no-win because it would *follow* a C major.

(If the chords don't change, you don't have a progression.) Then what are the other chords that contain a C-natural? I really ought to let you work that one out for yourself but I haven't got the heart. F major (which we've already identified as redundant) contains a C-natural but that's out for previously stated reasons.

What does that leave? Well . . . A-flat. There is a C-natural in an A-flat chord. But surely that won't work with those accompanying black notes, A-flat and E-flat, will it?

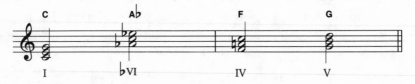

Substitution Ab major shares common tone
C with original A minor

Hmmm. Melodious. Much nicer than the A-major substitution in my humble opinion. Okay, add it to the list:

Original chord: A minor
Substitutions: A major
                        D minor
                        D major
                        A-flat major

Eventually you will also discover F minor. There's another right in front of your nose. Can you find it? Uh-huh—C minor.

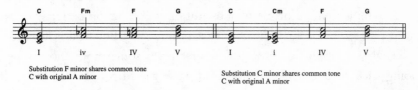

Substitution F minor shares common tone
C with original A minor

Substitution C minor shares common tone
C with original A minor

Are we running out of gas? Well, there's still that E-natural, the fifth tone in the A-minor triad. Any chance of hooking up with that? Remember our rule—if the two chords have a common tone the substitution is probably kosher. E-natural is common to both chords so, yes, an E-natural triad will work even if the results are less than sublime. It should be obvious that the E minor is the easiest substitution in this case.

Substitution E major shares common tone
E with original A minor

Substitution E minor shares common tone
E with original A minor

The other voices in the E-major chord—the G-sharp (it's the same tone as the A flat already used) and B-natural—*will not share a common tone with A minor* when expanded to a three-tone chord.

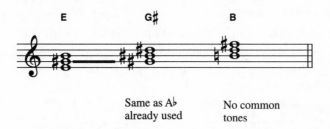

Same as A♭
already used

No common
tones

You can try it anyway if you want. You will find yourself listening to a dreadful half step that is not so much a surprise as a dull thud. Given, there are other kinds of substitutions, radical ones, dissonant ones, but our examples—arrived at mathematically—have a splendid pragmatic function for the songwriter. They will subtly alter the harmonic substructure which supports melody without necessarily changing the melody itself. It's that marvelous *common tone*, you see. No need to change a specific note of melody. Change the supporting chord to another that shares the same common tone.

Please remember that the I–VI–IV–V progression is only presented as an example. The principle of substitution will function perfectly in *any* chord progression on *any* chord in that progression. But to develop more challenging examples of progression first learn some more chord types. Going back to our first C-major triad, raise the fifth tone (G) one half step to G-sharp.

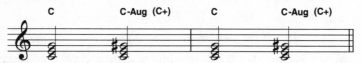

This is an *augmented* chord (technically an augmented or raised fifth) and usually notated in the studio this way: C aug 5 or C 5+. Play with it. Move the top voice up and down to resolve the augmented fifth. Put it through some inversions.

Its very close cousin is the C *diminished* which is arrived at almost as easily. Move the two uppermost voices (the third and fifth tone) down one half step (C flat 3, flat 5).

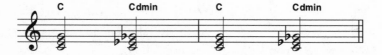

Goof with it—moving the voices up and down. Notice its relationship to C minor. By playing a C minor and lowering the top voice a half step—voilà!—you get the same animal (by playing any minor and lowering the fifth one half step, you get a diminished chord).

Play this progression a few times:

Now remember what we've learned about inversion.

Even inverted it's still pretty boring stuff. But not when it's put through a transformation that still surprises and delights me after all these years, applying the principle of substitution. I'll do one first.

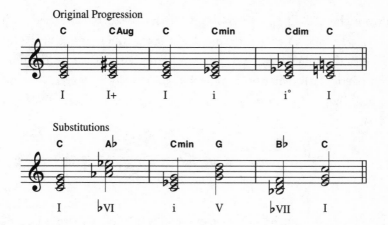

I like it better but how did I work it out? I made some informed choices based on the principle of substitution. The first chord (C) I left alone. In the second position I took the augmented fifth (A-flat) and made an A-flat triad out of it. In the third position I took the C and turned it into its close cousin, C minor. Ironically enough, the next chord in the original pattern *is* C minor so I *had* to change it. Borrowing a G—its fifth tone—I included a

G major. Now I know you're bright enough and yet you're perplexed by the B-flat in the fifth position. You are correct, there is no B-flat in the C-dim chord but we *can* find an *E-flat* and *the fifth tone in the E-flat triad is B-flat.* I nicked this B-flat and made a triad. *In this instance B-flat is two generations removed from the original chord.* In the end, I came back to C. Most of these decisions were made "by ear," choosing combinations that sounded good. Playing with the inversions I managed to create a melody—*a deliberate linear movement of specific tones*—along the top of the chord progression.

"Melody" derived from Substitutions

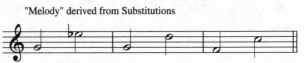

Now you try it. While the possibilities are not infinite I suspect that you will find them exhausting. Taking your time try several different combinations. Don't be afraid to go two generations removed from the original chord in your search for substitutions, or to try different inversions. In these inversion experiments, melodies will probably be discovered. (As an exercise try listing all the possible substitutions for each chord in the progression.) Whew!

More chords. The sixth chord (C-6) has been the dreaded ending of many a lounge band arrangement but surprisingly, the sixth tone in the scale is thought by some to have a mesmerizing effect on the human psyche particularly when it is repeated in a melody. It's easy to make this chord by playing a major triad and just adding the sixth tone to the rest.

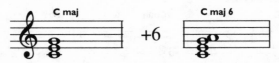

In a progression it has a rather innocuous quality as there is no innate tension that drives it toward a resolution or even another chord. This is no doubt why we often find it unnecessarily garnishing the climax of a Muzak arrangement. I remember it well from my childhood, eerily echoing in the twilight from the air horns of a distant diesel train.

Some scholar might want to explore the reasons why the six-chord so often accompanies the progress of massive, potentially deadly diesel engines. (It doesn't fit in very well with its *mesmerizing* qualities—or does it?) Anyway, what are we going to do with it? The impressionists (Ravel, Debussy, etc.) used it to good effect in creating dreamlike textures, as have Philip Glass and Steve Reich in more recent times. Extended into infinity it does have a certain somnambulistic . . . oops!—drowsed off! *Influence*, I meant to say. Seriously, it will lead us—however reluctantly—to the seventh tone which is a powerful fulcrum of the scale:

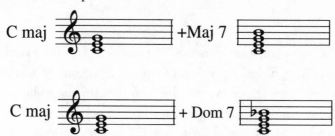

For now we will be grateful it provides more *common tones*, other junctions for substitution. We know that we can substitute at least *eight different chords* for any voice in a triad according to the principle of substitution.

Substitutions for C maj

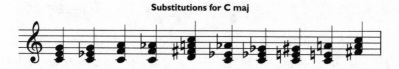

But the "six-chord" is not just a triad. It has *four voices*. This should give us at least another eight substitutions for each voice—32 in all—for a C-6. Let's see if our principle will carry us that far.

The first chord in Glenn Miller's "Moonlight Serenade" is a C-6 chord. The next chord is a C-diminished but the sixth tone is carried over (sustained) producing a C-diminished+6. Interestingly enough, this "C-diminished +6" is also known as a C-diminished 7th. The C-diminished 7th is "spelled differently," in fact C-diminished +6 is an "inharmonic" way of spelling or referring to a C-diminished 7th.

C dim7

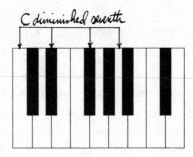

" . . . It is worth your knowing," Bernstein said to his Harvard students, "that a diminished seventh is the most ambiguous of all tonal formations and for that reason became the favorite harmonic ambiguity of all the Romantic composers." He goes on to point out that any diminished seventh chord is capable of "at least four different resolutions." He knows there are more than that of course. Here are the obvious ones, and remember that these resolutions can be "substituted" for one another.

For the time being, and for clarity, we will refer to and diagram the C-diminished 7th as a C-diminished +6. Back to "Moonlight Serenade." The *inner voices* then move downward another half step which creates the third inversion of the F-6. An F-augmented follows and the phrase ends on a G-dominant-7. This is simply a G-triad to which the seventh tone has been added, in this case a minor or dominant seventh, one half step lower than the major seventh. Perhaps we can understand this better by looking at the example.

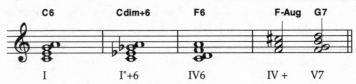

Learn to play the "Moonlight Serenade" progression. Notice how the inclusion of a fourth voice in most of the chords enriches the texture. The sound *buzzes* more. The mood is soft, seductive. (This represents what is called *close harmony,* four voices grouped together in the same octave.) Will the principle of substitution hold up when applied to this kind of chord? One thing that might cause us some legitimate anxiety is that there is only one whole step separating the fifth tone (third voice) from the sixth. We are flirting with a harsh dissonance. (A sound that on first hearing may be unpleasant, an extremely close interval.) Well, here goes. Let's leave the first chord as it is and attempt a substitution for the second position in the progression. (Having already explored the possibilities for the first three voices of C-diminished we could be smug and say that all of those chords will safely substitute for the C-diminished-6. Unfortunately, the fact that we have now added a sixth tone—A—to the C-diminished means that some of those chords may have become intransigent. (As a homework assignment determine which of the original substitutions may have been canceled out.) Concentrating on the sixth tone (A) of the C-diminished-6 and using it as a common tone we have these options:

Original Chord: C-diminished+6 (C diminished 7)
Substitutions: 1. A-7
                 2. D-7
                 3. C-minor+6
                 4. F-sharp minor-7
                 5. A-major-7
                 6. D-major-7
                 7. B-flat-major 7
                 8. F-major-7

Realizing that this process can be tedious, I would still like to explain how I arrived at a few of these alternatives. Obviously in the first instance I made the sixth tone (A) the root of a new triad, an "A" triad. Good enough, but since the second chord in the progression has four voices I would like for the alteration to also include a fourth voice. The fifth tone (G) in the original chord happens to be the dominant-seventh (G) of the A triad, so if I retain it (adding it to the A triad) the substitution will share three common tones with the original C-diminished-6.

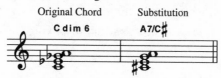

Original Chord   Substitution
     C dim 6   A7/C♯

The substitution is simply the second inversion of an A dominant 7. Check out the math. Make sure you understand it. Make sure *I* understand it.

The second substitution: The sixth tone (A) is also common to the D triad as it is its fifth tone. While using the D triad we notice that it also has another common tone less readily apparent: the root (C, or the first tone) of the original chord is the dominant seventh of the D-major triad.

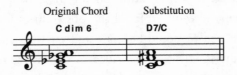

By including this note the convention is maintained of including four voices in each substitution and when we look at the way this chord is voiced in the progression we confront another basic law: *A chord has one less inversion than it has voices.* A triad (three voices) has two possible inversions. A chord with four voices like a D-diminished 7 has three possible inversions:

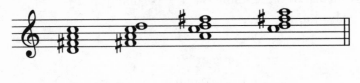

D7   1st Inv.   2nd Inv.   3rd Inv.

Our substitution is the third inversion of the D7 chord.

The third example is the simplest. Instead of playing a C-diminished +6 play its closest cousin, a C-minor+6.

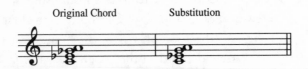

The last possibility—the F-sharp-minor-7—while mathematically correct is rather a strange sounding duck ("A," our common tone, is the third tone in the F-sharp-minor chord, its seventh tone "E" is in conflict with the "E-flat" in the original C-diminished).

However, it's passable, even interesting, if we voice it like this using its third inversion:

It is up to you to explain why an F triad or F-6 is not kosher even though it is a perfectly executed substitution.

The principle of substitution has come through with flying colors. Encouraging, isn't it? Especially when you remember the concept of "two generations removed substitutions." Extrapolating in search of "second generation" substitutions we unearth these "outside" candidates:

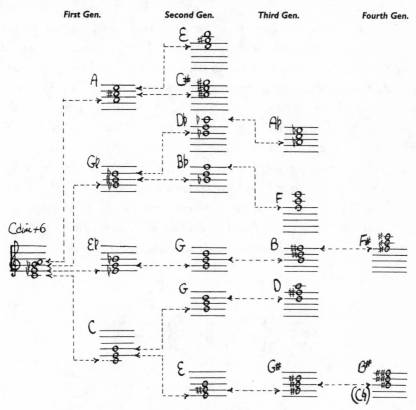

Make a chart like the preceding to help you keep track of potential substitutions. Remember that the choice to substitute for the second chord in "Moonlight Serenade" was an arbitrary one. Any chord in the progression can be omitted in favor of a substitution. Accordingly, try some different versions of the progression, substituting on different chords.

Another chord that has four voices is the major-seventh chord—in the C-major diatonic scale spelled C, E, G, B.

The B natural or major seventh is also known as a *leading tone* and one can speculate that the name comes from its predilection to resolve upward one half step, "leading" the diatonic scale to its octave (the same tone an octave above).

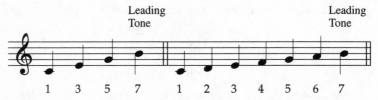

There is a story about a famous composer who could not tolerate the stoppage of a diatonic scale on its leading tone. Mischievous friends would often wait until the unfortunate man was in the bath or shaving or otherwise indisposed before loudly playing a diatonic scale on his living room piano, only to stop on the major seventh. He invariably burst into the room half-naked or covered with soap, cursing loudly as he rushed to the piano to complete the final half step.

If we continue "stacking" tones above the seventh tone, we get other exotic chords, commonly found in jazz arrangements, called 9ths, 11ths and 13ths. The sevenths in these 9ths and 13ths can be either natural or flat (cousin to the major 7 chord or funkier as in James Brown's "funky ninth"). The principle of substitution will apply to these as well.

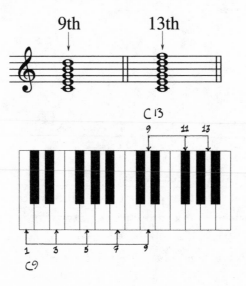

Those are some of the basic chords that are available along with a practical method for changing them to alternative chords within a progression. The technique will enable the writer to "spice up" existing chord changes, go on some exciting chordal journeys to unexpected places and one other thing: provide the tools to *harmonize* a melody. What does it mean to *harmonize*? Most often harmony is thought of as something that singing groups execute as part of a vocal arrangement, but more accurately to harmonize is to *add a chordal accompaniment to a melody*.

There are composers in the songwriting business who don't know a C chord from a snark. They whistle or hum or pick out a tune and usually rely on a trusted musician to fill in the chordal subtext. Seems mysterious enough, but how is it actually done? We need only to remember the contiguous properties of our old friend the *common tone*. Here are a few bars of melody, written just now with a decidedly cavalier disregard for the problems they will present to the would-be harmonizer.

(The numbers represent the position of the tone on the scale, in this case the key of C.) The very first decision we will make, and one of the most important in all compositions, will be what duration to assign each chord. In other words, how many notes of the melody will each chord be obliged to support? To change chords every time a note changes is akin to the college prank of trying to stuff the whole fraternity into a Volkswagen. At the other extreme not changing the chords with enough frequency will create a lazy, droning, unimaginative effect, reminiscent of Scottish bagpipes, etc. So here we are facing that duality again, Bernstein's blessed ambiguity. How much is enough? How little is too much? If we resist changing the progression on every beat—and I think we should—how about trying a chord change every two beats? A general rule would be: *If the melody is hyperactive, extend the chord underneath to support it. If the melody sustains or elongates then more movement in the chord progression is suggested.*

Right, down to business! We are in the key of C, the melody begins on C (I), so to keep things simple—you guessed it—a C triad would seem to be in order. In fact a C triad will harmonize throughout the whole first bar, all four beats, even though there is a note in the melody, D, that is not present in the C triad.

How is this possible? Because the D, known as a *passing tone*, is sounded for such a short duration and is so closely related to the C triad (it is its suspended second) that the effect on the ear is not inharmonious. Disregarding that happy circumstance for the moment, we want to change the chord after the first two beats, remember? The note that falls on the third beat is a D, the second tone of the C-major scale. We must find a chord that contains that D and shares at least one common tone with the C-major triad. I'll bet we can, using the same technique we used to locate *substitutions*. There are three possibilities that are readily apparent: F minor (IV minor), E-7 (III-7) and D-7 (II-7) without resorting to second generations.

I'm reluctant to go into a lengthy explanation of the derivation of these various tones. The C (first tone) is common to the IV chord, F minor. The second voice E (second tone) in the C triad is the E triad. The C (first tone) is common to the dominant seventh of the D-7 chord. Try them. Each has its sonorous qualities but my favorite is the D-7, though you may use one of the others if you prefer. Here is where my version stands:

In this example, as is common practice, the harmony is sounded or voiced *below the lowest note of the melody.* The range of the melody is left in the clear without undue interference from the harmony part. Think of the melody as the *right-hand* or *upper part,* the harmony as the *left-hand* or *lower part.*

Onward and—yes, the melody does move—*upward.* The next two notes are C (I) and F (4) in descending order. We need a chord to fit both. By now you should be able to figure out the options fairly quickly. The chords that share common tones with the preceding D7 are myriad, F minor, D minor, A minor, B major, G♭ or Major 7.

What complicates this choice is that the F (4) which follows the C (I) *will be sounding over the chord as well.* Our candidate needs to accommodate both tones. Perspective will be enhanced by playing the whole progression as it exists thus far with the melody and trying each substitution in turn. F major (4) and F minor(4 minor) will suggest themselves immediately as each contains both the F (4) and the C (I). Some of the others are less obvious and even strange-sounding. I settle for the F minor and look carefully at the subsequent D natural melody note (B-flat major, A♭, F7, etc.). Cutting to the chase, I am pretty sure of the simple B-flat major.

We might want to change a decision like this based on what turns out to be the next chord in the progression. What will that one be? Two of the most important objectives in the writing of interesting melody are the use of *repetition* and *variation.* To illustrate, when we next encounter the C (I) and the F (4) we find the F *above* the C. The melody is ascending, soaring. The C (I) fits with F major, F minor, D-flat-major-7, A-flat, A-flat-major-7 (not to mention the augmented and diminished chords that are available)— you're supposed to know how to do that by now. One of them is bound to give you a thrill. Remember that the chord should accommodate both the C (I) and the F (4). I'm extremely happy with D-flat-major-7. C (I) is the seventh tone in the D-flat chord and F (4) is its third tone, hence both notes are covered. The next two notes in the melody are E-flat (3 minor) and D (2) in descending order. This time I hope you will be able to list all the possibilities for yourself. The D (2) will more than likely be a passing tone. You will need a chord that contains an E-flat (3 minor) that will not cause an insufferable dissonance when the D-natural moves through it. I fancy C-minor-7 sharing its root with the preceding chord. The E-flat (3 minor) is its third. The passing tone D (2) is its suspended second. All the voices are a simple half step down from the previous D-flat-major-7 but the chord is pleasing in spite of its obvious adjacent quality.

You're on your own for the last two notes in the phrase. I arrived at F (IV) major followed by a G (V) major 7.

Obviously this progression does not constitute a complete musical thought. In a complete verse or chorus we might seek closure by working our way back to the C-major triad with which we started (the key center or tonic). In fact, the G is the dominant chord in the C scale and if a C chord is played immediately after the G-7, a tidy resolution back to the key center will result.

To make it more interesting, let's reverse the role of the melody versus chord structure. So far, the melody has driven the chord structure. Any confusion there? We have derived a chord structure from the melody by seeking out common tones in all the available substitutions. From this point onward we will allow the chord structure to drive the melody, and why not think of the new melody as a *chorus*? Our little four-bar phrase will represent a short verse, and now let's write a small chorus, only this time we will distill the chord structure first and let that structure suggest a melody.

At this juncture you may be forgiven your suspicion that we have strayed from the subject of melody. Actually we have not, because in modern songwriting melody is almost invariably *chord-driven*. Chord-driven melody is frowned upon by the traditionalists, vesting—as they do—a metaphysical quality to the stream of notes conceived with little or no consideration for what will lie beneath. The idea that a melody can be immediately exposed by the knowledgeable musician as "derived from chord structure" is presumably the same conceit that led Joe McCarthy to discover a Communist behind every science-fiction screenwriter. It is utter nonsense. These purists would have you believe that the melody comes first in all its liquid grace, hanging in midair, unsupported, and *because* of this it has some intrinsic superiority. It only remains for the composer to *harmonize* it, guarding all the while against the intrusive or overly complicated chord, *suborning* the harmony and keeping it in its place. For instance, Wilder says of Berlin: " . . . Most of these melodies one would say contain the implication of specific chord progressions"; and of Gershwin: "Having heard that he superimposed his songs on opulent harmonic patterns, I expected to find melodies often distorted as a result of the harmonic demands." And "I know from experience how easy it is to let chords guide the fingers that are choosing the melodic notes," and "In my experience, the better the piano player or orchestrator, the less pure or autonomous are his melodies." Mr. Wilder was suspicious of chords, a trait shared with a host of A&R men in Nashville. On the other hand, we have Stephen Sondheim: "If I am writing the music as well as the lyric I sometimes try to get a vamp first, a musical atmosphere, an *accompaniment* [my italics], a pulse, a melodic idea, *but usually the tone comes from the accompaniment figure . ."* (from a Dramatists Guild Special Projects session).

Many contemporary composers, myself included, believe that oftentimes the germs of beautiful melody exist in chord structure itself; that the chord structure leads us in interesting directions melodically, paths that might not be discovered otherwise.

I would not want to be accused of conjuring up some radical melody to accommodate the random banging of chords on the piano or guitar. I agree that it would be easy to recognize a creation so patently awkward. But when melody and chord structure develop in true symbiotic fashion, every opportunity is given them to complement each other. The whole, many times, can be greater than the sum of its parts. So, as brash as it may seem, it is my intention to approach melody from its substructure, the first element of that substructure being *mood.* Who will deny that different chord progressions create different *moods*? Is it to be a happy song or a funny song? A sad song or an *angry* one? Try writing a happy song in a minor key and see how far you get. How about a really sad polka? Yes, we could accomplish that with a well-honed sense of irony but the point is obvious.

The transition from a verse to a chorus most often implies a *continuance* of chord structure, meaning that our first decision will *not* be to return to the C-major triad with which we began our verse. To do so would be to create a finality, or a harmonic cul-de-sac, which is also called a *cadence.* (Of course it is *possible* to find choruses that began in precisely this way.) We will begin the "chorus" section on another chord, one that we can "substitute" for the C major. Forgetting about melody for the moment, the objective will be to string together a sequence of chords based on the way they *sound* in relation to each other. "Woodshedding" is an old musical slang expression that means kind of working things out by trial and error—fitting things together and discarding others as we go along. It is hard to imagine a better description of working out a chord progression by ear. It's rather an impulsive and random activity, substituting one chord for another, juxtaposing their order and waiting for the "buzz," that little physical thrill that is experienced when two or more chords lock together in a perfectly natural or even a totally unexpected way. Frequently these combinations will occur in "patterns"—perhaps four chords (any number, really) that will repeat in a pleasing endless cycle. Once one of these has been discovered the opportunity is presented to create a variation, and if it hasn't sunk in by now, I reiterate that *variations* and *transformations* are the wellsprings of all good musical art.

Follow me while I "woodshed" a typical chord progression that might be found in a chorus. Using the G7 (V) as a "jumping off" point, I try going to an F (IV) triad according to the principle of substitution and find that the sound is pleasing but it represents a return to a chord that I've only just left. It doesn't "buzz."

I then try A-flat major 7 (VI-flat) which conforms to the principle of substitution (both chords harbor a C [I]) and it sounds regal if not majestic, which is another way of saying pretentious and this is not a score for a sword-and-sandal movie. Worst of all, it places me *in a completely different key*. It is a true *modulation* which is something that is not yet on the program. (That is being saved until you are *completely* confused.)

What about A minor? That's what I finally settle on as it gives me the "buzz" and sets the chorus apart from the "verse" nicely, making it an acceptable starting point even though it shares no common tones with the preceding chord. We're *inventing* now, not substituting. After a few minutes of trial and error I have linked together four simple chords that please me.

I can repeat them at length and begin to hum or sing along with them to some degree, letting them push my voice around in one direction or another as seems fitting. While I'm doing this I decide that the second time through the pattern, to alleviate the repetition, I will end the pattern with a G chord (V) instead of the C chord (I).

It is time for a variation on this chord pattern—something that will drive the melody to another point on the compass. At this stage I could be singing some words that I've written along with this or "dummying" a nonsensical lyric as I blindly bumble along feeling for a tune.

Larry Hart's dummy lyric for "There's a Small Hotel" went like this:

There's a girl next door
She's an awful bore
It really makes you sore
To see her

Rpt.

By and by
Perhaps she'll die
Perhaps she'll croak next summer
Her old man's a plumber
She's much dumber.

> —Larry Hart,
> "There's a Small Hotel"

By now almost everyone knows that McCartney's "Yesterday" was originally "Scrambled Eggs." Anyway, I want the next sequence to be similar to the already familiar pattern, but noticeably different. Why don't you seize the opportunity to try a four-chord variation of your own at this point? I'll stumble along in my usual pedantic fashion: one technique would be just to "shuffle" the chords—start with the E minor, go to the F, then the G that we recently added to the mix, and *then* to the A minor.

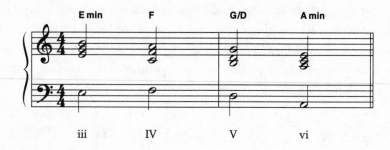

It only remains to create another four-chord pattern that will lead us home to the *tonic*—the first note in the C-major diatonic scale which corresponds to the C triad. Feeling wicked and somewhat mischievous, I believe I will introduce two new chords: D minor (II-minor)and B♭ (DVII).

The foregoing, frankly, constitutes a quick and arbitrary decision and is finally a *cadence* or closure to the whole chorus.

How on earth do we get a melody out of all of this? We play the chords over and over and sing along, altering the tune as we go, singing some words—any old words—to establish the rhythm of the syllables (scansion), changing direction in mid-stride if necessary to accommodate the next chord—or if the melody "takes off" in a delightfully unexpected direction, we search for a new and completely different chord or chords to accompany that flight of fancy—cutting and pasting, improvising and altering until we are hopelessly confused and hoarse, at which time we retire to the nearest pub for solace, submerging our faces in at least a gallon of cold, pale ale. The suggestion that this is an "easier" or "second-rate" way of writing melody angers me to no end. No method could be more strenuous, frustrating or corrosive to domestic bliss. Here is the melody that I "made up" to the chords along with a "dummy" lyric that reads as though actually written by a dummy.

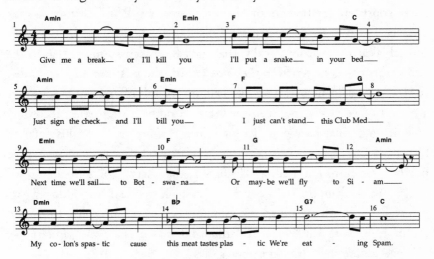

Let's recap! A melody can be sung, hummed or written in the clear either to an existing lyric or the lyric can be written afterward and added to the tune. This melody can be *harmonized* utilizing the principle of substitution to seek out the desired chords. Many different combinations of chords can be devised to fit the very same melody. On the other hand, a chord progression can be written *in advance of the melody or lyrics* and used as a scaffold on which to erect a melodic line which is accomplished pretty much by trial and error in a freewheeling interplay of improvisation and pragmatic substitution the aim of which is only to satisfy the composer's ear.

There are melodies like "Harlem Nocturne" (Earle Hagen), "Summer of '42" (Michel Legrand), or Antonio Carlos Jobim's "How Insensitive" that "feel" so perfectly natural that it seems like they must always have been. The first time we hear them they are "familiar"—not because they are derivative but because the order of the tones seems preordained. Ultimately this is what the melody writer strives for: uncompromised originality that is so carefully and logically presented that it somehow evokes nostalgia. "Now Webb has gone crazy," I can hear you say. Create something original that sounds familiar? Oxymoronic as it may seem, this is the mysterious territory wherein the great songs are discovered.

Our generation has contributed its share of beautiful melodies to the repertoire: Stevie Wonder's "All in Love Is Fair," Brian Wilson's "Don't Talk," the Addrisi Brothers' "Never My Love," Billy Joel's "She's Got a Way" to name a few. But McCartney is, without fear of contradiction, our most consistent craftsman of the deft tune: "I Will," "Penny Lane," "Maybe I'm Amazed," "Yesterday," "Blackbird," the list is as long as your proverbial arm. It's ironic, really, that Paul has taken so much flak in the latter years of his career from the same crowd who posthumously anointed Kurt Cobain a "genius." I have met Paul on several different occasions over a period of years, having been invited to a number of parties, recording sessions and what-have-you (I sent him a toy fire truck on his fortieth birthday). On these social occasions McCartney has a habit of seeing me before I see him, but I always recognize the cheery voice in the crowd behind me or from the half-seen figure casually perched atop a dusky garden wall. I have always heard the same phrase—a greeting that I prize all the more because Paul, his late father and myself share the same name. "Give us a tune then, Jim!" he always says.

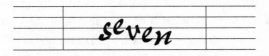

IN SEARCH OF THE LOST CHORD

He's the warmest chord I ever heard
Play that warm chord and stay baby . . .
—JONI MITCHELL,
"MY OLD MAN"

The inexperienced composer probably believes that there is a "right" way and a "wrong" way to write chords. One prevalent misconception is that a triad or even a more complex chord must have a bass note that is identical to its root.

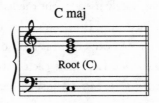

Bass note must be the same as the root?

If one is only familiar with the rudimentary arrangements found in church hymnals or the three-chord wonders heard on country radio, this is completely understandable. However, from a philosophical standpoint there is probably no such thing as a "wrong" note in a chord if the composer puts it there. ("Wrong" notes can only occur when a composer's work is misplayed.)

That is not to say that a lot of dissonance in a chord won't cause a frown on the face of an A&R man if it occurs in the "wrong" context—e.g., a demo for Garth Brooks. The pop music arena as a whole is not ready for intentional discord, no matter what the existential justification (though ugliness is deliberately incorporated in a lot of alternative/grunge/punk material, perhaps even considered essential).

Regarding the tendency of the inexperienced composer to rely on bass notes that are identical to the chord root (except for their placement on the scale, i.e., bass notes are most always an octave or two south of middle C), we must come to the conclusion that it is a limiting, restrictive practice. That such "bass" lines require no effort of any consequence is probably their best feature. In fact, there is a rich vein of sonority and resonance to be tapped by introducing *alternate basses* into the mix—and another benefit that relates specifically to the devising of interesting and even more fascinating chord progressions: An alternate bass often introduces a fourth tone to the simple triad which, according to the now familiar principle of substitution, furnishes another common tone which can be used to find another category of substitutions. But first, how do we find these *alternate basses*? As a prerequisite we have to know the difference between a "rub" and a "clash"—roughly analogous to the difference between a Japanese shiatsu and a head-on collision at an intersection. A "rub" is a level of dissonance that is tolerable and even pleasing. A "clash" is an immediate jarring assault on the ear. Know that if an alternate bass note *sounds* like an accident or a mistake, it probably is. "Good" dissonance doesn't startle the listener or cause discomfort even though we know that in so-called "serious" music and in an experimental context these jarring combinations can be deliberately used to put the listener under stress.

In the example the bass note is also a C. It "doubles" the root of the chord and is exactly the same note except it is an octave removed in what is commonly called the bass clef. Let's take each note in the C diatonic scale and put that note *in place of the C bass note* just to hear the sound.

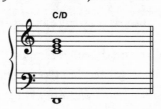

In the studio musicians frequently call this "C over D"—you could say "I (the chord) over 2 (the note)" and be accurate in any key. (Roman numerals will always represent chord symbol; standard numbers—Arabic—the individual notes on the scale.) Studio shorthand for this kind of chord is: C/D, easily jotted down above a lyric line or on a chord chart. Well, what do we have here? It is undoubtedly a nice warm sound. Play it. Savor it. It's the first chord in "By the Time I Get to Phoenix" (in the key of G), and in that context it displays an almost overpowering predilection: it wants to resolve itself to a chord corresponding to and built from the fifth tone below the bass note.

Why does it almost insist on this? Two reasons. The bass note D (2) is the dominant chord (V if it were a chord) and *wants to return to its tonic* (G or I). The C chord now floating above the D is in itself the subdominant (IV) of the G scale and has an impetus of its own to resolve or return to its tonic (G or I). This combined pulling power makes a return to the G tonic almost irresistible. (It should not escape notice that the melody in this case is the sixth tone of the C scale, a fact that is irrelevant to the chords and bass notes underneath.) Yes, there are other resolutions from this starting point. If you want to know where we are going with this, be advised that Jimmy Bowen once turned to an engineer while listening to one of my string arrangements and said, "What is that? Jazz or what?"

Moving up the scale we come to the third tone of the C triad, E (3). It looks like this:

E bass

"No dissonance here," you might say, since the note is already in the chord, and yet there is a subtle tension in the harmonic series that is almost subliminal dissonance. This is more obvious when the third is "doubled" or sounded both in the chord above and in the bass.

J. S. Bach as the inventor of the tempered scale was probably the first human being to identify this slight flaw or disturbance and established a rule that survives to this day, to wit: *The third should never be doubled.* If we humor the inventor of Western music and remove the third from the C chord then our C with an E bass looks like this:

Perhaps we could debate the issue but there is little doubt that the combination sounds better with no third in the right hand. Studio musicians will say "C no 3 over E" and notate it C no 3/E. The interval in the right hand between the root and the fifth tone is now an "open fifth" or "perfect" fifth. The open fifth possesses a kind of primeval buzz all its own. (Hollywood film composers decided early in the twentieth century that a pounding series of open fifths in the left hand most typified the "savage" nature of Native Americans.) A lot can be accomplished with open fifths and fourths moving in conjunction with each other. Later in the chapter we will find out just what. For the moment, where does our open fifth over a third in the bass want to travel? First and foremost it wants to resolve to the IV chord (F), the E-natural bass ascending an easy one half step to F-natural.

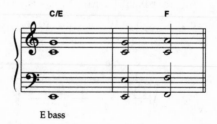

Why? Undoubtedly because the E bass is the "leading tone" or seventh tone in the F-major scale and we have already seen that the "leading tone" desperately wants to complete the F scale. To a lesser extent the F (IV) chord shares a common tone (C) with the C chord adding even more momentum. Applying the principle of substitution to the F (IV) chord, we find that the progression will move toward D-major or A-major. It will also move quite naturally to a G over D bass or to a C over F bass.

And there it is right in front of us—our next candidate—C/F or I/4. It's a wonderful, living, vibrating thing—bright with possibility. It will travel to F major of course, and just as easily move to B-flat or G-major:

C over G (I/5) follows. The G is already part of the C chord but when used as a bass has a rich power because of its relationship to dominant chord G (V) of the C-major scale. The chord itself rather wants to move to that G chord:

But it has many functions in a complete progression which will be explained as we encounter them. We are all familiar with C/A (I/VI) whether we know it or not. This dense chord could as easily be called an A-minor seventh and perhaps many musicians will prefer to use traditional chord terminology in referring to these kinds of combinations, but there is a method to my madness.

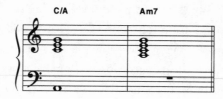

In this case the A (6) is an alternate bass for the C chord. We are going to think of chords and basses as *two separate things*—chords in the right hand, basses in the left.

The reason we are all familiar with this combination is because it so much wants to resolve to D-major (II).

Mantra-esque, isn't it? George Harrison must have thought so when he wrote "My Sweet Lord" and couldn't have been overly surprised when he lost a court battle with Ronnie Mack, who claimed infringement on his Chiffons hit "He's So Fine." (The court decided that Harrison had been "unintentionally" influenced by Mack's music, but Harrison still paid the fine.) Why is this chord propelled so hypnotically toward the II chord (D) and then back? The A bass is in the dominant position (5 on the D scale). There is a powerful reciprocal magnetism between the dominant and its tonic. This is the dum-de-dum bass part that plods through so much unimaginative, nondescript music. Tonic-dominant-tonic-dominant-I-5-I-5 to I to 5, all right already! One last stop on the diatonic scale, slot number 7, the B-natural or leading tone now becomes a bass note.

This is our most dissonant alternate bass so far. It seems not so much to desire a resolution toward another chord as to want to slide off a whole step down to an A (6) bass and leave the C chord in peace. I adore this sound even though some may find it disturbing. It is godlike, evoking images of towering pipe organs and scenes of awesome significance. It is what we might imagine a "lost chord" would sound like even though some will say, "What's all the fuss over a C-major seventh with the seventh tone in the bass?" Then why does it grind and pull on us so? Because of the close interval—the half step between the bass note (7) and the root of the C chord (I). The closer the interval between the alternate bass and any one of the notes in the simple triad, the more friction and psychic disturbance.

I have presented a fair assessment of the effect of alternate basses when they are taken from the diatonic scale and used beneath a simple triad. Obviously a bass note does not always have to be the same as the root of the chord. This fact makes it possible to construct bass "lines" in which bass notes because of their independence from the root of the chords will begin to take on melodic properties. Here is a simple progression where the bass line is a descending diatonic scale:

The latter is found often: in "A Whiter Shade of Pale" (Keith Reid and Gary Brooker), in "For No One" (Lennon and McCartney) and in "Piano Man" (Billy Joel) as well, but a bass line can display more movement than a simple diatonic scale.

If the previous bass line is played without benefit of the chords it takes on the characteristics of a "melody."

Another kind of bass line, the *ostinado*—which is a repetitive cycle often found in pop music—"Hit the Road Jack," "Peter Gunn," "Twist and Shout," "My Girl," "We Gotta Get Out of This Place," "Money," "Canadian Sunset," "Rescue Me," "Baby Don't Go," "Tequila" all illustrate that a complete song or instrumental can be organized over a simple series of bass notes cyclically repeated.

Create some progressions using diatonic alternate basses under your own chord structure. Think of the bass "line" as having its own melodic character independent of the chords above.

And yet some alternate basses remain. These are the "black" notes or chromatic tones that fill in the spaces in the diatonic scale. The first of these in ascending order is C-sharp (D-flat)—or 1+, 2- in any other key.

This one is an earful though not without a certain macabre charm. If passed through quickly, say on route to F/D, it has a gospel flavor.

Highly dissonant alternate basses should almost always be used as passing tones and dealt with quickly (at least in pop music). The next rogue in ascending order is E-flat or D-sharp (3- or 2+) and what we end up hearing is a major chord in the right hand and its minor or flatted third in the left.

Not pretty. The third is a vulnerable point in the triad as J. S. Bach first discovered so many years ago. Legions of studio singers have struggled to overdub thirds as precisely as possible because the least deviation from true pitch is immediately noticeable. (Depending on the harmonic context it is interesting to note that sometimes a third that is played or sung exactly on pitch will *sound* out of tune.) To invoke disaster in this way is not to court acceptance in ordinary pop music unless to underscore a particularly harsh emotion or lyric.

F-sharp or G-flat (4+ or 5-) comes next and again is not a sound that is comforting though it will resolve solidly to a C/G creating once more a satisfying "gospel" feeling.

The G-sharp or A-flat (5+ or 6-) is a clanker but nevertheless moves pleasingly to either a C/A or a C/G.

Finally the dominant seventh A-sharp or B-flat (6+ or 7-)—a wonderfully reedy noise, only barely dissonant, which is a busy junction of possibility.

... and so on. Try some other variations on your own. This last exercise has presented the possibility of a bass line that has not only diatonic melodic characteristics but chromatic ones as well. We could do this:

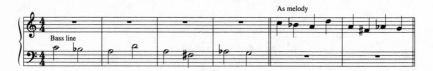

Now to play this bass line as a chromatic melody:

... which is only to demonstrate that with the addition of the chromatic elements the bass line is even more free-flowing and independent of the chord roots. So far we have moved the bass line around considerably while contenting ourselves with the playing of simple triads in the "right hand." But these simple triads have all sorts of variations in themselves as we remember suspended seconds, fourths, minor thirds, augmented/diminished chords and the like. Perhaps it is not too much a leap of faith to assume that minor chords also have viable alternate basses.

The C minor/D is a marvelous grainy creature that desires to resolve downward to a D-dominant 7th.

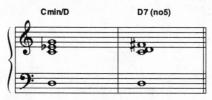

The ancient taboo against doubling thirds—even minor ones—applies to the E-flat (3-) bass and so the minor third must be eliminated from the right hand resulting in this:

The C minor with its third in the bass will gravitate toward D-7 as well, though we could change the right hand as we leave the E-flat bass in place:

. . . resolving to a conclusive B-flat. Or what about this:

C minor/F is a thin texture but could be the first element in the following cadences:

Sounding the fifth (G) under the C-minor chord does not create a particularly resonant effect and should probably be avoided except in passing . . . while placing the A-flat (6-) in the bass beneath a C minor instantly creates an A-flat-major-7 chord.

A C minor over a B-flat could just as easily be called an E-flat 6 with its fifth tone in the bass.

This one has all the passive-submissive traits of any sixth chord—wanting to be forced somewhere, e.g.:

The first bass that is chromatic—C minor/C-sharp—has great character, pulling strongly in the direction of C-sharp major:

C minor/E-flat natural is again that Achilles' heel of a dissonant third. Ouch! . . . and the F-sharp underneath is not a whole lot nicer.

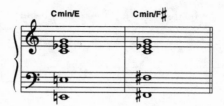

To put the A-natural (6) in the bass is in essence to play a C-minor 6 chord, dropping the sixth tone out of the right hand and sounding it in the left.

To see it perform rather typically:

More deviously:

C minor/B-natural (7) is strident and seems to want nothing more than to return quietly to the A-natural (6). When it does so the effect is persuasive.

With all this knowledge in hand we can to begin to experiment with ever more complex "right-hand" chords in conjunction with alternate basses to create "high-tech" combinations, many of which can not be quickly or easily named using conventional chord symbology.

Inversions and omissions now come into play strongly as a technique for altering the *voicings* of chords.

It is the opening accompaniment or "vamp" to "Sandy Cove" (J. Webb, ©1991 White Oak Songs). I made the decision early on to always play the F-major 7 *without its third*. Each time we hear the F-major7, the third is missing in hope of creating the same tension in the listener (the realization that something is missing) and the one time we do hear the third, in the penultimate F-major7 chord, it is in the bass and therefore remains alien and a little disturbing. (Samuel Barber used this chord to great effect in his moody "Adagio for Strings" along with the resolution.) In the above example, we see sustained chords, alternate basses, omission of notes and inversion of chords all working together to create a mood, one that is meant to provide a foundation for "Sandy Cove's" lyrical unease.

> *Out by Sandy Cove I thought about my life*
> *I thought about my children and a lot about my wife.*
> *About my Mom's old accordion and all the other things I've lost*
> *Like Grandpa's ship in a bottle . . .*

> —Jimmy Webb,
> "Sandy Cove"

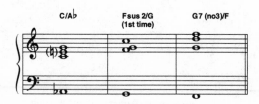

In the preceding example a chromatic, highly dissonant element has been incorporated. It is the A-flat bass in the first chord, an inverted sus chord and then an alternate bass on the second chord followed by an omission (the third) over an alternate bass on the last chord. The top note, F (4), is common to the two last chords and the inversion is used primarily to keep it in the uppermost position where it is most effective.

As a further comment the author finds that in general, common tones (the tones shared by different chords) furnish their most cohesive and seamless effect *when they do not change position on the scale from one chord to another.* More often than not, this will call for an inversion like the one illustrated.

Much energy has been expended thus far in describing the role of the alternate bass—that it changes radically beneath chords that only change slightly if at all, utilizing common tones, inversions, omissions, etc. The bass note can be altered to serve another function: it can stay right where it is while the chords change radically above it. In such cases it becomes, in the parlance, a *pedal tone.* Musical folklore has it that a pedal tone is so called because it was first discovered and utilized by Baroque organists who used their feet to sound bass notes on a pedal board leaving both hands free for the rigors of the mid-eighteenth-century fugue. The most simple way to think of a pedal tone is as our old friend the common tone, only played in the bass range as the lowest note sounded.

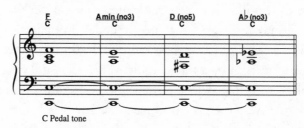

Notice that the bass note C (I) is sustained while the chords change above it, and that it is common to all the chords played: it is the fifth tone of the first chord, the third tone of the second chord, the seventh tone of the third chord and the third tone of the last chord. A pedal tone can be dissonant/chromatic as well:

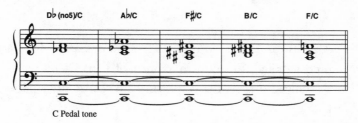

In fact a pedal tone is often heard in precisely this context—the big ending or fanfare—but can be used more subtly to create a song accompaniment, a verse perhaps.

Pedal Tone

In the preceding case the pedal tone is not sustained as on an organ's pedal board or a bowed bass (*arco*) but pulses rhythmically with the track. For purposes of description it remains a *pedal tone*.

(Dash some chords around above a pedal tone of your choice and see what kinds of scintillating effects or progressions you can bring to life.)

We've already discovered that we are under no obligation to play all the notes in a given chord as we have omitted the third on several occasions without being stricken by a thunderbolt. When the third is omitted from the triad altogether, that archaic yet splendid perfect fifth emerges (for reasons unknown, Westerners seem to have decided even before Gilbert and Sullivan that the Chinese "sound" or perhaps "look" like perfect fifths). The interval between the fifth and the octave (root) above is yet another "perfect" interval—the fourth.

Perfect fifths can be played in the left-hand or bass cleft to create an accompaniment though in so doing another of Papa Bach's verboten perversions is indulged, that is the employment of consecutive perfect fifths called *parallel fifths*.

According to the Maestro himself, a poor luckless soul could go to hell for writing parallel fifths though after Brahms the practice seems to have become more of a misdemeanor than a felony and in this century nothing more than a bad habit. Current laxity is due to the fact that marvelous things can be accomplished with juxtaposed perfect fourths and fifths in parallel and contrary motion.

Our blessed ambiguity surfaces again. Are these chords major or minor? It is very difficult to tell since none contains a third. Motion is "contrary" because the fifths are moving in opposite directions. Such a simple concept and yet what fantastic, even "lost," chords! Funnily enough, the first one when analyzed is only a lowly B-flat6 . . .

. . . but it is the widely separated "voicings" of each tone in the chord, a direct result of the perfect fifths, that excite the imagination. The second chord would seem to be in a strict mathematical sense only a C-sus4.

The third chord is a "cluster," not easily identified by rote and the last is an E-flat 11th sans the third and ninth.

In the example the descending parallel fifths begin on a G and the ascending ones on a B-flat. This is an interval of a sixth, and arbitrarily so. We could as easily begin them a fifth apart.

Fairly good results except for the obvious redundancy on the third chord. Fifths can be started in contrary motion with any interval separating the two lines of fifths at the outset, keeping in mind that redundancy may crop up from time to time (not that it is even to be avoided necessarily) and that some combinations (the interval of a second or third for instance) will be excruciatingly dissonant. Abandoning the linear or sequential approach and combining perfect fifths in skips opens up another aspect.

Or by using conventional materials in the right hand and parallel fifths in the left.

What about using perfect fourths *and* fifths together in this way? Being perfect cousins they should get along famously.

Experiment with parallel and contrary motion of fourths and fifths in different keys. While it is unlikely that a writer will want to create an entire song accompaniment in this mode, occasionally he or she may wish to draw on these exotic materials when a particular lyrical moment or emotion demands.

It has been successfully demonstrated that a chord need not duplicate its root in the bass, that tones can be omitted from the chord to create effects and most recently that whole chords with their thirds or other voices omitted can be played one above the other as in the examples of combined perfect fourths and fifths. What about playing complete triads? One above the other as in the following example:

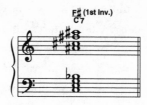

What have we here? A jazzy sophisticated sound first of all, and a difficult chord to spell or notate, second. Conventional terminology would label this chord a C-13 with a flat or diminished 9th and an augmented 13th, and might be written C- flat9 13+. The songwriter in a hurry with limited theoretical skills may simply want to write F-sharp 1st in/C7, once again thinking of the right and left hand as two entities, one chord in the right and one in the left, both combining to create a super chord. As Bernstein said, "the combination of two different chords automatically creates a third one, a new phonological entity." (From the Harvard Lectures, he is talking about Stravinsky's experiments with bitonality.) An unaltered C-13 could be pictured this way:

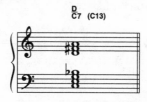

Which is to say as a D-major chord over a C-7 (dominant 7th). You say you want a truly dissonant chord like this one?

Even if the writer is successful in divining the proper traditional chord symbol for a chord of this complexity, it is doubtful that every musician who attempts to decode it will play it in the proper inversion or even correctly. It simply makes more sense to divide the chord into two parts, an upper and lower component marking the correct inversions, notes to be augmented, diminished, suspended or omitted, etc. This is most germane when the composer is after a specific *voicing*. Conventional chord symbols do not per se describe the precise placement of individual notes in relation to each other. The composer writes C-minor 6 above a lyric on a chord chart. The musician, depending on his mood or instrument or ability, may play the C-minor 6 in root position or first or second inversion. He may play it an octave higher than intended. The only unequivocal method to pinpoint the location of each note in a chord in its proper place on a wide frequency band like that of a piano keyboard is to *write out the music on two staves in traditional notation,* a laborious, and for some impossible task. Failing that, this right-hand/left-hand shorthand combined with a few simple symbols indicating suspended, omitted, augmented or diminished tones along with the proper basses and inversions provides a practical songwriting tool that reduces the time spent explaining oneself to instrumentalists in regard to *voicings.*

What do I mean by voicings exactly? As applied to chords, the term has nothing to do with tuning or pitch so forget that. To voice is *to locate the individual tones in a given chord in specific locations on the scale and in relationship to each other.* F-sus2/D can be voiced like this:

Or this:

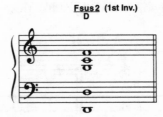

Or this:

Clearly the examples do not all sound the same though they are technically the same chord. When voicing is done correctly it introduces space between the tones and/or alters their position in relationship to one another in order to enhance the effect on the ear. This is neither a random process nor is it a formulaic exercise. (It is not Lotto and it is not religion.) It is, rather, trial and error in terms of listening to a number of variations and determining which voicing is most pleasing or appropriate to the material.

When we begin to "spread out" the tones of a chord at least two results are readily discernible. One is that dissonance is more tolerable when it does not occur in close proximity.

Normally the use of a Csus2 would preclude the use of the "third". In this case I indicate that it is to be used.

In the first part of the example the tones are clustered tightly together. They tend to interfere with one another. In the second representation there is a perfect fifth in the bass between the root (I) and the dominant (5). The third is a sixth higher and the sus-2 is a seventh higher. The dominant or fifth tone is doubled a fourth above that. Because of the spacing between the voices the effect is rich and yet uncluttered. I tend to voice triads in the left hand in just this way: root on the bottom, the fifth tone next and the third a sixth above the fifth tone. Because of my relatively large hands I can play this "octave and a third" rather easily with my left hand. If your hands are smaller you may need to "roll" the tone to achieve the same effect. With this big powerful triad firmly anchored in the left hand, I can get some interesting effects with the right.

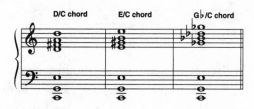

Here is an elegant way to voice a G over C:

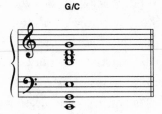

The G chord in the right hand is played "in octaves," a technique first taught me by Karen Goddard, an Oklahoma City piano teacher with a brilliant flair for improvisation and substitution. In her words the way this is accomplished is to "play an octave and fill in." The musician plays G and its octave above, then finds the fifth and third—the inner voices—and sounds them simultaneously. Voilà! A rich voicing and easily done. (Melody is often played in this way—each note in octaves and "filled in," which means simply that whatever voices are missing or desired are located and played between the octaves.)

The second result of widening the scope of chords—putting more air between the voices—is almost cinematic in nature. To do so spreads sensory input right and left as human beings hear in stereo. A single chord voiced in close harmony, played dead center on the keyboard, simply does not have the dramatic punch of one dispersed left and right with plenty of daylight between the voices. Furthermore, it is my instinctive belief that the harmonic (overtone) series is more excited by chords that are widely dispersed over the keyboard than by close harmonies and tight crowded clusters. For that reason I most often play a bass note in octaves and "fill in" octaves in the right hand, particularly when I want power.

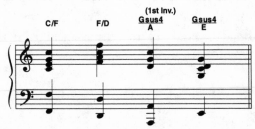

As an exercise try revoicing some of the familiar chords you've been working with, playing the basses in octaves, using octaves in the right hand and "filling in," playing widely spaced triads in the left hand while widening the intervals in right-hand chords and experimenting with different inversions. See if some of these alterations make your progression sound better or even inspire you to a better melody.

We have found that one chord can be substituted for another, one bass for another, one individual chord note for another, one voicing for another, but did you know that we can actually substitute one *key* for another? What is a key? A key is nothing more than a *scale*, and convention and practice dictate that the chords of a typical song will all be derived from the notes on one given scale with a view to eventually returning to the tonic chord (I), the first note of that scale, with a satisfactory plunk. However, it is child's play to effortlessly move from one key (scale) to another in the course of the same song or piece of music, and such a metamorphosis is called *modulation*. Modulation is in disrepute. Suggest modulating to a contemporary musician and you are likely to be sneered at if not banished in perpetuity to the boneyard of the un-hip. Your invitations may begin to wander mysteriously in the mail. Why is this so?

In pop music modulations—for the most part over time—have represented unabashed attempts to hype the audience. A chorus is repeated a couple of times at the end of a record and then, voilà!, modulation!! The chorus is now repeated a half or whole step higher, the vocalist stretching for the highest note possible as the violins attempt to induce bleeding from the ear. The climactic conclusion of a Caesar's Palace headliner is invoked—anathema to the folk-rocky singer/songwriter crowd and perhaps rightfully so. Though we might think of modulations in this rather unflattering and obvious way, the cold hard fact is that much of modern music modulates, sometimes constantly. Sting rarely writes a song that doesn't modulate at least in a "transitory" way. What do we mean by a *transitory modulation*? A transitory modulation leads to another key for a time and then back again or from that key to a new key altogether. The number of bars spent in each new key might be nominal. We could be two bars in one key, four in the next and eight in an entirely new key before returning to the original. (Sometimes these different keys or key signatures are called *key centers*.) What seems to bother the contemporary ear most is the *final modulation*—modulating without returning to the original key, usually for suspect, overly dramatic reasons. Nevertheless to reject the very suggestion of modulation as some kind of rock 'n' roll heresy is to ignore a kaleidoscopic shift of musical light and color, an opportunity to diversify melody, enhancing the emotional impact of a song. It is fairly common in pop music for a verse to be in one key and the chorus to be in another and equally common for one or two verses to be in one key, the bridge in another and the closing verse in yet another key.

For the composer entrenched in the single key signature mentality, the idea of moving from one key to another may seem mysterious if not terrifying. But it's easy! There are three ways of moving from one key to another plus a wild card that we will play last. There is the *chromatic modulation* and if you are the type who is confused by academic double-talk, let me straighten you out once and for all on the subject. If while moving from one diatonic scale to another diatonic scale (key center) a chord is employed that is based on a note that is not diatonic (i.e., "black notes") then a chromatic modulation is being employed. Wanna see some?

Up a Half Step

The example represents a common and frequently used modulation from the key of C to one half-step higher or C-sharp. The A-flat7, which connects the two keys, *shares common tones* with both scales. When searching for a chord to serve as a connector between two different keys the writer should find one that shares common tones with both keys. Bernstein loved the diminished seventh chord for its versatility, citing its "minimum four-way ambiguity," and the fact that it "can resolve to four different tonics: to A, to F-sharp, to E-flat, to C. What's more, each of those four tonics may be major or minor; and there are even more possible resolutions I won't go into" (pg. 232, Harvard Lectures, ex. 68).

Obviously a chord with these awesome capabilities must be considered an important tool in the process of modulation. Let's consider these other examples of chromatic modulation:

Up a Minor3rd (or Down a Major 6th)

Up an Augmented 4th (or tritone)

Up a Major 7th or Down a Half Step

Up a Minor 2nd

OLD KEY   CONNECTOR   NEW KEY
C   Ab7   Eb

Up a Minor 3rd

OLD KEY   CONNECTOR   NEW KEY
C   Bb7   F

Up a Perfect 4th

OLD KEY   CONNECTOR   NEW KEY
C   C#7   Ab

Up an Augmented 5th

OLD KEY   CONNECTOR   NEW KEY
C   Eb7   Bb

Down Whole Step

Note that some connecting chords of these chromatic modulations share common tones with both the key center they are abandoning and the one to which they are traveling. In the C-major diatonic scale all these connecting chords are based on the "black notes" making them true chromatic modulations. As an exercise pick two different key center "chords" at random and try to come up with a chromatic modulation, a connecting chord that shares common tones with both.

You knew this was coming, didn't ya?! *Diatonic modulations* are modulations effected by building the connecting chords from the "white notes" on the scale like this:

Up a Whole Step

Again, it is evident that some "connecting" chords share common tones with both the original and the modulated key centers.

OLD KEY   CONNECTOR   NEW KEY

Up a Major 3rd

No attempt is being made to represent all the possible modulations from a C-major diatonic scale to any and all other keys or from all the remaining keys to yet other keys. Rather experimentation is encouraged, particularly when the songwriter is trying to solve a specific problem, i.e., "How do I get from *here* to *there?*"

The *enharmonic modulation* sounds by far to be the most complicated of the three but in fact it is not. Suppose we hold just one note over at the end of a verse, chorus or other passage that ends with the tonic chord C. Let's hold the fifth tone (G) over. Once the tonic chord C has died away and the G remains alone, let us decide that now the G is the third of an E-flat triad and that E-flat is a new key center and that we intend to finish out the piece in E-flat.

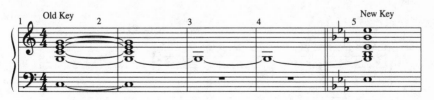

Enharmonic Modulation

Simple, isn't it? It is our dependable common tone, and of course the maneuver can be accomplished instantly with no interruption whatsoever in the flow of the music.

I promised a wild card but actually there is more than one joker in the deck. It is not necessary to have a connecting chord or common tone to move from one key to the next. A composer can quite arbitrarily launch into a new key if he so desires. (Charles Ives, among others, frequently composed in two different keys at the same time—not recommended.) We might call such an occurrence an *arbitrary modulation* or *skip modulation* (also called an *abrupt* modulation).

Arbitrary Modulation or Skip Modulation

At the opposite end of this spectrum the composer may want to use *more than one chord* to effect a modulation and this may take the shape of a small interlude or instrumental or it may take place subtly in conjunction with the melody as the song progresses. In "Skywriter" (Jimmy Webb ©1987 White Oak Songs) there are two modulations, a pronounced interlude, and then a third.

In "I Don't Know How to Love You Anymore" the first modulation occurs in the chorus and the second quite arbitrarily on the first note of the bridge.

There is another modulation between the end of the bridge and the instrumental chorus.

And then something rather interesting occurs:

The ascending notes in the upper register convince us completely that we have modulated yet again to a higher key when in fact a quick perusal of the chord structure beneath . . .

. . . reveals that we have returned to the original. "To what end?" you might well ask. In this particular case it was done because the singer wanted the drama of a modulation to a higher key but didn't have the vocal strength to sing any higher. The singer was me ("Suspending Disbelief,"

©1993, Elektra Records). Finally, there is J. S. Bach's "Circle of Fifths," a kind of musical elevator from any one key to any other. A composer can "enter" on any one key and then travel through the intervening keys to a point of exit.

Circle of Fifths

Many musicians and producers in our business don't believe in chords that have more than three voices. Some only believe in three chords altogether. Songwriters quickly become accustomed to hearing their chord progressions "ironed out" in the recording studio, i.e., sanitized, simplified and de-sophisticated. Being able to write down music or a chord structure on paper is not thought to be of much consequence, especially since the chords will probably be changed anyway.

When Harry Nilsson was at RCA, and the Artist in Residence in their giant Studio A, I chanced to stop by one evening, and upon opening the control room door encountered one of the strangest scenes I've ever witnessed in thirty years of booth-hopping.

A host of musicians were visible through the double glass—all kinds of horn players, percussionists pounding away on steel drums as somewhere in the back of the room Brian Wilson could be heard doodling on a B-3. In command of all was Van Dyke Parks and it was readily apparent that he was attempting to teach the orchestra by rote. He was *singing* the parts. During an appropriate lull in the cacophony I dared to speak to Harry.

"Hey, Schmeel, why is Van Dyke humming the parts?"

"Because I told him to."

The chaos continued at double volume—he had turned up the monitors to discourage my input. For an hour or so the situation continued to deteriorate in spite of the good maestro's best efforts to hold the cheerless and demoralized troops together. Finally when things had broken down altogether I had another chance to speak.

"Harry, why didn't you just let Van Dyke write all this stuff down?" I asked.

"You *would* ask a question like that," he growled.

Songwriters don't have to be arrangers but a little shorthand will keep confusion to a minimum on recording dates.

Shorthand System
Chords Over Alternate Basses

Major Chord	Sus Chord	Dim. Chord
C/D	Csus2/D	Cdim/D

Aug. Chord	1st Inversion	2nd Inversion
C+/D	C 1st Inv./D	C 2nd Inv./D

It also helps to be able to count to four, locating the individual beats in a bar of music in order to place the chord symbols correctly.

As to the importance of the "lost chord" in the first place, in country music for the most part and in much of mainstream pop music complex chord structure does not seem to have the slightest significance. Gene Lees maintains that civilians are completely oblivious to harmonization anyway, and short of that I can attest that I have known chord-deaf people, many working in important positions in the industry. As incredible as it may seem some of us believe that if you've heard one chord, you've heard them all. Consider Arthur Lange's (former Head of Music at MGM, 1954) run-in with studio head Irving Thalberg. Lange tells the story about how Herb Stothart, who had written the underscore for *The Wizard of Oz* in 1939, had subsequently written a very modernistic main title for a picture called *The Census Taker:* "One of those with terrific, dramatic things in chords, a very modern type of thing. So Thalberg heard this title and he got all burned up about it because he didn't know anything about music; in fact, he hated music."

The story continues that Thalberg sent a memo down the chain of command to the effect that owing to the difficulty the public had in understanding complicated main title music, "kindly refrain in the future from using minor chords." Thalberg had actually banned minor chords and "discords" from the studio. (Lange and his assistant made themselves some big badges inscribed Chord Inspectors and went around to all the arrangers to insure that their scores were minor chord–free.) As for myself, if it were not for grainy, disturbing, interesting, colorful, dissonant, poignant, sweet and sour chords, I would be working as a deckhand on a tramp steamer.

If the chord progression is—as I believe it to be—the foundation that lies under the form on any song, then there should be little difficulty in imagining the chords as stones or footings (perhaps one of them may even be a cornerstone) and the common tones, modulations, pedal tones, alternate basses, sustained tones and the like as being the mortar that binds chords together in good order thereby supporting the whole superstructure. Why else have generations of composers referred to this matrix as chord *structure*?

YOU AND THE WORDS AND THE MUSIC

I got a song that ain't got no melody
I'm gonna play it for my friends
Will it go 'round in circles
Will it fly high like a bird up in the sky . . .
—BILLY PRESTON,
"WILL IT GO 'ROUND IN CIRCLES"

Rodgers and Hart would pull a gag on reporters by asking for telephone numbers and allowing each digit to correspond to a note on the musical scale. (Eubie Blake is said to have written "I'm Just Wild about Harry"—©1921 from a phone number.)

They would sing these melodies with great glee to journalists foolish enough to accuse Dick of borrowing from himself or others—the implication being: why would a composer brilliant enough to fabricate melodies from random phone numbers ever find it necessary to steal?

Arthur Schwartz seems to have had a similar attitude toward his lyric writing. Once while sitting with some young Songwriting Turks at dinner he bragged that he could instantly sing a lyric to any tune that they could name. One of his companions—quite sure of victory—proposed that he try his hand at "The Tango of Love." Scarcely had Schwartz heard this formidable challenge when he began singing:

Cyd Charisse, get off that mantelpiece
You're such a shock there, we need a clock there.

With all due respect to such a feat, what I have done is to write the lyric down first (referring to Chapter Five and "Problem Child"), and now I want to create a tune for it.

I have the option of changing the lyric if I so desire and in fact I intend to fine-tune the words as I go along (there is always the chance that a wonderfully inspired melody will cause a drastic change in the form or scansion of the lyric). It is important to not guard against the melody's evolving influence over the words provided this influence causes some improvement.

I begin by exploring a set of chord changes that seem to create a mood and tempo and after a while I arrive at a progression, or more precisely, a *cycle*—a pattern that I can repeat ad infinitum, and why (you might ask) would I want to do that? Here are a couple of good reasons:

1. As I am now at an embryonic stage, searching for the very first notes of melody, this circular pattern is an effective device with which to sing along at length testing different notes as I try the words over and over again.

2. A circular pattern like this makes a great intro. It can be utilized between verses or after a chorus if so desired and is a kind of harmonic DNA code for the whole song. When the harmonic and melodic nature of the music changes—as it must—it will change in *reaction* to this established pattern in the form of a variation, substitution or other transformation.

PROGRESSION: Problem Child

This pattern is very similar to a Latin tempo, but it is also "slow rock 'n' roll" identified by the prominent accented eighth note pulse . . .

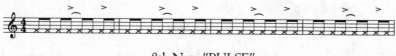

8th Note "PULSE"

. . . and the "push" between the first and the second beat of the bar which is created by "tying" the fourth eighth note to the fifth one and accenting it.

8th Note "PUSH"

Variations on this eighth note pulse constitute the basis for most of the slow- or medium-tempo pop music of our era. We don't swing any more. We don't even rock much anymore. We pulse. The first thing that needs to be established in the quest for the melody, then, is to determine what relationship if any this "pulse" has to the written word. It might be a good idea to set up the metronome or drum machine to play this eighth note pattern or pulse.

When you <u>cross</u> that <u>line</u> between <u>brilliance</u> and <u>madness</u>

I've marked the syllables in the first line of "Problem Child" that receive the most stress in normal conversation. It's not that the remaining words are without importance—notes will have to be written for them as well—but it is essential that these accented syllables have a corresponding rhythmic stress or accent in the "beat" to which they will be synchronized.

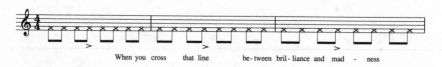

When you cross   that line   be-tween bril-liance and mad - ness

This is the rhythm that feels most natural to me but it could be executed in another way.

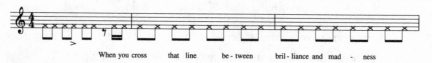

When you cross   that line   be-tween   bril-liance and mad - ness

There is nothing "wrong" with the foregoing except that it's quite square. Pushing the first two syllables into one beat seems awkward and, more importantly, will make the listener strain to hear what's being said. It is wise to avoid jamming too many syllables together on the same "small" note like an eighth or, God forbid, a sixteenth.

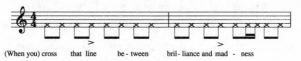

This is wrong. *"When"* does not merit three whole eighth notes at the beginning of the phrase. *"Cross that line"* is pushed together very clumsily in a traffic jam at the end of the first bar. Starting *"between"* on the first eighth of the second bar places an accent on the first syllable when it belongs on the second syllable in normal speech, etc. In other words the apportionment of time values to each syllable is a significant task and can be egregiously blown by the composer who doesn't pay close attention to the natural rhythms of speech. (It is barely necessary to point out that the lyricist is responsible for arranging syllables over the melody by the same criteria in the event that the music has been written first.)

If I write out the natural rhythm of this first line in conventional notation it looks like this:

Now obviously this is not a melody because the notes don't change but it is the *shape of a melody.* To be technically precise it is the *rhythmic profile* of the melody. If the writer sings along with the circular chord pattern described earlier, using the prescribed rhythm for the words and trying different combinations of notes, discarding some and retaining others, then he has begun to write a melody.

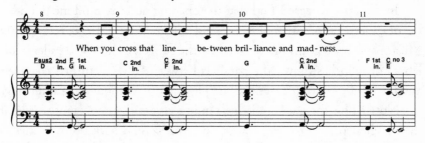

Here it is necessary to insert a brief disclaimer. There is no known shorthand for *rhythmic* notation. John Thompson's first-grade piano book among other instructional texts for beginners describes quarter notes, half notes, eighth notes, dotted notes and notes that are tied to others, etc. Most composers and arrangers spend a great deal more time dividing and charting the rhythmic pie that constitutes each bar than they do choosing pitches or devising chord progressions. There is little point in attempting to teach rhythmic notation in the space that I have available. I suggest that you either learn to do it by consulting an appropriate teacher or text or work with someone who already knows how.

The one thing that I find myself unable to explain after decades of contemplation is why a composer will or should choose one note over another. In my practice it is an entirely subjective response that—I almost regret to say—seems to originate in the source of my emotions, wherever that is. In an objective sense, the composer is able to read the words and to attempt making the music mirror or intensify the meaning of them. As mentioned earlier he or she can take heed of any obvious physical characteristics that are described in the lyric—i.e., up, down, gentle, rough, etc.—and utilizing dynamics, dissonance, chordal textures and intervals of various kinds, try to describe these. But at the end of the day—as the British like to say—the soul makes the hard decisions utilizing its emotional ears. Only one postscript might be added: If the composer has heard a sad song and been moved by it, his criteria for expressing "sadness" may in some way be molded by this experience. Over a lifetime he or she may compile an extensive library of these kinds of emotional references. I admit that I have many times decided in favor of a certain tonal sequence because, as I say to myself, quite self-satisfied, "That sounds like Barber." To elaborate, I have approached the emotional problem in a way that I believe Samuel Barber would have, and sometimes we make our decisions by emulating great brilliance and that's okay.

In this specific case I find that the opening notes remind me not a little of "Desperado" (Don Henley and Glenn Frey, ©1973 Red Cloud Music) and once again I'm amazed by the subconscious—that silent collaborator who has drawn the parallels between "my" disturbed character and the loveless wretch described in "Desperado" without any prompting.

Notice how the chosen pitches tend to accent the important words, at their highest point on "*line*," lowest on "*between*," and back up to "*madness*."

The word *"between"* doesn't sing very well and I can't seem to find an accent or rhythm that enhances it much. What if I change *"between"* to *"from"*?

When you cross that line from brilliance to madness

The result is a much cleaner melodic line which is one syllable (note) shorter and perhaps the meaning of the lyric is even made clearer. I've also added a touch of melisma, some sixteenths on *"to"* and the last syllable of *"madness"* which amounts to simple ornamentation.

Then you're out there on your own

Again the melody ascends to accent the important words *"out there"* only to subside under *"on your own."* How come? *"On your own"* is a mournful thought and the melody mirrors this by moving downward. The chord progression has now completed one cycle. I could continue writing in the same vein if I chose by repeating it again. Instead, I decide to break away from the circular pattern and send the chord progression in a different direction.

Just when you're overjoyed, you might be destroyed

The lyric is cautionary. The melody descends over a somber, almost religious cadence. The important words *"overjoyed"* and *"destroyed"* are given emphasis by the prominent space or rest that follows each, augmented by the "push" or anticipation on the important syllables, *"-joyed."* and *"-stroyed."* As for the underlying chords themselves, the first one, C/A, moves smoothly away from the established pattern by virtue of the fact that the new bass note, A, is adjacent to the G which has preceded it. C-Minor/A-Flat follows, the bass note moving down a half step, again striving for a seamless quality. Finally the A-flat bass temporarily becomes a pedal tone while the triad above descends from a C minor to a B-flat. All this could be called "organ technique," that is, moving the chords and their basses to adjacent or near adjacent destinations, sometimes sustaining the basses or the chords above and almost always sustaining common tones.

Like Icarus too close to the sun

I have moved the melody upward into a higher vocal range for three reasons:

I. Heretofore the melody has been quite low and it's simply time for a change.

2. The lyric speaks of Icarus "*too close to the sun*" which implies a physical gaining of altitude.

3. The chorus is imminent, will in fact arrive at the end of two more lines—my idea being to gradually ascend to a much higher note and to change key right at the beginning of the chorus for a hoped-for dramatic effect.

Let me explain why there is a 2/4 bar under the line "*too close to the sun*" (2/4 means simply that there are two beats, both quarter notes, in a given bar). At the end of the line "*just when you're overjoyed*" the syllable "*-joyed*" falls on the first beat of the bar and the next line, "*like Icarus,*" could be delayed until the end of that bar like so:

It is obvious that such an arrangement creates a tremendous gap in the lyric line. We must wait three whole beats for the sentence to resume. This "hole" is accentuated by the fact that the chord progression is static for the same period. To correct this I begin the line "*like Icarus*" immediately over the last two beats of the bar and finish out the line, "*too close to the sun.*" "*Sun*" is an important word and completes the meaning of the entire sentence. It should fall on the first beat of a 4/4 bar so that there is a natural three-count pause between this line and the next, i.e., "*sun*" 2/3/4. Therefore, "*too close to the*" becomes a truncated bar and the two unneeded beats are simply discarded. In traditional notation this necessitates temporarily changing the time signature from 4/4 to 2/4 and then back again. In your own writing it may become necessary from time to time to drop beats out of certain bars in order to accommodate rhythmic shifts of various kinds pertaining to the lyric. This practice is not only acceptable but is a legitimate transformation or variation, part of the very process of melding words and music.

It's so hard to come down from that dizzying height

"*So hard to come down*" does precisely that by very deliberate steps. "*From that dizzying height*" climbs higher than the melody has yet dared. This line and the one that follows represent a kind of staging area from which the chorus can "take off!" In the chapter on form, this transitional component was identified as a "lead-in," a section that both lyrically and musically prepares us for the advent of the chorus. The chord progression represents part of that preparation, laying the groundwork for a modulation as the bass line ascends in deliberate whole steps, leading inexorably to a new key.

Burning alive just like a meteorite

"*Alive*" climbs higher still, and then finally with "*meteorite*" the melody of the verse reaches its zenith as the chord structure modulates from C major to F major, a key that is a fourth higher. (Notice that the key signature changes from zero sharps or flats to one flat which is the key signature of F-concert.) It is now time to write a part of the song that should be—in a perfect world—memorable, tuneful and supportive of the message expressed, in short the chorus, which only has to be written *once* because being a chorus, musically and lyrically, it will repeat itself. In this fact there is a measure of comfort.

Problem Child why do you run so wild?

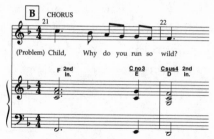

This lilting descending line is a consequence of having built the verse up to such a high—both in pitch and in dramatic intensity—that the melody needs to subside. Add to that the metaphor of Icarus tumbling downward and away from the sun, beautiful wings melting, and it seems proper to continue a kind of inevitable decline. The bass descends in thirds and in parallel motion with the melody, anchoring it and guiding it downward.

What struggle deep inside you is so unreconciled?

Poignant and appropriate as I believe this last descent to have been, now I must change direction or risk destroying by overzealousness what has been accomplished by a modicum of taste and good fortune. (The chord progression continues to cushion and carry the melody downward.)

What are you running from? Where are you running to?

The musical phrase provides natural breaks (rests) that correspond to the question marks in the lyric mimicking, in a sense, the tendency of a speaker to pause briefly after a question. The second half of the line is a variation on the first—same rhythm but different notes—one of our much discussed transformations. Since the rhythm of the next two lyric lines is substantially similar if not identical to these, perhaps it would be advantageous to continue with additional variations on the same pattern.

Whatever will become of a crazy kid like you?

I have changed "*mixed-up*" to "*crazy*." I will not deny that there is a private joke here but primarily the change has been made because "*mixed-up*" is a ridiculous combination of vowels and consonants that are together almost impossible to mouth. I am only concerned that "*crazy*" might be perceived as mean-spirited. At this point—I must admit frankly—the chord progression has taken over the melody, much to my delight, in its shivery romantic movement. But is this appropriate to the lyric it underscores? The words are meant to be tongue-in-cheek and at the same time a very affectionate nudge. To my way of thinking the warm, romantic chords defuse any possible misinterpretation, i.e., that the line represents any serious rebuke. Thus far the variations on the original melodic phrase are working like gangbusters according to my taste which explains why I continue inventing in the same vein.

Do you feel exalted, or do you feel defiled?

There must be at least one of you out there reacting somewhat petulantly to the fact that "*exalted*" travels downward on the scale instead of upward.

Horrors! *"Defiled"* also went the wrong direction. What gives? Please remember that these so-called rules are only guidelines, practices and habits and that they are *meant to be discarded on a whim or at a moment's notice if instinct dictates.*

Opposites again. Chord-wise we are straying from the key of F. We have strayed so far in fact that it has become necessary to modulate to the key of B-natural on the syllables "-alted." The main reason we go to all the trouble of physically changing the key signature instead of merely posting each note with a sharp (#) flat [♭] or natural [♮] is that in a key like B with all those sharps (five) it becomes highly problematic not to mention messy, confusing and space-consuming to label each note with its own little traffic sign. The *key signature* enables the composer to label only those notes that need the musician's specific attention called *accidentals*. (My piano teacher was fond of telling me that the reason these notes were called accidentals was because if I happened to play one of them correctly, it must surely have been an accident.) Neither am I strictly adhering to the rhythmic pattern that has been so emphatically established—one reason being that even though *"do you feel exalted"* has the same number of syllables as *"whatever will become,"* for instance, the emphasis on *"exalted"* must fall on the syllable"-alt" and this means that the final two syllables will fall on the downbeat of the next bar. The rhythm of the second line is bunched together at the end of the bar before it suddenly shoots up high in imitation of a David Sanborn sax riff. Why are these rhythmic variations creeping in? Because the repeated phrase with its familiar rhythm has just about played out its initial appeal and my instincts tell me it is time to move on.

After the syllable "-ild" notice the answering (ascending) figure in the bass part. This is what producers like to call "hooky" and would probably be heavily emphasized with additional instrumentation or dynamics, etc. on the actual production.

How long since you laughed or even smiled?

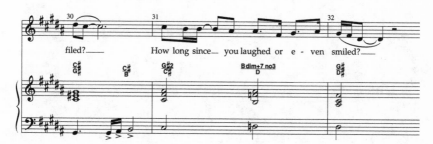

I find that I have abandoned the repetitive pattern in which I so freely indulged when it suited my purpose. Look closely at the example above. What does it remind you of? A throwback to the opening notes of the chorus—the *"Problem Child, why do you run so wild"* theme that descends in thirds with the bass? While here the bass is rising up to meet the melody which is another transformation, a way of changing the context of the familiar. In my mind this restatement of the opening theme is a significant development and signals the approach of the ending of the chorus.

You may not give a damn but baby here I am

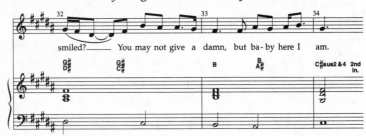

The notes that accompany *"you may not give a damn"* amount to a fractional restatement of the opening theme of the chorus, moving downward and weighted by the emotional cargo of the lyric. The rhythm has been changed slightly to bring *"damn"* down firmly on the first beat of the bar for emphasis. *"Baby here I am"* is in the affirmative so here the melody turns upward slightly in support and *"am"* is located squarely on the beat—a subtlety, but one that strongly reinforces such a positive statement. The chord structure beneath these two lines has been deliberately restricted to a simple hymn-like cadence. Since this is the "message center" of the entire composition, I want the listener to accept the message as sincerely as it is being offered. Fancy voicings, suspensions or crafty substitutions are not warranted. It only remains to wind things up and tie off the loose ends.

Tell me what's the Problem Child?

Here on the last line there is just a hint of the chorus's "secondary theme"—the rhythm that was repeated so many times (perhaps too many times) aside from a little turn, three-sixteenth notes on the word *"problem,"* there is nothing fancy or complicated nor should there be. At the end of a song the composer's primary concern should be to make the meaning of that last line clearer than day. The modulation at the end of bar 36 is worth notice. I have enthusiastically modulated well off the map, from C to F and then to B. There is some irony at work since B is a half step lower than the key in which I started (C). Considering these revolting developments carefully, the crafty composer is aware that the next musical event on the horizon will be a *repetition of the verse* (Verse II). Will our genius stay in the key of B and simply transpose the entire song downward a half step? Two drawbacks:

1. For most people, including expert musicians, transposition of any kind is anything but simple. (Not a great reason.)

2. More importantly, the song and particularly the *singer* will lose their head of steam if the second half of the song proceeds in a lower key than the one in which it began. It would be possible to modulate to an even higher key but at the very least we want to return one half step upward to the key of C. (I am aware that the class is passing some sort of crumpled paper back and forth at the back of the room; I would ask you to please control yourselves.)

The shortest musical distance between the F-sharp chord which begins bar 36 and the C-major chord which begins bar 37 is an F-natural with a G bass. Some may find this quick shift a teeny-mite jarring, but since I've been using it for years, familiarity has taught me blasé contempt. The writer who is offended by this fast-food modulation is invited to read Chapter 7 and explore some possibilities that are infinitely more complicated. As for myself, I intend to use the quickie key change.

The important words are *"what's the problem"* so these are the highest notes in the phrase. The note that accompanies *"child"* is nothing more or less than a good resting place as a proper last note should be.

For the life of me I can't explain exactly why a lot of these decisions were made. In the words of Richard Rodgers, "Perhaps if the reader sees the bare words *'the corn is as high as an elephant's eye'* ["Oh, What a Beautiful

Mornin',," Rodgers and Hammerstein, ©1943 Williamson Music] and remembers that *the proper music had to be provided for these words* [my italics], he will gain some understanding not only of the problem posed the composer by the words but *the solution of the composer's problem provided by the words themselves.*" [My italics.]

In my opinion no one has ever been able to articulate exactly what is going on here nor is it possible. Oscar Hammerstein came very close when he said, " It must be understood that the musician is just as much an author as the man who writes the words. *He expresses the story in his medium just as the librettist expresses the story in his.*" [My italics.] He goes on to use the word "weld" as exemplary of the process as I have often used "meld," implying that there is a superheated area between words and music where the two must melt together. What would be the source of all this heat? It would have to be a fusion reactor of sorts, a crucible where the differences between language and music could somehow be broken down or ameliorated. Leonard Bernstein said, " . . . The notion of a world-wide, in-born musical grammar has haunted me . . . " He continued, "I would never have dreamed of basing a lecture series on a notion so ill-defined, and apparently non-verifiable, if it were not for the extraordinary materials that have appeared in recent years on the similar idea of a universal grammar underlying human speech." (He is referring to ground-breaking research by the great semanticist Chomsky.) Is this superheated area between words and music where syllables and frequencies go white-hot to become a third thing defined and fueled by a "universal grammar" that is common to both language and music? Such was Bernstein's passionate belief.

We have noticed especially in the chorus of "Problem Child" that a certain rhythmic pattern was repeated—perhaps even at too great a length—but certainly we must look upon repetition as a kind of "tip of the musical iceberg of aesthetics" as well as a common code which interacts with many linguistic formulae. Bernstein said, " . . . The repetitive principle is at the very source of musical art (and of poetry)."

It has been said that a little knowledge is a dangerous thing. For a young writer to infer at this stage that repetition, any old repetition, any kind of mundane repetition, literal repetition as in *rote* repetition or just repeating some inane phrase ad infinitum, that any of this might in some way be related to the "essence of creativity" would be making a grave error.

It ain't that easy. It ain't that easy. It ain't that easy. Bernstein says, "The *idea* of repetition is inherent in music even when the repetition itself is not there at all . . ." Such a quotation would not be surprising if we found it in a quiet corner of author and philosopher Alan Watts's *Watercourse Way*. The Tao is ever present in the twisting and turning path of a melody. That old cliché "going with the flow" becomes somewhat functional. Radical or overly cerebral melodic moves are usually not innately pleasing, an idea that Alec Wilder reinforces in his book: " . . . Because I'm a musician and I know how enormously difficult it is to write a bone-simple song, within the range of an octave and employing neither artifice or cleverness." He also seems to hint at the Eastern approach (composition as Zen) though it is hard for this author to imagine writing a very good melody without being slightly devious. Here are some things to keep in mind when writing melody:

1. Never stifle an impulse. You are not editing. You are composing. (Quincy Jones calls this "choking the baby in the crib.")

2. Either write down or record every note you play. Fortuitous accidents happen more often than one might expect. It can be exceedingly difficult to remember one of these serendipitous "mistakes" after the fact.

3. Don't be reluctant to write a "dummy" tune with the idea of refining it afterward. Get the *rhythm* of the melody in sync with the lyric, avoiding what Sondheim calls *mis-accents*.

4. If your melody has "stalled" and you don't know quite what to do with it try some substitutions. A new chord or even a modulation will oftentimes kick the melody off in another direction.

5. Sing along with your melody constantly and avoid writing anything that is unsingable. (If you can't sing it don't assume someone else will be able to.)

6. The composer should be careful to avoid writing more than one note on the same syllable (melisma)—but should not be so fanatic as to sacrifice a gorgeous turn of melody for the sake of a technicality.

7. " . . . A composer setting words to music [I believe Bernstein actually means to say "music to words"] seeks those notes

which he considers most condign to the semantic values of the words he is setting." —Leonard Bernstein.

This must be a highly individual struggle to derive from the writer's own experience and level of technical mastery a matrix from which to assign each syllable a note of specific frequency and duration. Some of the more obvious decisions can be related to movement in the physical or emotional plane, i.e., up, down, happy or sad. Others to the natural accents of words and the arrangement of their vowels and consonants as well as to their overall importance in relation to inferior words, specifically as regards duration. Still other decisions will have to be based on more ambiguous and subjective criteria, perhaps so much so that the mode of making such decisions will be of necessity inherent in the individual's personality.

8. "Turning a melody 'sideways' merely requires changing a few notes in the original melody while keeping most of the same rhythms and note values. In many cases it amounts to plagiarism." —Michael Feinstein

Musical thievery is to be avoided if for no other reason than it is so much more vexing to steal than it is to write something original.

9. "Roger Englander, who was a close friend of Leonard Bernstein, once made me aware that one of the themes from a Vaughn Williams composition inspired the main musical phrase of 'Cool' from *West Side Story* just as a theme from Benjamin Britten's *Peter Grimes* became 'A Boy Like That.'" —Michael Feinstein.

Don't be so timid of being called a copycat that you do not allow yourself to absorb and mirror and be influenced by the music and melodies of the great masters. All the beautiful things you've ever heard can find legitimate new expression as they move through you and are influenced by your taste and experience.

10. Avoid repeating the same note excessively or returning to the same note too many times or too often. There is no cut-and-

dried formula for determining how much is too much. Antonio Carlos Jobim wrote a captivating song called "Waters of March" (a.k.a. "A Stick, A Stone," ©1973, Corcovado Music Corp.) in which he deliberately repeated the same three notes over and over with good effect. Two other cases where diversity has been flaunted with an ear toward humor are in "One Note Samba" (N. Mendonca and Antonio Carlos Jobim, ©1961) and "Johnny One Note" (Lorenz Hart and Richard Rodgers, ©1937).

It shouldn't be overly difficult to set the second verse to music. The melody is extant as well as the lyrics and if we have been careful with the syllable count—hopefully using a template for insurance—the elements should line up perfectly. At this point, however, I always check the lyric of the second verse against the melody of the first verse for discrepancies.

Whoops! I seem to have an extra syllable at the end of the second bar. My options are to either add an extra note or try for another word with one less syllable or perhaps to eliminate the conjunction "*and.*" In this case, "*and*" contributes significantly to the grammatical integrity of the line. What else then could I possibly "cross"? I could cross my *heart* except that it's a promise, not a hex against misfortune. Cross my *legs*? The more I mull it over, the less sure I am of the first line. Both verses begin with "*When you cross*" and while there is nothing specifically erroneous about this, it may be a case of too much symmetry. You see how the melody has got me to thinking twice about the lyric. After a little thought I decide that "*when you tempt your fate*" is a strong candidate. The line gets me well away from the overly symmetrical beginning and is exactly what I would like to say.

The lyric fits the existing melody perfectly and the song has been improved as well.

hope for sal - va - tion——   You're on thin ice in a heat - wave——

This line is in big trouble. It doesn't fit the melody of the first verse even slightly and this fact presents me with a real artistic dilemma. I am passionate about this line and want to keep it in the worst way, even though I have some alternates that will fit the melody like a glove: *"You're just dangling in the wind,"* *"Pride comes just before a fall,"* or *"You are gambling with your soul."* (Admittedly all clichés.) No doubt there are many others but I can't bring myself to move in that direction. I intend to very cold-blood-edly throttle a "rule." Keeping the line *"You're on thin ice in a heat wave"* I rewrite the melody of the second verse. If I was writing a song for a Broadway show I might not want to flaunt convention so blatantly but in a statement this personal some degree of idiosyncrasy can be justified for its own sake.

hope for sal - va - tion——   You're on thin ice in a heat__ wave

The new melody is not so different from the original. The rhythm has been adjusted to accommodate a couple of extra syllables, that's all.

You're on thin ice in a heat__ wave—— 'Cause when you think you've got it

made That's the time to be a - fraid——

I've been overly casual about this entry, I'm afraid. The melody of the first verse accommodates eleven syllables. In this case I am attempting to burden it with fifteen.

> *'Cause when you think you've got it made, that's the time to be afraid*

Initially, let me delete *"'cause"* as non-essential, which leaves me two syllables over. *"When"* can be disposed of if the first line becomes a question in the vernacular.

> *You think you've got it made? That's the time to be afraid.*

The audience can't hear the question mark of course, though its existence can be hinted at in this way:

You think you've got it made? <u>Then</u> you better be afraid

I'm still two syllables over. While such penny-ante malfeasance is forgivable in the pop milieu, especially if I lump *"then you"* together on one beat, I would like to steer out of these amateurish straits. After a good deal of trial and error I settle on:

When you've got it made it's time to be afraid

Both lines fit the melody perfectly. Happily, they also convey the proper note of caution.

Next we find that *"God knows when you're having too much fun"* shares exactly the same number of syllables with *"like Icarus too close to the sun."*

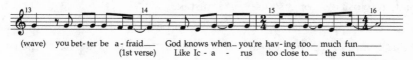

While this is technically correct there are a couple of awkward moments: *"knows when you're"* falls on the sixteenth in an unchewable way. *"Much"* coming off the sixteenth to the word *"fun"* is likewise very nearly unpronounceable. It is more in the idiom, clearly understandable and easily sung to write *"God knows it when"* (*"you're having too much fun"*). The rhythm can be rearranged slightly to provide a little more room for *"too much."*

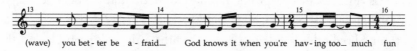

Jerome Kern is probably howling in his grave out there somewhere but I prefer to think of minor rhythmic alterations to the melody as *interpretive.* If singers are going to do it anyway—and they most certainly will—then why not the composer?

These two lines—I'm proud to say—are a perfect match.

cir- cu- lar— stair—   I know you're in - dif - f'rent but the   de - vil may care.   Prob - lem

This also fits extremely well. A couple of nonessential syllables were dropped— *"and you're . . ."*—but while considering this line carefully one last time I have unaccountably discovered a better one. How about:

I know you're indifferent but the devil may care

Please allow me a few comments about this virtually complete second verse. Most of the melodic changes made to accommodate the lyric were minuscule. This is as it should be. In one instance only I flagrantly broke the rules to include a line that I felt was essential to the very character of the song. This was a judgment call and in fact no serious attempt was made to gloss over or disguise this "mistake."

It takes approximately three minutes to perform "Problem Child" in a realistic tempo, which is to say not too fast or too slow. As part of the end game of completing this song I will take that fact into consideration. There is no arbitrary or abstract reason why the song needs to be any longer. The only valid question that can be asked is "Has the composer said what he set out to say?" If the answer to the question is "no" then I have encountered one of two situations where I might at this stage consider adding a bridge. Go ahead and ask. "A bridge to what?" It must necessarily be a bridge to either a final chorus or *in extremis* a verse/chorus.

In this instance except for fine-tuning and subtle adjustments I do believe that I'm finished. "Problem Child" will forever be a verse/chorus/verse/chorus form. Should the piece ever be recorded the artist will probably end the song outright after the second chorus or "repeat and fade."

What misgivings, if any, do I have about what I have wrought thus far? There are at least two lines in the lyric that fall short at first glance. The penultimate line in the chorus, *"How long since you laughed or even smiled?"*, is more an attempt to achieve a rhyme than it is a graceful sentence full of meaning. I now feel the constraints of having committed to this *"-ild"* rhyme scheme in the first place and prepare to pace the floor for a good long spell in order to think of something better. What I would really like to indicate is that the subject of the song is a person who has trouble recognizing emotions positive or negative. This person is shutting down real feelings. I decide on:

How long since you've shed a tear or smiled?

After this marginal improvement I address the next sore spot which follows forthwith:

You may not give a damn but Baby here I am . . .

The rhyme is obvious and the inclusion of an imprecation like *damn* always creates problems: Is it gratuitous? Or is it just overly dramatic and a little corny? A writer should have some damn good reasons for swearing in a lyric and even better reasons for using profanity. It will be necessary to procure a note from God when employing naked obscenity.

I decide that in any case this couplet will have to be different in each repetition of the chorus. It will be monotonous to have both choruses end exactly the same way. (This is strictly a judgment call but the scholar will discover that many so-called "identical" choruses will differ in one or perhaps two details, these usually concentrated near the ending or "payoff" line and are meant to create variety and additional impact.) I decide to conjure up as many alternative couplets as is reasonable. Let me illustrate a neat way to do this in order to avoid rhyming "*helping hand*" with "*understand*" and other filthy habits. Randomly select and scan different columns of one-syllable rhymes in your dictionary at a relaxed yet methodical pace. Look for *related rhymes* that can be paired in order to say in so many words: "I'm here if you need me. You can talk to me about your difficulties." It's easy. All you have to do is remember what you want to say and then make the logical connections between the two rhymes without forgetting the line that follows. In this case the line that follows being:

Tell me what's the Problem Child . . .

Is it such a big cliché? That it's something you can't say?
(Tell me what's the Problem Child)

Are you really so blasé? Is your life in shades of gray?
(Tell me what's the Problem Child)

Are your demons held at bay? Are they silent when you pray?
(Tell me what's the Problem Child)

Can I come to your aid? Do amends need to be made?
(Tell me what's the Problem Child)

What mystery have you made? That makes you so afraid?
(Tell me what's the Problem Child)

Is it living in a cage? Is it boredom, is it rage?
(Tell me what's the Problem Child)

Will you bend before you break? Will you speak for your own sake?
(Tell me what's the Problem Child)

Will you open up your heart? Since you seem to be so smart . . .
(Tell me what's the Problem Child)

We could literally do this all day long but I'm beginning to realize that the solutions I like best are the ones that relate to communication.

Is there nothing you can say?
Will you speak for your own sake?
Will you open up your heart?

I decide that this tributary is most worthy of exploration as long as I avoid the word "tell" because "tell" will be redundant . . .

(Tell me what's the Problem Child)

I know souls aren't made of steel, you can show me how you feel
(Tell me what's the Problem Child)

"Speak" I have already used. "Tell" will be redundant. Most of the other synonyms—*convey, impart, suggest*—sound lofty and/or pompous in this context. What about:

This is not a third degree, can you simply talk to me?
(Tell me what's the Problem Child)

Forgive me if I ask, so what's behind the mask?
(Tell me what's the Problem Child)

If you'll say what's on your mind I will answer you in kind
(Tell me what's the Problem Child)

Writers can toy with a lyric in this way right up to and including the moment when the "red" button is depressed on the actual recording date and they often do. Many nitpickers with self-confidence disorders—myself included—never stop rewriting their songs even long after they have been recorded by famous or infamous people and may have even found a place on the charts. (Annoying as this trait might be to the average historian, it is of an inestimable virtue in the lyricist.) Other changes may come about at this stage because the artist or producer has found fault with a particular line or turn of melody. It is up to the writer how sanguinely he or she wishes to treat encroachment on their creative territories. (As a personal observation I might say that I have rarely seen a more pathetic display than that of a lucky amateur eliminating the possibility of a first recording with an important artist through ill temper or intractability.)

Problem Child

Music & Lyrics by Jimmy Webb

To CHORUS 2

cir-cu-lar stair.—— I know you're in-dif-f'rent but the de-vil may care. Prob-lem

CHORUS 2
Problem Child, why do you run so wild?
What struggle are you making that so unreconciled?
What are you running from?
Where are you running to?
Whatever will become of a crazy kid like you?
Do you feel exalted or do you feel defiled?
How long since you shed a tear or smiled?
I know soul's aren't made of steel, can't you show me how you feel?
Tell me what's the Problem Child?

As I consider the whole I am suddenly aware of another criticism that could be levied. I haven't lived up to my charter in perfect detail. The resulting song ends up being as much about *me* as it is about the "Problem Child" for whom it was intended. Despite this sudden realization I'm not either overly surprised or dismayed. In our racket the messenger is always subtly intertwined with the message. If I have failed to accomplish my objective precisely, then I must hope that a second, perhaps subliminal goal will have been reached and cherish the thought that this inadvertent achievement may be of even more value. Such an occurrence would not be unique in the affairs of artists in general and songwriters in particular.

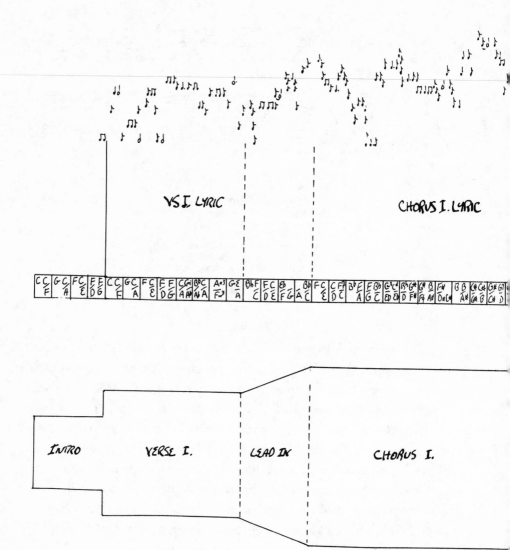

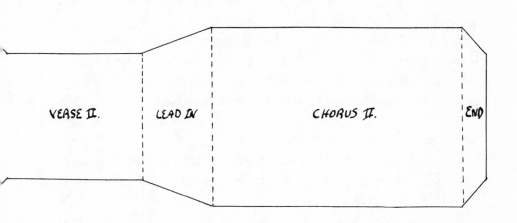

VS II. LYRIC

CHORUS II. LYRIC

VERSE II.   LEAD IN   CHORUS II.   END

My house is complete though constructed in a somewhat unorthodox way, the walls (lyric) first, foundation (chord structure) second, and the roof (melody) last. Don't let this important fact escape you: *These components could have been assembled in any order.* Unlike construction on the earth's surface, gravity was not a factor. Embrace the marvelous freedom that is afforded by being able to combine these main components in any order. "Problem Child" was created by one sequence. There are two others—completely different—readily apparent in this model and probably countless more subtle vareities if we let each section or even individual line or bar in the composition be approached in a different order (it gives me a headache just to think about it).

When I reflect on what I have learned from analyzing my own songwriting technique the word that comes to mind is *substitution*. We have seen how useful the *principle of substitution* can be in the alteration of mundane and predictable chord patterns into vivacious ones. What may not be so obvious is the role substitution plays in the development of a melodic line where fresh notes and phrases are freely *substituted* for ones that are tiresome or unsatisfactory. In the pursuit of the perfect lyric we *substitute* descriptive words for others or even entire phrases. When rhymes are stubborn in their resolution we go to the thesaurus and *substitute* another word that is more amenable. The principle of substitution seems to extend even to other aesthetic endeavors. The artist makes a rough pencil sketch as a guide and then *substitutes* other lines that improve on her initial vision. The actor searches for an accurate portrayal of the character by developing a first impression and then *substituting* refinements of mannerisms, speech patterns and appearance. The choreographer visualizes a dance routine or ballet and realizes it by *substituting* countless movements for others in an extended process of trial and error. Whatever the discipline, it is the facility that the artist possesses in connecting him- or herself to the next most desirable *substitution* that separates the women from the girls and the men from the boys. It is the skill with which this cerebral game of chance is played that most closely defines the true nature of the twin chimeras, talent and creative genius.

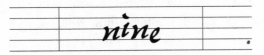

AT ODDS AND ENDS

You say eether And I say eyether,
You say neether And I say nyther,
Eether, eyether, neether, nyther,
Let's Call the Whole Thing Off!

—GEORGE & IRA GERSHWIN,
"LET'S CALL THE WHOLE THING OFF"

To be able to write words *and* music that allows the freedom to travel light and press onward without consultation, the opportunity to shape one's own vision in its entirety combined with feelings of immense satisfaction when the whole complicated process is over and done with, is an unparalleled experience. Even so, if America's songwriting heritage only consisted of works by autonomous composers, more than half of our musical library would instantly go missing. In my view collaboration has always been something of a necessary evil, which is no doubt why I have never been particularly adept. (A strapping friend of mine from Louisiana once told me that we should definitely get together soon and "clobberate." I declined, as it sounded very much as though I would be getting the worst end of the deal.) Either because they are compelled by necessity or because they have been told that it's the preferred method, many writers continue to collaborate even as we approach the twenty-first century. I have had the pleasure of writing with some very nice people: Kenny Loggins ("Traveling Man"), Gerry Beckley ("Stereo"), Toto's David Paich ("Home of the Brave"—also written with Steve Lukather and Joseph Williams), Carly Simon ("Film Noir") and Alan Silvestri among others. "A Dream Worth Keeping" (from the 20th Century film *FernGully: The Last Rainforest*) inspired Silvestri to such exertions that during the writing session he found it necessary to remove his shirt. Every collaborative experience is, by definition, unique. The up-close and personal ones are portrayed in many an old movie: two sweaty bodies in close proximity for a number of hours, locked in what amounts to a protracted argument, gulping down cheap food, consuming vast amounts of coffee or something even more vile, so the stereotype goes. In days of yore, tobacco seems to have been an essential ingredient in the process. (Wilder goes on to the point of tedium about certain songs bearing the unmistakable "odor of cigar smoke.") Today's amateur tunesmith will soon learn that cigarettes are about as welcome in recording studios, musical homes and publishing offices as polecats are at baby showers.

When setting up a collaboration for the first time it is excellent advice for the suitor to be pristine in all matters of hygiene, religion and politics, as what is proposed is remarkably similar to a marriage contract and, therefore, any obnoxious traits should be carefully concealed—at least until it is way too late for the other party to turn back. There is no cut-and-dried method for two people to work together. Does the lyricist approach the session with half a dozen verses written out on a KFC bag and a definite suggestion for some of the melody? Does the composer show up with a barely finished tune and some dummy lyrics which he then bellows in his best imitation of the village idiot? Or do they both arrive empty-handed and stare at each other with the same expression of lachrymose self-pity? Many are under the impression that for a writer to be successful in collaboration he or she must enjoy the process and be fond of his or her partner. History will indicate this ain't necessarily so. Jerome Kern's unfortunate workmates found themselves in the company of a martinet who refused to change his music to accommodate the slightest deviation by the lyricist even when an alteration might have made the song better! In his excellent Lorenz Hart biography, *A Poet On Broadway*, Frederick Nolan quotes Dick Rodgers on the subject of his sidekick Larry Hart: "I think the interesting thing . . . [was] the fact that he would not work without me in the room with him . . . on the other hand, I could write without him, and frequently did." Nolan's next comment is chilling. "In a hundred similar interviews over the years following Hart's death, Rodgers fashioned the legend of his partner's unreliability, his reluctance to work, his drinking, his dislike of the business end of their business, his inability to write without Rodgers there to make him." With such friends one might consider writing with an enemy.

In the lobby at a 1947 Boston theatre tryout Alan Jay Lerner, lyricist of immortal classics like "Brigadoon" and "My Fair Lady," was heard screaming at his partner Fritz (Frederick) Loewe, "Don't touch me or I'll kill you!" Dissonance prevails in these sometimes precarious relationships from the distant past to the present.

In his book *Blackbird*, Geoffrey Giuliano isolates the catalyst in the Lennon/McCartney songwriting chemistry using the classic rock 'n' roll *mea culpa* "Getting Better" as an example. "Paul has often commented that the song is a textbook example of how the Lennon/McCartney compositions were *strengthened by the collaborators differing* and complementary perspectives [my italics]. When McCartney sang, 'I've got to admit it's getting better,' Lennon caustically added, 'It can't get no worse.'"

Lennon was wrong of course. It got much, much worse. Evidence of this exists in the Beatles' former publicist, the late Derek Taylor's priceless if unpleasant collection of warring postcards written between the Lennons and the McCartneys during their ensuing estrangement. The feuding partners went so far as to trade musical insults on alternating solo albums during this period and what is quite surprising to me is that all in all the heyday of this most significant collaboration lasted a scant two years. (In a catastrophic development scores of their songs were apparently unceremoniously placed in a dustbin by domestic staff at McCartney girlfriend Jane Asher's home. Amazingly enough McCartney ended up owning none of the copyrights for the songs he co-wrote with Lennon.)

The book *Shout*, by Philip Norman, suggests that songwriting between Lennon and McCartney began as a rivalry to see who could write the best, and continued in that vein as they egged each other on.

Stephen Schwartz, a meteoric influence in the film musical firmament and composer of *Godspell* at the tender age of twenty-three, had mixed feelings about co-writing from the very beginning:

Well first of all, I'm shy . . . it's kind of like, okay I'll write but not in front of people. Plus the fact that when I first started out it was all instinct, I had no idea what I was doing. Once I went to Bernstein with an entire lyric, "The Word of the Lord," and he set it to a Brazilian folk tune and even though the words "fit" they didn't "sit." I made a mistake going back and rewriting the lyric after the music was done. Lenny was extreme in everything. He had fixed the date for his *Mass* to open the Kennedy Center in September of 1971 and three months before the performance he had almost *nothing!* Well, he had a little quatrain by Paul Simon, which probably remains the best lyric in the whole piece. I ended up devising a dramatic structure for *Mass*, which I'm prouder of now than any of my lyrics for it. How could I know I was capable of something like that, except that when we write we tap into abilities of which we're normally unaware?

Charles Strouse seemed to be very flexible as to whether music or lyrics should come first or whatever. So when we started collaborating, I would bring a finished lyric to him, and a week later he would play me the music, and the lyric didn't fit at all! So ultimately, we ended up writing *Rags* all music first. From this experience, I believe I learned my lyric writing craft. And ultimately the songs were better. Why? Because music has to rule. If the music is dominated too much by the lyric, the song doesn't come off. This is a function of what you might call "the collective emotional unconscious"— the power of music that is cross-cultural and deeper than words. I remember jamming at the piano in Bernstein's apartment one day working on a song for *Pippin*, just slamming chords together and playing with melodies, and I turned to realize he was standing in the doorway listening to me with a wistful expression on his face. "You know I used to do that," I remember him saying, "but now when I write, I put one note after another and I think: 'Are those two notes worthy of Leonard Bernstein?' " We have to—despite technique—get to that unconscious wellspring of creativity.

Peter Yarrow spoke to me carefully about a sensitive process:

I've worked with Barry Mann, Noel Stookey and Tim Hardin among others, and it's a kind of synergy. You trade positions. One person writes while the other is editor and critic and then the roles are reversed. You have to be able to absorb the criticism and understand that in the end everything has to please everybody. That's the way it always was with Peter, Paul and Mary, even when it came to an arrangement.

One cautionary note: When you've finished, when it's all done, there's a tendency to inflate the estimate of one's own contribution. Tunnel vision, when there's intense involvement, is not uncommon. Try to "sleep on it" before discussing the split of the creative contributions. Then, if your partner does not seem really comfortable with your suggestions, ask one of your songwriter friends to privately give you a "reality check" on your assessment. Erring on the side of generosity will serve you well—and assuredly bring back good karma as the years, and songs, roll on.

In the book *Heroes and Villains* by Steven Gaines there is a conversation supposedly taken from a cassette tape between Brian Wilson and Van Dyke Parks:

Wilson: "Hypnotize me, Van Dyke."
Van Dyke: "Cut the shit, Brian. You're a songwriter, that's what you do, and I want you to sit down and write a song for me."
Wilson: "Hypnotize me, Van Dyke, and make me believe I'm not crazy. Convince me I'm not crazy."
Van Dyke: "Cut the shit, Brian, and play the tune."
Wilson: "What's the name of the tune?"
Van Dyke: " 'Sail On, Sailor.' "

In addition to that memorable hit Parks went on to help create some of the more adventurous of Brian's later works but his rhapsodic surrealism eventually got him into trouble with Brian's cousin and fellow Beach Boy, Mike Love. Particularly vexing were the lyrics from "Surf's Up," Van Dyke's gorgeously evocative but literally incomprehensible flight of fancy above and through a ruined dreamscape. After a trip to Europe during which one may assume that the Beach Boys were asked on numerous occasions by picky journalists just what the heck the great opus was about, Love demanded a literal explanation for each line in the lyric from Parks, obsessing over the lovely but puzzling *"columnated ruins domino."* After enduring this third degree for longer than I would have, Van Dyke dourly responded, "I have no excuse, sir."

When attempting to write a song with another there is nothing more disconcerting than to discover that somewhere in the woodwork there is a third sounding board and opinion maker. A few years ago I was goaded into attempting a collaboration with a hot young performer by an artistic misanthrope who is no longer a part of my career management team. Nothing would do but that I would make overtures to this newsworthy persona and get the old collaborative ball rolling. I admired the man's talent and so with great reluctance and a tiny spark of hope I went to a meeting where, after all the outward rituals involved in the forging of a new friendship, it was decided that I would write some lyrics to my new workmate's prerecorded track. We wrote using the telephone, him at his home in the San Fernando Valley and me in my office at Broadway and Nineteenth Street in New York City. Most often we would talk about the lyric for a few minutes on the wire, he would indicate a general direction and even some preferences for specific parts that I had done, and after hanging up I would concentrate on his taped track and do my best to fill in the verses and choruses. It was interesting to me that he wanted certain preexisting lines incorporated into a surrounding of added lyrical material. We went on like this for a number of weeks, me reporting faithfully like a subordinate and my alter ego enthusiastically supporting my efforts with oohs, aahs, cries of exhortation and general flattery until I was convinced that I was nothing less than the first long-distance lyric-writing genius. A fool's electronic paradise can be brutally fragile. One afternoon he called me without fanfare and informed me in so many words that our happy songwriting ship had run rather suddenly aground. My oh my—to what unknown forces did I owe this sudden hammering of fate and all that wasted time?

"Well, my brother just doesn't hear your words coming out of my mouth," he explained. I was thinking to myself that perhaps he should just sing them a bit louder but before I could point this out he slammed the door on such a faint hope. "And my wife doesn't like it either, and neither does the band."

I was speechless. In the space of sixty seconds I had learned that for four weeks I had not been writing a song with one person but a minimum of seven. The chances of pulling something like this off are slim to none in direct proportion to the size of the crowd. The beginner will want to evaluate the prospective partner carefully to determine whether this sort of anomaly exists. It's hard enough to write a song with one person. For me, this long-distance telephone stuff just hasn't worked out very well. A similar situation occurred when some friends of mine who played in a well-known band sent along a "dummy" lyric and assured me that the somewhat patchy and sparse wording was entirely disposable if I would consent to write a new lyric. Once burned, I looked at these lyric fragments with a rather jaundiced eye but after voicing my concerns was reassured that these had only been "thrown in" by the lead singer (we will call him "Sean") for a sense of shape and some syllables to sing to, nothing more. "Then if I understand you correctly," I focused carefully, " it's okay to just throw these few lines out and go in a completely different direction, is that about right?"

"Oh, absolutely," came the reply.

Two weeks later I sent them a hard-won epic about someone dear to all of us who had taken one too many joyrides on the white powder and had failed to return. It was about as good, hard-hitting and honest as I can write. I was proud of it, or as proud as one can be of the flat, blunt, ugly good looks of a .44 auto mag. The call came quickly.

"Hey, what happened to *Sean's* lines?"

Certainly your songwriting counterparts are allowed their opinion and are perfectly entitled to say that they simply don't like your lyrics. I would like to think that I'm still friends with every person I've ever written with, successfully or not. But one must be careful not to proceed with a project until the requirements, perimeters, final authority and most intimate details of the collaborative process are clearly understood by both parties. In the previous two examples the fault for failure lies unequivocally with *moi*. How so? One of my new rules—and it probably should be one of yours—is that I don't work as a lyricist on projects which include lyric *fragments* from another writer that are meant to be used. Of course if you are one of those persons who believes in immortality and thinks of wasted time as a matter of no importance then go as carelessly as you please. I have never hesitated for instance to collaborate when offered relatively large amounts of money to do so, even though on two separate occasions great floes of time and Herculean efforts were expended in creating long operatic-styled pieces for musical cinema without the songs ever being used, recorded, heard, etc. (Once with a wonderful guy named Jules Shear.)

It still gives me a queasy feeling to do all that work (no matter how well paid I may have been) and see no appreciable result. It's enough to put you off the whole business except that, to be fair, there is a brighter side. Many in-person encounters go smoothly. Harold Arlen said to Alec Wilder: "If the composer has good judgment in editing, a lyric writer can help you find a way you hadn't thought of before—it's nip and tuck." Arlen worked very flexibly with super-lyricist Johnny Mercer, extending or truncating his musical phrases to accommodate changes in the story, syllable count, scansion, etc. Oscar Hammerstein liked to hear a composer play a melody over and over in the belief that such repetition could inspire an unusual mood or train of thought. He got along well with Richard Rodgers (it was probably just as well that he did) and cited many examples where the two men had written using lyrics first. "Collaboration is the biggest word in the theatre," Hammerstein once said. (Larry Hart, perhaps more cautionary, said that "tenderly nutured ideas are only allowed to live when they are worthy.")

Carly Simon once wrote a song over the phone with Michael McDonald which resulted in a number called "You Belong to Me" that was a hit on both their albums (Michael's album with the Doobie Brothers, *Livin' on the Fault Line*, released in September 1977, and Carly's, *Boys in the Trees*, which was released in April 1978). Simon's album went platinum the following August. The songs for the Beach Boys' *Pet Sounds*, one of the milestone albums of the late '60s, were written in a notably smooth partnership between Brian Wilson and Tony Asher, who made up dummy words during daytime writing sessions and then fine-tuned the actual lyrics during the evenings on his own time. (The next day Brian would pick and choose his favorite parts.)

In a remarkable anecdote Del Shannon described how one of the great rock songs of all time, "Runaway," was written on stage at a nightclub with his organ player Max Crook. Crook is said to have played the brilliant and distinctive organ solo ad lib on the very first try.

Perhaps this is the primary advantage in collaboration, being influenced by a completely different perspective, which implies a certain level of psychic discomfort, if not a little therapy and cod-liver oil. Lerner and Loewe would talk about their stories and songs literally for weeks before writing a single line, intentionally relaxing while emphasizing the preliminary and nonspecific nature of the work.

The trick is to somehow integrate two different ways of doing things into a single coherent method. As Walter Becker said about Donald Fagan in Paul Zollo's *Songwriters on Songwriting*, "We developed a way of working together that really combined our sensibilities. There were a lot of things that I never learned because Donald already knew how to do them. I could manipulate elements of his technique without having to master the same things myself. A lot of the themes we developed, we developed together . . . over the years, just bouncing things off of each other in ordinary conversations we'd be having . . . I think that our collaboration was so well integrated that we weren't sure ourselves where one guy's contribution ended and the next guy's picked up."

Much as I deplore being confined in a small space with another writer for extended periods of time I think it is probably essential to begin the writing relationship in close proximity. The physical meeting is semiotic of serious commitment and defines the relationship in real terms, not in glib turns of phrase that may flow all too easily through the telephone. Once a collaboration is under way, practicality indicates that there has to be a way of working at a distance. The mails are probably too slow but what about E-mail or the fax machine? With these modern miracles we can use what I call the "tennis ball technique." My partner sends me a tune or tune fragment on a tape or through the telephone. (He could also send me this musical phrase via computer using a process I frankly do not understand.) I make an initial lyrical contribution and fire it off on my E-mail or fax. After evaluation perhaps he calls me with changes, suggestions or criticisms after having made some changes or additions of his own. I make notes and go over his comments carefully, refining my ongoing contribution before I "hit" it back at him. At intervals during the process we physically meet in the same space (like going to the net in tennis) and hack out major differences face-to-face. Each party has the opportunity to work privately and serenely while mutual respect and input is also provided for. There is a certain kind of writer to whom this writing at a distance will be anathema. That is the aggressive type who wants to establish a physical dominance over the work itself. In other words, a person who wants to be in charge. Collaborations where one partner is successful in subtly bullying or controlling the other by any means—no matter how understated—are probably destined for failure. Irving Berlin hired pianists to pound out chords for him—apparently he had someone in this capacity for most of his professional life—but never pretended that this "collaborator" was

anything other than an employee. This approach is more honest than that
of a person who selfishly uses someone else for the other's abilities.

When I discussed this "dominant partner" theory with Felice Bryant
she seemed to disagree, at least when it came to her late husband,
Boudleaux:

> You have to have a leader, someone to make decisions, and he pol-
> ished and changed everything that I wrote first, you know he was a
> genius with his chords. I got there with pure luck and a prayer. When
> he didn't like something he flat wouldn't write music to it, like "Take
> a Message to Mary," "I'm Not Afraid," "We Could." I wrote the
> music to those . . . But Boudleaux could do everything too. "All I
> Have to Do Is Dream," and "Devoted to You," those were his ideas.
> I'd cook and he'd strum. While I was paintin' the walls he'd follow
> from room to room with his guitar and his chair and make sure I
> didn't miss a spot.

Though all collaborations are marriages of a sort, the dynamic of co-
writing in a literal state of matrimony presents its own problems and pecu-
liarities. Let's pretend we're sitting in the kitchen with Alan and Marilyn
Bergman.

Marilyn: The most important elements are trust, respect and
            a willingness to sound stupid. Sometimes a silly idea when
            put forward by one of us will trigger a really good idea
            from the other . . . How is working with your
            husband/wife? Well, we have the above elements licked.
            Another big advantage is never having to make an
            appointment to work. But conversely, it's sometimes diffi-
            cult to know when to stop!

Alan: I believe that there must be a genuine connection between
            you and your collaborator(s). Marilyn and I, of course, have
            that! I don't believe in collaborating with someone I don't
            like, truly enjoy being with. The process must be joyful. In
            the last analysis, that's all we really have, all we can always
            count on being within our control. After the work leaves
            our hands it "belongs" to artists, producers, etc . . . As far as
            any difficulties in working with your mate, as Marilyn said,

here is where respect and trust come in. If one of us isn't happy with a word or an idea, we explore other alternatives. And the more you work the more you realize the alternatives are endless. And of course the flexibility extends to being ruthless with the work. I think what separates the amateurs from the professionals is the ability (and the willingness) to rewrite.

In a recent phone conversation with Barry Mann and his wife, Cynthia Weil, they reminisced about their early days together, as well as the highs and lows of collaborating:

Cynthia: Yes, it's true that I met Barry at a songwriting session with Teddy Randazzo. Teddy and I were writing a little dumb song called "Cherie." It was okay for its era, I guess, and what's interesting about it is that Barry and I ended up with the A and the B side respectively. Working together? It's been fun and difficult. There's no question that the work feeds the other part of the relationship although sometimes I think Barry may have been served better by another kind of wife, someone who didn't react to the all too frequent setbacks.

Barry: On the other hand, we could always savor the triumphs together and how many other marrieds could say the same? Unfortunately, most creative people tend to be in the depressive area so there have been times when we have just sat down and waited it out.

Cynthia: That was in the old days, of course. I mean, my rebound time is about a hundred times faster than it used to be. Songwriters tend to think that's it, I'll never get another chance, and then of course after a few years, you see that so many times you were worrying over nothing.

Barry: Lately I don't give a damn. I'm very conscious of trying not to base my sense of self on my output.

Cynthia: That's an occupational disease. In a true collaboration you're on the same creative wave length and I firmly believe that you have to find the best person for you. Some people, no matter how well respected or successful or agreeable on the surface, are just not for me. Barry on the other hand, could collaborate with a stone. (She laughs.)

Barry: There are people I can't work with. There was a guy, for instance, very famous, who wanted to sit back in the armchair and critique me as I demonstrated what I could do. Picking and choosing, you understand. I found it very disagreeable. I need more participation than that, and I never worked with him again. The major impediment to collaboration is *fear*. Every collaboration begins with this sense of unwillingness to reveal ourselves as in Oh my God, he's gonna find out, he's gonna know I'm a fake, that I don't know what I'm doing.

Cynthia: On the other hand, we just worked with Hanson, a group consisting of an eleven-, thirteen- and fifteen-year-old, and we all had a great time.

Barry: For the record, Cynthia is the only writer I ever slept with.

One of the most spectacular "marriages" in songwriting history is the forty-seven-year connection between Jerry Leiber and Mike Stoller encompassing a whole genre of American songwriting including "Hound Dog," "Love Potion No. 9," "Jailhouse Rock," "On Broadway," "I (Who Have Nothing)" and "Stand By Me." Their music is currently featured in a Broadway musical called *Smokey Joe's Cafe*.

Jerry: It wasn't unusual for us to write four or five songs a day. In those days we wrote exclusively for black performers . . . Jimmy Witherspoon, Amos Milburn, Little Esther, Charles Brown, Little Willie Littlefield, "Big Mama" Thornton.

I met Mike Stoller indirectly through a mutual acquaintance. He gave me his phone number. I called him and we made a date that day to get together. After a long session of Mike trying to convince me he wasn't interested in writing songs, he asked to see my spiral notebook. I handed it to him, and on the way to the piano he started thumbing through the pages. When he got to the piano he turned to me and he said, "These aren't songs . . . I mean, these aren't *pop* songs . . . these are the blues. I *love* the blues." He sat down and played some very funky stuff. That day we wrote five songs.

Toward the end of the session, I walked around and stood behind him, and there on the wall above the old upright piano was a photo of George Gershwin . . . and in the right-hand corner of it was an inscription, "To my dearest Adelyn, with love, George." I asked who "Adelyn" was and Mike said, "My mother," and I said, "You're kidding? Your mother knew George Gershwin?" He said not only did she know him, she was in one of his shows. I was awestruck, and I remained that way for all the years that the two of us worked around that old upright piano under that picture that hung so heavy over our heads.

Mike: Jerry and I have collaborated in a few different ways. Initially, it was like spontaneous combustion—I'd start playing some kind of rhythmic stuff on the piano and Jerry would pace about, shouting out phrases until something happened that sounded good—then we'd work on it, arguing over a note, a word, a syllable, but it was a very fast process. Of course everything we were writing then was in a boogie-woogie or blues bag. "Hound Dog," "Kansas City" and "Ruby Baby" were all written pretty much that way.

"Hound Dog" was written for Willie Mae "Big Mama" Thornton. It was a big R&B hit in 1953. Three years later I went to Europe for the first time. I was returning to New York from Naples on the ocean liner *Andrea Doria*. Less than twelve hours out of New York it was struck by another ship and it went down. I was picked up from a lifeboat by a freighter. When I finally got to New York, Jerry was waiting for me at the dock. He said, "Hey, man, we've got a smash hit." I said, "What's that?" He said, "Hound Dog." I said, "No kidding—Big Mama Thorton?" and he said, "No—some new kid named Elvis Presley." . . . Well, they'd changed it around a bit 'cause it was originally written for a woman and it was too fast, but a funny thing happened: the more it sold, the more I began to like it.

Anyway, these days we tend to begin writing separately. Jerry will have four lines of lyrics or I'll have eight bars of music before we get together. Sometimes he'll have an entire lyric or I'll have a complete melody. I have to tell you this story about "Is That All There Is?" Jerry had written these spoken vignettes and I'd set them to music. One day Georgia Brown came over to Jerry's house with her conductor, Peter Matz, and they listened as Jerry recited the vignettes while I played the piano. Georgia said, "I love it!—but it needs a chorus," so we quickly added some old thing we pulled from the trunk and they said, "Wow, that's great!" Well, after they left, I looked at Jerry and we said almost at the same time, "It doesn't make any sense" . . . we'd think about it. The next day Jerry said, "I've got some words," and I said, "Wait a minute, because I have a tune," and immediately I started playing the melody of the refrain . . . Jerry got really quiet and he said very seriously, "Play that again," and as I played it again he sang the entire lyric to the refrain of "Is That All There Is," and it fit perfectly—we didn't have to change one note or syllable.

Down the hall and to the right a couple of doors we can hear "Walk On By" seeping through the plywood along with echoes of "Anyone Who Had a Heart," "A House Is Not a Home, "Alfie," and fifty or a hundred other significant works including the Broadway show *Promises, Promises*. We knock hesitantly and step inside for a few moments with Hal David and Burt Bacharach:

Hal: Collaboration is based on mutual respect for the art and craft of the other person. In my life I've only had one aborted collaboration and that's because the other person, very brilliant, was communicating with me through an intermediary. I realized that if he was not straightforward, that he was not for me. I just collaborated with Burt on a new song for *Promises, Promises*—which will open on Broadway in a new version soon—and you know, every thing with Burt was good. I would give him a lyric idea and he would say, "Are you sure of that?" and after a while I would come back and say, "I'm sure." And he would play me a melodic idea and I would say, "Are you sure of that?" I kept throwing him lyrics and titles, he came with phrases. We would "show each other our wares" and try to match them up. Even though we worked a lot separately, we must have worked together every day for ten to fifteen years.

Burt: My association with Hal David was a very long one. Once we got started we just didn't write with anyone else. Carole Bayer Sager was the one who promoted the idea of a third person. Sometimes Bruce Roberts or Neil Diamond. There's something really good about a third person. It makes you reach a little further because you are almost in a performance mode. Perhaps it's not exactly the same but it's almost like having an audience. When you're by yourself it's too easy to find excuses to quit or go off to the refrigerator or the telephone or whatever. I've always been uneasy about a face-to-face meeting when I didn't have anything prepared but eventually I got to be comfortable with a lot of other people. In this modern era you know you can dazzle with drum machines, synthesizers and other technology, but when you strip away the glitz there still has to be a tune in there somewhere. My nonsymmetrical phrasing has never been a conscious effort to break the rules or even a reflection of Hal's lyrics. In fact I never realized anything was complicated until I wrote it down and looked at it. "Look at that—that's a five-bar phrase!" or "That's a 7/8 bar." In other words the music sounded good to me, not strange, you know? But there was this one time when Dionne [Warwick] was playing at the Apollo and the band was really annoyed at the score to "Anyone Who Had a Heart," actually *angry* at the way it had been written and I said to them, "*Feel* it rather than read it."

[Note: "Anyone Who Had A Heart" is unique among pop songs because of its long sequence of irregular bars.]

Hal and I recently wrote a new song for *Promises, Promises,* after quite a few years apart, and he brought in a completed lyric and I looked at it and thought, "Man, this guy is really a helluva writer." He's very flexible and it was nice work; it was a situation piece for the book and it wasn't like trying to run a song past Clive Davis. Neil Simon was the key listener. It's so different when it's not a marketplace kind of thing.

After my first few songs were recorded I was surprised at how popular I suddenly became with persons seeking to "collaborate," many of these being staff producers or other employees of the record companies and publishing houses where I worked. On one occasion I sat at the piano and played a song for a staff producer who made a couple of diffident suggestions—one of which I thought was not too bad, and which I subsequently incorporated rather absentmindedly into the finished product. He recorded the song, sang it himself, had the recording pressed up before I knew it, and there under the song's title in parentheses, his name was included with mine. The sexual metaphor stirs uneasily in this tale as collaboration; when it is not willingly engaged in by two consenting adults it is musical rape. The reader is more than likely aware of unethical persons in the industry who will try by various means to interject themselves into royalty situations by preying on newcomers. What may not be known is that these people are often quite attractive, sympathetic and winsome in every possible way. Persuasive as the very devil, one might say. Be wary of surrendering a royalty position on a song without being convinced that a transforming contribution of real significance has been made by the would-be "collaborator." This may necessarily force a conflict between the desire to place a song quickly and easily by overlooking a bending of the rules and walking away from a sure thing, expensive dignity intact. For instance, in the (January 29, 1998) *New York Post* there was a nauseating story about a well-heeled diva/husband/manager team who demanded and got up to twenty percent of publishing royalties from most of the songwriters who had cuts on her last album. Even Carole King, Bryan Adams and the Bee Gees were called on to tithe but demurred. The songwriters involved would only speak anonymously—afraid of being blacklisted—saying in the newspaper article, "Basically we were told it was the only way we could get on the album." "It's tacky," said another writer. "How much money do they need?"

In this general context we are drawn slowly, we are curving inexorably into the gravitational pull of a favorite forbidden planet of mine, a strange environment where only persons of cast-iron constitution dare disembark, the strange land of Untalented Spouses Who Want to Write Songs, and there are plenty of them! The signs are all too familiar. The successful husband or wife linked with a helpmate who begins the relationship in a more or less conventional manner. The next thing you know the marital partner has abandoned the hearth of home and is standing in the middle of the recording studio yelling at the producer. Mysteriously, this person will now almost inevitably decide that they have been endowed by their creator with certain unalienable songwriting skills.

Why is this? Why do otherwise perfectly normal people who would never think of barging into their neurosurgeon mate's operating theater and snatching the scalpel from his or her hand during a brain transplant dare to meddle in the delicate manipulations of a discipline so arcane and shrouded in secrecy, subtlety and nuance as SONGWRITING? (Sadly, this is a subject for another very large book and will have to be unceremoniously shelved.)

Anyhow, curious, nonsensical, kindergarten-level compositions suddenly begin to appear in the repertoire of an artist known for their dead-level seriousness of purpose and competency. Music may eventually become a sideline, even a nuisance to more serious pursuits such as attempting to break the world's record for the Naked Bungee Cord Marathon while raising college monies for the Eskimos.

Not very long ago—in the scheme of things—a brilliant composer was lambasted with a huge lawsuit by a publisher unwilling to accept his musically untrained spouse as a co-writer on a number of songs that were involved in a royalty dispute. And what does it mean to you? Simply this: If you have the strength of character, it might be best to hold your spouse or significant other at a distance from your songwriting business. Of course you may just be the one person in the world who has by chance managed to marry a larval Joni Mitchell or James Taylor or you may have intentionally wed a formidable and talented collaborator with all the knowledge of and respect for composition one could imagine as part and parcel of your relationship. That would be nice.

Even if one has managed to keep a marriage free of artistic intrusion there are other influences that are less blatant than that of the explicit collaboration. Do you have a *silent collaborator?* If you bottle up emotions or censor your writing out of fear that the person who lives closest to you will respond negatively to certain subject matter then you already have a collaborator, if purely a reactive one. I first encountered this problem during the '70s when attempting to flak material to successful and ostentatiously married male recording stars. Certain story lines, those dealing with heartbreak or the consumption of alcohol or even vague feelings of unfulfillment, were simply out of bounds. The songs submitted had better be positively themed, praising a certain special person and promising a lifetime of unblemished fidelity. I am the first to admit that I have written precious few of the latter, nor do I know very much about the subject, and so was placed at a decided disadvantage. (Sammy Davis Jr. once threw me out of his suite at the Riviera Hotel in Lake Tahoe and told me not to come back until I had some happier tunes.)

But if the recording artist is self-censoring when it comes to selecting a piece of material for a long player then how much more so is the song*writer* living in close proximity with a love interest? Overhearing virtually every line sung, the significant other may be unable to mute an understandable curiosity and, most unfortunately, may be powerless to stifle or even disguise feelings of hurt surprise at the direction certain songs may seek or the suspicions they may innocently arouse of their own accord. The writer attempting to preserve both artistic sensibility and the Peace of the Home may become as secretive as an alcoholic, hiding controversial songs behind trick panels of the heart. Ladies and gentlemen, this is a very real problem. What do we do about it? In my view, a person doesn't have much of a relationship with someone if they cannot go to them and say in so many words: "Look, I am an emotional creature. I make my living by sorting, organizing and playing with emotions. Some of them are very real. Some of them I synthesize the way a painter achieves gray, by mixing a bit of black with white. You may choose to take everything I write to heart or you can believe, because it will be better for both of us if you do, that I am an artisan in the pursuit of certain abstract objectives that have nothing to do with *the way I feel about you.*" Will this fly? It had better, because if you are the real deal you will not want to spend the rest of your life writing songs with someone who hasn't actually been a part of the process.

Whether or not we write words or music or both, in a very real sense we all collaborate, if only with our "other self," our subliminal co-writer. I converse with my subconscious collaborator constantly and out loud. "Hmm, why don't *we* do so-and-so?" or "We-e-e-l-l, *we* could try *this!*" I swear sometimes a voice replies with an answer or suggestion. Am I schizophrenic? We definitely are not! It's just that I've trained myself to be very sensitive to the subconscious voice. Sometimes I think that "writer's block" is nothing more than a breakdown in communications between a writer and his or her subconscious co-writer. Here's a suggestion: When writing alone treat your subconscious as a living, breathing collaborator by providing moments of relaxation and introspection, opportunities for your "partner" to talk back to you. You can see that when two people collaborate there may actually be a quartet at work. (The royalty split could get very complicated.)

Unquestionably the "platinum age" of collaborative arts was the first half of the twentieth century. Rodgers and Hart and Hammerstein, Lerner and Loewe, the Gershwins and many other finely matched duos honed the technique to a fine edge. They used their formidable instruments to carve immortal works for the theatre that will—unfortunately—probably never be equaled. In the '50s Leiber and Stoller continued the Tin Pan Alley tradition in their songs for Elvis Presley and the Coasters, etc. while Felice and Boudleaux Bryant created an enviable body of work for the Everlys among other Southern artists. Bacharach and David set new standards for lyrical and musical sophistication in the early '60s. Later in the decade, of course, Lennon and McCartney dominated the collaborative field although the Adrissi brothers' "Never My Love" seems permanently moored in the number-one position on BMI's "most performed" list of the last fifty years. Tommy Boyce and Bobby Hart wrote many gems for the Monkees that have never received their proper due. In the '70s, Crosby, Stills, Nash and (sometimes) Young in various combinations created substantial works that mirrored the social ergonomics of their era. Disregarding for the moment the contempt of the elitist for mainstream music and that Lennon and McCartney were Englishmen, it is evident that our generation—at the very least—kept the tradition alive and well.

As we approach the twenty-first century collaboration is nothing less than "hot." Many successful writers journey to (manager of David Bowie) Miles Copeland's French castle to attend his biannual workshops for professionals with muses on the fritz. Rarely do I talk to another writer who doesn't include an offer to collaborate in the conversation. Janis Ian, who began a brilliant career as an autonomous songwriter, has co-written almost exclusively since 1986: "After about fifteen years or so, you develop your own style and your own boring routines." Carole King told me not long ago that co-writing had jump-started her out of a recent creative slump. Carly Simon is doing it, though she is cautionary on the subject of men. "Only a man will change your lyrics around without asking you and present you with a fait accompli." C'mon guys. Carly once collaborated with Alan Jay Lerner posthumously when she finished a lyric fragment from a song called "Over the Purple Hills" to a tune by Arthur Schwartz. Oscar Hammerstein's first notable success, *Carmen Jones*, was written with the deceased composer Bizet. Barry Manilow wrote an evocative and haunting tune to deceased lyricist Johnny Mercer's wistful "When October Goes." There is little doubt that much less friction is involved in co-writing with someone who doesn't talk back.

The art of collaboration is a special gift. Some writers are simply too egotistical and self-centered to ever do it right. It involves a great deal of genuine selflessness and dedication along with an inexhaustible tolerance for the peccadilloes of one's fellow man. I once heard what is perhaps an apocryphal tale about Sammy Cahn writing with Harry Warren. Harry was playing a tune for Sammy for the first time, just to see what he thought of it, and Sammy pulled out his notebook and started scribbling madly along. Warren turned to him exasperated, stopped playing, and said, "Sammy what the hell are you doing for Chrissakes? I'm trying to play the tune here," and Sammy said, "Relax, I'm rewriting the lyric."

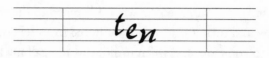

GETTING TO FIRST BASE

And there used to be a ballpark where the field was warm and green
And the people played their crazy game with a joy I'd never seen
And the air was such a wonder from the hot dogs and the beer
Yes, there used to be a ballpark right here.

—JOE RAPOSO,
"THERE USED TO BE A BALLPARK"

In an old movie about Alan Freed and the '50s (*American Hot Wax*, 1978) there is a curiously affecting scene in which a number of teenage music groups and individuals are gathered in the anteroom of Freed's studio receiving advice and encouragement from Alan as they attempt to write hit songs on the spot. For someone like myself, who came along a decade later in the '60s, this was already naive nostalgia. In my day radio had become big business, jocks were media stars, and would-be songwriters didn't just walk into a station without an invite though warm relationships with disc jockeys did figure peripherally in my personal development. As a high school student I would call Lynn Bryson (a jockey on the graveyard shift) at K-MEN, San Bernardino, in the early hours of the morning seeking advice or a job or just a spin of "Baby, I Need Your Lovin'." I was to K-MEN, San Bernardino, what Jack Ruby was to the Dallas Police

Department, a hanger-on, a voyeur and a beggar-of-crumbs from their star-strewn table in an era when a personal appearance by a local disc jockey could draw a damned respectable crowd at the Piggly Wiggly.

> For me it started out in the '50s when I listened to the radio all the time, and would turn it on when I got home from school and wait for "Tequila" to come on, and when it did, I would call my brother into the room and say, "Quick! Quick! 'Tequila' is on!," and he would be doing the same thing with "Oh, Venus . . ." in his room. And while I'd go running to his room to hear that, he would be running back to mine to hear "I Will" from the movie, *Bye, Bye Love*. It was an event— delicious anticipation—waiting for your favorite song to be played on the radio!
>
> —Carly Simon

During the '60s the music "business" quickly became the music "busy-ness." Big corporations realized suddenly that the record industry was a humongous money machine with mass appeal, not merely a loose confederation of small specialty labels that were patronized by their respective ethnic or sociological constituents. Since songs are the raw material that power the reactor of a large part of the entertainment busi-ness, it is only natural that opportunities for songwriters in the mid to late '60s first multiplied and then came thick and fast. Ironically enough, the major problem for songwriters of my generation was in being heard over this beehive of unceasing commercial activity. It was hard to persuade a harried executive to sit still long enough to listen to a three-minute song, even though sooner or later someone almost always did. A person with real songwriting talent would have had a better than average chance of placing a song with a major recording artist in the decade bounded by 1965 on the one hand and 1975 on the other. After that, impediments began to interrupt our free and easy progress. Self-contained groups proliferated, wise to the subtleties of including their own published works on records for financial purposes. The overall quality of long players declined dramat-ically as listeners began to settle rather too easily for an LP containing only one or two cuts of real worth. In the mid to late '70s the pure singer— such as Linda Ronstadt, Glen Campbell, Sinatra, Kenny Rogers and Dionne Warwick—began to encounter a wall of diminishing returns that could only be breached by massive and unceasing television exposure, a problem exacerbated by the advent of elitist and age/demographic-driven video music outlets like MTV. The Olivia Newton-Johns, the Bee Gees, the Fifth Dimensions, the Petula Clarks, the vast pantheon of Motown acts and even sensations like Crosby, Stills and Nash, not to mention many of the traditional giants of country and western like George Jones, Buck Owens and countless others, began to slowly but unmistakably fade from the spotlight. And what was the line of disembarkation? It was drawn mainly at the radio station that would or would not play a certain artist; a new kind of discrimination directed not at the sound coming out of the speakers, but at the source of the noise—the age, color and even politics of the recording artist. It is interesting to note that the encroachment of the exclusive "playlist" superimposes neatly over the rise of the "independent programmers" whom I blame mostly for the disappearance of democratic Top 40 radio which gave birth to rock 'n' roll in the first place. Even as early as 1967 the writing was on the wall. In June of that year Brian Wilson drove down to KHJ on Melrose Avenue in East Hollywood with his brand-new single "Heroes and Villains," *avec entourage et acoutrement*, only to have the DJ on duty (Johnny Williams) refuse to play the record because it wasn't "on the playlist." By 1971 one programmer, Bill Drake, a guy who looked more like a professional linebacker than an arbiter of teenybopper taste, was deciding what was to be played on virtually every Top 40 radio station in the whole country.

There were suddenly fewer artists interested in recording a song (any song) written by a pure songwriter. Imagine the state we're in now, thirty years later, when we can count the number of viable nonwriting recording artists on the fingers of one hand, when the playlist holds unchallenged sway over those "free" frequencies once devoted to a dispassionate dissemination of white/black/slow/fast/sweet/angry/Chicano/Japanese/rock/R&B/ballad/classically influenced/jam/jazz/novelty/bubble gum/country/folk/fusion and what-have-you. But that was before "compartmentalized" radio whose stations are dedicated exclusively to one kind of music or another, carefully aimed at a certain specific age group and/or ethnicity. In the '90s this phenomenon has gone so far as to separate "old" country from "new" country, the upshot being that songwriters interested in airplay had best get focused on one listening mode, be it "ska" (not "reggae," mind you) or "death metal" (not to be confused with the more archaic "heavy metal") or some such ilk, and create a music that will pass a close inspection according to the criteria. This state of affairs also serves to make songwriting a lot simpler or a lot more complicated in direct proportion to the writer's IQ, and has impacted significantly in at least two ways.

1. On the quality and integrity of the American song
2. On the general welfare and future prospects of the *pure* songwriter

Things are harder now for the songwriter, especially the beginner or amateur, than ever before. We can immediately take the position that in an environment so bereft of proper singers who record songs written by others the young writer may as well attempt the logarithmic leap to singer/songwriter with all the promotional difficulties attendant. Should you try to be a singer/recording artist? I honestly can't think of any reason why you shouldn't, considering that vocal talent in today's market seems to be more a matter of "sound" than "technique." Almost everybody has a "sound." Only a baker's dozen of male/female divas all clustered together at the top of the charts have what could properly be identified as "voices." As an alternative, the writer might hide him- or herself in a self-contained group like one of the current crop of embarrassments that dominate late-night television, the ones that rub the noses of the sleepy American public in the fact that nobody showed up after the Beatles. My point is that if there is any task more difficult in the known universe than establishing an identity as a songwriter/recording artist, it must be the assumption of the mantle of the legendary and almost extinct "pure" songwriter. Assuming that by now your feet must be nearly frozen solid, I prepare to offer some minimal and carefully considered encouragement.

Current technology provides an efficient and inexpensive means of creating professional quality demos at home. There is no excuse for the writer not to have a clean, competent demo of each song. But what are you supposed to do with these demos? Three decades ago writers and publishers would "shotgun" them—just send out as many as possible in all directions and pray. While this may have provided a windfall for blank tape manufacturers, it can be debated whether or not such a strategy ever resulted in even one song being recorded by anybody. Oh yes, it did provide a ready source of free cassettes for other songwriters and publishers as well as giving them plenty of new ideas for songs.

There is an axiom for improving your chances of song placement, and as daft as it may appear on first perusal, read it carefully and hearken ye: *A songwriter should play his wares for someone who's listening.* At any given moment the ears of half or more of potential publishing sources in the industry are deafened because the people in question already have what they need. Many publishers have a writing stable on salary and are understandably eager to justify their investment by utilizing their "in-house" material for ongoing projects. I have already mentioned that an unprecedented number of today's recording singles and groups write their own material (for better or worse). This state of affairs has given rise to the rather ominous term "outside material." It is vital that the writer does not waste precious time and money in sending demos and lead sheets to perfectly hopeless destinations such as other songwriters or groups that write their own or to record labels. Rather, the writer should work in two distinct areas that provide an element of rational control over a process that is notorious for its random qualities. First, *intelligence.* Not intelligence as in IQ, but intelligence as in cloak-and-dagger information about one's objective. The writer has to know who is looking for material, what kind of material they are looking for, and why they are looking for it. For this, there are most obviously "tip sheets," industry publications like The National Academy of Songwriters *Musepaper,* which lists "Pitchathons" and "Cassette Roulettes"—open forum listening sessions with industry professionals actively seeking material or writers. Many publications have up-to-date information on who's doing what and sometimes include addresses or phone numbers for first contact. Don't underestimate the importance of trade publications like *Billboard* and *Variety* or turn up your nose at the entertainment sections of local newspapers or "entertainment television" programs. All of these contain nuggets of intelligence about artists who may be needing a certain kind of material immediately. When you contact the people who will be representing these recording artists, producers, music supervisors or A&R personnel, it is important to begin with confidence. Don't say, "Gee, I've never done this before." You are talking to the enemy. Be supremely cool and say your name as though you are saying "Irving Berlin." Most of the time the intermediary in question will not be sure exactly who you are anyway, but they will be looking for telltale signs of insecurity or ignorance of well-known facts and procedures so that they can label you as an amateur and shunt you to Limboland. (And for God's sake, when doing a mailing, don't send out lyric sheets scrawled on loose-leaf paper with your cassettes. The only thing dumber is to send out lyrics on notebook paper without a cassette.) The naive, innocent faith involved in such an act would be amusing if its utter futility was not so pitiful. The writer of lyrics should not seek a collaborator at a major record label or publishing house or with another established songwriter. Rather, he or she should find a collaborator close by and submit finished songs on neatly labeled cassettes with the proper and vital information—your contact number, the song title, etc. (And by now you should know better than to send out un-copyrighted material.) Approach a first phone call like this:

> Hi, this is Leonard Flortnoy, the songwriter. [*As though the person should know who you are.*] I understand that Flippy Hardbottom is doing an album of upbeat love songs and I've got two pieces of material that are right on the money. Have you picked everything yet?

Be nice. Be friendly. Be confident. If you sense that the other party is impatient don't push it or stay on the phone a moment longer than necessary.

> Well, listen, thanks a lot, if you can help me it would be great. I've tried to take a fresh approach on this and I wrote the songs especially for Ms. Hardbottom. May I leave my number?

Or:

> I thought "Shotgun Rhumba" was the best, in fact I loved it so much that I wrote something that might be almost as good. I'm sure Flippy would want to hear it.

Don't try to force yourself into a face-to-face meeting. Don't call back and pester. Sound as though you have busy, important things to do. (It would be especially nice if you actually did have busy, important things to do.) Got it? Do this ten or twelve times a day and I guarantee that someone, somewhere is going to listen to one of your songs. The only thing is— after this pitch, it better be a damn good song.

Another area where it is important to concentrate is the world of personal contacts. Ninety-five percent of all songwriting business is conducted face-to-face. It is more important to know the artist's bass player than it is to know the producer's home address and phone number. There is a theory, well known to you I'm sure, that there are only six degrees of separation between any human being and any other (you know someone who knows someone who knows someone who knows the queen of England).

There is nothing scurrilous, underhanded or sleazy about promoting oneself via personal relationships in this blatantly political industry and in fact—to put it plainly—you must get to know as many famous and influential people as is humanly possible. Speaking of those, my friend Michael Douglas has said to me on more than one occasion, "James, shyness is not a virtue." What he did not say but what is undoubtedly true is that self-effacement just might be the most fatal character flaw in one who desires a career in the entertainment business. How is one to go about shameless self-aggrandizement? Well, there are nightclubs, and there are ways to get backstage, and there are charity events and organizations. There are seminars and industry happenings like Tin Pan South in Nashville, or South-by-Southwest in Austin, as well as Hall of Fame dinners and various interactive events sponsored by ASCAP, BMI, SESAC and a plethora of other songwriting organizations coast-to-coast (you probably have some such organization in your immediate area). There are musicians who play in the bands of famous people and personnel who work in recording studios and other sound technicians as well as roadies, groupies, wives and girlfriends. In short, there is a whole songwriting social swimming pool. The emphasis throughout brazen self-mongering should be on getting into a live performance situation with guitar or piano or paper and comb in order to play your songs for as many onlookers, off-listeners and overseers as feasible. It doesn't matter if your voice sounds like a lovesick loon caught up in an outboard motor accident, or if your instrumental technique was learned from a video purchased off late-night television, or if your stage fright is so acute that you curdle the milk of human kindness, you must play and sing anywhere, anytime, any way you can. Self-promotion is the only promotion you've got. Got a job as a restroom attendant? I guess I don't have to tell you what you need to do. While pursuing social contacts in any circumstances, however, it is inadvisable to press a cassette into the hand of a notable personality whom you have known for only five minutes. New friends and acquaintances will eventually want to hear your music and will ask you to play it for them, which brings us to the next topic: You're not going to make it in Idaho. In the past few years there have been secondary songwriting markets developing in provinces like Seattle, Minneapolis, Austin and some say in Branson, Missouri, but essentially the business of songwriting is still conducted as it mostly always has been in New York, Nashville and Los Angeles. I'm not suggesting that in order to be a successful songwriter one must move to one of these three locations, and in fact, that might be the worst decision a person could ever make. That doesn't mean it would hurt to have a presence in one of the Big Three, perhaps a representative, post office box or answering service.

A "representative" would of course be the most desirable and difficult, a publisher who has a vested interest in promoting your music, or in rare instances, a "manager/agent" who is paid a percentage of gross, or rarest of all, a friend who would help out for free. A local P.O. box or answering service is simply a way to remove the onus of "small townism" from a return address and make a homegrown operation seem more credible and professional.

New York City, widely accepted as the birthplace of modern American song, location of the hallowed Brill Building, the Big Apple, the traditional hub of the nation's musical theatre and Valhalla to the advertising trade, has always been a favorite destination for hopeful songwriters of all kinds. A casual scan of some recent headlines, "Slumping Sales a Sour Note for City Music Biz," "In Music Industry All Signs Are Bad," "Stores Stop the Music: Mounting Losses Force Mass Closings," "Lloyd Webber's Last Act?," might suggest that New York City is not the mecca for music writers that it once was.

Take Broadway, please. Now that Andrew Lloyd Webber's English operettas seem to be losing a grip on their charmed lives, it is hard to imagine what all those magnificent theaters are going to be filled with. Daytime talk shows? Late-night talk shows? Dance and supper clubs, casinos and churches? How about an "All Revival Broadway"? The music or drama major who steps off the plane at La Guardia even slightly wet behind the ears imagining a steady, fun-filled educational journey from workshop to Off-Broadway, to the stage of the Nederlander Theatre and fantasizing that this should only take three years or so (if that long) had better bring plenty of Daddy's money.

What the starry-eyed hopeful will find instead is a wasteland populated by only half a dozen well-known book writers, perhaps half that many marketable directors and choreographers, and an unknown number of terrified producers-in-hiding trying to figure out what to do next. Of investors not much has been heard lately. Scientists are beginning to quietly circulate the theory that they have become extinct. This is dark humor and not very funny, but it is ludicrous to see the Tony Awards committee trying to decide which among the season's two original musicals is "the best"; a community of critics who can't seem to grasp the concept that when the last show closes for good, there won't be anything left to review; or a coalition of unions tightening their grips around the long, thin neck of the gorgeous swan that sang the golden songs even as she musters her last quavering note.

Will a rank newcomer and outsider find a warm welcome in this cynical and almost panic-stricken community? Might he or she hope for a nurturing and guiding fraternity of mentors, philanthropists and other Good Samaritans? We-e-e-ll, the performing rights societies have always provided workshop formats for beginners in an attempt to bridge the gap between college theatrical departments and professional opportunity. BMI's Lehman Engel Musical Theatre Workshop is one of the most ambitious programs in the country. Mr. Engel was a veteran of the musical theatre and this extraordinarily knowledgeable man directed the organization until his death in 1982. The program requires that applications be submitted each year by an August 1 deadline. Omitting for the moment some of the details—certain compositions are submitted on cassettes as well as lyrics, and there are different categories for composer/lyricist or composer and lyricist alone—there are auditions and composers are required to perform or recite, etc. The first year consists essentially of a training program wherein composers and lyricists are often given partners and asked to create specific songs for scenes from various sources. Pure book writers study the subtleties of the libretto. There is much discussion and analysis. During the second year partnerships are formed to work on actual musicals with lots of criticism and group discussion, etc. Exceptional students may be asked to join an advanced workshop; there are no restrictions on memberships and no fees. (Applications should be made in writing to BMI, 320 West 57th Street, New York, NY 10019; 212-830-2515.)

ASCAP has two workshop classes devoted to musical theatre, both run by Stephen Schwartz:

We do have some super-luminaries among our alumni, including Jonathan Larson (*Rent*) and Doug Cohen (*No Way to Treat a Lady*), but our success rate depends a great deal on what standard you go by.

Schwartz emphasizes that there is a much larger percentage of graduates who go on to a "small production here or there," but as part of the process—and most importantly—gain immeasurably in terms of "process, mores, manners, connections, and entrees into the community." Finally Schwartz admits:

> We unabashedly provide special help for those we deem to be unusually talented, and a lot of what we pride ourselves on is a kind of "post-graduate" or "job-placement" service for people who are no longer with us.

The New York workshop has been in existence for some time while the West Coast version (located on the Disney lot) is only two years old at the time of this writing. There are annual workshops, each approximately two months long, and these are free of charge with no special requirements. Applicants mail in a cassette of four songs from one specific musical that they're working on, a copy of lyrics for each song, a brief outline of the show and a brief bio with their name and address. Schwartz and a panel of celebrated theatrical lights including Stephen Sondheim judge the works in progress. A spokesman at ASCAP told me that many wannabe writers and composers are helped enormously by simply auditing these classes. (Details can be obtained by writing ASCAP, Musical Theatre Workshops, I Lincoln Plaza, New York, NY 10023.)

When I first arrived in the city with my well-polished Grammy Awards and gold records, I figured it could only be a month or two before I would be "hired" to write a score for some terrific producer or what-have-you (this in spite of the fact that I knew good songwriters such as Lambert and Potter—"Rhinestone Cowboy"—who had gone east in a blaze of publicity only to return to California quietly and under the cover of darkness). After a few months of floundering, frankly perplexed that my obvious talents had not been seized upon by David Merrick, I determined that the best way to get into this "musical" racket (how hard could it be?) was just to write one. The first idea that blew through my head was to write a musical about

Tuxedo, New York, my place of residence, and specifically about its founder, Pierre Lorillard. I hired a researcher, hunched my shoulders over the grand piano and proceeded to create the book, music and lyrics. (I even did little drawings of the stage sets!) When I played the songs for my neighbors, they thought they were just wonderful. By the by, the libretto was sort of a Horatio Alger Becomes Jay Gatsby by way of *Gone With the Wind*, if you get my drift. No one else did. The producers of *Nine* came to the house most enthusiastically to collect the script, but quickly sent it back via regular U.S. mail. Thus began my great and continuing search for a writer—a "book writer" mind you—the most important yet least paid and recognized person on Broadway. Book writers are always busy, they are likewise inevitably excited about one's subject matter, but they hardly ever write a word until a production is capitalized. It was while searching for one of these rare and highly strung creatures that I happened to speak with David Geffen and mentioned that I had been struggling with the theatre for two years to little or no avail, and before you could say "Schubert," I was sitting in Amagansett beside a kidney-shaped swimming pool talking to Michael Bennett. I left with two scripts ("books") in my hand. I moved into Michael's building and was settled into an office next door to his. Our musical, *Scandal*, with Treat Williams and Swoosie Kurtz (written by Treva Silverman), went all the way through the workshop process, was beautifully choreographed and directed by Michael, while spectacular sets were constructed by Robin Wagner, and was one week from dress and technical rehearsals at the Mark Hellinger Theatre when the ax fell. The hundred-and-fifty-some-odd people who were working in the show recall the day as "Black Monday." There were a lot of reasons. Most of them were none of my business and therefore, probably none of yours. On the surface, AIDS had made the cover of *Time* magazine and the musical was a hilariously orgiastic tour de force if not an endorsement of slapstick promiscuity. On the surface, Michael had developed a heart condition. On the surface, there were serious creative differences between many of the principal contributors. But when a show closes before it opens the surface reasons don't begin to expose the appalling degree of heartwreck behind the scenes. My first experience on Broadway had literally been a showstopper. I went to Tahiti—unadulterated escapism admittedly—but when I flew home to New York and walked down the ramp at JFK, it hit again hard, as though someone had dropped the entire Helen Hayes Theatre on me. The only person who ever made me smile about the debacle, Robby Lantz, said, "It could have been worse . . . it could have opened." The moral to this somewhat depressing tale is that on Broadway there is no longer any cut-and-dried way of doing anything. While I was moping around and grieving over *Scandal*, my good friend and fellow Oklahoman Roger Miller rafted quietly into town with *Big River* and a few weeks later sailed away triumphantly holding every Tony that wasn't nailed down. Much of what finds its way to Broadway in this day and age isn't conceived and developed there. The shows are born and come of age in unlikely places like Nashville, Palm Beach, Tulsa, Toronto or Duke University. It is as though the city has become an overly hostile environment for a fetal idea in all its vulnerable innocence to survive. I talked to Mac Pirkle, artistic director of the Tennessee Repertory Theatre, about a local music writer's chances in a regional theatre company.

If somebody already has a collaborator, and they come to me and our theatre, yes, they can get started in Nashville. For me everything depends on the material. Like most of the other programs that concentrate on developmental processes for writers based on original material, reactions are very subjective. Something I might love in terms of subject material, the brilliance I might see . . . Paulette Haupt who runs the musical theatre program at the O'Neill might not see. Or the person at the New Harmony Project in New Harmony, Indiana, might see something totally different. Same thing with the New Musical Project, which is a consortium of three theatres: the Ordway Music Theatre in St. Paul, Theatre Under the Stars in Houston, and the Fifth Avenue Music Theatre in Seattle. They have about a hundred fifty thousand dollars a year earmarked to develop new writers and new musicals. Part of our mission is to identify not only new, but also established writers who are working on new pieces. These kinds of programs take a little probing and quite a lot of incentive on the part of the writer. Even assuming that the material is worthy of respect and deserves a real shot, there's a lot of legwork for the neophyte. The theatre world has its own little membership, rituals, mores and etiquette, none of which is written down. Developmental money on the commercial side is very different than what I do, because we're on the nonprofit side. Independent producers like

Margo Lyon and Elizabeth Williams are looking for people, and there are going to be some programs from the larger producers like the Shuberts who are looking for commercial hits and are going to try to find the writers who can do it. When you come to a company like mine, though, it's more of a process that starts with me and the tapes, boxes and boxes of tapes and books (scripts). Some people submit the classic tape of the composer sitting at the piano and singing (with a tape recorder) through the music, but generally speaking, the demos are becoming rather impressive. I will know if I like it after fifteen minutes with the book and three or four songs. Here's an example of something that just came over the transom, so to speak, just came out of nowhere. *Battleship Potemkin* actually lay on my couch for at least six months because we're a small operation. (I try to warn people, "If you think you're gonna send something to me and get a two-page feedback on what I liked in two weeks, it's just not gonna happen.") And I said to myself, "You know? This is pretty intriguing," because it was an opera, it was through-composed, and it was the Russian Revolution, I mean, my God! What American writer is writing about the Russian Revolution?! I called the agent and I just said, "You know, I'm kind of intrigued by this, where are you in the process? Has it ever been produced?" One of the writers was in New York, and one was in L.A. Neither Eric Allaman, who has scored some movies and television productions, nor Jeffrey Couchman, the librettist, have a huge music theatre reputation by any means. They said, "This sounds pretty far out . . ." and I said, "If you're willing, we'll give you a spot at camp." [Mac Pirkle does a summer camp in Tennessee every year where he workshops a number of projects.] They came back to camp a second time and then they were part of our Musical Notes Workshop in January. Since then they've gotten other offers. They're on their own journey now to see if they can do a full production. It is a complex process when your bread is being buttered by another full-time job.

What remains of the Great White Way are the glorious theatres, the cachet, the bright lights and the big money or what is left of it. John Bucchino is a brilliant young composer/lyricist who is dedicated to the theatre, reasonably well connected and whose exquisitely crafted songs are frequently recorded:

Four and a half years ago I was living in Los Angeles and wanted to be a pop writer, in fact I thought it would be easy. But it really wasn't. I guess you could say I came to New York looking for a place where my work would fit in. It was here that I found out I wrote theatrically. People like Stephen Schwartz, Stephen Sondheim and others heard my songs and encouraged me to move toward the theatre. I was a piano accompanist at the time with a political singer Holly Near, and I found out that cabaret is a very real link to Broadway. In fact, it's almost the next best thing. If your songs are appreciated in the cabaret environment, word gets around, people begin to come in to listen and your reputation as a potential Broadway writer begins to be established. If someone expresses interest in me and my work, any interest at all, I give them a tape right away. Perhaps I'm careless in this, and there have been times when I've passed out uncopyrighted material, but I have discovered that people in the music theatre world are looking for new talent to nurture. I left a tape for Stephen Sondheim at the Director's Guild after a panel discussion and, lo and behold, he called me back! He of course is very close with Mr. and Mrs. Hal Prince who I met through Hal's daughter, Daisy, and I feel that a lot of what I do is to build a network of converts, preferably important people who know of me and will recommend my work to others. Hal is also someone who encourages new talent. For instance, he has been known to take young director-hopefuls into an internship. Now let me stress something: You have to be good. You have to have your craft together in order for someone of this caliber to disrupt their personal life to show an interest in you. As for me, it's finally coming together. I have a project called *Urban Myths,* with book by James Waedekin which looks like it's going to happen Off-Broadway. All the theatre companies and production organizations are looking for exciting new materials . . . the frustrating thing for everyone is that Broadway shows have to be huge! They have to be "titanic" in scale. And oftentimes it is the very size of the production that causes it to fail. There doesn't seem to be any market for the middle-sized Broadway show. But I'm very happy to write the inward personal things. [Author's update: *Urban Myths* premiered in Wichita in February '98; John is currently working on songs for an animated film for Dreamworks.]

Adam Guettel is thirty-two years old and has already won the coveted Stephen Sondheim Award from American Music Theatre Festival in Philadelphia, a circumstance which resulted in a commission and eventually the production of his highly praised *Floyd Collins*. He also happens to be the grandson of Richard Rodgers.

Because of *that*, musical theatre was really the last thing I wanted to do. I always admired him and was proud of him and respected what he had done, but not until I started doing it myself did I truly understand what he had accomplished. The fact is, I didn't know him terribly well, though I remember him as a very warm grandfather. I still hold on to those initial misgivings about the theatre. I believe musical theatre today is marginalized and deservedly ridiculed. In the last thirty years—with some prominent exceptions—there really haven't been many works of merit. Where are the pieces that resonate socially? (I'm not talking about Clifford Odets.) There are four or five pieces from Stephen Sondheim—well, I would put *Sweeney Todd* at the top of the list, and then *Sunday in the Park*, of course *Pacific Overtures* . . . *Company* is an incredible score. I try not to imitate them.

My first instrument was piano. I was a music major at Yale and I hated it, but had one good teacher. Before that I was a professional boy soprano when I was ten to thirteen. *Floyd Collins* is based in large part on things I am able to do with my voice. I am a words and music guy but lyrics are increasingly difficult. I have one eye towards finding a partner because I'm aware that [lyric writing] is another discipline and I don't have the same innate gifts.

I've gotten some terrific advice, I think, first and foremost from my mother [composer Mary Rodgers], as she was very direct about what was good and bad and knew much about line and economy. I'm in a very special situation because I have money to live on, and I'm blessed by that circumstance to be able to pursue those projects that really mean something to me, the ones that give me a "hot response." I have friends who take all kinds of jobs to support their writing— I'm very lucky.

Years roll by disguising one's own almost imperceptible inertia when working on a Broadway show. Children are born and their elders perish. Musical styles change, burning political issues cool and become yesterday's causes célèbres, slang is invented and discarded, child actors mature and outgrow their comfy juvenile parts and with the regularity of the changing windows at Bloomingdale's, the cast of mannequins rotate, old power wanes, but few wunderkinds ascend and astonish while theatres are closed and torn down. In this continuum, one cannot work quickly enough or make decisions with too much alacrity. Succeeding in this genre is much about the smooth use of power and an unaffected social ease. The iconoclast, no matter how brilliantly gifted, will not fare well.

The Players please.

The Producer: This person or persons is supposed to have the wherewithal to secure the underlying rights in a case where the musical is based on a preexisting play or other scenario. He or she is additionally hoped to possess the diplomatic skills and professional clout necessary to organize a competent team and ensure that the creative aspects of the show are completed successfully. When it is time to open the show in addition to engaging a theatre the Producer(s) must "produce" enough cold cash to meet the staggering costs of the opening including publicity, and must even have reserves in hand should reviews be lukewarm so that the production can be "kept open" for a few days or weeks. (Until, hopefully, it creates its own audience by word of mouth.) Finally the Producer is supposed to possess the business acumen necessary to manage the show on a firm economic foundation through its entire run.

Investors: Most Broadway shows are financed by more than one entity. These Investors (once called "angels") can be from any walk of life with varying stakes in the show from as little as five thousand to five hundred thousand dollars. Except in highly exotic and almost unheard of circumstances, investors have zilch to say about what goes on. The limit of their influence is usually defined by their dibs on the house seats. They recoup their investment if and when the show goes into profit and begins to pay dividends.

The Director: This person is responsible for the interpretations of the actors onstage, the selection of the proper musical material along with the "look" of the production, its ambiance, the casting of the parts and to some degree, the style of the costumes and sets. All the major artistic decisions are made by the Director provided he does not lose a fight with the Producer. The Director will in most cases be intimately involved with the creative team from the very outset and is often paid a royalty for artistic contributions made during this phase. Historically the Director has often functioned as the show's choreographer as well. (Michael Bennett, Bob Fosse, Tommy Tune, Gower Champion, etc.)

The Choreographer: Choreographers exert a powerful creative influence over the "look," style and ambiance of any show. He or she is an integral part of the creative team and may even receive a royalty as a result. This person will not only design the dance routines and body language but will, on occasion, steer the Director, Book Writer and Composer in the proper direction when it comes to presenting the human body most effectively on stage. There will almost always be a powerful and significant interaction between the Choreographer and the costume and lighting designers.

The Composer: Very rarely is any money paid "up front" to a composer writing a Broadway show. When money is wrung from a producer for an advance the amounts are usually so modest as to not remotely begin to reimburse the poor fellow for the hundreds of hours he will spend in collaboration with each and all of the show's principal contributors. I have heard the writing of music for Broadway shows described as a "tedious hobby." The Composer can only complete the music with the unanimous approval of his partners. In some cases he will write the lyrics as well. His is a strong royalty position.

The Lyricist:	One might as well say that writing lyrics for a Broadway show stands completely apart from any other lyric writing. The Lyricist serves the book and its characters only. There is a sophistication, a deft narrative knack and an expansive vocabulary both literally and emotionally that is missing from most other pop writing. Often the Lyricist will be asked to take whole pages of dialogue and distill them into a few well-chosen lines that cover the same dramatic distance. The job of Lyricist is at least the second most important in a show. Poorly crafted lyrics have been the Achilles' heel of many a pristinely mounted and hellishly expensive production. His or her royalty position is strong.
The Book Writer:	The Book Writer can hardly be blamed for resenting a composer who handles both music and lyrics as this leaves him with only a third of the pie. Book Writers have been known to lyricize and since their prose is frequently boiled down to a few succinct lyrics, they have also been known to negotiate themselves a few extra points from the Composer and Lyricist. Without a doubt the most important member of the creative team is the Book Writer. Observe carefully the elegant economy of the little scenes that piece together *The Sound of Music* (book by Howard Lindsay and Russel Crouse) or *My Fair Lady* (book by Alan Jay Lerner) and think how easily either show could have been ruined by a verbose or clumsy misstep. When the Book Writer is doing his job well, his presence is invisible and the Stars are allowed to shine.

It has occurred to me recently that the only thing separating you or me or the bandleader at the local high school from an opening on Broadway is money. One does not need any special pedigree to stage a production in

New York. To my knowledge there is no examination that one need pass or license required that entitles one to hire the small army of actors, singers, dancers, set designers, stage managers and hands, costumers, choreographers, musicians and orchestrators that make up a tantalizing hors d'oeuvre for critic Clive Barnes. It's just money. To put it simply: If you've got the *talent* and someone will give you the *money*, you don't need this book or John Simon or anything else except a crackerjack creative team. For instance, old timers were skeptical when the Disney organization came to town with the unconventional idea of adapting existing animated features into stage productions. Lynn Ahrens commented, "I'd hate to think that anything is doomed because of what it is derived from. I think it has to do with each individual piece of writing, and of theatre. Each piece of work has to stand alone on its own merits because a theatre piece is a unity of all kinds of elements from design to music to acting to costumes. Nothing stands alone." Stephen Flaherty adds, "I personally believe that *The Lion King* musical became stronger than the animated film by going back to the original roots of African storytelling and 'call and response.'" The Disney stage productions have been runaway financial phenomena. Norman Rothstein, a successful producer and general manager, describes the "deal":

> Generally speaking, (with *great* variation) a typical Broadway show's financial structure is a "two/two/two" situation with each of the three categories (composer, lyricist and book writer) receiving two percent of the gross on a weekly basis. As start-up costs are colossal sums, the producer needs to scale and price tickets accordingly so that (by way of example) the show can gross at least a half million dollars a week to offset weekly operating expense and yield (one hopes) a profit. Total percentage royalties include royalties to director, choreographer, orchestrators, arrangers, designers, etc. and can easily reach 12 to 20 percent of the gross receipts. Were a production to gross (for example) $800,000 weekly, the weekly royalty cost would range from $96,000 to $160,000—sums likely to "cripple" a production. As a consequence, there has been devised a royalty pool which establishes a relationship of interest between all the creative royalty recipients (author, directors, choreographers, designers, etc.) and the actual operating expenses calculated against the actual gross receipts whereby

the surplus (if any) of gross receipts above operating expenses will be divided among the parties in lieu of actual percentage royalty.

It would be in the express interest of a "new" song writer to negotiate as high a percentage royalty as possible because (in the event of a pool) his share of the pool would be greater. Pools are normally structured so that a fixed dollar value per percentage point is agreed to and paid as a weekly guarantee. Obviously, the greater the percentage, the higher fixed dollar value. Further, the interest of an individual royalty recipient is calculated by dividing his individual percentage amount by the total number of all individual percentage points in the pool. Once again, the greater the individual percentage, the higher the share.

Another musical empire makes its headquarters and carries on its endless intrigues along these same rows of monolithic buildings and it too attracts its fair share of pretenders and dreamers, modern-day prospectors hard on the heels of easy-money myths and urban folklorish tales of quick advancement. This would be the advertising industry. There are two components in the complicated world of advertising that concern the composer directly: the "jingle house" and the ad agency. There are probably a dozen top jingle houses in Manhattan, like Chris Crushing Enterprises, JSM, Three Three and Look & Co, that handle ninety percent of the business at the largest of the ad agencies, small bureaucracies like J. Walter Thompson, Ogilvy & Mather, DDB Needham, BBD&O, Young & Rubicam, Chiat Day, Omnicom Group, Inc., and Bocell Worldwide, Inc.

Fairy tales told around campfires portray the ad industry as a land of milk and honey for the enterprising and clever composer. (I deliberately use the word *composer* because rarely, if ever, does an ad agency seek outside help for "lyric" writing.) These stories are inspired by the handful of jingle writers who have scored with huge national campaigns such as the "It's the Real Thing" Coca-Cola pitch that ran for the better part of a decade. Another, almost mythic success was the "You deserve a break today" ditty which Barry Manilow penned for McDonald's. Wide-eyed, the raconteur describes the million and a half dollars per year earned for merely writing "thirty seconds of music." The familiar phrase will almost always recur: "How hard could it be?"

Now for the difficulties: Ad agencies do not strike up relationships with composers who walk in off the street. I've tried this myself and believe me, they respect my accomplishments and treat me most courteously but nothing ever comes of it. This is because the big agencies have what amounts to fiduciary relationships with their favorite jingle house or houses. When the proverbial push comes to the metaphorical shove, they will go to the people with whom they share a track record, however patchy. Mind you, if General Motors tells Ogilvy & Mather, "We like Webb. We like this new song off his album," then the agency will almost certainly come after me, but even then, the initial contact might be made by their favorite jingle house. Here are the Players:

The Client:	This is the company that manufactures the product—could be soap, medicine, automobiles or exercise equipment. The Client is God because they have the most money. They don't have to make musical sense but can be surprisingly specific about what they don't want to hear. It is common for them to have "fine arts" executives on staff to advise them on aesthetic matters, particularly if they are oil men or if they manufacture machine tools or fishing gear. They hire . . .
The Agency:	This is a gray-flannel suit factory, a bunch of people sharing office space under the same roof and competing with each other and other agencies for power, prestige and money. Unless they have recently acquired the client, they have probably dealt with the same company for a number of years. Their creative staff (fine arts executives) will come up with the "pitch," the storyboards, "lyrics" (they insist on calling them "copy") and a handful of musical concepts. These are the guys who can get tears in their eyes telling you about a new name they've come up with for a douche. They hire . . .
The Jingle House:	A suite of offices surrounding a state-of-the art recording studio or studios inhabited by a few hollow-eyed key board junkies (probably six or eight) under the supervision of a leader/owner or two with houses in Connecticut or Long Island

and better than average golf clubs. After the
Agency sends over the new "douche" campaign,
two or three of these "in-house" composers will
start trying to bang out a catchy (unforgettable,
hummable, clever) tune to a set of falsely rhymed,
grammatically indefensible "lyrics" that would
gag the guy who wrote "There's a Town in France."

The last act of this drama is always a horse race. The jingle house (or
the agency) can and will swear vertically and horizontally that you are the
only hollow-eyed wretch working on their commercial, but they speak
with forked tongue. There are always five or six different composers working on the same sales pitch. This is in case the "waterfall" theme doesn't
wash in the big client/agency "douche" meeting they can fall back on your
rip-off of Harry Nilsson's "(Put Da Lime in Da) Coconut" (© 1972
Blackwood Music, Inc.).

Let's assume the newly arrived sixty-second maestro has come hard on
the backstretch and been selected as the big winner. Part of his fee will
always go to the jingle house. The fee will always be a *buy-out*. Composers
are not paid for broadcast performances of television or radio commercials. This means the agency will pay you one time and you will sign a
paper swearing that you won't annoy them anymore, even if they play your
music on television for the next fifty years, even if somebody writes a good
lyric to it and it bubbles onto the *Billboard* Top 100, even if they finally get
tired of those ridiculous skips in the "Star-Spangled Banner" and make
your music the new national anthem.

Frank Di Minno, executive producer of No Soap Productions, had
this to say about advertising fees for composers:

The situation with jingle houses is not a straight percentage as it
would be with an agent. There are some established music houses
which have exclusive composers/arrangers on the payroll. However,
they hire "freelancers" if the workload is too heavy or the project is in
a form (for instance, jazz, rap or classical) that is outside their specialty. When this happens, the arranging fees and other payments are
usually split sixty-forty in favor of the company, naturally, or fifty-
fifty although it can be as disparate as seventy-five–twenty-five.

Many new music houses [jingle houses] are one-man shows with the producer doubling and tripling as the musician and vocalist.

There are fears that this might bring the advertising music industry as we know it to an end since buy-outs undercut union musicians.

The trick, you see, is to sing on the commercial. People who sing on big national commercials get rich. It is amusing sometimes to observe a composer standing amid a choir of nightingales, mockingbirds, canaries and thrushes, opening and closing his mouth like a confused crow with nary a note issuing and the client and the agency rep standing there beaming, tapping their feet and patting each other on the back.

We were doing this one afternoon (I was playing the part of the confused crow) when the agency rep came breathlessly rushing in fully a half hour late. He apologized profusely. It seems he had been recording toilet flushes at another studio—trying to get that exact—well, he began to describe all the different sounds. Some toilet flushes, well, they just sound *indelicate*, you know? It's hard to chance upon that Golden Pond, Disney-esque, Hygienically Acceptable Flush if you know what I mean. (Michael Feinstein says that according to Robert Montgomery, trustee of the Cole Porter estate, "by oversight a Porter song was once licensed to the maker of a toilet bowl cleaner with the lyric *'I've got you under my rim.'*")

Things are a bit different nowadays. Agency reps peer at you sagely and whisper in hushed mysterious tones of "sound design." To hear them tell it, a lot of the cutting-edge crop of commercials are done by "sound designers." I've never met one of those but I'm assuming it's just another hollow-eyed ink-stained keyboard geek living with a bathtub in their kitchen and not making enough money. *Someone will just have to explain* the difference between "background music," "sound design" and "underscore." Film and TV composer Irwin Fisch:

> Sound designers? Well, there's a real division in the business between song-type jingles (pieces with lyrics and vocals) and underscore. And it's more skewed now than ever toward score as opposed to songs. There are a lot of reasons for that; one is that the idea of singing about a product has become anachronistic in our culture and hokey to some people. The creative decisions at the agencies are being made by a younger, ostensibly "hipper" crowd, no longer the baby boomers for the most part.

There used to be underscore which was musical in the traditional sense; *the notion of sound design is this contemporary thing—the merging of musical content and sound effects; either the sound effects are used musically, or music is used as effect, or some combination of both.* [my italics] They want something that is inextricably wedded to the editing style of the picture. It usually speaks more to the surface of the visuals than to emotion or subtext. They needed a label to throw on it; in the interest of being contemporary, people began saying, "I don't want a score, I want a *sound design.*"

How many ads have I worked on? My guess would be a couple of thousand . . . in different capacities; initially as a player, and then people started saying, "Can you arrange?" and I said—completely lying—"Of course I can." Then after arranging for awhile, clients started tossing scripts and storyboards in front of me, saying, "Why don't you try writing on this?" And eventually I found out that where there used to be a line of work called "arranging," there's little call for it in the ad business anymore. That's because writers pretty much do it for themselves. So, you become a writer by default, whether you have the aptitude or not. That's where the path leads . . . it's less specialized. There are still cases where they need to get somebody with traditional orchestration skills, but usually—because of the technology having taken over and the capacity of anybody in their living room with a synthesizer to do something that sounds like the radio—the production and writing have become merged. And, just as in other areas of the business, people are expected to be able to realize their own material.

Overall I think there's a lot less work [available]; there are fewer commercials with music being produced. It's also a lot less New York–centric. And unfortunately—because I'm affiliated with a big jingle house—it's gotten to be more of a cottage industry where anybody with a synth can do the work. There's also more licensing of existing music—such as old records—for new commercials.

The big agencies still give out the work although I don't have much awareness of them. If you're a writer working through a jingle house, you get to be insulated a little bit from that particular politic—the good part of insulation is that you get to focus on the music more. The bad part is that if you're working for a jingle house and insulated, you don't develop the direct contact that would some-day enable you to go out and steal their client.

They bill a creative fee for a song which is anywhere from five to thirty thousand dollars for some little regional thing to more for a car campaign . . . Then they bill an arranging fee between three to five thousand dollars for a spot, and then they give the person who actu-ally does the work between a third and a half of that.

My Song of the Year, "Up, Up and Away" (1967), was one of the first "hit" songs that ever found its way off the pop charts and into a television ad campaign. Jerry Della Femina wrote about those prehistoric times in a book called *From Those Wonderful Folks Who Gave You Pearl Harbor* (Simon & Schuster):

> Long about then, a skinny kid named [Jimmy] Webb with a lot of hair was out on the West Coast starting out as a songwriter. If this kid knew what chaos he caused in New York, he'd break up. One of the songs he wrote was called, "Up, Up and Away" and it's got lines in it like "[would] you like to fly in my beautiful balloon?", and stuff like that. Well, a chase develops for the commercial rights to this song . . . the in-fighting over that song! Also, word leaked out that TWA hated their current song and this one seemed ideal. Anyhow Foote, Cone somehow latched on to it but as soon as the others [competing agencies] heard that Foote, Cone had a song, then every-one else had to have a song.

The situation inspired some confusion. When I first met Barbra Streisand she asked me if I was "the guy who made a hit song out of that commercial?" The artsy-craftsy-songs-are-politics crowd really got on my case. I had "sold out to the establishment," and so forth, even though when I think back it didn't seem quite that earthshaking. Perhaps out of ignorance I perceived no moral dilemma, not then or even when I was writing Chevrolet commercials and being reimbursed annually with a brand-new silver and totally loaded Corvette. In spite of an occasional groan from the back rows ("This Note's for You," Neil Young, ©1988 Silver Fiddle), pop music and rock 'n' roll have—in the years since I com-mitted my little sociocultural boo-boo—become fair game for the big advertisers as catalogs have been sold out from under their original owners and creators, which is why not long ago we heard John Lennon singing "Revolution" accompanying a spiel for Nike tennis shoes. (You can thank Michael Jackson for that.) The source of the real "easy money" in the ad business is in selling the old horses to the glue factory. But writing jingles is an exacting and tedious discipline. Even more so than in songwriting per se there is an electron microscope focused on every note and chord. More money is spent arranging, performing and recording a thirty-second spot than most recording artists spend on their whole album. Give honor to the jingle writer when you hear one of those deceptively simple yet annoyingly unforgettable petite airs. Think of the pressure-driven atmosphere where it was created and the difficulty one has in verbally communicating musical ideas to people who, for the most part, know best what they don't want.

The original Tin Pan Alley, the alley itself, was probably behind a row of townhouses on West Twenty-eighth Street—houses that had been abandoned by families one by one as post–turn-of-the-century publishing houses encroached on the neighborhood with their "questionable" clientele (black folks and musicians) and their clanging and tintinnabulating tack pianos, hence "Tin Pan." Not even echoes of those competing keyboards remain along Twenty-eighth Street today although if you walk in front of the Baudouine Building at 1181 Broadway and close your eyes real tight, it is easy to imagine what a contrapuntal Charles Ivesian nightmare of conflicting musical opinion this might well have been. This street once sweetened by love songs and contaminated by silly novelty numbers drifting from balcony to fire escape is now perfumed by stall after stall of exotic flowers and small stores dealing colognes, bath oils and other fragrances. Today's pop music business has moved uptown, and upstairs. Part of it resides in a towering spaceship at 1290 Sixth Avenue in the very heart of the city. Longtime friend John Titta (senior vice-president, creative services, for Warner-Chappell Music) spoke to me recently about newcomers and their chances.

> Here at Warner-Chappell we have eight to ten pure writers and another thirty writers who we've signed in view of cultivating record deals. In the latter case, I'll give you an example, I signed a girl here four years ago and brought her along, got her a couple of significant covers and recently a deal at Sony Records. We literally construct a career.

As far as our policy on co-publishing is concerned, most of the time when a writer comes to us with significant covers or say they've already had a hit record of their own, whatever, we will do a co-publishing deal. Recently I made a deal with a couple of guys from a band that was a little bit over the hill and some of the guys, I won't mention any names, said, "Hey, don't you kind of think you missed the boat on that one?" And it really made me mad, I mean, hey, these guys were good songwriters, they are good songwriters, they're always gonna be good songwriters, and I think we should make them a good deal. Six months later we had a big smash with Joan Osborne. To get to our eight or ten pure writers we literally listen to hundreds of tapes, that is, me and about four others. I have a bag of tapes in my car all the time. I will always listen to the first song. Whether I listen to the second song or not, or the third song, that's up to the writer. If I was a young writer getting off the bus at the Port Authority at New York City for the first time, I would go straight to ASCAP, BMI or SESAC. They will supply connections to people like me. They have no interest in ripping anyone off. They provide seminars, panels, conventions and consultation virtually free of charge to the novice.

I'm from the old Tin Pan Alley school. We have two writing rooms at Warner-Chappell, one called the Jule Styne room and one called the Sammy Cahn room. A lyricist and a music writer, you know? It's such a great atmosphere in there, with guys coming and going all the time, and it gives me such a great feeling to put a couple of guys together and hear them write a great song.

The songwriter fledgling can sit outside one of the sidewalk cafes adjacent to ASCAP at One Lincoln Plaza and gaze in a daydream at Lincoln Center's Avery Fisher Hall just across the way. Nowhere else in New York City is he or she more likely to be surrounded by birds of a feather like Lindy Robbins:

My contact with Rodgers and Hammerstein I made through a friend who was related to someone at the company, but truthfully, it wasn't any kind of nepotism. I sent in my tape to the appropriate person, just for evaluation. I thought, "Hey you know, the worst I'll get out of this is some helpful advice." Well, the lady just went crazy for my tape which contained about six songs and all of a sudden I was looking for an attorney to help me negotiate a deal. Believe it or not one of the attorneys I talked to wanted ten percent of my publishing to make the deal and I thought, wait a minute there's just something wrong with this. Anyway, through another attorney I ended up with a three-year writing deal, a fifty-fifty deal meaning that we shared the publishing equally and it was a *step deal*. [Meaning if the writer is successful, a greater amount of money is paid each time the option is renewed.] Three substantial figures in the five-figure range. I also had a neat clause in my contract called a reversion clause which means that if they don't "get records" [if they don't place it with a major recording artist] the copyrights are returned to me, and I ended up paying about three thousand dollars for legal fees, which wasn't bad. We lasted about two years and I must have written at least forty songs but in the final analysis we were incompatible. Their only other unknown writer wrote grand opera and they weren't able to get me any cuts, even though they really did love and appreciate the music. At least they tried. I don't know of a writer in this town who has ever heard of a big publishing company who ever did anything for anybody. The only beginners I've ever heard of that are being signed by a major are writer/artists (with good looks), writer/producers or people who have gotten at least one big cut on their own. In my view it is fairly easy to negotiate a co-publishing deal in New York City: Nashville is the only place I know where it's almost unheard of—except for writers there with pop catalogs. [Note: Since the interview Lindy Robbins has moved to Los Angeles to try her chances. She is now co-writing with established songwriters and recently got a "cover" on an album by the group Kai on Geffen Records.]

The conventional publisher/songwriter relationship is alive and reasonably well in New York City, offering the young professional entry-level opportunity at the price of surrendering a share of the publishing. And now the Players.

The Publishers:	There are a score of huge publishing concerns in New York City, most of which have a staff assigned to listen to submitted tapes. Before concluding a deal the young writer should have an experienced entertainment attorney go over the technicalities in the contract.

The Performing Rights Societies:	ASCAP, BMI and SESAC may as well have been created when God created the heavens and the earth. Don't ask. They collect millions of dollars from countless "customers," restaurant operators, jukebox operators, radio stations, television networks, record manufacturers, Muzak, and just about any other business concern that uses music for any reason, and then pay the writers they represent an approximation of what is due them. They provide certain educational functions and limited support to inexperienced persons wishing to become songwriters.
The Composer & Lyricist:	Viable deals for "lyrics only" are in the realm of fantasy fiction. The Lyricist needs to be paired with a music writer. Sometimes the Publisher will arrange these relationships. The songwriter(s) delivers finished professional quality music and sometimes the Publisher pays for competent demos and goes after recordings.
The Artist:	It is difficult to penetrate the security barrier around most celebrities but not impossible. No promotional gimmickry in the world compares to an unforced and genuine friendship with a successful Recording Artist.
The Producer:	Record producers like Robert "Mutt" Lange, Jimmy Jam and Terry Louis, Sean "Puffy" Combs and Walter Afanasieff have at least a one-third vote on which song will be chosen to appear on a long player (the Artist and Label Chief will often split the other

	two-thirds votes). If the Producer is powerful and "on a roll" he or she may even have complete autonomy over the chosen songs.
The Label:	Because of the fragmentation of the radio station audience these days it is difficult or impossible for one record to be heard on enough stations to appeal to the wide cross-section a label needs in order to create a million seller. This has sliced the songwriting market into many smaller pieces of pie. Hopeful songwriters hardly ever make a physical appearance at record labels anymore, though labels do receive tons of unsolicited tapes and there are still some hearty souls like Jay Landers who try to listen to them all in hopes of finding another Lennon and McCartney. Most labels look to the big publishers to "screen" material and save them time.
Artist & Repertoire:	The label employs A&R people specifically to screen material for upcoming projects and sometimes to sign new acts. Obviously these are important people to know.

The view from the top versus the bottom of these big rocket-ship office buildings is strikingly different. It is interesting to note that sometimes acolytes who are native New Yorkers don't go near the big publishers but work doggedly in their own strata, retaining their own publishing and hoping to catch some lightning in a bottle. Jane Arginteanu pursues her own career as a writer/vocalist while working as assistant to a legendary songwriter:

> I've been a songwriter for twenty-six years but I was always behind the scenes. Usually in one band or another with other people performing my songs. Still, I have to say it was always a thrill. That was in the days of the Lone Star, Ritz, Tracks on Seventy-second Street . . . I've never had a publishing deal and only recently started getting my first tape together as a writer/vocalist. Yes, I work for one of the most successful songwriters in the business. Is that good or bad? Well

it's hard to find the time to pursue my goals sometimes but it's an advantage to be an insider, great to be able to meet such exciting people. I suppose the danger is that it's all too safe a place to have vicarious thrills . . . The part of my job I like the least is having to send back tapes to people who expected something wonderful to happen. I have sympathy for the sender. I can't decide whether to seriously sing my own songs or not . . . record deals seem to go to younger people and I'm not the confident type. I'm drawn to Nashville—like it or not it's true music. "Eighteen Wheels and a Dozen Roses" pretty much says it all. I'm making a country tape and Nashville beckons. I've always had shyness about being good enough, but now I'm ready to deal with my demons and teach them a lesson.

So what's the attraction down in Nashville? Songwriters have been drawn there from the bright lights of both coasts as though by a giant musical magnet for as many years as I've been in the business. During the '50s just across the alley from the Ryman Auditorium (the Grand Ole Opry) in Tootsie's Orchid Lounge songwriters like Willie Nelson and Hank Cochran would waylay Opry stars while they wetted their whistles between shows. I doubt if there's ever been a significant improvement on this direct and wily strategy. In other words, songwriters go to Nashville because that's where the stars are.

Henry Gross, hit songwriter and founder of Sha-Na-Na, came to Nashville from New York more than eleven years ago and sums it up this way:

> Here's the deal. All you have to do is show up with five great songs, by that I mean undeniable songs, and you'll get a publishing deal in Nashville. It won't pay much, maybe ten to fifteen thousand dollars a year to start, and that might be for all your publishing. People who dream of being songwriters will do anything they have to do to support themselves. Let me put it this way, everybody who ever painted my house was a songwriter.

Renowned former housepainter J. D. Souther has a different take:

> Here's the thing about Nashville—it's a company town, but it has *always* been a company town. As such, if you toe the line you have a better chance of getting a well-supported release. However, radio is

tending to fragment around it [the overall product] because too much of the stuff sounds the same. No wonder! There's only a dozen or so big-time producers in town, most of them writing songs, so they want to co-write the songs on the album. There are only a few guys (top musicians) who get hired for the "A" sessions, so, gee, it's no surprise the stuff sounds similar. The good side of that, if there is any, is reminiscient of that old axiom about the tree of democracy needing to be watered occasionally by the blood of patriots. The fact is that cracks are appearing in that wall, great music is seeping through. There's really strange, edgier material. I've heard everything in the last year from unique original ballads, other songs that sound more to me like early Celtic music, and gorgeous pop '50s country, that Patsy Cline sort of thing. I've even heard country thrash bands.

There has been a modern-day exodus from L.A. to Nashville that started in earnest in the mid '70s when session musicians like bassists Joe Osborne and David Hungate and blues legend Al Kooper made their moves culminating recently with the arrival of Michael McDonald, Neil Diamond, who stayed for a year, Bob Gaudio, who is a sometimes resident, Peter Cetera, who owns a home here, and so on. The city is a charmer with its folksy small-town ways and hilly forested surroundings. The weather is good by and large, save for a couple of desperately hot and humid summer months about which the locals say, "You get used to it." Still, over a period of years the regular visitor gets an impression of restless turnover. Faces appear and disappear and reappear among the songwriting community with the same ephemeral transience of dancers in Las Vegas or actors in Hollywood. On more than one occasion I have considered packing up my mule and moving down to Nashville, particularly after one of those visits when I've been loved back to life, hugged nearly to death, standing ovationed into a daze, fed into a stupor and flattered to sleep. Something always holds me back. It's the sensation that these visits are singular events and that this outpouring of Southern hospitality would not hold up if I moved in across the street and started mowing my own grass with my gut hanging out. Perhaps this attitude is terribly unfair and even cynical, but the amateur historian in me cannot forget what happened to Captain James Cook on the Big Island when the Hawaiians inadvertently discovered that he was not a god. [Note: Up until that time the islanders had never tasted white meat.]

Joyce Rice's accent is to the ear what honeysuckle is to the nostrils. After a successful career in banking where she saved many a songwriter's bacon, Joyce joined BMI as head of writer/publisher relations where she continues to dispense advice and hospitality to the weary and heavy-laden. She has her own views on Nashville's changing cast of characters.

I don't agree with what you're saying—I think that what happens is that the people who move here stay here and I think they're very happy with it. I know a lot of people who have come here to do projects and just didn't really get their roots in; they just did the project and left. They just wanted a little bit of the creative strength from Nashville, and they would come in and record, or use the producers or the studios to get a little bit of a different feel and after their project was over they'd go back home where their roots are. But I can't even think of anybody who came here and left except Mentor Williams and he went to Texas—but he's not one to stay in one place anyway! Oh, one person who didn't stay—and I don't know the situation—was Jimmy Buffett. I think he just missed Florida, being near the ocean and all. There are many people who have moved here from L.A. and made this their home . . . Bob Gaudio, Peter Frampton, Brett Michaels, Donna Summer, Michael McDonald, Kim Carnes, John Bettis, Luke Perry, Steve Winwood, John Hiatt, Adrian Belew, Gary Tallent, Larry Carlton, Bernie Leadon and John Kay of Steppenwolf. Katie Sagal, who played Peg Bundy on *Married With Children*, also writes. These are just some in the pop field; there are too many country stars and writers to mention. But even Buffett was here for a year or two . . .

When wannabe writers come to our front door we try to help them. We usually encourage them to go first to a roundtable service that we have, a two-hour session. We have it twice a month and we have these new writers attend in order to see what the music industry's all about, what a publisher does and what they should do to get their act together, and how to conduct themselves, and what a performing rights society does, what the labels do, what the publisher does, descriptions of all the important roles. We alternate the teaching responsibilities. I'm one of the executives, along with David Preston and Mark Mason and Thomas Kane. Usually about twenty-five or thirty writers attend, all ages, all nationalities, and from all over the United States. We have elderly people, very young people, students, men, women—it's just a big variety. What we're in the process of doing is putting together a workshop which will have two different levels, the roundtable for the first-time writer and the second level where there is a paid professional who knows who to critique and can tell more experienced writers how to compose and what's needed. This will be a three-hour session for mid-level writers.

When I ran the Music Industry Office for First American National Bank, based here in Nashville, most of the writers didn't know or care about business matters. At one time one of my customers, a well-known writer, depended on me for advice so much that he interrupted a meeting to ask *where* he should take his wife on vacation, not if he had the money to go. My assistant would put a sign on my desk when she saw him coming that said, "I'm not your mother." He loved it. Don't get me wrong, I loved that part of my job, especially being close to creative people. But it's amazing how the business has changed since then, and I think for the better. Today's songwriters really educate themselves to what's going on, from legislative issues to business matters, and they keep track of their own affairs. It seems they have learned some lessons from the people who went before them.

My advice to a new arrival would be to get a job to tide you over—you've got to want success so bad that you're willing to spend the time and effort to learn the business and make the contacts that will help you get where you want to go. Do not pay anyone any money—there are lots of demo and publishing schemes that are only designed to take your money. . . . This is an estimate, but a good professional quality demo with singers and everything should only cost in the neighborhood of $250. I see a lot of newcomers make their move too soon. . . . sometimes you only get to go through that door of opportunity one time, and if your material is not up to par, there's no second invitation.

You can hang around the 'ville for a long time waiting for a break. One time I was leaning up on my car by the gas pump waiting for the oldest little old man I'd ever seen to finish filling up my tank. He was making a career out of it. He looked up and focused one bright blue eye on me, the other busy with the task at hand.

"What's your business, young feller?"

I find it difficult to tell lies to my elders.

"Well, I dabble in the music business."

He thought about that as the pump rang merrily.

"How long you been dabblin'?"

This is my least favorite subject but I obliged him.

"Oh, twenty years or so."

He jerked the nozzle out of the tank and carefully began to wipe the spillage off my fender.

"I've been writing songs down here for . . . oh . . ." He stroked his grayed and weathered chin and then looked me straight in the eye. " . . . Oh, for about sixty-five years I 'spect."

He flashed me a near-toothless grin when I handed him a twenty and as I told him to keep the change he fished a greasy cassette out of the bib of his overalls and smacked it into my hand.

"Dabble on that, son," he laughed.

My good friend Tommy Riggs has been an institution in the Nashville nightlife scene for over a decade with his rich, Prysockian baritone and legendary sold-out shows at the Stockyard's Bullpen. Recently he left the stage to concentrate on his lifelong preoccupation with songwriting.

> Sometimes people move here and then they get scared because it's not "easy fast" and they leave. Then they realize they should have never left and they come back and stay. A lot of people come into this town and they're just blown away by the fact that there are some of the best writers in the world here . . . it's like salmon swimming upstream. It seems as though there are more salmon in the stream every year. It gets harder and harder to get cuts because you have to get past the artist's publishing company and all of his writers, and his producer and all of his writers, and the label and their writers, it's like a mine-field or an obstacle course, but still, just being part of the game is exciting.
>
> It doesn't really feel strange not to be in the club every night. I'm gonna be fifty-four this Tuesday. I really like just getting to write and

still staying plugged into music, it's kind of like I traded one high for another. When I realized the club thing was coming to an end, I went to Marty Gamblin [Glen Campbell Music Company] first because Marty and I have a co-publishing agreement on songs that I own with a partner, and he wanted very much to sign me but he had to justify it by hopefully getting me a cut or something, and he made me an offer of four demos and made the agreement that if I, in the meantime, found a publishing home, that all I had to do was just repay the demo cost. He wasn't able to get any cuts on those songs but it hooked me in with a new studio—Texana Sound—and I began to write with Barbie Isham, who just had her first hit record with a Leann Womack song called, "Never Again, Again." Then a gentleman I've known for a lot of years, a wealthy and honorable man who has been champing at the bit to get into the music business, hired me to produce all the demos for an artist that he manages, as well as produce demos for the songwriters at his company, Caption/ALV. Now he has connections with Mike Curb and you and I know how important connections are to helping a good song reach the bull's-eye. I'm very optimistic about the future—I think I've landed a song called "Love's Last Stand" with Reba McEntire. [Update: Tommy didn't get the Reba cut, but he co-wrote a song called "Not a Brick Out of Place" with Curt Ryle, which is to be the title track of a new film.]

Because of its tremendous expansion and popularity as a tourist spot Nashville has been demeaned by the flippant and unthinking as "Nash-vegas." The truth is that it remains our only citadel of pure songwriting. Our profession is respected there as it is in no other corner of the world, and Nashvillians demonstrate a wide appreciation of diverse writing styles and performers; however, the immigrant will find that most Nashville A&R men like their chords simple, their rhythm strong and two-steppy, and their sentiments conventional and to the point. A snappy title based on a cliché with a double entendre or pun repeated at the end of each cho-rus will still open doors.

I've basically given up trying to get a cover. All my hits by other artists have been because the artist knew me and came to me, having already found that hit song before I knew who they were. I know that people still get covers in Nashville but I'm not part of that community because I'm an artist and I'm on the road, and I'm not here for that everyday Music Row clique.

—Nanci Griffith

The Players, y'all:

Publishers:	Publishing houses are like the sands of the sea in Nashville. A good songwriter with several solid, finished works of brilliance should not have a lot of trouble signing a modest deal. It will be rather difficult for the first time professional to retain one hundred percent of publishing and still "get records."
Producers:	Producers like Tony Brown, James Stroud and Scott Hendricks are powerful godlike figures in Nashville. They can wave a magic wand over your song and make it appear on a top-of-the-line artist's album. Unfortunately, most producers have their own publishing companies and usually a favorite cadre of writers.
Artists:	Recording artists are probably friendlier and more accessible in Nashville than any other celebrities in popular culture. Top recording artists employ dozens if not scores of people in their publishing operations, studios and tour support. Some artists will be encountered who have only recently signed their first deal and are on the lookout for hot new writers and co-writers.
Labels:	Nashville labels are always looking for young, attractive singers, male and female, who write and co-write to sign to artists and publishing agreements. Vocal talent in country music has traditionally been

	stupendous; therefore, mediocre or uninteresting vocal chops will probably not fly.
Performing Rights Societies:	BMI, ASCAP and SESAC are at their most active in Nashville and an integral part of the community. There is essentially an open-door policy to all comers. (The Nashville Songwriters Association is one of the best outfits in the country.)
Live-Performance Venues:	The Bluebird is small and famous, Cafe Milano is new and not so famous. Others are 12th and Porter, Henry's Coffee House, Station Inn, Courtyard Cafe, Jack's Guitar Bar, the Fiddle and Steele Guitar Bar, etc.

Lucy's El Adobe Cafe sits across the street from Paramount Studios on Melrose Avenue in East Los Angeles. There used to be another restaurant directly across the street called Nickodell's with more things on the menu than Musso Franks. Ninety-three KHJ, the best damn radio station in Southern California, was next to Nickodell's and most of the time there were a couple of jocks, the real Don Steele or Ron Jacobs sitting in one restaurant or the other. I remember the first time I ever walked into Lucy's. It was 1965 and I had just done the Lloyd Thaxton Show with my all-girls group, the Contessas. We were looking for a reasonably priced meal. Instead we found a sweet slice of life as Lucy and Frank Casado not only dispensed the best chicken tacos and guacamole in the Southland but also love, friendship, encouragement, clothing and an occasional free meal to anybody with a guitar strung across their back. J. D. Souther will attest to this, as will Linda Ronstadt and Joni Mitchell and a hundred others. From Lucy's my stomping ground extended north along Gower some ten-odd blocks up to Sunset where I would make a left at the Columbia Cafe and walk down past RCA on the right to the corner of Sunset and Vine where Bob Ross—diminutive, goateed, grinning magician of a copyist—ran his publishing and recording operation out of an old white farmhouse, dwarfed by the Los Angeles Federal Savings & Loan skyscraper that skewered the smog and housed Jobete and Motown Records. It was in this building that one of my life's seminal moments occurred, in a matter-of-fact way, which, as I have learned, is the way most milestones are approached and passed.

I was still trying to attend college in San Bernardino and driving up to L.A. on the weekends with my "clipboard waving flags of tattered papers," carrying my reel-to-reel tapes (in a paper sack) made on a roommate's wavering Silvertone Recorder and selling songs door-to-door. Every weekend I made the rounds. I would go to Dick Glasser's and get turned down. I would go to Warner Bros. and get turned down. Verve, same story. I would hit the studios, Sunset Sound, Western Recorders and storefronts that didn't have names searching in vain for a singer who needed a song. I will never know what possessed me that one day I decided to go over to Motown. A guy who played drums in a pickup band with me from time to time, named Jimmy Stotler, with a sculpted Italian pompadour (he was a real scream) said, "Hey man, whatchoo goin' over dere for, cracker? You know you don't know nuttin' about soul music!" I just laughed and went over there with my paper sack. Big buildings were new to me and I guess that tall gray and chromium shaft all vertical and modern was about the biggest one I had ever seen. I ascended the elevator to the twelfth or even the fourteenth floor. It was the highest floor I had ever been on. The doors stood ten feet high, extending down the corridor, in a sort of Albert Speer intimidation-through-architecture thing. I finally found the one that said "Motown Records West/Jobete Music, Inc." in raised gold letters, and then knocked softly. A Miracles record was throbbing so loudly on the other side of the door that no one could have heard me even if I had kicked it off its hinges.

I decided I would pound on it with all my strength and just as I did, the music stopped as someone had obviously lifted the needle off the disc. The door opened with an angry swoosh and there was the receptionist, an Amazon with stormy brown eyes and chocolate skin whom I was later to know as Vicki. "*Can I help . . .* " she paused, looking at this white bag of bones clutching a paper sack. "Are you sure you're on the right floor sweetheart?" She laughed with a big, hearty, rumbling chuckle that started somewhere below her feet and ended up rolling out the top of her head. "I'm a songwriter," I peeped, trying to decide whether to run for it or pretend to faint. "Well, just come on in here, then . . . you poor, scrawny little thing," she said as she laughed some more and my face turned cherry, burgundy and then magenta. She sat me in a chair right in front of her desk and ate her lunch looking at me. Every once in a while she would give out laughing so hard I was afraid she was going to hit me with a chunk of banana. While she ate, she discovered where I was from, and so on. She got my name written down and said, "Well, I suppose you'll be wantin' to leave a tape." She had suddenly decided to look at me seriously and I was nervous, fumbling in my paper sack for a tape. Her eyes were looking right through me and it was a long moment, with a beginning, a middle and an end. She said, "Honey, you give me that tape!" and I swear to God there were tears in her eyes. The Motown sound continued to pulse beyond the door and inside the inner office, but she arose, as pretty as you please, and went over to one of those ten-foot doors and walked right through it. Junior Walker and the All Stars came to a screeching halt. I sat there in fearful trepidation, conscious of the muffled sounds barely audible through the door, and then suddenly in its wide and wavery splendor, I heard my own voice singing "This Time Last Summer"—my song, maybe not my best song, surely not a great song by any means, but mine—and someone was listening and they listened all the way through. A pause ensued. In the waiting room I was thinking, "Now you've done it! Now you can go back to Oklahoma and drive a tractor with a clear conscience." The ten-foot door marked "Private Office" opened slowly, first just a crack, and then the suggestion of a beautiful face, an angelic, serenely peaceful male face, surely an African American face, did appear there. A pair of large brown eyes focused on mine and I could see Frank Wilson's mouth moving, though I could not hear him—he was a man who spoke very softly—and then finally I realized, as though in a dream, that he was saying, "*Will you come in here please?*"

Diane Warren: When I started, L.A. didn't want anything to do with me . . . I was rejected a lot—I wanted to be you [Jimmy Webb]! Look, nothing's ever easy, sometimes I think I have a great song for somebody, and they don't do it. The people who say that music today isn't as good as it was, well, in some ways they're right. In the '60s you had a lot of classic songs, but you also had plenty of novelty records and junk. By and large I think there were more significant copyrights, whereas if you look at the Top 10 today, you see a lot of rap and a lot of things that aren't really songs. Concerning today's writers, it's a song-by-song thing with me, there's not a "Jimmy Webb" who I really idolize. There are surely fewer songwriter "personalities" because it's harder to break through now. I got lucky. Today it's definitely more slanted toward the producer/songwriter or the artist/songwriter. Then again, in the '60s, when Carole and Gerry, Barry and Cynthia and everybody else—and the Beatles—came, it was similar; all these English groups running their own songs, but somehow Barry and Cynthia could write "We Gotta Get Out of This Place" for the Animals, so there was the "outside" song that you could get in. You can't fight rap, I don't write it but . . . I do like some of the records production-wise . . . I like some of the material Dr. Dre does; his records are good, they're not really songs but it's like listening with a different head, checking the rhythm out. If something's successful you want to pay attention. I'm a total melody person, one thing that seems to be missing from the charts—but the stuff you can get from checking this new music out, production values and so forth, are important. As for me I'm just going to keep writing songs with melody and lyrics. They will always survive any fad or trend. I believe that.

I'm sure there are huge numbers of songwriters out there right now, I don't think they went away, but they have to rethink their approach. Publishers aren't what they used to be. They mainly sign artists or groups or a producer/writer or an artist/writer, someone who they know is going to recoup their investment. And you know what? I think it's really too bad.

I was a regular fixture around Motown for a while. Frank Wilson turned out to be a great producer and a real nuts and bolts songwriting whiz. He knew about all the basic parts and how to rivet them together. We wrote together and worked with Billy Eckstein ("I Did It All for

You," Webb and Wilson, ©1965), Tony Martin, and Brenda Holloway, who had etched an exquisite regional hit called "Every Little Bit Hurts" (Ed Cobb, ©1964). Marc Gordon ran the place and second-in-command was Hal Davis, a sweet guy with a pronounced limp and lisp who sang under the nom de plume of Danny Day. The Contessas (Suzanne Weir, Alyce Wheaton, Susie Horton and Sharon Johnson) were my pet project, all white and all blond, the cream of the crop of a century of cheerleader gene pruning, all dressed in identical little blue gingham dresses, and when I walked into Motown with them, Vicki started laughing harder than ever. She put her head down on her desk and cried. The Executive Suite became a free range for the girls. They came, saw and conquered, though as far as I know, nobody ever gave anything up. Marc and Hal decided to organize some orchestra sessions for me across the alley at Bob Ross's farmhouse studio. They must have been dazzled by blue eyes, white teeth and blond hair because I knew about as much about orchestrating as I did about fornicating, which is to say, I had never actually put my baton to any practical use.

The night before the session I laid down on the floor in front of my daddy's hi-fi and listened for hours to Teddy Randazzo's arrangements of "Hurt So Bad" and "Goin' Out of My Head" while I scribbled out the chart for "This Time Last Summer" on lined notebook paper. I had for-tuitously suffered a singular stroke of genius; I had decided to use all con-cert (C-clef) instruments: trombones, flutes, violins, vibraphone and so forth because then I wouldn't have to transpose. At the session Bob Ross came over and tsk-ed, tsk-ed, tsk-ed at my scrawls. "Next time bring these to me," he growled, "I'll show you how to do this. You can learn to write for *all* the instruments!" The session sounded pretty good for a first time out—more like a miracle—while the Contessas gyrated around the con-trol room, four angelic look-alikes. A handsome, intense Italian-looking dude was playing drums on the date and afterward he came over to me and said, "You should keep this up, kid." As he walked away, Frank Wilson whispered in my ear, "That's Hal Blaine." (Blaine subsequently played drums on seven NARAS Records of the year in a row, including "Up, Up and Away.")

One day me and the Contessas are driving into L.A. to go to Motown, and listening to K-MEN, San Berdoo, and lo and behold, "This Is Where I Came In" comes on the radio. The girls almost killed us all, shrieking, and hopping up and down on the seats, hugging each other, and pounding on my head while I tried to keep the car under control.

It was along about then that through the auspices of my friends at Motown, I got a cut with the Supremes on their Christmas album (*Merry Christmas*, ©1965), though to be truthful, "My Christmas Tree" was never a serious threat to "Rudolf the Red Nosed Reindeer." Motown West was not a priority item with Berry Gordy (the guys up there knew that and made fun of his high, squeaky voice all the time) and Marc Gordon had decided to move on. He wanted to manage a promising new group called the Versatiles. The Contessas' career had been sweet but short-lived, and they were beginning to drift toward dancing careers or families. I myself walked out through the ten-foot door one day and never went back, although I left more than forty songs behind me. I was anxious to find some steady work but I paused to say good-bye to Vicki and hugged her and cried a little because I would never be able to forget that she had opened the big door for me.

I found a job at Audio Arts, a small studio on Melrose where I could see Lucy's El Adobe Cafe through the blinds in the front. It was a room-and-board job. I lived with the proprietors, Madelon and Jack Baker, and Madelon fed me and even bought me a new suit (oh so cheap) and yelled at me when I left the refrigerator door open, even the tiniest little bit. Bob Ross had been true to his word. He had taught me to do some quite spiffy lead sheets and I erected a table in the lobby at Audio Arts and put up a sign that said "Transcriptions, $5.00." It's a good thing I didn't have that many customers considering it took me at least three hours to do one job. I also picked up a little money playing the piano on demo sessions that came through, like the Lettermen and Rod McKuen. McKuen came in one day and did fifty-three demos in eight hours. I was paid twenty-five bucks, and then allowed to sweep out the studio. After one of these marathons I would go down to Lucy's and have a chicken taco and Frank Casado would frown at my money and grin that big south-of-the-border grin and throw my check into a shoebox.

Stephen Bishop: I first signed a publishing deal when I was eighteen with Edwin M. Morris in 1969. In the publishing world they were very big on musicals like *Bye Bye Birdie, Hello Dolly*—they had a lot of hits—but in those days it was evident that there were more artists on the charts. It was a different era in that you wrote songs for artists and your chances of getting a cover were a lot better than they are now, where there are mostly artist/songwriters.

I remember my dad saying, "Y'know ever since Bing Crosby, music hasn't been the same." I would say, "Ouch!" I like Alanis Morrisette and a lot of other writers but generally the melodic content is just not as rich and fulfilling as it was in earlier pop songs. It doesn't excite me. I have written or sung about twelve or fourteen songs for films—but boy! that's really gotten tough now. The competition in L.A. is just huge. Even with my track record it's mostly "What have you done lately?" I've hired different agents [film music agents] throughout the years and I don't know why, but it never really helped much, so I don't do that anymore. I do understand this: Of course moviemakers put all the newest groovy acts like No Doubt or Smashing Pumpkins or Jewel in, to help sell the movie. There was a movie recently that one of my songs was almost used for, and then it wasn't, and then I heard the song that had been chosen and it was so lousy and I thought, 'Well God, that would be different if it was a good song beating me out . . . " I think a lot of movie makers don't always have great taste in music, and of course that is sour grapes—but I don't think they have the ears they used to. Music supervisors? Well in some cases they do have the ears, but mostly they have to please the director, producer, etc.

I've always considered myself more of a songwriter than a singer but as I kept at it, I started feeling like I was ready for a record deal, thinking at least some people would hear my songs. Truthfully I always felt that I was the best interpreter of my songs. Some versions by other artists are just so disappointing! Roy Halley gave me my first deal—signed me to ABC

Records—and that was through my manager at the time, Bob Ellis. I was also connected with Art Garfunkel back then and it helped, because I had the B side of Art's single "I Only Have Eyes for You." I had two songs on *Breakaway*, "The Same Old Tears on a New Background" and "Looking for the Right One," and that whole time was very pivotal.

Networking is really important. I think there's a kind of "pushy etiquette." For example, if you're a smart songwriter you'll always have a couple of things [cassettes] on your body wherever you go because you never know when you're gonna bump into somebody. I was at the Troubadour once—this was before my pushy-etiquette knowledge—and I ran into, of all people, David Clayton Thomas of Blood, Sweat and Tears, and I just walked up to him and went "Hi!" I was just off the turnip truck, and I said, "My name is Stephen Bishop and I've written two hundred songs! I know who you are and boy, I'd really like it if you recorded one of my songs! What's your phone number?" He gave me a number like "500-0000" . . . Now I get hit up by a lot of songwriters . . . one night I was getting really drunk in a Greek restaurant and this tall guy named Randall Kirsch, he was about six nine, and he handed me a tape and said, "I really like your stuff . . . " He was very nice, which I think is important—nice and considerate, not overly polite and self-demeaning, but cordial. I thought to myself, "Oh boy, here's another tape to throw in the bin"—but I always listen because you never know when you're gonna hear something like "Yesterday . . . " So I put it in my car on the way home and it was just great! Really innovative . . . You [Jimmy Webb] once said to me, "Y'know, Bish, the only problem with writing a song with you is that you're in the room!" You really said that!

I think that the '60s had such an overwhelming amount of nourishment and richness of content, melodic structure and meaningful lyrics that it's hard to rise above that. We had Motown, the British invasion, Marvin Gaye, and Dylan. It was just a hell of an era. Now, maybe people are doing some kind of valid and revolutionary antimelodic structure thing. I just don't get it. But every generation separates itself from the last through its music and it will probably continue to happen. Maybe the next generation will be singing Bing Crosby songs. When I ask artists what they're looking for, they always say, "A good song. A really good song." I think there's so much anger in this culture, and so many successful songs that are angry, like "You Ought'a Know," that sky-rocketed Alanis Morrisette.

"Angry" material for me? It would depend on what happened in my personal life, or if a movie called for it, but my basic philosophy is just to deal with my emotions. I wrote an angry song once called "Separate Lives"—I wrote it about a girl I was in love with and I was so angry and full of emotion, that when I wound up playing it for her a month later she said, "Oh that's beautiful!" And I went, "WH-A-A-A? What do you mean 'that's beautiful'?!" She saw it as beautiful and loving . . . We "mature" songwriters? I guess we're all just trying to get laid . . . I don't have a "live-in" right now, but the escort service should be here any minute. Her name is Marsha. Are you editing this?

Living with Madelon and Jack of Audio Arts hadn't really worked out. She quickly "adopted" me and began to treat me very much like some orphan carelessly left at her doorstep. Not that I didn't appreciate her somewhat clumsy attempts to "love" me, but my real mother had only been in her grave a scant two years and I had not yet attempted to deal with my grief. We fought over things that I did to deliberately annoy Madelon, bringing girls into the studio at night without permission, throwing my clothes all over my bedroom floor or leaving the mayonnaise jar out on the cabinet. (She said it would spoil and make us all sick and I knew for a scientific fact that it would not.) It's not recommended that a teenage writer live with his or her publisher.

I had a contract with Madelon and in spite of that fact, had just about made up my mind to run away from "home" for the second time in my life, when Marc Gordon arrived one day at our little storefront studio in company with a small, finely sculpted young man wearing a mustache and goatee below a straight nose and a pair of piercing blue-green eyes. His hair was curly and dark and his hands were like Dresden china. He was wearing a leather jacket that cost more than I had made since high school. Marc introduced him to me as Johnny Rivers. The two men sequestered themselves with Madelon in an inner sanctum for what seemed like hours as I paced the lobby fighting the impulse to simply walk to her office door and put my ear to it. After a while she called me in there and asked me to sit down and smiled that Maggie Thatcher smile of hers and spoke. "Do you want to go with these fellows?" she asked, eyes shining as she bit her bottom lip. It was one masterful example of self-control that prevented me from yelling, "Whoop-de-doo!" or perhaps "Thank God!" and doing a pirouette right in the middle of her office, but I strained my acting chops to the limit and feigned concern and nostalgia for the unforgettable year I had spent studying at her knee and partaking of the fragrant bread of her table. I knew that she would have to be utterly convinced that I loved her and really did not want to leave her for there to be the slightest chance of her letting me go.

Johnny cut himself quite a deal that day. For fifteen thousand dollars he obtained my exclusive services, "Up, Up and Away," "Didn't We?," "Galveston," "By the Time I Get to Phoenix" and a half-dozen other choice copyrights. Marc had reason to be happy. His Versatiles were now called the Fifth Dimension and were the first act signed to Rivers's new label, Soul City. Madelon had her money, though she would live to regret her impatience, avarice and frustration with my teenage angst. I had what I grossly overinterpreted as my "freedom." Abe Somer was Johnny's razor-sharp showbiz attorney, and in the days following, he proceeded to disavow me of any remaining postadolescent illusions about getting rich quick. My seven-year contract with Johnny Rivers Music hinged on the fact that the cash money Rivers had laid out to Madelon Baker would be reimbursed to Johnny out of *my royalties*. All I had done was to pay for the privilege of trading masters, and consequently, though my situation had cosmetically improved, in reality, it stayed the same.

John Ramistella (Johnny's real name) lived in a beautiful rambling

Spanish house, high in the Hollywood Hills above Doheny Drive and Trousdale Estates and it wasn't long before he had asked me to move into the spare bedroom. With a momentary lapse of good judgment I had accepted. I was now getting one hundred dollars a week advance, and through Johnny Rivers Music I was allowed to lease a brand-new buttercream-colored Camaro convertible Rally Sport. God help me—I thought I was pretty hot shit, cruising Sunset Boulevard, top back, with a couple of my college buddies, Mike Reilly and Glen DeLange. Going down to the Whiskey A-Go-Go at midnight with Johnny to see Smokey, or the Four Tops or John Lee Hooker and watching the light show squiggling around on the wall. Playing piano in Johnny's band at the Monterey Pop Festival (yes, we were there too). Meeting Janis Joplin at the Fillmore West and a hundred other important stars and finally getting laid (by a stewardess as it happened). John and I were tight. I remember one night both of us sitting in our bathrobes in his living room beside the massive fireplace, listening to *Sgt. Pepper's Lonely Hearts Club Band* and smoking sinsemilla, higher than a couple of satellites, when a fire broke out in the house next door. Half the fire trucks in Beverly Hills arrived in the street and on the driveway with sirens screaming and mirrored colored lights revolving madcap. Johnny thought it was a bust and threw everything we had down the toilet in a frenetic attempt to avoid capture. We still laugh about it.

Things were going along pretty smoothly. John had been voted the number-one male vocalist in America twice in a row. We made a record called *Changes*, on which he recorded one of his new acquisitions, "By the Time I Get to Phoenix." There was a shop on Sunset across from where Le Dome sits now called DeVoss, Ltd. We would ride down there on John's Harley, me hanging on the back, and he would buy hippy-dippy-chic long-sleeved cotton shirts with silk ribbons stitched down the front and round brimless corduroy hats à la Dick Gregory made by a guy named Leon Bennett and suede pastel boots and bell-bottom trousers, all very expensive. John went overseas to the San Remo Song Festival and left me in charge of the Fifth Dimension's rehearsal schedule. Billy Davis ("Junebug"), one of the best guys in the world with the chops of an Otis Redding, would tease me unmercifully about the holes clean through the bottoms of my tennis shoes. One day I tried out this song, "Up, Up and Away," on them (Billy Davis, Marilyn McCoo, Lamott McLemore, Ron Townsend and Florence LaRue) and they went nuts over it and got me so excited that I started showing them some parts. When Johnny came back from Europe we presented him with a fait accompli, a finished version of the song. This presumption he took with good grace, conceding that "Up, Up and Away" might be a good name for the group's album. Beneath the surface, however, he must have been thinking that his new protégé was getting a bit out of hand. He let me know one day that I wasn't up to par as a houseguest, which didn't come as a complete surprise. He told me that there were problems with my proximity to some of his girlfriends, one in particular, and that in general terms he had decided to curtail my activities in a Big Brotherly kind of way. In the studio he was constantly castrating my chords, removing the inner voices and alternate basses and I think that's what needled me most: seeing it in a Freudian context with all its attendant symbology. As we worked on the first Fifth Dimension record ("Up, Up and Away," ©1967) I began to chafe under his leadership and to resent his authority. Sometime around then I decided to move up into Laurel Canyon. Once a week I would go into the company office at 9200 Sunset Boulevard and pick up my check from Patti Dennis. There was an older character in charge there who I will just call Harvey whose job was to handle the most intimate details of John's business affairs. Harvey was in his second childhood surrounded by all of us flower children as he had been an intimate of Lenny Bruce and part of the first wave of Bohemians who hung out at a joint called The Renaissance in the late '50s (which used to be across the Strip from where the Comedy Store is now). Harvey liked to smoke dope and hang out with young girls in miniskirts and dispense "beat" wisdom to anyone who would listen—some of which wasn't half-bad—and he would usually talk to me for a few minutes every time I went in there about . . . oh, stuff. Stuff like one day when he asked me if I knew that the option was almost due on my contract. "What does that mean?" I asked innocently. He explained patiently that Johnny had to "re-up" the option on my contract every year or so in order for it to remain in effect. "What . . . "—he put the tips of his fingers together in his habitual gesture and stared just above them out the window and across Doheny Drive—". . . do you suppose would happen if for some reason that option wasn't picked up?" he seemingly asked of the gently waving palm fronds and frolicking birdies. "I dunno . . . What would happen?" I responded. "Well, my boy . . ." his inner struggle was not too well fought, "you would then be as free as one of those birds out there." I was silent. "Of course," he continued, "if something so catastrophic were to occur here in the office I would be in dire need of a position." He swiveled his chair around to look me straight in the eyes, with just the hint of a smile tweaking at one corner of his mouth.

J. D. Souther: I came to Los Angeles from Texas with a band I actually wasn't a part of but they needed a lead singer, and I needed a ride. I had a band in Texas called the Senders, but the rest of the Senders didn't want to be sent to California. So I came with another Texas band, The Kitchen Cinq—very clever!—we had a few gigs but as we broke up everybody found their own way to survive. I built houses, painted houses, roofed houses, painted apartment buildings, and if you ever need help you can call me. I won't do the work but I'll be sympathetic.

I only had access to a few small publishers, and to tell the truth I wasn't writing songs yet. I was astonished to find that publishers would pay money to someone for learning to write songs. I played with lots of musicians, including Norman Greenbaum in a band called "Natty Bumpo." Then I met Glenn Frey and we had nothing, no jobs when we met. We played guitars, and he played me rhythm and blues and I played him Hank Williams. So we were learning how to write songs, which I'm sure was more agonizing for the guys who were giving us publishing money than it was for us. I can't actually remember who the publishers were because we never stayed that long. They didn't really like the songs—a little too "minor key" for them. We started playing hoot-night gigs, acoustic nights; there were a few then: the Troubadour, the Ashgrove, Folk City, In the Alley and a little bitty place in Hollywood called Arty Fatbuckles, where Glenn and I actually had our first paying gig. We'd go to the Troubadour and listen during the week. We saw a lot of musicians but Tim Hardin had more to do with me turning a corner acoustically and shaping my songwriting. And I loved all that whole Blue Note scene.

You know, Miles, Coltrane, Horace Silver, The Adderlys, Herbie Hancock, Lee Morgan, Art Blakey and all those guys, and the amazing Wayne Shorter, who still writes the best melodies. And we had our own circle like that. We were all in it together . . . Jackson (Browne), Don (Henley) and Glenn (Frey) and Bonnie (Raitt) and Linda (Ronstadt), Lowell (George), Warren (Zevon), Ned (Doheny), Jack (Tempchin), the late, wonderful Judee Sill. . . . There was some competition but there was also a sense of esprit de corps. We were all going into Lucy's in those days. There you go, you start out lookin' for a good, cheap Mexican meal and you end up finding church.

Glenn and I made a record for Jimmy Bowen's Amos Records but they didn't understand us and besides, we weren't very good. We were only beginning to learn how to write. The group was called Longbranch Pennywhistle and we were listening to the Flying Burrito Brothers, Poco, Dillard & Clarke, the Byrds and Dylan, of course. I never feel like I can describe my own music, but it initially was a kind of blending of country music with Glenn's R&B thing. The contemporary songwriters that I listened most to then, to be perfectly honest, were you [Jimmy Webb] and Bob Dylan and Tim Hardin. I still listen to you guys and it still moves me the same way.

Eventually we met David Briggs, who had just produced "Everybody Knows This Is Nowhere" for Neil Young and Crazy Horse. We recorded with him for a couple of days and took it in and played it for the guys at our record company, and it was obvious they we were just going in different directions. Glenn and I laid low for awhile but then Jackson (Browne) met David Geffen and introduced all of us to him and things really began to fly. Most importantly I was getting more confidence as a writer. It seemed Asylum was a writer's label for artists who had something in common. David bought off my old contract and gave me enough money to rent a house. Before that, Jackson, Glenn and I were living in a little stucco box in Echo Park for something like sixty-five dollars a month.

I don't draw any big distinctions between what was going on then and what is going on today. There's still a ton of places where songwriters can go and play here. And I'm not really sure that it's true that all publishers are looking for dual roles in their songwriters. The biggest negative is that today, publishing companies are so focused on their acquisition business that they are concentrating on buying the Motown catalogue more than beginning writers. I know they still sign them, 'cause somebody's always calling, saying, "Listen, we've got a young writer, would you be interested in writing with him?" I don't know any publishers that aren't signing young writers. For instance, there's Bug Music, which has a lot of writers who are not well known and are eccentric and young. They don't give big advances, they tend to just administer the catalogue or take a piece of them, and they seem to be very active. I get their newsletter and they're always getting cuts for their people—but the big companies are signing, too, and working with their new writers.

The kid who has just arrived in L.A. should first fortify the body and soul with a chicken tostada and a kind word from Lucy (Lucy's El Adobe), and then just go play all the open-mike nights. Playing every coffee house and bar is more important then walking into people's offices and playing them tapes. I didn't get a deal because I walked into David Geffen's office or Jimmy Bowen's office. I got a deal because we played all the time . . . and after we played enough, we got better and the musicians themselves started talking, and sooner or later someone from a publishing company came to see us, then another publishing company came, and finally somebody from a record company came. If you want to

be good at making music, make music. If you want to be
good at walking into people's offices and playing tapes,
do that. The point is it's the music that's important.
Musicians that are twenty years old shouldn't have to get
their music from Jackson or Don or me or Tom Petty, or
you [Jimmy], or for that matter Jacob Dylan, or Boyz II
Men, or anybody else, they should be trying to make
their own. That's how this music bubbles up from the
street.

There was trouble in Paradise. Somehow, God only knows how,
Johnny Rivers had failed to re-option the contract on his thoroughbred
songwriting star. "Up, Up and Away," by the Fifth Dimension was rocket-
ing up the charts (even though it had been banned in Oklahoma City
because it was suspected that it dealt with the subject of drug use). The
song had also been covered by a group on Liberty called the Johnny Mann
Singers and even *their* version was ascending the charts. I was hiding in the
Beverly Wilshire Hotel. I was hiding because I had failed the first great
moral test of my life. I hadn't *done* anything. As far as I know to this very
day, *no one* had *done* anything. (It may be safely assumed that no one had
called Johnny Rivers and informed him that my contract was about to
lapse.) One of Isaac Asimov's Laws of Robotics stipulates that an intelligent machine could not "by inaction allow harm to come to a human
being." On this occasion, we could have made any number of machines
superior to me.

I believe that I committed intimate, irreparable self-injury when I
allowed this conspiracy of silence to proceed against my friend, however
unpleasant and onerous I may have found the situation. But what choice
did I have? Seven years of indentured servitude or my own publishing company? I am sorry for it and glad for it in the same breath. I took no real joy
in it even then. I skulked around the hotel for a couple of days and when
Harvey came by to check on me I couldn't look at him. Again, I had over-
estimated the virtues of freedom. I re-imagined scenarios in which I had
looked Harvey straight in the eye with a steely glint and said, "You'd better
make damn sure you exercise this option, Harv!" Alas, I had not.
Innocence was lost and for the life of me I couldn't bring myself to face
Johnny Rivers.

The 9200 Building sits on a slice of pie bounded by Doheny Drive on one tangent and Sunset Boulevard on the other. There is a traffic signal on Doheny that prevents merging traffic from carrying into the apex of the V formed by the two streets. Who knows what inconsequential errand or obtuse twist of fate brought Harvey and me down Doheny that afternoon in his antique Maserati and to a stop in the left-hand lane at that particular signal? I only know that with a smooth, gliding purr, a sleek red Ferrari pulled up parallel to us in the right lane and when I glanced in that direction from my passenger's-side window, I was looking straight into the face of Johnny Rivers. It was not a pretty sight. We sat like that, the three of us, for the eternity that it took the light to change . . . an eternity in which I could meditate on how a single moment, as sharp and ferocious as a carefully honed cleaver, can sever us from childish concerns, and what it means to be banished forever to a world of real actions and painful repercussions.

PolyGram Music Publishing's Linda Newmark:

My advice to a songwriter who is a newcomer to the music business is to get involved with some of the professional songwriter organizations, such as the National Academy of Songwriters, the Songwriter's Guild, and other music industry organizations such as NARAS (the organization that puts on the Grammy awards), and a performing rights society (ASCAP, BMI or SESAC). These organizations and other music industry groups provide panel discussions, workshops and other opportunities for people who are serious about the music industry. I think it is also important to hook up with other songwriters. As a songwriter you should first and foremost focus on working on the craft of songwriting. You should also create opportunities to learn about the business and to get to know (and learn from) people who are successful at what you want to do.

I think that one of the more difficult paths to a music publishing deal these days is for the person who comes to a publishing company as a "pure" songwriter. In other words, a songwriter who is not a "recording artist-songwriter" or "producer-songwriter." Our Nashville office signs many more pure songwriters than our offices in New York and Los Angeles. A lot of the major artists in country music record songs written by outside songwriters, whereas in some other areas of music we see bands that are more self-contained and tend to write their own material. Since it's harder today for a publisher to get a cover in the rock/pop world than it was a number of years ago, I think that makes it harder for a pure songwriter who writes in the rock/pop area to get a publishing deal. Of course there are always going to be exceptions. Diane Warren is a pure songwriter who gets her songs recorded in rock, pop, country, and other areas of music, and I'm sure most music publishers would love to sign her to a publishing deal. Although there are no specific rules, if a writer comes to a publishing company saying, "I've got a record deal with this major record company, the record is coming out at the end of the month, and here is a copy of the songs that I wrote that are on the record," well, that's an easier sell to a publishing company, as is a situation where the writer comes in saying, "I've produced Artists A and B, and I've co-written three of the songs on Artist A's next album and two of the songs on Artist B's album." When someone comes in with that kind of activity, then we can say, "Okay, you produced and co-wrote for Artist A, we've got connections with Artist C, let's put you two together with the concept that if it works creatively, maybe you can co-write with Artist C for Artist C's next album.

While most publishers will sign a limited number of "development" writers who do not yet have commercially released songs or a record deal, it really does help when a writer "brings something to the party," because in this business having *some* activity makes it easier to generate *more* activity. Getting the first break is the hardest part. A publisher can help in a lot of creative areas, including setting up collaborations with other songwriters and pitching songs to record artists. Our company has also been very active in working on additional ways to get our writers' songs recorded. For example, we have several staff members who work full time pitching songs for use in motion pictures, television programs and commercials. Motion pictures, television programs and soundtrack albums are a great way to get exposure for great songs and for emerging artists.

A few years later I would get an invitation to stop by David Geffen's house to talk about a possible managerial relationship. David was having a busy day. Graham Nash and David Crosby were there—angry and intense—striking their acoustic guitars with a fury and singing "Four

Dead in Ohio." The events at Kent State had unfolded only hours before. Geffen also wanted me to hear a new writer, a young kid who was living in the spare bedroom, a sensitive-looking kid with large brown eyes and good hands named Jackson Browne. I had known from the first glimpse of the wrought-iron gate and its brick driveway that the rambling rancho was none other than the very same one that had once belonged to Johnny Rivers and had been my temporary home. I walked in and sat crossed-legged once again in front of the massive stone fireplace across from Jackson as he played for me the elegiac "Opening Farewell," which is my way of saying that in Hollywood, only the names change. It is a tough town for all its balmy breezes, palm trees, and sunny afternoons. It's easy to make mistakes when you're young, easy to be cocky and look around you and say to yourself, "Well, if they're doing it why can't I do it?" The answer is they aren't doing it, they're only pretending to do it and if you try to do it you'll get caught and you'll be sorry. Hollywood is not an ideal proving ground for mistakes because among all cities it is the most hypo-critical. The young writer will not want to be saddled early on with a label such as "difficult," "substance abuser," "attitude problem," "misogynist," "sloppy" or any other pigeonhole. He will not want to talk back or tell people to go "fuck" themselves. He will want to be a team player, perfectly meshed into the health-conscious, tennis-playing, World Gym mentality. Clothes will matter and so will wheels. It would be wise to practice speak-ing earnestly and convincingly about everything without saying anything. Ass-kissing is good. Getting laid by the right person is even better. Hanging out in the right place with all the right people who have laid all the right people? Forget the piano lessons, kid, you're on top of the world! (P.S. And never put anything in writing.)

> With film work these days they'll solicit twenty writers, and they might take the material of five of them. Usually I would meet with the musical director of the film and try to discern what they would want, even though it feels like you're in a big horse race. So I'll go back to my fifteen albums and see if something exists there, or to my unrecorded material and see if there's something else, but I'm not going to put my heart and soul into a piece of writing that's not gonna get used.
>
> —Nanci Griffith

As far as my own experience writing songs for the film industry, I may as well confess to my checkered and perhaps even polka-dotted past. My first serious writing project was with Garry Marshall, and he was the funniest guy I ever worked for, but it was only one song and I really didn't know what I was getting into. I can still remember the old sound stage on the MGM lot, though, those rotary pan pots and forty-some-odd single-track machines all running in sync at the same time the live orchestra and vocal date was going on outside. Someone told me it was the same stage where *The Wizard of Oz* had been recorded. I worked on Hugh Hefner's first feature, Playboy Films' *The Naked Ape*, as much because of Victoria Principal's buff starring role as anything else. It was my first experience with a Broadway director, Donald Driver, and I learned that I didn't know beans about reading a script. It is so very important to be associated with something good right out of the box, say for instance the way Paul Simon had his beautifully crafted tunes laid into a jewel of a film like *The Graduate*. A writer can work steadily in hundreds of bad movies for decades and nobody cares.

One of the strangest things I ever tried was to write a song a week—sometimes even *two*—for police drama producer David Gerber, when he remusicalized *Seven Brides for Seven Brothers* and made it into a TV series. I was writing songs about mountain lions, Mexican cooking and bucking horses, about anything it seemed, as long as it wasn't a particularly suitable subject for a song. Suffice it to say that the show didn't run nearly long enough for all seven brothers to get brides.

I worked on a musical film with producer Joe Wizan called *Voices* and met one of my life's real soul mates in actress Amy Irving. I was devastated when the studio picked Burton Cummings over Ted Neely to overdub Michael Ontkean's vocals. I had lobbied for the star to do his own vocal stunts. Be advised that usually when the producer or the studio wants your opinion, they will give it to you. (The movie tanked.)

My best experience thus far was with animation producer Jules Bass while composing a score for his full-length feature *The Last Unicorn*, with Gerry Beckley and Dewey Bunelli (of the rock group America), who sang the vocal score . . . and it was a lovely piece (six-year-old girls still swoon over me when they discover that I'm the composer of "Man's Road" and other unforgettables). But the distributor bellied up and the picture ended up being "four-walled" in second-rate movie houses and monotracked after we had moved heaven and earth to cut a lively, delicate score in Dolby stereo.

In recent times I sold an unrecorded Christmas song of mine to a studio (the studio shall remain nameless) for an end title, and they tacked it onto the picture, apparently with little or no thought of releasing a soundtrack album. They were selling the picture short, but Lo and Behold, it took off as though it was being towed by all eight tiny reindeer. The studio could have sold a skillion CD's because they had a damn good record in the can and their own label. Instead, they rushed the record onto the racks in mid-January. I'll always hope that some smug little yuppie got fired for that boner, but I doubt it.

Traditionally the studios have been just so ill-equipped to deal with the realities of including songs in film. Countless times, studios have obtained an expensive vocalist, like, for instance, a Sheena Easton, and spent themselves into a nosebleed to get her recorded properly, only to "discover" that once the picture hits the theatres no one has thought to contact her label in advance to arrange for a single release. Oftentimes the label will outright refuse to do it (incredible but true). The songwriter for film learns to appreciate the taste of stomach acid, because there is so very much that is completely out of control.

You're nobody till you've been fired off a picture. Carly Simon, Andre Previn, John Barry, and Wynton Marsalis have been, just to name a few, and I have to tell you, I'll bet you a Learjet in most cases the firees will tell you that they're glad it happened! Why wouldn't they be? It's a rite of passage, like crossing the equator for the first time. Something to look forward to.

Every songwriter dreams of writing a musical for Disney. Songwriters are literally lined up around the block to work for Disney, but even though we're talking about animated films, it is Broadway chops that land these jobs. Disney, Fox, or Dreamworks, be advised that no major studio will hire a writer for less than half the publishing. Of course, many writers clamor to make this sacrifice, reasoning that the trade-off will come in fame and future fortune. So much of the film marketplace consists of working "on spec." Recently, a well-known Hollywood producer advertised in full page ads in the industry trades, enticing out-of-work songwriters and composers to feel free to submit their music for use in his next film. It seems that it would almost behoove the serious songwriter to fill a war chest with pre-prepared songs, lots of end title "wind and wings" numbers and quite a few Homeric "Eye of the Panther-martial arts" type things and just wait 'em out. When they tell you you're the only writer working on the project, you can look them straight in the eye and say, "well, in that case, I'm gonna write this song especially for *you*."

The Players:

The Managers:	Managers are more powerful in Los Angeles than in any other part of the world. Geffen started out as a manager and Gallin, Azoff, Kragen, and Asher have all molded the careers of extraordinary writers and artists. Super Manager/Agents like Ovitz, Peters and others "package" the talent that goes into major motion-picture musicals and other projects.
Film Music Agents:	One or perhaps two Hollywood music agencies exercise a virtual monopoly over the songwriting and film scoring talent used in all the significant films made in the industry. It won't take you long to find out who they are. Not many songwriters will attest to having ever been helped by such an agent. "Hot" writers or groups hardly need help getting film jobs. As far as the newcomer is concerned, as in other aspects of the business, "personal contacts" are almost the only way to go.
The Director:	Film Directors can be notoriously unable to articulate specific aesthetic requirements when it comes to music. They often use "temp tracks," existing music that is dubbed onto the rough cut of the picture. Once ingrained in their subconscious however, the "temp track" becomes the ruin of many a poor boy (and God, I know I'm one).
The Film Producer:	His duties are similar to those of a Broadway producer and he can always decide that his daughter's boyfriend or his Aunt Marge is going to score the picture or write the title song, though he will almost always go with a writer who has an enviable track record or is coming off a big hit.
Studios:	The studios are the Client when it comes to songs or other music for movies. The Studio, the Dir-

ector and the Producer often play the "shell game" when it comes to making a decision on a composer or a piece of music. (The person you are negotiating with will almost always say that the final decision lies with someone else, ad infinitum.)

The Heads of Music: Each major film studio has an executive in charge of hiring composers and songwriters for film and television projects. Beneath them in the hierarchy are Music Supervisors who do roughly the same job as A&R people at record companies. Burt Berman is head of music of Sony Pictures, Gary LeMel at Warner Bros., Matt Walker and Bill Green at Disney/Touchstone, and so on, although the cast of characters changes with confusing regularity. As a matter of routine, I send my latest projects, records, demos, etc., to the Heads of Music at the studios. Your publisher should be interfacing with studio music departments on your behalf.

Music: The same dynamics are in play for the scores and songs used in television programs as pertain to feature film except on a smaller scale. You will find that certain agents specialize in handling composers and writers for television. Some composers and writers are "marooned" in the television field almost in the same way an actor in a series becomes typecast and unable to break into the big screen; however, one successful theme song for a runaway series like *Cheers* or *Seinfeld* can set a songwriter up for life. In television it is more likely that the producer will make most of the vital decisions concerning casting, score, and may even pick the theme song. Television shows are usually the progeny of any one of a hundred "production companies." Each production company will have an executive on staff to screen tapes

	and interview writers about potential musical contributions.
Record Producers:	In L.A. the top Record Producers are powerful, highly paid and likely to have ready access to hot new films in progress as well as label projects. Don Was, David Foster, Baby Face and Glen Ballard are active as we go to print. The careers of record producers are mercurial at best, and the list of "hot" producers changes almost every time a new issue of *Billboard* hits the stands.
The Label	Every major record label except Sony has recently gone through an intense period of consolidation, reorganization and re-evaluation of their executive ranks on both coasts. This has created a ripple effect of instability and confusion in the songwriting market. The marketplace has diversified to the point where labels have to make ever more careful decisions about where and how they spend their promotional money. They are now trying to decide how to make the Internet work for them as well as the retail outlets who will be in danger if they do not adapt quickly. The entire situation is in a state of flux.
Live Performance Venues:	According to J. D. Souther there are plenty of places to sing and play in Los Angeles: Highland Grounds, Genghis Cohen Cantina, Largo, the Un-Urban Coffee House, the Crooked Bar, as well as the Troubadour, the Ash Grove, McCabe's Guitar Shop, and at least a dozen others.

One last thing: The single unforgivable sin that one can commit in Tinseltown has nothing to do with drugs or infidelity or alcoholism or irresponsibility, or surprisingly enough, even failure (some people have gotten away with murder). But mark me well—do not ever in an unguarded moment betray to anyone, even your closest friend, the tiniest hint of *fear*. About five years ago, in the convulsions of a particularly difficult divorce, I was speaking to an old family friend who still lives in California and works in the film/music industry. As we were talking on the telephone I confessed that I had been shaken to the core, that I didn't know where my career was going, and I told him, money was in question for the first time in my professional life. I even felt out of touch with my creativity, I told him. "To tell you the truth," I said, "*I'm afraid.*" I haven't heard from him since.

eleven

LIVING WITH IT

I'm the innocent bystander
Somehow I got stuck
Between the rock and the hard place
And I'm down on my luck
Now I'm hiding in Honduras
I'm a desperate man
Send lawyers, guns and money
The shit has hit the fan . . .

—Warren Zevon,
"Lawyers, Guns and Money"

The difference between being able to write a song and not is a precarious balance between caring too much about what one does and not caring enough. Hack writers don't get writer's block and paradoxically neither do hungry ones. Writers who are flush and experienced enough to be jaded are bound to get it. "Composers should never marry rich women," renowned Broadway agent Robby Lantz said to me about one famous writer's lack of productivity. A divorce will trigger it or an illness or serious accident. The most unfortunate thing about the blockage is that it grows worse over time. There is a palpable suspense as the weeks and months elapse without any significant work being done, an increasing anxiety that exacerbates the paralysis until one fears and dreads the moment when sitting down at the piano can no longer be postponed. I know this because I haven't written a song in over a year.

Songwriters are particularly vulnerable prey for many diseases of the spirit. Their finely tuned emotional nature is a delicate engine, a high-performance racing type but not particularly efficient and prone to break-downs and costly repairs.

The writer may tend to be in love perpetually and then after a series of bone-jarring affairs may become aloof and spiritually armored. I wouldn't think marriage particularly easy for most songwriters. Even when one's heart isn't engaged in some phantasmagorical flirtation one's mate will likely be watchful and if not continually suspicious, then at least wary. How can she/he completely trust someone who writes and thinks about romance all the time? There's not much that can be done about this state of affairs. It comes with the territory, as the expression goes. But all of this is trivial compared to the onslaught of serious depression. It is there in most of us, an uneasy doppelganger flitting in and out of the periphery of consciousness, but when it sets in with a vengeance, people die as surely as if they had contracted the Ebola virus. The true poet understands this strange mood shift all too well—walking out the front door onto the porch on a glorious spring morning, serenaded by the liquid songs of birds, only to find that the day has taken on a darkly sinister aspect and that there is a uranium slug suddenly buried in the pit of the stomach—all made worse by the fact that the victim knows all too well that the cause lies within. William Carlos Williams was on at least one occasion ("Waiting") unaccountably propelled into a depressive state by the sound of his children laughing and playing as he arrived home from work. William Styron related a harrowing tale of his struggle to maintain a tenu-ous grip on not only his sanity but even his will to live for a period of years. In his book *Darkness Visible* Styron lists by name a small community of fellow writers, poets and artistic types, who lost this struggle with self only to commit suicide. The effort involved in holding this monster at bay creates other vulnerabilities: the temptation to self-medicate along with the addictions that may follow, as well as related professional failures that may destroy a person's faith in their own future.

As I mentioned at the beginning of this book, songwriters as a species are most likely to be loners. Their whole social whirl may consist of one or two close friends and one of those may be their collaborator. Even the gar-rulous ones, the raconteurs and entertainers, are more than likely putting up a smoke screen to obscure the fact that a large part of their lives is spent in self-contemplation. It is a narcissistic business and a full-time job, this constant evaluation of one's emotional state, this sensation of watching from a safe distance one's own joy or pain. For this reason songwriters are not great joiners. I was speaking a few years back with an acclaimed songwriting diva of our trade and holding forth perhaps at too great a length about the ridiculously inflated profit margin of the record companies and saying that we should all get together as a group and make them turn over some of that excess money to the wretched and hungry around the world. If we all got together and threatened to QUIT WRITING we could force them to do some good. She agreed that we most probably could do something of that nature and then added, "But I mistrust crusaders." I would as soon organize a parade of certified schizophrenics as to try and get a herd of songwriters headed in the same direction. For the most part they suffer the inevitable defeats and indignities of their ephemeral profession in stoic isolation. This solitude is seen as a necessary evil to most of us. To betray any weakness is to tinker with the delicate clockworks of our careers. It seems to be a practical matter that we continue to suffer in silence. But slowly the songwriting community is awakening to the need for a therapeutic outreach.

Sims Ellison was born the year "Up, Up and Away" became a hit, 1967. He was a bassist with the talented band Pariah, who were signed to Geffen Records in 1993, making the album *To Mock a Killingbird*. June 6, 1995, he shot himself. The band had recently been dropped from the Geffen roster. He was working at a clothing store in Austin, Texas, at the time.

On August 11, 1995, SIMS (Services Invested in Musicians Support) was established as an organ to provide "low-cost mental health services to the Austin music community." In their own words SIMS is a "one of a kind grassroots organization, founded in the memory of Sims Ellison." They offer "programs of personal and professional development," mental health education, spousal support groups and are proud of the fact that they "take requests." (The group maintains a web site at http://sims foundation.org.) Whereas this organization is not aimed exclusively at the songwriter, I spoke with Peyton Wimmer, one of the founders, about their relationship to the songwriting community.

It seems around town that I'm the only person who did not know Sims. He was very popular, compassionate, caring . . . very emotional, which may have been a contributing factor to his suicide, along with getting dropped from the label. He had been battling depression his entire life. Mostly, with being dropped, I think it was the fact that his friends and brother were in the band. Seeing their disappointment and the way they were treated—that hurt him. We get a lot of calls from songwriters. For example, I got a call from someone last night who is bipolar—which is a hard gig. His fear—and this has been voiced so many times—is "What if I go to therapy? Will it affect my writing? Where will my inspiration go?" That's one thing I would like people to understand. Therapy doesn't end your creativity. Freud had a term, "sublimation." We take some of the pain we feel and turn it into art as a way to deal with it. That understanding of themselves will help them to be able to use that sensitivity and that feeling to write and not be run over by the pain.

It seems to me that this effort represents an auspicious beginning in the potential development of a nationwide network of referral counseling and therapy support for songwriters and other musical creators. One can envision a toll free crisis line and perhaps a national web site where professional volunteers might intervene to prevent tragedy, as well as an open forum for writers interested in interacting with others of their profession. (SIMS, P.O. Box 1622, Austin, TX 78767-1622; 512-494-1007.)

Of course since 1989 there has been MusiCares, established by NARAS (the people who give out the Grammy Awards) with the sole purpose of "ensuring that music people have a place to turn during their times of financial hardship." They provide financial assistance grants, substance abuse intervention and referral program, national health insurance, and other assistance to music professionals. (MusiCares, 3402 Pico Boulevard, Santa Monica, CA 90405; Phone: 310-392-3777, Fax: 310-392-2187.)

Generally speaking there are more songwriting events than ever before where songwriters get together simply to play their songs and get acquainted with one another. The National Academy of Songwriters, a Los Angeles–based support group, established one of the first of these annual get-togethers and it quickly became a sentimental favorite of many of us because there were no awards presented, the only pressure being a subtle impetus to try and play as good a song as the other person. Backstage, songwriters sat together in easy camaraderie, discussing their mutual problems, families and concerns for the future, and in the case of many of us, it was the first time in our lives we had discussed such issues with other professional songwriters. Tin Pan South, a week-long annual songwriting festival, has become a real celebration of our profession not only because of the educational opportunities provided by the Nashville Songwriters Association but primarily for the outpouring of love and respect songwriter to songwriter. For a few all too short days the pressure of making a living recedes in favor of a tangible spirit of unilateral support and encouragement. All of this may just be too sappy for some in the profession. There is a certain constituency who will say that songwriters don't need to be happy and secure, that in fact that's just about the worst state a songwriter can be in. I can't in good conscience argue. The connection between emotional upset and the creation of a powerful song is simply too well established. In a broader sense, unfortunately, this says that most civilians are *unhappy and frustrated* because they provide an insatiable appetite for our depressive effluence. On the other end of the spectrum, "happy" songs too often represent a mindless Pippi Longstocking sentimentality that perpetuates while validating most intellectual criticism of pop music. In the middle ground there are good songs about being in love that have both a sense of reality and a literate, romantic quality. The best of these reflect the mental health and spiritual maturity of the creator. Too bad there's not much of a market for them.

The writer is in a position where an overdose of sanity might be commercially and even artistically lethal. On the other hand if the imagination lives exclusively in a dreamworld populated by brokenhearted losers and is helped gently down this declining path by alcohol or some other substance, then who is to wonder if the mind begins eventually to falter and the body follows suit?

There are many factors in the business world that are calculated to drive songwriters crazy, especially when taking into consideration the fact that most of these "right brain" people are ill disposed to deal with monetary distractions. It is so much easier to let someone else write the checks, suggest the investments and make the "hard" decisions. Not only is it "easier," it is morally justifiable! After all, this art of ours is important work. Who wants to be worrying about money all the time? Beyond that, we are without a doubt a privileged caste so that the gods look kindly upon all our endeavors. Even our fellow human beings must be moved to some degree by our emotional sacrifice and surely they look benevolently upon our carelessly attended schemes. As Joni Mitchell is quoted in *The Great Rock 'n' Roll Quote Book* (St. Martin's Griffin), "You wonder about people who made a fortune, and you always think they drank it up or stuck it up their nose. That's not usually what brings on the decline. It's usually the battle to keep your creative child alive while keeping your business shark alive. You have to develop cunning and shrewdness, and other things which are not well-suited to the arts."

Let's talk about how much money songwriters make. When a song is played on the radio, called a "performance," the BMI writer makes either six or twelve cents a shot (depending on whether it is a Class I or Class II radio station)—ASCAP writers earn about forty bucks every time it is picked up—providing he or she owns the entire copyright. If this is not the case, then it's usually "halvesies" but not always. The BMI writer doesn't get paid if the music is used for a background, cue, or not played in its entirety for some other reason; ASCAP writers get a lower amount if the music is used for a background, cue, or in commercials. On local television stations the BMI writer gets a buck fifty if somebody sings the song on camera; ASCAP writers get four bucks per station if somebody sings the song on camera. On a network station this swells to either five dollars or nine dollars (depending on the class of station); with ASCAP, a network television "theme" song can earn you two hundred fifty dollars— which could swell to twice that if it's a "supertheme" (one that is used in opening and closing and lasts fourteen weeks or more) in prime time! For a television "theme" song the BMI writer gets either fifty-eight or seventy-two cents per station (a "supertheme" will earn you two bucks!). Background music for announcements and whatnot earn zilch. Genuine underscore (with BMI) pays either fifty-two or seventy-two cents per minute (per station); genuine underscore with ASCAP pays one hundred forty dollars per minute on a network. Underscore for motion pictures (both feature and made for TV, series, specials, etc.) pays the same on television, whereas BMI pays seventy-two cents per minute when shown on television. ("Live" performances in actual movie theatres don't count.) In addition to these, there are certain other technical categories, "bonus payments" and what have you but basically that's the ballgame.

As this book is published, songwriters and creators of all stripes are facing perhaps the challenge of the century with the proliferation of the

Internet (a.k.a. the World Wide Web. I have my own web site at www.jimmywebb.com). Many futurists believe that electronic money will eventually replace any form of coinage and that the great bulk of goods transfer, even the trading of staples, will take place on the personal computers of individual households. This means that, eventually, entire record albums or perhaps even first-run feature films will be downloaded to recordable formats by satellite for a fee, which is paid electronically via credit card or some other code. From the outset many literary anarchists have seen this wide-open electronic frontier as a no-man's land within which to shamelessly plagiarize and decimate the writings, poems, and yes, even song lyrics and music rightfully belonging to others.

In a recent issue of *Time* magazine (*Time Digital*) the late Sonny Bono responded to the question, Is content on the Net "ownable"? "Absolutely. The concept of owning intellectual property is firmly established in our legal system. Your question really asks whether authors, composers, and artists deserve the same rights as individuals who produce more tangible products. In truth, we arrived at the mystical Digital Age through the hard work of all the intellectual-property owners who led the way." Bono was stalwart in his insistence that songwriters' rights be protected into the new millennium no matter what mode of dissemination, introduced the Copyright Term Extension Act of 1997 and continued in the article to say, "In no way should the freedom of access offered by the Net abolish or disregard the rights of creative people."

Record producer and company executive Jay Landers had this to say:

> You have to make things like the Internet work for you, and right now it's all so new that we're trying to figure out how we can make it work for us. I think the person who asks me [will the Internet be a threat to record companies and put them out of business?] reminds me of the same person who asked if television would be the death of movies. It had an impact but the fact is that movies now make more money than at any time in the history of the cinema, and TV is watched by more people. My view of the Internet and whatever new technologies that come along is that we need to embrace them because 1) they're not going away and 2) any mechanism that can bring more music to a wider audience is ultimately a good thing. It's for the record companies to figure out how to integrate with not only

the Internet but with retail to figure out how all of this can work. I think the retail stores will be in danger if they do not figure out how to embrace the technology, and rather quickly. The main retail stores are going to be at the forefront. While the technology and the delivery systems for music may change in ways that we can't even fathom for the moment, and we may all be listening to our CDs on things that look like the heads of pins, the fact is—and will always be—one person or a group of people sitting in a garage somewhere, trying to come up with something that is inspired musically. And that is a long-winded way of saying it will always be creatively driven. And it's a major cliché, but it always does start with the song.

The songwriter whose primary living is writing songs as opposed to writing and producing their own songs, or performing their own songs, is in a very challenging situation. To those who succeed with brilliant regularity, it's quite a testament to craftsmanship.

"It's not the singer, it's the song."—Conway Twitty
"It's the singer, not the song."—Mick Jagger

There has always been considerable skepticism in the ranks, with all due respect, about any humongous organization's abilities to keep track of all these performances spread out all over the United States every minute of the day.

Now for the "mechanicals." Mechanicals are the small sums of money paid to a writer as a share of the monies received when an actual physical object like a cassette or CD (in ancient times, records and sheet music) is sold. Practically speaking, there is only one organization, the Harry Fox Agency, to license phonograph manufacturers to reproduce copyrights on mechanical devices. Yes, there was a real Harry Fox, and though it is a perennial puzzlement as to why there is no competition for this agency, there are no particularly sinister aspects to the quaint tale of how this came to be. Let it suffice to say that Harry Fox pays at the current rate 6.95 cents per composition or 1.25 cents per minute of playing time, whichever is the higher figure (and they take a four and a half percent commission). How are we going to get rich doing this? With superhuman effort and extreme care if at all.

One of the larger flies thrashing around in the ointment is the professional—the manager, accountant, lawyer and the like—who may be presented, even unwillingly, with a *conflict of interest*. One of the most famous examples of an alleged conflict of interest occurred in 1977 when the Eagles, Don Henley, Glenn Frey, Randy Meisner, Don Felder, and ex-Eagle Bernie Leadon took David Geffen to court insisting that he had promised upon signing them not to sell their publishing to a third party and then had proceeded to do just that. The dispute eventually evolved into a more pertinent question: "What was David Geffen doing with an interest in the group's publishing in the first place?" Irving Azoff asked. It seems obvious that it is not in the writer's best interest to sell or assign publishing to a lawyer or manager who is active in influencing other aspects of that same career. In one huge case which originated in New York, a songwriting superstar unknowingly allowed his copyrights to be used as collateral in connection with a hefty loan from his own record label. The deal was handled by his acting manager . . . his *former brother-in-law*. Though the copyrights were temporarily lost in the dispute and the songwriter eventually sued the manager as well as his own law firm (who were privy to the transactions), his property was eventually returned by the head of the label in a rare display of good manners and conscience.

The Beatles' first manager, close friend Brian Epstein, presented the group with an almost insurmountable publishing handicap when he made a deal with publishing chum Dick James to form a company called Northern Songs. McCartney and Lennon would share 40 percent of this company and Epstein would forego his management fee of 25 percent in order to own 10 percent of the publishing end. Dick James apportioned himself 50 percent of the total earnings. He received this unimaginable windfall for an investment of precisely *nothing*. The Beatles eventually lost control of their publishing interests in Northern Songs.

The *Cardozo Arts and Entertainment Law Journal* (©1991 Hal I. Gilemore) states, "The continued existence of conflicts of interest in the music business, and their resulting negative effects, is largely attributable to two factors. First, no statutory, administrative, or licensing requirements clearly define the role of, or regulate, personal managers. The second reason . . . is the hesitancy of American courts to intervene." The journal goes on to say that rarely if ever do such disputes find their way into a court of law.

Legend has it that in 1972 Bruce Springsteen, largely unnoticed by the music business establishment, signed a deal on the hood of his car with

Mike Appel, an up-and-coming record producer. All such agreements being service contracts, Springsteen obligated himself to write and record for several companies that Appel either owned or in which he had controlling interest. In certain exotic circumstances the agreements paid Appel commissions as high as 50 percent. Eventually, Springsteen's compositions were sold outright in a split publishing deal. Abuses on the recording side of the agreement—too lengthy to recount—resulted in Springsteen's obligation to record ten albums for CBS records, receiving only ten cents per album sold while Appel (Laurel Canyon Ltd.) was getting forty cents. Eventually an audit revealed that over a four-year period, while Laurel Canyon Ltd. had received between one and two million dollars from Springsteen's efforts, he had bagged only $100,000. (Still "The Boss" did not file suit until Appel spurned his choice of record producer Jon Landau in July of 1976. The suit was settled out of court.)

In my singer/songwriter days at WarnerRecords, I was often on the road doing promotional stints at the same time as the late Jim Croce. Frequently we found ourselves sitting face-to-face in the lobbies of the same dismal little radio stations. Croce's guitarist Maury Mulhausen shared the bill with me at the Main Point in Philadelphia the night before he flew off on the tragic tour that was to end his and Croce's lives. In September of 1968 Croce had signed several contracts for recording, publishing and management with an outfit called CP&W. (One of the owners was a college chum, the other an attorney Croce had never met "prior to signing the contracts.") All Croce was to receive was $1,200 a year and other monies described as "royalty payments." He signed without consulting independent legal counsel, apparently believing he was being covered by his "friend's" attorney. Unaccountably, the court eventually concluded after considering a suit by Croce's widow that there had been no wrongdoing. Croce's lack of bargaining power, lack of his own attorney, and the shrewdly "negotiated" terms of the agreement did not cause the court to award his widow any damages.

In another—this time near mythic—encounter between Albert Grossman, the manager, and Bob Dylan, the artist, Grossman is said to have arranged, at the outset of Dylan's career, for a publishing deal with M. Witmark & Sons Publishing, which provided a paltry $1,000 advance for Dylan and 25 percent of the publishing for Grossman. When the contract lapsed, Grossman inspired Dylan to establish his own publishing company, increasing his own take to 50 percent of total publishing income. Since Grossman's 20 percent managerial fee came out of Dylan's publishing share, Grossman was having it both ways. In a snit, Dylan eventually refused to publish music of any kind for about five years in order to deprive Grossman of these swollen commissions.

A recent issue of the *New York Daily News* (February 19, 1997) tells the sad story of the last two remaining members of the Teenagers, a '50s vocal group whose biggest hit was "Why Do Fools Fall in Love?" with wunderkind lead singer, Frankie Lymon. Herman Santiago and Jimmy Merchant failed in their attempt to stake a claim with the U.S. Supreme Court on back royalties dating from the song's 1956 debut. The article states, "They sued to get credits and royalties in 1987, long after the three-year statute of limitations expired. They argued they had been intimidated by Morris Levy, who bought the rights to the song in 1964. In 1995, a jury awarded them back royalties amounting to an estimated $570,000. Last August '96, however, a federal appeals court ruled the statute of limitations had expired before Levy allegedly made his first threats in 1969."

As we approach the "zeros," as my children are fond of calling the new millennium, the role of the personal manager is becoming multilayered and harder to decipher in the cut-and-dried terms of "good guy" versus "bad guy" that we find in most of the previous circumstances. As *Forbes* magazine states in the September 25, 1995 issue, "As entertainment becomes more and more big business, the scope for making money as a manager grows. . . . While talent agents can handle only bookings, there is nothing to prevent a manager from partnering with a personality in making movies, records, or TV shows. . . . Essentially, managers have found a loophole in the law. Managers are unregulated, not subject to the rules created to protect entertainers from predatory agents . . . the managers can book, advise, and own."

Even though state law in California, for instance, clearly states that all negotiations regarding bookings are supposed to be handled by a state-licensed talent agent, in the real world anything goes. A clever and motivated manager, it must be said, can be of immense help to the songwriter in today's multifaceted business environment, both in the area of arranging covers, introductions to recording artists and others, and specifically, in an instance where the songwriter wishes to morph into a recording artist.

Many courts and judges seem to have difficulty with the concept of the intrinsic worth of a given copyright. Obviously, a "hit" song, one that has sold millions of records, is an "object" of value even though songs are not three-dimensional and don't actually exist anywhere except in the air when they are being performed live or played on equipment. But what about another song by the same writer that has never been recorded? What is this "new" specimen worth?

My advisors and I searched at length for the answer to this question in 1973 when Madelon Baker came out of the woodwork, suing me for breach of contract and chopping off a sizable portion of my royalties at the source with a writ. She claimed that in my Johnny Rivers Music contract, in HOAP (Head of a Pin) Font, there was a clause stating that I had promised her I would record a certain number of her copyrights on one of my subsequent solo albums, even though when I went over to JRM my prospects as to the making of a solo album were so remote as to constitute the wildest speculation. (As it turned out, Mike Reilly, Glen DeLange and I did in fact make a single on Soul City Records, "(I Can Feel the) Love Years Coming" (Jimmy Webb ©1967, Johnny Rivers Music) as the Strawberry Children. Regrettably it became necessary after a few weeks as starvation closed in—she was holding up nearly four hundred thousand dollars of my royalties—to point out that none of my records, not *Words and Music, And So: On,* or *Letters* had sold even twenty thousand copies let alone come close to recouping their cost. There had been no "hits" on any of these recordings; therefore, how were we to attach a punitive value to the copyrights that admittedly had not appeared on my records and whose erstwhile identities in any case were unknown?

Madelon's argument, or at least that of her attorney, was that the judge should assume that every song in question (they may have claimed half a dozen altogether) would have had an estimable value equivalent to the performance of a song like "Up, Up and Away" or "By the Time I Get to Phoenix." We were suddenly talking *millions!* My attorney argued that songs are intrinsically worth only the paper they're written on and the ink with which they are written. Her side then argued that professionals like herself could tell the difference between "hit" songs and those other kind. If she had picked out the songs (told me what to sing), then due to her expertise surely they would have been "hits." We countered with "River Deep, Mountain High" (Jeff Barry, Ellie Greenwich and Phil Spector,

©1966), a surefire "foolproof" hit that Phil Spector had failed to bring home with Tina Turner. The song was never a bona fide hit, even for a substantial number of artists who continued to cover it, convinced that somebody had made a terrible mistake. The judge was apparently stymied by the insubstantial nature of a song in and of itself, but he did understand that songs as viable commercial concerns could be "made into hits" by promotion, hype and payola, etc. His thinking was leading him in a dangerous direction by our estimations, to wit, that since any song can be a hit even though some misfire—that one song is just about as good as another, in other words—any one of them could or might be worth a lot of money. Madelon was beginning to smile at me like Thatcher again. She wore a lot of red.

Heading up Warner Bros. Music at the time was a young executive who had the uncanny knack of being affable and brooking no disrespect at the same time. Ed Silver wore a triumphant red handlebar mustache and faded blue jeans into his office, traditionally a posting for a white-collar establishment type. Since Ed was widely acknowledged as an industry authority, indeed almost a legend for his prodigious publishing feats, we didn't hesitate to approach him about a court appearance to provide us with expert testimony. (It goes without saying that he was not offered any remuneration whatsoever, nor to my knowledge was he coached in any shape or form.) The day came for Ed's court appearance and he calmly ascended to the witness box in his blue jeans and was sworn in. Did songs in the abstract have any intrinsic value, he was asked. None that had attracted his notice, he answered. Was any song more likely to become a hit than any other, he was also asked. "Some people seem to think so," he replied, "but in my opinion it's a crapshoot." That's exactly the expression he used: *crapshoot*.

Madelon lost her case and had to relinquish her stranglehold on my royalties. The judge ruled that she couldn't to a certainty have been harmed by my failure to include a handful of unspecified songs on my markedly unsuccessful solo albums. One could infer from his rulings that my contracts with Ja-Ma Music *may not have been a valid agreement* because I was only eighteen years of age and had not been represented by my own attorney when I signed with Madelon. It is interesting to note that on at least this one occasion the law took a good close look at the "song" in all its abstract glory and decided that beauty—or at least value—is in the ear of the listener. As a postscript, one day not long afterward, Ed Silver arose from his desk in his office on the Warner Bros. lot and, legend has it, walked out never to return. The last time I saw him he was on the deck of a sailboat off Virgin Gorda heading out to sea and not looking back.

When harm is done to a writer in the publishing business it is many times accomplished with the deft anesthetic flair of a female mosquito. In other words, the event may not be noticed until it is too late. By the mid '70s "Up, Up and Away" had made a tortuous but profitable journey through several different publishing companies. Johnny Rivers had wasted no time in selling the Webb catalogue and I can't say I blame him though "Harvey" had summoned Johnny to his deathbed and confessed that the deception had been his idea and inspiration. (I am sure this unselfish act saved my friendship with Johnny Rivers who has since forgiven me, and I will always be grateful to Harv for this final kindness.) Anyway, Charles Koppleman at EMI had acquired the copyright for what it was worth . . . a standard to be sure, but slightly past its prime. The TWA commercial hadn't aired for years and aside from a perfunctory Evelyn Woods speed-read of the royalty statement when it came in, I paid little attention to my BMI catalog. (I had recently joined ASCAP.) An audit of a writer's pub-lisher is not unlike a biannual visit to the dentist to have one's teeth cleaned. You may be wasting your money but then again, you never know what might be hiding in some neglected cranny. Still, it is something that, like the dentist, is usually put off as long as humanly possible. One night at home lying on the couch with my eyes half-closed, listening to the tele-vision and trying to drift into a nap, I heard the familiar strains of "Up, Up and Away." I cracked one eyelid open and looked at the screen. No big deal, just a TWA commercial. Holy shit! A TWA commercial! I sat bolt upright on the couch—a TWA commercial no less. "Come and fly away on a winter holiday." They were singing it, albeit with a couple of copy changes, more than ten years after the initial fact. I called my business manager who, for a sizable chunk of time, had difficulty comprehending the import of my tidings. "We've got to slap an audit on Charles Koppleman," I said to my then-attorney, Leonard Marks, "right away, now!" When the audit was completed it was discovered that Trans World Airlines had been paying quietly and consistently, indeed ever since 1967 they had been paying a substantial amount of money annually for the express purpose of *preventing any other airline from using "Up, Up and Away" as a theme song.* I was owed in the neighborhood of three hundred thousand dollars. If I hadn't seen the one-time regional ad urging New Yorkers to head down to the Keys for a break from the intemperate weather, I have no idea when the EMP company (the copyright owner for this song) would have seen fit to notify me of my good fortune. Here is as good a place as any to describe one of the most prevalent scams in the publishing/recording business. THEY, whoever they may be, will always wait as long as possible up to and including your death to pay you. This is because as long as they have your money . . . they are collecting the interest. If they get caught with some of your money that they shouldn't have, you can bet that it's only an unfortunate oversight on their part. In other words, you'll have to sue them to get the interest they owe you. Got it?

There is much of this sort of thing going on constantly in our trade disguised for the most part as benign neglect. "Oh, we're just all so busy and important, millions to earn, companies to buy, loads of things to do! Can't be bothered with your little piddling hundreds of thousands of dollars, sorry." One of the major problems that makes this sort of "sin of omission" possible is the rapidity involved in the transfer of one's publishing from one company to another. It became necessary during the writing of this book to trace the publishing "lineage" of a certain song because I intended to quote it and needed permission. None of the publishers listed as ever having handled the song professed any knowledge of it whatsoever. The performing rights society involved couldn't find the rightful owner either, though they volunteered the cheerful if useless detail that the writer, as far as anyone knew, was still alive. We started trying to find HIM. As I write this, a few weeks before going to press, we have not found the unfortunate author of this piece of well-known music, a "hit" by any measure and possibly even a "standard." Do you know what is most worrisome about this situation? It is unlikely that the writer is receiving any payment.

When a writer's publishing is owned by a company that sells to a foreign-owned one or is even licensed in a foreign country, the chances of an author receiving an accurate accounting diminish in direct proportion to the distance between him and the new publisher. Foreign rights is a great sinkhole for royalties no matter what your domestic publisher tells you. The publishers themselves have a tough time riding herd on their foreign interests as new markets open up in the post-glasnost era. The vast territories of the former Soviet Union and China, among other inscrutable places, defy collection of royalties in a traditional sense. China, for instance, has no performing rights society and pays no one for anything except the manufacturers who off-load tons of outdated plastic there. What is the point in all this . . . well . . . negativity? The writer must know that he or she is ultimately responsible for seeing that fair payment is made. No grandfatherly attorney, accountant or publisher is likely to beneficently preside over all these complicated matters for any compensation imaginable, short of a full partnership—and then we must remember our old nemesis, conflict of interest. Songwriting is not a dreamlike, passive, artistic pursuit. It is hands-on business practice, and the bleached bones of those who have foolishly mistaken it for something else line both sides of the metaphorical stairway to songwriters' heaven.

Businesswise, the people who made it when I was coming up had it comparatively easy. BMI and ASCAP (SESAC was not really a player until recently) were in a constant bidding war to pick off the top earners. Here's how it worked: A writer with a medium-sized catalog and a couple of hits who looked prosperous in the short term might be snug as a bug in a rug at BMI. He knew about ASCAP, the word was out that they paid slower but that they had a more "legitimate" cachet. Gordon Jenkins was with ASCAP, Paul Francis Webster was too. An ASCAP representative would come around and take the writer to lunch. It would be a pleasant conversation during which he would be reminded that at the end of his current contractual obligation to BMI the writer did have the choice of "re-upping" or he could come over to ASCAP. A dignified spiel would follow about how ASCAP was in the process of revamping its accounting procedures, had these very interesting new bonus provisions coming into effect and *we'll give you a half-million-dollar advance, which amounts to an interest-free loan if you'll cross over! And I'll take that tab!!!* Most writers didn't agonize over this decision for any great length of time.

After all it was a bloodless affair that only involved signing one's name to a short paragraph of boilerplate. Beyond that, we quickly learned that in a short two years or so when renewal time rolled around again the president or vice-president of BMI would call with an invitation to lunch and we could repeat the whole lucrative process in reverse. This practice soon escalated into a full-scale perennial bidding war. And How Awful! The top ten or twenty writers were crying all the way to the bank. Make no mistake about it, we were not taking candy from babies. ASCAP and BMI were sitting on huge reservoirs of songwriting money.

Well, the party had to come to an end sometime. It's just not right that a bunch of shiftless songwriters should be able to capriciously exercise that kind of financial power. One bright, sunny day, each of us pen-wielding, side-switching song jockeys received the same mournful telephone call from our respective attorneys. It seemed both BMI and ASCAP had pulled the plug on big advances, loans and guarantees. Right off the bat we know that this is one hell of a convenient arrangement for ASCAP and BMI! This is gonna slim those entertainment and expense accounts right down! Now for Pete's sake, how were we going to finance those cabins in Aspen, those ketches and yawls on the Cape, those Harleys and Ferraris not to mention those getaways to Bora Bora? In other words, how were we to live beyond our means? In a more sobering vein, what were we going to do when we hit a White Squall, a life-threatening disease, IRS beef or even an earthquake, one of those catastrophes that is at any moment only a phone call away?

I asked Frances Preston, president of BMI, how it happened that both societies had made the same drastic cutbacks almost simultaneously.

> It came to an end so suddenly because of a lawsuit referred to as the "Buffalo" case. This was a struggle with some independent television broadcasters that BMI and ASCAP fought for approximately ten years. During that period of time the legal fees were so tremendous, and not knowing the outcome of the suit we closed the door to advances and guarantees. It was unfortunate because advances were very beneficial to songwriters. Even though the money for the larger songwriters was coming out of all songwriters' pockets, these large catalogs boosted the market share so that the organizations were able to acquire more from the users, which benefits all writers and publishers.

Marilyn Bergman, president of ASCAP, thinks the practice quietly continues. She seems to feel that BMI has always had the advantage in the "switching game."

> ASCAP and BMI both operate under consent decrees with the Justice Department, but the decrees are quite different. ASCAP's consent decree is much more stringent. For example, an ASCAP member has

and must have the right to resign, or "re-up," at the end of every year. BMI can tie up affiliates for two-, three-, or five-year deals. That the playing field is not level is unfair to ASCAP and the writers, who should have the freedom to join whichever organization they prefer.

The beef between ASCAP and BMI goes all the way back to 1940 when, according to Frederick Nolan's biography of Larry Hart, "the radio networks and the songwriter's union, ASCAP, became involved in a life-or-death struggle over performance royalties. ASCAP raised the performance fees they charged broadcasters to such heights that the networks responded by forming their own Performing Rights Society, Broadcast Music, Inc., which in turn resulted in the banning from broadcasts of all songs by ASCAP members. Not until late in February 1941 did ASCAP accept a Department of Justice consent decree which resolved the deadlock." ASCAP itself originated twenty-six years previously when, angered by decades of abuses (E. P. Christie of the famous Christie's Minstrels was said to be a blatant thief who put his name on many Stephen Foster songs), Victor Herbert and his attorney, Nathan Burkan, founded an organization to guarantee composers payment for live performances.)

The 1960 occurrence that changed the rivalry between ASCAP and BMI was the Payola Scandal. In early January, hard on the heels of an antitrust investigation against it, ASCAP asked the FCC not to renew the licenses of 557 radio stations unless they divested themselves of BMI stock, claiming the stations would plug songs in which they had a financial interest. Legendary disc jockey Alan Freed's career was ruined in the crossfire.

This is a good juncture to point out the differences between ASCAP and BMI. Believe it or not, BMI is owned by *broadcasters*. Ms. Preston clarified this relationship for me.

Our board does not enter into any of our licensing negotiations.
They depend on management to bring in as much money as possible
from all users, to keep our costs down and that the money we receive
is paid to our writers and publishers.

She went on to explain that the formation of BMI and the open-door policy for all songwriters brought on the explosion of American music in the '50s and '60s, and debunks the myth of a "secret circle" of big broadcasters.

It's no secret who serves on the board. It's not *big broadcasters!* [her emphasis] There are some small owners, some middle-sized, and several very large ones, but not more of a conflict than you have on the ASCAP board, with Time-Warner, MTV and VH-I all sitting.

Marilyn Bergman is proud of the fact that ASCAP is a membership organization.

What we cannot do is give a writer a guarantee, as BMI can, because this is our members' money. We can legally advance money against a writer's royalties, as long as that advance is recouped. Unlike ASCAP, BMI is a corporation owned by broadcasters rather than a membership society run by writers and publishers.

Whatever the real origins of this "restructuring" of the songwriters' "banks" and "best friends," there is no minimizing its role in the absorption of small, individually owned publishing companies by huge and often foreign multinationals. There is something decidedly unpatriotic about Congress, BMI, ASCAP and SESAC standing by with their hands in their virtually bottomless pockets while small, family-owned publishing companies are gobbled up.

Congress is always teasing us with the prospect of reducing our meager ways and means. The strong impression is gained that many members of both houses feel that if a person's name is familiar in the celebrity sense, regardless of that individual's line of work, then that person is bound to be rolling in it. In other words, Jewel? Oh yeah, I guess she's in the same financial bracket with Jodie Foster! Right. The result is that when something like copyright term extension comes up like it did a few years ago (a bill that would extend a writer's or heir's ownership of a given work) a not very subtle effort is made by the competition (the people who want your music to go into the public domain, the sooner the better, so they can use it for free) to characterize "we all" as rich celebrities with more than we need who don't really work for what we have. The truth being that songwriting is a cottage industry much like a family farm. Good fortune ebbs and flows and there are some rich farmers and maybe a few rich songwriters. Of course everyone else should be able to pass the works of their hands—their companies, inventions, farms or literary works—along to the grandchildren . . . BUT NOT SONGWRITERS? Are we really of an entirely different social caste that our grandchildren and heirs into perpetuity shouldn't inherit a portion of what we've struggled so hard to achieve? Allow me to acquaint you with another such slight in the law. Did you know that a songwriter is probably the only citizen of this country who cannot sell his property, that is, *his publishing company*, without the okay of his spouse and children? The only legal precedent I can think of for this might be a mental patient in an asylum. What if I hate my children and don't want to consult with them about the selling of my company? What if my spouse has tried to poison me? Where along the way did songwriters show themselves to be so irresponsible as to not deserve the same rights as other businessmen?

As this book nears completion bills H.R.789 and S.28 have been placed before Congress for the third time in a row. The people who introduced these bills must have balls of brass to entitle them "Fairness in Music Licensing." Passage of these bills would cost all songwriters, composers and music publishers millions of dollars since writers would not be paid when their music is played in bars, restaurants, retail stores, etc. Think about that the next time you are sitting in a romantic restaurant, listening to a Mercer and Mancini ballad and chewing on a ninety-dollar filet mignon. Isn't the music worth a couple of extra cents? (The busboys are getting paid.) Oh yes, religious radio stations are protesting as well, the ones who claim they are nonprofit while soliciting billions of dollars in tax-free money. Maybe they would like to switch over to a Middle Eastern format for a while!

When I was a young songwriter both societies faced one of their greatest challenges in the form of the jukebox operators, the guys who bring coin-operated Seeburys, Wurlitzers and the like into bars and restaurants. (Since 1934 and the repeal of Prohibition, virtually every bar, beer joint and honky-tonk on the American landscape has had at least one coin-operated record player on the premises, giving rise to the nickname "juke joint.")

"It was a direct performance for profit," said Frances Preston. "You put a quarter in the machine and hear the record of your choice. There was no question as to whether a song was a public performance for profit."

I remember well the position the jukebox operators took on this issue. They had purchased a piece of plastic and they felt like they should be able to play it forever.

"The truth was," Preston continued, "most jukeboxes were given free records for promotion."

At the time, Frances and others placed a diagram of a big "quarter" in front of the congressional committee and showed them graphically how the songwriters only ended up with half a cent if there were two of them.

"I can remember there was a senator who was backed by the Longshoremen of Hawaii, and he threw us out of his office—he didn't even want to hear our story!"

After this pitched battle was won by our side I chanced to encounter a young fella named Jim after one of my live shows, and he told me he worked for BMI. He said his job was to go out to bars and wherever and make sure the jukebox operators were complying with the new regulations. When he found a bar where the owners weren't paying for live music and jukeboxes, he was supposed to gently instruct them in the error of their ways. I didn't see him until a few weeks later, but when I did, he was on crutches and had his arm in a cast. He didn't work for BMI anymore.

SESAC, BMI and ASCAP are not heartless institutions. ASCAP has a hardship advance set up for members with a royalty history and allows one advance every twelve months. Covered in the advance are medical emergencies, tax liens and death, although they are adamant about informing members that they employ "case-by-case" criteria. BMI has a loan program with NationsBank and is working on an insurance plan. SESAC offers advances depending on the situation and the writer, and details are usually worked out between the member and his or her SESAC representative.

It is, however, poignant beyond belief that these incredibly wealthy companies—because that is what they are—can't find a way of making large sums of money available to writers on short notice in order to help them save their publishing from absorption by large publishing houses and then being installed in overblown "collections" for the most part only to collect dust on some top shelf. A less kindly and understanding person than myself might look askance at such a situation and imagine conspiratorial quid pro quos, especially when all the parties concerned know that loaning money on a reasonably significant catalog amounts to a *guaranteed* return and profit.

Success, even a measure of it, has a way of throwing the hardworking, long-suffering songwriter a curve. It becomes hard to remember that writing a song was once almost as much fun as riding an old wooden roller coaster—the kind that are already creaking and ready to fall apart. "Be quiet kids! I have to work!" you will hear yourself saying instead, because of success you see. . . . You're up on that big horse and for some reason afraid to fall off. I reminded J. D. Souther that neither one of us is getting any younger and asked him if he felt at all like trying to compete with some of today's hot youngsters.

> You ask what I think the future holds for us older cats? I don't think we have to chase Beck. I don't think it's a race. I think part of reinventing yourself as an artist is realizing that the world doesn't revolve around you, and that actually can produce a more revelatory kind of work, a more examined life in art. It doesn't mean we're going to sell ten million records; the chances of that happening anytime are small . . . but someone will always be making records that have good songs on them.

There is an old Portuguese proverb that haunts me when I catch myself hopelessly entangled in the success and lifestyle game and it goes like this: "The road to Paradise is paradise." I have to remind myself that writing a good song is worthwhile in and of itself, that at the end of the day if it is only me that has heard the music, wadded it into a tight ball and thrown it in the wastebasket, then it still ranks as one of the better days that life has to offer.

Most songwriters I know are tense, nervous types who have to "work" at relaxation. Obsession is always nudging at our elbows and can only be countered by allotting specific time for play. Yes, play! Modeling clay and model planes and white-water rafting and painting and travel and birdwatching and softball and aquarium keeping and kids and dogs. PLAY. If simple old-fashioned playtime seems too unstructured for the well-disciplined songwriter then what about another discipline? Tennis, cross country skiing, bicycling, flying, sailing or playing another musical instrument. It helps to get outside oneself by interacting with friends who know nothing about the music business. One of my lifelong friends is a Hollywood stuntman who especially enjoys setting himself on fire. Another runs a lobster boat out of Booth Bay, Maine. Another teaches senior citizens how to run computers. What a relief they are!

They used to say about Richard Nixon that he always had "one eye on history." It seems to me that if one eye is always focused on the back trail, it's only a matter of time until the traveler comes to grief on a hairpin turn.

It might be helpful to remember that no one is going to put up a statue of any songwriters we know until a long time after we're all dead. You will never be in a position to look over your shoulder and see your bronze likeness sitting on someone else's piano. So forget about it.

You might even luck out and get to be famous—it could happen. People have gotten famous for throwing cow pies further than other people, at least in Oklahoma. If such a novel and distracting experience occurred in your own life, one would think that you would at least want to look back upon it as a happy time.

With success so—well to be frank—*unlikely* most writers are remarkably unprepared when the lightning does end up in the bottle. Success attracts sycophants and yes-men in droves and many are quite accomplished actors and storytellers. I have paid publishing reps fifty thousand dollars a year to "get records" (get my songs recorded), who never got *one*. I have signed administration agreements with publishers who faithfully collected their twenty percent and otherwise sat on their fannies for the duration of the contract. I walked out onstage at the Dorothy Chandler Pavilion and played a catastrophic concert unprepared because I couldn't summon the gumption to tell my then-manager and attorney to stick it. I loaned money to anybody who came through the door and never really thought too much about getting it back. I supported bands and their entourages along with permanent houseguests. I played "Elvis" and bought six Cadillacs and gave them away to my staff. I took my friends into the studio and cut records with them when I knew their chances were minuscule. I have picked up more three-hundred-dollar dinner tabs than a deer has ticks. There were excesses. They called the private dining room at Benihana's on Ventura Boulevard in Encino the Jimmy Webb Room. If I wanted a lobster in the middle of the night I would send Don Gee (owner of Starlite Limousine) to The Palm and have him order two. He would eat one and bring the other to me. Money flowed out in a wide rushing river. It was inexcusable and if I could go back in time I would probably spend every dime exactly the same way. I don't advise the newly successful songwriter to follow in my footsteps. A man can accomplish more for others in this world from a position of strength than weakness. Guilt is not a virtue. It does not even the playing field when one has been fortunate enough to accomplish more than most of his friends or family. Guilt can be carried to the point of fiscal self-destruction.

The songwriter, of all people, should be financially conservative with a clear understanding of what another songwriter once wrote: "*Nobody knows you when you're down and out.*" Longevity is where it's at. Being able to make money doing a variety of things, being a sideman, an arranger, a performer, a producer, even a copyist, anything to surf over the inevitable "corrections" in our marketplace. Sometimes the bottom just drops out. A certain fastidiousness in regard to taxes would not be out of place. The IRS likes to pick on show business types and make examples of them—put them in the stocks so to speak—so they will often audit a songwriter instead of, for instance, a guy who makes more money but runs a large shoe store. Do I need to say that money needs to be put aside for college, retirement and such? Oftentimes a songwriter is so caught up in the excitement of this big wonderful business of ours, so distracted by the cyclic windfalls that always seem to arrive just in the nick of time, that a concept so simple eludes them. Would it be unfair of me to suggest that the traditional support mediums available to the writer—or for that matter, anyone unfamiliar with the narcotic effect of heavy cash flow—such as banks, lawyers, accountants and other financial advisors are many times less than zealous in their pursuit of a frugal approach to the client's lifestyle? When a songwriter or recording artist is making and spending huge sums of money a long trough is provided at which to feed. It is a season of plenty for all the farmyard animals. Favors are bartered back and forth, often in secret. Volume creates a lower per-unit price which any decent general can tell you inevitably gives birth to a black market. From the client's viewpoint an excessive and incessant flow of money is always obscured. Checking accounts, plastic, electronic drafts, CPA's with power of attorney, all lend an air of unreality to transactions, an unreality that would not be present if the big spender was *actually touching the money*, physically had to count out eighty-four thousand hard-earned dollars for a new Mercedes. It boils down to this: The more money you have, the easier it is for someone else to slide it away from you.

I believe that at the same time a songwriter exercises vigilance over money matters he or she can make their most important long-term investments in the form of kindness to others. Short of being a card-carrying saint, there are few of us who will manage to live an entire life without leaving a couple of enemies in our wake. Sometimes, diabolically enough, we create these enemies out of the clay of kindness. As some smartass once said, "No good deed goes unpunished" (attributed to various sources). Generally speaking, however, the music business will be found to be peopled with good-hearted, well-meaning folk who will respect and remember genuine goodwill. Our village is a small one as towns go. Word about behavior and treatment of others travels fast and is rarely questioned, though to be sure, the type of person who would take such advice solely for the good it would do them probably does not stand to benefit from it.

It is a good policy to refrain as much as possible from "show business gossip" and unfounded speculation. I blabbed once for a couple of weeks about how unfortunate it was that old so-and-so, the songwriter, had died, until he called me up and ordered me to keep my mouth shut, else he would come over and kill me. It was hard enough finding employment, I believe he said. Gossip is, to me, a substance as volatile as nitroglycerin in the vibrating engine room of the music business, so let the purveyor beware. Talk is not cheap. Talk is bloody expensive for fools.

Failure is inevitable. It is best to confront this terrible fact at the outset. If a writer's every twentieth song were recorded and became a hit, it would constitute a phenomenal, if not unequaled, record. Virtually every writer of any stature has had a red-hot streak and then a brain-numbing, white-knuckling downward slump during which he or she may believe that nothing of any consequence will ever again occur in his or her career. It is an American way of thinking, originating perhaps in our preoccupation with sport and athletics. "There are no second acts in American life," said F. Scott Fitzgerald. When I was twenty-one years old the only career I could imagine for myself was an endless string of hits. I was convinced that I had the magic and was surprised that more people did not understand the same obvious strategies that I had memorized. My first professional appearance was at the Desert Inn Hotel in Las Vegas as part of the Connie Stevens show. At one point in the evening I would go onstage with Connie and we would sing a duet of "Didn't We?" I was a shaky, untrained singer at that tender stage of my career but the crowd invariably went nuts. One song, tentatively sung, and yet they whooped and hollered for ten minutes every night! "What's going on?" I asked Connie one evening as we walked into the wings. She looked at me with the most adorable expression and her cerulean blue eyes twinkling. "People love a fresh face." She smiled. "Enjoy it while you can," she said as she led me back out to the apron for another bow. Bill Cosby was probably a more honest audience. He leaned in my dressing room door one night and asked, "Hey kid, are you really gonna be a singer?" I laughed. I was twenty-one years old and having fun. But when the spotlight really and truly swings away to focus on some newly arrived Phenom, it can be demoralizing and exceedingly hard to take. It's galling to write your heart out, work fourteen months on a solo album, release it to critical accolades all over the world only to have some half-crocked TV star at a cocktail party ask, "Are you still writing?" *Still writing?* That's like asking a shark if it's still swimming. Even when success condescends to tap on your shoulder a second or third time that klieg light is so much slower to swing in your direction. A person has to jump up and down and stamp their foot and yell, "I'm still here! Look at me! I'm Number One on the country chart! I'm still here!" You may be asked to do a few interviews and be paid a watered-down, detached sort of attention but something will have changed. You're not a "fresh face" anymore. If the writer is depending on reinforcement from the media to bolster the old *ego cogito* at this stage, he or she is in some real trouble. It's time to get tough. Time to strip away the extraneous showbiz bullshit and find out who we really are under all that flattery and hype. I call it "doing a Gregory Peck," after one of my favorite actors and particularly for a scathing lecture he delivered to the character played by David Niven in a movie called *The Guns of Navarone*. To go the distance a songwriter has to take the hard hits and maintain a stubborn self-esteem. Most of the time when an experienced songwriter is trying a song out on a new listener and says something like "Hey, listen to this and tell me what you think," he already knows what he thinks, he knows what kind of a writer he thinks he is, and if the truth be known, he doesn't much care what the other person thinks if he's already decided it's a good song. That's what it takes. When I was a contract writer at Jobete, I had a little song that I thought might be good for an artist they were trying to develop. His name was Paul Petersen and he was a cute kid who had appeared on *The Donna Reed Show*. I played the song for Hal and Frank and they criticized it roundly. The fact that it was a three-verse form and almost a true ballad turned them off. Everything at Motown was choruses and hooks. "Put a big chorus after each one of the verses and you've got something," they ordered. I went home and toyed with the idea halfheartedly but could never make the changes and ended up missing the boat on the Paul Petersen release. The song was "By the Time I Get to Phoenix." That's what it takes. I don't believe in writing songs by committee.

This stubborn self-esteem can't, to my knowledge, be learned or taught. It is a gift that one gives to oneself and once freely given and accepted can never be taken away. There are a couple of people out on the West Coast in positions of considerable power in the musical side of the film business. One of these gentlemen in postadolescent days was a would-be songwriter when I was at the zenith of my notoriety. He decided to send me some unsolicited material, and fool and egomaniac that I was, I sat down at my desk and wrote him a critique. Though I honestly do not remember what I wrote or whether the songs were particularly distinguished one way or the other I am assuming he was disappointed by my comments because this same person has bad-mouthed me around the business ever since. He has told close friends of mine that he doesn't understand what all the praise for my work is about. He's told others who have reported directly to me that he does not think my music or songs have any place in films. I have been told by a close friend who was working on a project with him that he had called a producer who had just hired me to write a song for a major motion picture to tell her that she could do much better than me. (My song eventually was literally and mysteriously squeezed out of the picture.) Do his antics disrupt my life plans? Or enrage me enough to put me off my game? They do not because he is a fly and I am an elephant. And like Mikey Douglas says, I also have the *memory* of an elephant. That's what it takes. Talent will out. That's what it takes. Turn the anger, fear and frustration into a new song better than any you've ever written. That's what it takes. "Do you still write songs?" Hell, yes, that's what it takes. "You're in it up to your neck now, mister!" That's what it takes. Find a hot young artist. Go around the bastards. Sell your solo album door-to-door and get on *60 Minutes* and let them laugh at you. But make 'em cry when they listen to you. Become a real man or a real woman. Pour out a part of your soul that no one else is willing to reveal. That's what it takes.

The nemesis of creativity is stasis. When we are cowed, sullen and emotionally dead in the water, when the career seems to be stalled and no part of life is going very well, a violent, arbitrary and radical change of direction is called for. Perhaps a pop songwriter should then write songs for a rap project (as John Bettis is known to have done). Or write a modern symphony. (Billy Joel is contemplating the creation of several symphonic works.) Or do what I'm doing—write choral settings for weather forecasts. Stasis must be destroyed by any means, because in today's entertainment business an artist over forty years of age will only be appreciated for his or her iconic value, as on the memorable evening when filmmaker Oliver Stone looked at me for the first time with an expression combining equal parts discovery, amazement and revelation, saying, "So *you're* Jimmy Webb!" What has worked before is never as good as something that has never been tried before, even if it doesn't work. I would like someday to write a suite about the island of Majorca based on Catalan folk music and flamenco influences and rhythms. I know little or nothing about such music except that I like it. There is no one more qualified to write this piece of music than me. I am uniquely qualified if only because I have an open, excitable mind. A Catalan composer may by necessity or accident of birth bring a certain stasis to the work. He will be set in his nationalistic ways. I or perhaps someone else will make something new out of it! It might be wise to immediately cease and desist in any creative task that has become tedious and depressing to strike out in a new direction. If it turns out that the writer literally does "strike out," then at least there will be consolation in the temporary banishment of Tedium and Depression, even though these ugly sisters will eventually return. It may become necessary to change course many times during a creative life. It is a good thing, a thing not to be feared, and strong medicine.

When something bad happens to a bus driver or a school teacher or an insurance adjuster or architect, there is not much from an emotional standpoint that they can do about it. They can sue or grieve or drink or swear vengeance against those who have caused them pain. A songwriter, on the other hand, can write a song about it. A great song, unlike most other forms of recourse or sublimation, can put the world back into focus. It can make silent phones begin to ring again, return money to a depleted bank account and sometimes even bring someone back into a life who might have been thought gone forever. There is unimaginable power in a great song. Fortunately the stuff that songs are made of is nonpolluting and recyclable. The grief and frustration that easily grinds up and destroys ordinary mortals is grist for the songwriter's mill. Something to remember when feeling down and helpless: You're a songwriter and have power over the demons. I encountered a young husband outside the stage door of the Royal Albert Hall one night after a performance with the London Philharmonic. We stood in a misty rain. "This is my wife, Ophelia," he said, his arm encircling a lovely young woman who smiled and said in turn, "This is Giles and Diedre," her arm around two white-haired, rosy-cheeked English children. "I want you to know," the young husband continued, "that eight years ago when I was in public school I had a horrible row with Ophelia here, and she cursed me and swore to never see me again." Ophelia blushed at this and cupped her hand around her forehead. "I took *this!*"—he triumphantly produced a 45 r.p.m. record out from under his mac—"over to her flat and taped it to her door." Meanwhile I stood there utterly confused. "Will you sign it for us please?" he beseeched me, brandishing a pen and pushing the plastic disc into my wet hands. In the dim light and half rain I could just make out a scratched copy of "All I Know," recorded by Artie Garfunkel. I took another much closer look at Giles and Diedre, smiling, expectant and apparently *grateful* in the Knightsbridge drizzle.

A song can heal. It can close wounds between lovers, friends and families. Perhaps in some cases songs have even cured diseases. Music is being used increasingly as a therapy by certain farseeing persons active in the treatment of autistic children with surprisingly positive results. As for us, songwriters may be the only "physicians" who actually have the power to heal ourselves. Writing songs is probably the best autopsychotherapy ever invented. In fact, the infamous "writer's block" may be nothing more than a stubborn unwillingness to cure ourselves, a psychomasochism caused by our refusal to confront the truth and put it into the air regardless of repercussions.

Paul McCartney said about his touching song to slain collaborator John Lennon ("Here Today," ©1982), "Songwriting is like psychiatry; you sit down and dredge up something that's deep inside and bring it out front. And I just had to be real and say, 'John, I love you.' I think being able to say things like that in songs can keep you sane."

It is ridiculously easy to become bitter in this trade, so hard not to resent in at least some small capacity the success of others. The real problem is that envy and bitterness are such poor materials for a songwriter to work with. A person can write one, perhaps two songs on the subject and even if the pieces are well-crafted, probably no one will want to hear them. I capsulized insults and aimed them at specific living individuals in some of my early music and now regret those acts more than any others in my creative life. I still wake up at four o'clock in the morning in the pitch black of my bedroom, staring at the ceiling in horror at some deliberate and carefully constructed ridicule wrapped like poison in an old lyric. As a weapon in the pursuit of personal vendettas the song lacks elegance, at least in my hand, but in a sociopolitical sense it has and will continue to provide a keen edge for the evolution of change. As Dick Bradley says in *Understanding Rock 'n' Roll*:

> It is no accident that in many radical journalists, musicians and so on, from Adorno through to the NME [New Musical Express] columnists of the 1980s we see both *consolation* and *resistance* as popular music possibilities often tending to disapprove of the former and seek far and wide for the latter. Yet music *must* do both . . . but, of course, it is to be hoped that the resistant side of the process, music as a potential weapon for freedom, is developed more and more by the working and middle-class listeners, amateurs and professional musicians themselves.

Bradley is not talking politics per se, as much as hoping that socially conscious music might someday point the way to a kind of Utopia.

Once a songwriter has come up with a couple of hits (and the people who write about such things just can't resist stating that he or she has found "the formula"), there is just tremendous pressure from the label, the fans, the media and even family to keep doing it. Just keep churning them out. Look what it did for McDonald's! There is a lot that is wrong with this tack but let's consider a couple of the deadlier ones. The dynamo that powers the music of "kids" (the younger persons who buy most of the records) according to Dick Bradley is "resistance." This resistance constitutes an ever-changing underground club with its own secret rituals, organized or disorganized in such a way that you and I will never manage to be members. By the time we complete our pathetic study of the current rules the culture will be miles downstream building and hiding a new exclusivity even harder to understand and to penetrate. That is why the beloved "follow-ups" of our youth are no longer effective or even needed. The parameters of this "resistance" are now changing so rapidly with such literally *blinding* speed that today's howl of rage is tomorrow's creamed-corn fart. To repeat oneself is to resign from the match and there is another reason this is true. One of the primary—indeed perhaps the single most important—functions, even *duties* of the pop media en masse is to pin donkey tails and Kick Me! signs on the backs of writers, singers and actors dumb enough to get pigeon-holed. The public wants to know *what something is*. After they find out *what something is* they want to know how to get *it*. I rented a summer house almost every year in a town called Poipu on the dry side of Kauai in Hawaii. Down below the house in the dunes was a beach called Mahalapu, scene of horrific battle and slaughter during the reign of Kamehameha the Great. One summer, primitive paintings or pictographs had been found there beside an old temple after a winter storm swept half the beach out into the Maui Channel. News of this find had leaked into *National Geographic* magazine. That summer was hell. Thousands of tourists parked their Jeeps and mopeds on our little private road and made the pilgrimage through our back yard and down into the dunes. We sat out in the back on lawn chairs, my friends and myself, stoically sipping our mai tai's and watching the crowds trek through the view. Virtually every besotted, Bermuda-shorted, cooler-carrying son of a gun who passed that way would squint up at us and yell, "Where is IT!?" We would point down toward the old Hawaiian graveyard and off they would hike to see *it*. They would return a half hour later, sweaty, cooler half-empty, frowning at us as though we had bum-steered them. You see, once people have seen IT or heard IT or bought IT, they get instantaneously bored and want to go find *another* IT. That's why an artist moves in a zigzag course so as not to end up like the cruiser *Indianapolis* foundering and surrounded by sharks. Did anyone ever know what the Beatles were going to do next? Or Dylan? Or John Cage? Nope, I don't think so, hence their endless and transcendent appeal; they avoided the dead-letter box. They were always . . . well, George Carlin said it better: "An artist has an obligation to be en route somewhere." God bless his ass. Or as Martha Graham wrote in a letter to Agnes deMille, "No artist is pleased . . . there is no satisfaction whatever at any time. There is only a strange, divine dissatisfaction, a blessed unrest that keeps us marching and makes us more alive than the others." Joni Mitchell, perhaps the most artistically restless soul of our generation, said in a 1979 *Rolling Stone* interview:

> You have two options. You can stay the same and protect the formula that gave you your initial success. They're going to crucify you for staying the same. If you change, they're going to crucify you for changing, but staying the same is boring. So, of the two options I'd rather be crucified for changing.

If one has taken care of oneself, thereby living long enough, then Glory Days can always return provided that too many bridges have not been burned. "The same people you abuse on your way up, you might meet up on your way down." So goes the lyric by Allen Toussaint ("On Your Way Down," ©1972). There is a difference between having a sense of self-worth combined with a reasonably firm attitude toward those who may or may not be trying to take advantage and going berserk every time something doesn't pan out perfectly as planned. There is always the temptation to write "The Big Letter." The Big Letter is always packed with superlatives: "the worst," "I have never," "ever again," "as long as I live," "in perpetuity," and so forth. It has been noted that the pen is mightier than the sword. As a supplement be advised that the pen is even harder to retract.

I did a Christmas interview for a network morning show a few years ago as a last minute favor, or so I thought. I was out of bed at five A.M. and sitting in front of a camera at six. We taped a seven-minute segment in support of a holiday album I had just recorded with Art Garfunkel and Amy Grant. All the following week I rose early and flipped to the proper channel anxious to see how my new blue sweater showed up on the tube. The interview never aired. I will spare the reader a description of my consternation and the colorful expletives I hurled against the persons who had so blatantly insulted my project and so callously wasted my time. I sat right down and wrote The Big Letter. Contained in the letter was an ill-conceived threat/promise to never appear on the program again even after reincarnation, in parallel dimensions if any or in any other time-space continuums. And so I haven't. Not because I haven't *wanted* to, but because the people who are running the show remember me and remember the letter.

I would like to contrast such a display of ignorance and pride run amok with another difference of opinion that I settled face to face. When I was a recording artist at Reprise Records in the early '70s, I was extremely dissatisfied with the way the label was promoting my record. Like, they *weren't* promoting it, or that was my impression. I drove over to the Warner Bros. lot one afternoon and walked into the label president's office, a gentleman named Mo Ostin. Mo smiled at me from behind his owlish black-rimmed glasses and asked what he could do for me. "I need you to spend an hour a day on my record, Mo, either on the phone or in person. I really need you to put in the time," I pleaded. He smiled again.

"Jimmy, we put out forty-three albums this month alone and I'm afraid I just don't have the time available to make that promise."

"Well then," I replied, "I would like to ask you to release me from my contract." I owed Warner Bros. Records in the neighborhood of a quarter of a million dollars in unrecouped royalties and had privately resolved to pay it back if necessary in order to make my escape. Mo stood up and took my hand. "You're free to go." He smiled. I found out later that he had absorbed the loss so I could start out somewhere else with a clean slate. As far as I know to this day there has never been a hint of animosity between us. So much for The Big Letter.

As mentioned previously it won't be possible to live and work in the music business without making enemies, at least if one wishes to conduct themselves with any degree of integrity and self-respect. What is to be avoided is the flagrant insult that makes it impossible for the other party to exit the confrontation with a modicum of face. Somebody has said that diplomacy is giving the other guy a way out. It is also about giving *yourself* a way out and that means keeping bridges intact if possible. An important part of keeping our bridges intact is periodic maintenance. In other words, a bridge does not have to be burned down for it to become impassable through neglect. A close friend of mine likes to use the expression "There are friends of the road and friends of the heart." In my view it is unfortunate that so many songwriting friendships are ones of the road, because we ourselves are our greatest asset in this passive war of survival and sanity. It helps immeasurably to know that there are others in close proximity who understand exactly the vexations we endure, not in the sense that "misery loves company," but because it is simply too difficult to excel at what we do and travel in such dangerous emotional terrain completely alone.

The first time I met Tommy Boyce and Bobby Hart was while working down on Melrose in Madelon's joint, and no doubt they had come in to make some cheap demos since that was about ninety-five percent of our business. (We had top-of-the-line equipment: a three-track Ampex that worked at least half the time.) Tommy and Bobby then seemed a lot older than me; they were real professional songwriters after all, but when I think back carefully and put it in perspective all I see is a couple of kids who had graduated high school maybe three years before me. Bobby confirms that.

"I came out to California right after high school in about '58 or '59 to go to disc-jockey school and maybe backtrack into singer/songwriting and that's where I first met Tommy," he told me a few weeks ago on my fifty-first birthday. The two kids worked for a while with a manager/producer named Jesse Hodges who told them they were going to need some original songs. "It wasn't the kind of collaboration where one person was the composer and the other the lyricist. We switched back and forth and had a lot of fun."

Boyce got The Big Break. He went to New York City to write for Stan Shulman, Ray Peterson and some others. Eventually Bobby joined him in the East and they had their first hit together ("Come a Little Bit Closer," ©1964). "I first worked Vegas in '64 or '65 as a back-up singer for Teddy Randazzo at the Thunderbird Hotel and what a blast! We'd start at eight o'clock at night and get off at seven in the morning."

It was during this period that Tommy got signed in New York by Screen Gems and came west to open the California branch office. The two friends reunited and the good times began to roll. They practically fell into the Monkees project, the brainchild of buddies Burt Schneider and Bob Rafaelson. "We wrote the theme walking down to the park from our house, you know it was kind of a walkin' groove."

The people in charge underestimated their abilities as producers but the tenacious partners eventually landed the producing chores on the first Monkees album (*The Monkees*, put out by Colgems/USA and RCA/ British). "It [the publishing] all had to be Screen Gems' and of course [Mike] Nesmith wrote some things but we ended up with ten cuts. Except for 'I Wanna Be Free,' everything we wrote was under some kind of deadline."

Eventually Tommy and Bobby signed with A&M as recording artists and charted five records, even a couple of Top 10s, the biggest of which was "I Wonder What She's Doing Tonight" (©1967). I ran into the two of them in Las Vegas about that time. I traveled up there every time Elvis played and they were usually around, wildly dressed and having a better time than strictly necessary. I remember Tommy in a crazy hat, laughing and hanging with songwriters Paul Anka, Paul Williams, John Phillips and others. Beautiful willing women were always nearby. "I think back about my career. The Monkees' stuff was what we were probably best known for—and I think about how all that happened occurred in just a year and a half. You don't know if the stars are lined up right or what, but something just clicks. There are other periods of my life when I just *know* I'm writing great stuff and nobody hears it . . . Maybe I'll get one cut that year."

From *The Tennessean*, 11/25/94:

Tommy Boyce shot himself early on Wednesday, November 23rd, in the living room in his home in Hillsboro Village, a Nashville suburb. Caroline, his wife of two months, had been sleeping upstairs and found the body.

There wasn't too much talk in the industry about Tommy's death. Unfortunately when someone in our line of work goes down I suppose certain suspicions inevitably arise, though as I inquired about the tragedy most people seemed either not to know the details or to not want to speak of it. There were some dark hints about Boyce's temper. When a contemporary commits suicide there is little doubt that it makes us feel safer in our skins to believe his own demons claimed him.

I was going down to Nashville once or twice a year to write with some people. I've always loved country—what they called pop music in the early '50s—I couldn't stand it! At that point though, Tommy lived in Nashville and we had not been writing together.

We were all so young, in a whirlwind. Because of the business we're in life sometimes takes us over. You're running on to the next thing you have to do. You go in different directions.

> *Boyce lived off his royalties and dabbled in the country music scene but it "wasn't coming together for him here," according to BMI/Nashville Vice-President, Roger Sorvine.*

Frances Preston talked about Tommy:

I talked to him about three days before he died. I talked to him all the time! I knew him back in his Monkees days and he hadn't changed. He was still joking around. When I first met him he lived in London and he would pull crazy jokes on his friends. One time he bought a rag doll and he called the rag doll "baby." He wrote postcards from all over the world, pictures of him and the rag doll. He would hold the camera out in front and take a picture of himself with the doll. He would put on wild clothes and pick up a guitar and go running through an audience any chance he got.

> *Jack Keller, Co-Producer of the first Monkees' album, said Tommy Boyce had suffered an [brain] aneurysm the previous year and "since then I've noticed he was sort of slightly a little bit different."*

"He did recover," Bobby explained, "although he probably could have died that night. It was Christmas Eve and Tommy was fifty-two years old. Instead, he was nursed back to health by his new wife, but I don't know that he ever really got his energy back."

At the time Bobby didn't know that Boyce continued to be a very sick man. "He'd be on the phone with me for an hour and a half, laughing and screaming and telling great stories."

Unbeknownst to Bobby Hart, afterward Tommy would take to his bed to recuperate, knowing the aneurysm could happen again and probably would.

He left a suicide note but the contents were not revealed.

So he just figured he'd check out, though for Tommy it couldn't have been an easy decision to make. He made farewell cassette tapes for certain people and bought roses for the occasion. He was a great guy. He was one of a kind with a heart of gold. We were buddies as well as partners and that meant a lot because it [the profession] can be very lonely.

I talked to Bobby for a while longer and he wished me a happy birthday as we both agreed that it's a shame songwriters can't stay closer and help each other out more from time to time.

"The only thing worse than missing Paradise is a short trip through it," so goes the old proverb, and for many songwriters the trip is a very short one. They have one record, or two, and spend too many years trying to recapture that elusive butterfly. It is a sad romance indeed when Fame falls out of love with a person, because they will always love and remember that short sweet ride. It is one, only one, of the hazards that lie alongside the songwriter's path.

And in the end, the love you take
Is equal to the love you make...
—LENNON & McCARTNEY,
EPILOGUE FROM "ABBEY ROAD"

Every generation of songwriters hates the next. The offspring are not usually so viciously opinionated as their predecessors as they can afford to be generous, even effusive in praise of a bunch of Old Farts who are either deceased, retired or struggling at making a living (i.e., not much of a threat). As for the Old Farts, they inevitably toast the encroaching generation with Chateau la Sour Rothschild. As early as 1939 Larry Hart complained to a reporter, "Where are the good new musical comedy composers? Whom can you think of that's come along in the last thirteen years?" Consider 1992, when Billy Joel was to be inducted into the Songwriters Hall of Fame, and toasted with a truly unforgettable vintage.

Irving Gordon had had a fortuitous season. His 1951 standard, "Unforgettable," had been a smash for Natalie Cole, singing a duet with her late father, the legendary Nat "King." Clever video computer wizardry had put father and daughter together on the video screen and that and

MTV and a striking performance from Natalie had generated phenome-nal sales. One would have expected Gordon to have been delighted by this surprising if unlikely turn of events and it was probably in anticipation of some salutary and good natured, even gracious, sentiment that he had been selected to receive a Song Citation and say a few words to the assembled multitude in advance of Mr. Joel's being presented with the small acrylic block that contains a faux bronze medal emblazoned with the logo of the National Academy of Popular Music Songwriters Hall of Fame. Directly preceding Mr. Gordon's speech, renowned rock 'n' rollers Mort Shulman and Doc Pomus, authors of such classics as "Save the Last Dance for Me," "Why Must I Be a Teenager In Love," and innumerable other genre hits had posthumously been inducted with much fanfare, including a special tribute from Frances Preston of BMI, a musical tribute from Arista recording artist Curtis Stiger, felicitations from hostess Leslie Uggams, and in a particularly poignant touch, eulogized by their surviving children as awards were presented on stage.

It fell to legendary songstress Margaret Whiting to introduce Mr. Gordon. Inauspiciously when presented with his plaque, the elder states-man of songwriting complained that, "it isn't right-side up." First, Gordon seemed to make an oblique apology for his previous remarks at the Grammy Awards (earlier that year, Gordon had maligned the Beatles, the Rolling Stones and others, preening in his acceptance speech, "It's nice to have a song come out that doesn't scream or yell or have a nervous break-down") and confessed that as a result of his speechmaking, many people had accused him of being "out of touch." On this evening he admitted to that. "That is true, I am completely out of touch. I feel like I came from another planet," he began in a gentle, almost self-demeaning tone, but it soon became apparent that the audience was in for a bumpy blast-off. In *his* galaxy, far, far away, Gordon insisted that the words and the music were "happily married," not "going through a violent divorce." He went on to say that in today's songwriting world melody is "looked at now like it was cholesterol. It's a *malady*, not a melody. And you have drums—cold-blooded drums on drums!" Gordon then found an ally in William Shakespeare, asserting that the Bard must have been referring to rock 'n' roll when he wrote the words, "sound and fury signifying nothing." The crowd in the Sheraton Hotel Ballroom had become malevolently quiet and sensing unease in the air, Gordon managed to mount another half-apology.

"I hope I'm not offending too many people," he smiled sweetly as murmurs of mutiny rumbled through the cheap seats. Margaret Whiting unsteadily grasped a supporting column in the background as Gordon ripped into The Artist Formerly Known As Prince and referred to his dropping of the Royal Drawers and "revealing his split personality." Sammy Cahn, possibly fearing that Gordon might eventually get around to lambasting the Chief Inductee and Guest of Honor (one could presume that "Allentown" hadn't been one of Mr. Gordon's favorites) leaped from the wings, grabbed both microphones on the podium and attempted to verbally persuade Gordon to "cease and desist." Gordon was having none of it. He was a man on a mission, insisting that "music is important in this culture." As Cahn grasped his shoulder Gordon shouted that the Songwriters Hall of Fame was not meant to be "some kind of Mutual Admiration Society." By now the men were physically grappling over possession of the mike booms and Gordon's speech began to fall apart in references to "violence in the streets," along with protests over the fact that his picture had not been included in the program, and so on. Eventually, he willingly left the stage after conducting a democratic poll to determine whether or not he should continue. An overwhelming majority was adamant in their preference. (At least two persons, Paul Simon and myself, felt that Gordon should have been allowed to finish his remarks.)

It may as well be admitted that many distinguished veterans insist that somehow the Beatles and others of their ilk—but especially the Beatles— were fundamentally to blame for the demise of the "Silver Age" of American songwriting. The "Golden Age" was already dead and gone, presumably dispatched by Leiber & Stoller, Mae Axton, and Jeff Berry, but mostly, we must assume, by Elvis Presley. In writing about Buddy Holly, Bill Haley, Eddie Cochran and Elvis, Dick Bradley cites several "Afro-American" practices that served to create what he called a *codal fusion* in the music of young, white Americans of that era, predominant among these, "the downgrading of melody . . . in the traditional tonal code sense," and goes on to describe "the abandoning of the tradition of melody which had characterized earlier [Caucasian] light and popular musics in Europe and America." Now this is the good part: "Furthermore, these records *demystified songwriting*. [Author's italics.] Holly, [Norman] Petty, Allison and one or two others were the authors of almost every hit the Crickets made, and there was nothing about the records [songs] which suggested they had employed any complex specialist skills . . . " A whole generation of mature American songwriters fancied that they possessed exactly those "complex specialist skills" and were anything but enthusiastic about children with electric guitars "demystifying" something as arcane and sacrosanct, mythic and metaphysical as The Craft. Rock 'n' roll musicians, Bradley elaborates, engineered the "downgrading/rejection of the instructions in the score." He says their electric technology "played a role in the movement away from large bands towards smaller ones . . . in the late 1940s and after." As for the lyricists, ". . . fast, dance-designed, loud music is very limited in terms of the types of lyrics which can be sung with, or within it. Simple exhortative phrases, lines of nonsense or brief conventional love lyrics which require and demand little attention are the most common lyric types found in early rock 'n' roll." It is easy to understand how threatened the Old Guard must have been by this perilous descent into what they could only perceive as anarchy. Oh indeed, they believed that some great tragedy of Atlantean proportions had occurred. According to Gene Lees, "The kids with guitars, who knew three or four chords and were devoid of literate sensibilities. They in turn affected not only the quality of the work of the next generation of 'composers' but that of the lyricists who weren't exposed to the words of Johnny Mercer and Yip Harburg and Howard Dietz, but only to those of the songwriters who supplied Elvis Presley."

There is no getting around Alec Wilder's contempt for "pop" songwriters. "I am convinced that movie music has always been one grade up from pop music and one grade down from theatre music," he wrote.

And in an epitaph that speaks eloquently of heartbreak and despair: "In just about the span of twenty-five years, the whole lovely, warm-hearted, clear-headed, witty, bittersweet world of the professional song-writer was gone." (All Wilder quotes from Gene Lees's *American Popular Song: The Great Innovators 1900–1950*, Oxford University Press.)

As early as 1957 Frank Sinatra (a songwriter, mind you, "I'm a Fool to Want You" with Jack Wolf and Joel Herron, ©1951) laid down this withering barrage:

> It [rock 'n' roll] is sung, played and written for the most part by
> cretinous goons; and by means of its almost imbecilic reiterations and
> sly, lewd—in plain fact, dirty lyrics—it manages to be the martial

music of every sideburned delinquent on the face of the earth . . .
— (*The Great Rock 'n' Roll Quote Book*, St. Martin's Griffin)

He went on to say that the music was "rancid-smelling," which if nothing else was a first for sound waves.

In his book, *Nice Work If You Can Get It*, Michael Feinstein recounted a story about Yip Harburg attacking contemporary lyrics in a 1978 lecture at UCLA and ranting, red in the face, about the Beatles and the damage they had done with their "bad" lyrics. Michael explained, "Most if not all of the great popular songwriters felt threatened by the new sounds of rock 'n' roll and the new openness about sex, gay and straight, that went with it in the 1960s. The overwhelming success of rock had pushed them out of the picture and they were angry and bitter about it." Whatever other achievement Irving Gordon attained on the night of May 27, 1992, there is reason to believe that he managed to fire the last live shot in the reactionary struggle between the Traditionalists and the Don't-Cares. Gordon died on December 1, 1996.

The British Invasion of the mid and late '60s with its emphasis on self-contained, autonomous writing groups, and an ensuing stampede of American imitators all together became a significant aftershock to the original rock 'n' roll earthquake. This proliferation of small, frequently amateurish bands began to put the squeeze on "light pop" writers who had previously supplied artists such as Pat Boone, Brian Hyland, Bobby Vinton, Sinatra, Little Anthony, Connie Francis, Dionne Warwick, Johnny Tillotson, the Everlys, Brenda Lee, Skeeter Davis, and even Paul Anka (who was a singer/songwriter before the fact!). This tilting landscape provided niches for veteran female writers like Carole King and Jackie DeShannon to become successful performers, something that might not have happened otherwise. Most songwriters of my own generation realized in the aftermath of Carole King's *Tapestry* (©1971) that if we did not begin to sing we were probably finished. The era of the "singer/songwriter" had dawned, and quickly on the scene and in charge were Joni Mitchell, Elton John, Paul Simon, Kris Kristofferson, Bob Dylan, Dan Fogelberg, Jackson Browne, James Taylor, Billy Joel, Laura Nyro, Carly Simon, David Gates and Randy Newman, among others. One has only to admire the financial elegance of the single singer/songwriter, traveling in an automobile or on one plane ticket, recording without the help of a cumbersome and expensive band or orchestra, writing words *and* music and recording only their own songs on album after album, *producing* themselves more often than not, to understand the precipitous decline of the traditional Tin Pan Alley "cigar smoking" songwriter/impresario.

The Old Guard has passed away. Irving Gordon, Sammy Cahn, Jule Styne, and Burton Lane were among the last of these and one might be forgiven for assuming that with them went the last vestiges of Professional Snobbism in our fair trade. Think again. Professional Snobbism is enjoying a resurgence in some altogether unlikely places. Rock 'n' roll has its own Hall of Fame these days and the once-maligned "cretinous goons," now lucky to be in their early fifties and ambulatory, are decanting their own Grapes of Wrath. In a recent issue of *Entertainment Weekly* (October 3, 1997), Keith Richard (guitarist/songwriter) groused, "I'm rapped out. I'm sick of 'Mary Had a Little Lamb' with a heavy handed drum machine going. I wish those guys would all shoot themselves." The latter in reference to recent murder and mayhem in the gangsta' ranks. "Carry on boys," he added.

In July 1996 *Details* magazine, Joni Mitchell responded to the somewhat loaded question, "what do you think of music these days?" "It's appallingly sick for the most part. It's boring chord movement and bad acting." Later she sounded off in *Rolling Stone* (March 7, 1997):

> [The new music is] building off something that wasn't very good in the first place. Back before the singer/songwriter, a very competent musician did the music, and a very competent lyricist did the words. But everybody does both now, so you've got a lot of mediocrity.

(Had Irving Gordon only lived a few more years he may have finally found an ally . . .)

John Cougar Mellencamp in the *New York Daily News* (April 9, 1997):

> There's not a lot of artistic development anymore. A record company puts out fifty records a year, figures a few of them will be hits and forgets about the rest. That's why very few artists from the nineties are going to be around in 2000.

We can credit Mellencamp with a more balanced, even benign overview than producing legend and songwriting collaborator, Phil Spector. The notoriously irascible and eccentric gun-toting inventor of the "Wall of Sound" who allegedly once ordered a passenger jet liner back to the departure gate because there were "too many losers" on board was typically outspoken when being presented with the TEC [Technical Excellence and Creativity] Hall of Fame Award on October 6, 1995. He first complained that "the Songwriters Hall of Fame will never induct me even though I've written little ditties like 'You've Lost that Lovin' Feeling' [with Barry Mann and Cynthia Weil] and 'Spanish Harlem' [with Jerry Leiber] and 'Be My Baby' [with Jeff Barry and Ellie Greenwich] and 'Da Doo Ron Ron' [also with Barry & Greenwich] and 'Chapel of Love' [again with Barry & Greenwich] and then I find out—of all things—that BMI sponsors the Songwriters Hall of Fame! And Frances Preston is like, one of the heads! [Preston is an Honorary Trustee of the Songwriters Hall of Fame along with Hal David and Marilyn Bergman among others.] So I congratulate you people a little bit, for proving why there are more horses' asses in this world than horses . . . " (In spite of this ill-temper, Frances Preston and BMI notwithstanding, Spector was inducted into the Songwriters Hall of Fame on June 10, 1997.) He went on to castigate today's music makers:

> The only way I can still answer that question "do you love it, still love it with a passion?," is if I didn't love this music and recording [it] with a passion, where would all the hate come from for all these people who do it badly? I hope I'm not offending too many people . . .

Spector smiled sweetly.

(Had Irving Gordon only lived a few more years he might have found *another* ally.)

> I get calls from the press about the deaths of everybody . . . and John [Lennon] of course was my closest friend for years and when Kurt Cobain died I got a lot of calls from the press telling me "oh, I haven't been this moved since John Lennon's death, would you like to make a comment?" And I said, "Excuse me, you don't know the difference between John Lennon and Kurt Cobain?" And they say, "no, no, no," and I say, "that's too bad, because Kurt Cobain did."
>
> —Phil Spector (TEC Awards, October 6, 1995)

Trent Raznor of Nine Inch Nails laments:

Rock 'n' roll should be about rebellion. It should piss your parents off, and it should offer some elements of taboo. It should be dangerous . . . but I'm not sure it really is dangerous anymore. Now thanks to MTV and radio, rock 'n' roll gets pumped into your house every second of every day. Being a rock 'n' roll star has become as legitimate a career option as being an astronaut or a policeman or a fireman.

We should have known we were in for trouble when a character in *Airheads*, a 1994 movie about a disgruntled rock band taking over a radio station, brags, "I'm screwed up and average enough that I could write the song that would live forever." Around about the same time this author heard an aspiring young musician postulating on a documentary-styled television program about a provincial rock band, "technically you can't have a band without music and stuff like that." He was apparently caught up in the heady camaraderie and testosterone-rich atmosphere of a four-way friendship that included as a peripheral activity some toying around with musical instruments out in the garage. (This is the mind-set that has resulted in CBS Orchestra leader Paul Shaffer referring to the present day as "the era of the non-playing band.") Concurrently the author observed a mature and intelligent young artist rhyming "misconstrued" and "destitute" with "you" in a song playing during NBC's *The Tonight Show*, heard advertisements rhyming "city boy" with "cowboy," "God" confidently rhymed with "slob," by a Top-10 writer, and in a recent song by the band Sponge, heard the phrase *"sixteen candles down the drain"* repeated ten times after each verse. As Noel Coward opined, "how potent cheap music is."

Paul Simon commented in the October 3, 1997 issue of *Entertainment Weekly*:

The *formats* are boring. None of the formats on radio apply to me, with the possible exception of public radio. Almost *none* of the mainstream interests me. So where do you go if they're not interested in what *you're* doing, and you're not interested in what *they're* doing?

This schism of taste between the generations has driven a wedge between most labels and their traditional strong sellers. Hall and Oates recently left Arista Records taking their album, *Marigold Sky*. Perhaps they were even "pushed" a little bit to release it on a label called "Push," which they partly own. David Brown said in the same issue of *Entertainment Weekly*, "Hall and Oates aren't the only veterans who no longer find themselves a priority for major labels. Former mega-sellers like Supertramp and Pat Benatar now record for Indie labels; some musicians like Arlo Guthrie and John Prine own and operate their own companies. This year, Crosby, Stills and Nash ended a twenty-nine-year relationship with Atlantic Records after a series of low-selling albums and are considering starting their own label."

Wynton Marsalis during a television interview:

> When you hear the same beat on every piece of music in our society it tells you something is wrong.

Is something wrong? Or is this just the age-old struggle between tradition and rebellion in its newest incarnation? I discussed this with Michael Stipe, who has a fairly even chronological perspective at the age of thirty-seven—somewhere between the "real" hippies and the current spate of imitators.

> Regarding today's music, I do think there's just a whole lot of crap out there. I'm not saying that it isn't valid for people to start bands and write songs, but a lot of it is not terribly inspired and I don't flatter myself that I'm speaking from on high because I don't particularly consider myself [to be] a great songwriter.

The overly modest Stipe sounds a note of tolerance in the generational Battle of the Bands:

> I wish that bands had more of an opportunity—as we did [R.E.M.]—to write those first thirty or forty songs before playing clubs, getting picked up by a label and turned into whatever. There's a point where one finds one's own voice and that's when it really starts to matter. The things that inspire me as a thirty-seven-year-old are very different from what inspired me as a twenty-year-old. Hopefully, at forty-seven or fifty-seven or even as a sixty-seven-year-old my desire to create music and to sing will lead me on my own path.

He goes on to say:

> We didn't feel we had to slay our elders necessarily in order to find our own voice and so our inspiration from the get-go was everything we had grown up listening to and admiring.

Each generation's songwriting comet seems to rise to its own peculiar zenith and then descend. On the twenty-first of June, 1966, Leonard Bernstein wrote:

> God forgive me, I have far more pleasure in following the musical adventures of Simon and Garfunkel or of the Association singing "Along Comes Mary" than I have in most of what is being written now by a whole community of avant-garde composers.

(Few if any of my own generation are unaware that Bernstein once showcased a young singer/songwriter named Janis Ian, who sang a racially charged ballad about premarital sex in the suburbs on his *Young People's Concerts* towards the end of the sixties.) By 1976 at the high tide of the singer/songwriter's heyday, Bernstein was disenchanted. He wrote:

> In the few years that have elapsed since [I wrote that] everything has changed. First of all, pop music is what I listen to least these days. What seemed fresh and vital then is now jejune and commercially grotesque.

Today's young songwriters are in their infancy. And as they find their mature voices there is little doubt that they will someday reach their own potential in spite of the pessimism and outright arrogance of preceding generations. One can't help but be confused, for instance, by Mike Greensill's (a virtuoso accompanist cum historian and curator to Weslia Whitfield and others) insistence that he detests "rock 'n' roll in an almost paranoid way. It's music for the crotch—they've taken away the melody." The sexual allusion is all too familiar, the complaint about missing melody now a tiresome cliché, but how then to deal with what follows? "I don't want to offend young writers," he dubiously asserts in the June 2, 1996 edition of *The New York Times Magazine*, "but we *have* the repertoire. It's 1920 to 1965, give or take, and there's a lifetime worth of material there . . . No one shouts, 'Why aren't they writing more Schubert songs?' because there's Schubert." (Classical composer Franz Schubert wrote over 500 songs.) This represents a fascinating quandary for a young person desiring to be an advanced songwriter. *"We hate what you're doing now but don't try to do anything better because at a certain point we will slam the door in your face. All the music has been written. And incidentally, the world is flat and if and when you get to the edge you will fall over. Now piss off."* In the same article by Jesse Green (with the inspiring title

"The Song Has Ended") Weslia Whitfield insists:

> Everytime I open one of those envelopes with a tape in it, I pray it will contain a wonderful new song. It rarely does. Most of it [the new music she has heard] is so sincere, so lacking in irony, so dreadfully intimate in the wrong way, it would be like getting up there and singing, "Now I'm going to kill myself and you're going to watch me," no thanks, I'll stick to the standards.

How interesting that the intelligentsia can complain so vociferously about the state of the Broadway musical and American songwriting in general without providing a bit more encouragement for the up-and-comers. As Jesse Green sums up the *New York Times* article, one full of disturbing transients (Barbara Cook slamming '60s singer/songwriters who "didn't know what they were doing," John Kander half heartedly blaming the Beatles yet again for something or other, unprovable assertions such as "by its nature, guitar-based music is harmonically limited, rhythm driven and . . . rigidly metrical," the eyebrow-raising insinuation that it was only the Jewish guys who were any good at it), then this, "the paradox then is that cabaret, despite its almost total dependence on nearly ancient material, is thriving, while new material in the standard tradition can't even get heard." [What a shame.] And finally, in what would seem almost an apology for all this bile, "partly it's the jealousy an older sibling feels for a younger sibling's greater success. Partly it's dismay over the inevitable dilution that occurs when an inheritance is passed on to too many heirs."

Whether it is an old-timer bitching about the chutzpah of some thirty-five-year-old Noel Coward imitator or an ex-long-haired hippie smashing the Pumpkins and hooting at the Blowfish, all could learn a lesson from the calm wisdom of Oscar Hammerstein II:

> Everyone is kicked around during his apprentice years and in fear and ignorance he makes silly blunders and does silly things of which he is ashamed later. If every successful man were to confess these past errors he could do a great service to those young people who are trying to follow in his footsteps.
>
> —*Notes On Lyrics* (©1949 Simon & Schuster)

(Hammerstein went on to confess grievous errors and illogic in some of his early lyric writing.)

If we were (are) an overly sentimental or saccharine songwriting generation, if we have (had) too much Vermouth in our collective Martini, who
can blame us? We grew up in the shadow of a real perceptible threat of
nuclear annihilation in a society which—in our time—began to slowly yet
methodically poison the ground beneath our feet and the rain that fell
from the skies. Our predecessors can't defend their glib, nonchalant, prissy,
over-rhymed savoir faire without admitting that top hat, white tie and all,
it comprised an elitist divertissement for wealthy and shallow people, who
were graduated by Ivy League colleges, cross-dressed in amateur chorus
lines and looked down their long thin noses at plebeians who didn't possess either the means or insincerity for such intellectual charades. The
Innovators were an unhappy, unholy bunch of coconuts for the most part.
Hopelessly self-involved, helplessly jealous of each other and inclined to
depraved addictions, self-disillusionment and most of the other ills
attributed by their champions almost exclusively to Rockers of my own
generation. They were Snobs, as were the people who bought expensive
tickets and went to glittering theatres to revel in that Snobbism.

Our generation has no more justifiable business in pointing the finger
at youngsters who grew up inundated beneath our whining obsession with
self, sex, and social injustice (what Jann Wenner once deftly dubbed "sob
stories of the rich and famous"), for striking out in some direction, any
direction, to seek new ground, even if the early results have been uneven.
These have been saddled with a record industry that doesn't give a flying
fart for artistry, which in fact would prefer a series of discardable bands to
"*Another Beatles*," that old song they like to sing every half-decade or so after
they've signed the wrong people and pulled the ripcords on their golden
parachutes. But the most unforgivable sin of our generation? We don't listen. We shamelessly criticize music we've never listened to. We brag about
it. "Oh I don't listen to that Shit. I don't listen to Rap! God, I hate that
Heavy Metal Shit! Oh man, I can't stomach the Reggae Shit! Oh, I never
bothered with any of that New Wave Shit! Shit, that Classical Shit makes
me want to go . . . well shit! Not to mention that Old Jazz Shit and that
Techno-Pop Shit. I fucking hate that Celtic Shit and that phony Hip-Hop
Shit! The only Shit I can stand is my Shit!" We have been playing this
game quite unsuccessfully for the longest time. As Gene Santoro, music
columnist for *The Nation* (December 4, 1995) frankly stated, "Many of
Rock's eighties' sub-groups loathed one another. Not surprisingly such

divisions resembled the ethnic politics both conservatives and liberals have played with such devastating, divisive results since the sixties."

> The most exciting contemporary music I've heard comes from the rap and hip-hop mode. It seems as though that's where the real energy is as those kids don't seem to be striving for anything except the interest of their own peer group. There's so much talent there, I'd like to be turned on to the melodic hip-hop.
>
> —Carly Simon

I, on the other hand, don't like listening to most of this shit better than anyone else of my generation but I do it anyway. I am a religious devotee of WFDU, Teaneck, New Jersey, which is an oracle of Fairleigh Dickinson University, for the last twenty-five years a voice of variety, an unbiased dispenser of disparate musical and sometimes political taste at 89.1 megacycles, "The right place to be on the left side of the dial." I have my suspicions that WFDU was born as an "underground" station—one of those fabulous organs of esoterica—in the late sixties or early seventies and though the programming has been subsequently divided into neat pie-shaped wedges—Vicky Sola who for sixteen years has presented her hot Salsa program on Saturdays from 12:00-3:00 P.M., Bob Westfield, who presents his new music alternative program on Saturdays from 5:00 P.M. until sign-off and again on Sunday from 6:00 P.M. until 12:00 A.M. under the banner "where new music begins," and of course Bill Halin and Ron Obrico with their "Traditions" program, and others, "Musicamerica," lots of blues, R&B/soul music and even a poet's corner (check your local listings)—and Lynn Crystal on Saturday afternoons at 3:00 hosting "Carnival of Song," a format that once might have been called "folk rock" with an emphasis on new songwriters, the ones that appeal to the current college-age crowd. I listen to all of the programming on KFDU if I am in my vehicle and this is why: One's ears are like any other muscle of the body, when they are not used they atrophy. No pain, no gain. It may shock that I would suggest that a sensitive individual subject themselves to the Chinese torture of listening to an entire program of new music/alternative (a genre that at times can sound surprisingly similar to a 1937 semi-automatic Maytag washing machine being attacked by a deranged army of shit-house rats armed with tire irons and chain saws) while the entire body squirms and the bile rises in the esophagus and the head begins to throb. It's essential for a few reasons. First, it is an antidote to ignorance. One can actually converse with a young person and understand, however vaguely, what branch of the current musical tree they are swinging from. If one wishes to criticize, then such criticism can be organized according to the principles of Aristotelian logic—not levied indiscriminately the way Dick Nixon condemned all of the music of the late '60s and early '70s as "drug music." Secondly— medicine is not famous for the pleasure we derive from its application. Vitamins which prolong life and lend a sharp edge to the gusto with which we attend our daily activities, taste like crap. I've never seen anyone accost a health freak on Venice Beach and say, "Hey! Could I munch down on some of those B-I's?" Eclectic and unfamiliar, even unpleasant musical genres are vitamins to the musical physique. If nothing else, they help us to immediately affirm a past belief. New music can even function as vaccine—we can aesthetically inoculate ourselves against some unperceived threat to our individual musical development—a process very easily—if simplistically— defined by the way we avoid repeating something that's already been done—a title, a lyric, a riff, an attitude or any intellectual property that rightfully belongs to someone else. Lastly, it is unlikely but remotely possible that we just might hear something that we *like!* In the last couple of years I've discovered some remarkable songwriting talent—if not new, then new to me which is the point entire.

There is Dan Byrne (album: *Self-Titled*) writing what has been described as folk for the skate punk generation, Susan Werner (album: *The Last of the Good Straight Girls*), Kate Jacobs, a little girl voice carrying some very heavy, dark songs, Terry Binion, formerly with the costume department of Disney World (album: *Shinola*), the well-thought-of Richard Shindell (heavily recorded by Joan Baez) and possibly the best of the bunch, Dar Williams, on Razor and Tie Records, writer of great songs like "Mortal City" (album: *End of Summer*). One of the best new songs I've heard is "There's Another Bruce Springsteen" by Frank Tedesso, a sweet man whose fog-horn of a voice seems to carry well across the dark and lonely harbors of the soul. I spoke with Lynn Crystal about the state of modern music and she admitted she sometimes has problems finding consistently great material.

> I had a hell of a time at first . . . musically at a loss. It may seem strange but I pick my music by reading lyrics. There have been times I haven't even heard the songs until they were on the air.

I asked her if she could think of any contemporary artists who write exceptional music (melody):

When I tried to think of someone on a level with, let's say, Paul McCartney, frankly I can't think of anybody. There's a kind of across-the-board complaint that I hear from a lot of people—WHERE'S THE MELODY?

The truth is that every songwriting generation has its good and bad talents. Much of what was written in the '20s, '30s, '40s was unabashed nonsense, *"boop, boop ditem datem whattam chu"* ("Three Little Fishies" ©1939, by Sayre Dowell), *"hidey, hidey hi, hidey, hidey, ho"* ("Minnie the Moocher," ©1931, by Cab Calloway and Irving Mills), *"mairzy doats and do-zy doats and liddle lam-zy div-ey; A kid-dle-y div-ey too, wouldn't you?"* ("Mairzy Doats," ©1943, Drake/Hoffman/Livingston), *"abba dabba dabba dabba* (etc.) *said the monkey to the chimp"* (Aba Daba Honeymoon," ©1914, by Arthur Fields and Walter Donovan), all stand-outs.

In the world of songwriting life goes on pretty much as usual as this book nears completion. Macey Lipman (Marketing) said in his Christmas message, December, 1997: "The record industry however, is on the upswing again, led by a beautiful mix of music from Streisand to Puff Daddy and from Spice Girls to LeAnn Rimes." Though Lipman lamented a declining cassette market, he insisted it was "still viable."

Among other things Lipman said that holiday business was up by 10.4 percent, that average soundtrack sales were up 7.5 percent and that, as a whole, there was "almost a 50 percent gain in retailers reporting business 'up' this year."

Tot-Pop is in. In *Time* magazine's 1997 May issue, Christopher Farley notes that "after pushing waves of twenty-something alternative rock bands in the early nineties, some record companies are turning to even younger groups . . . Hanson has just come out with *Middle of Nowhere* (Mercury). The youngest Hanson is only eleven years old. Pop-grunge band Radish (led by fifteen-year-old singer Ben Kweller and the object of a bidding war) has issued *Restraining Bolt* (Mercury) and sixteen-year-old Jonny Lacy has sold more than 150,000 copies of his debut album, *Lie to Me* (A&M).

"It's unfortunate," Farley sums up, "that all three acts have come up with immature, mediocre albums that are as much fun as a wet sandbox . . . it's too bad Dr. Spock never wrote a book on raising rock stars."

"There are more than 100 music copyright infringement cases in federal courts across the country today," said Ward Morehouse III, in the *New York Post*, September 23, 1996. Andrew Lloyd Webber, for one, is involved in a David vs. Goliath struggle with Ray Repp, an unknown songwriter from Maryland, who claims Webber stole "the Phantom song" from his religious number, "Till You," which has, to date, had no sales to speak of. Lloyd Webber counterclaims that Repp stole "Till You" from "Joseph and His Amazing Technicolor Dreamcoat." Despite the degree of the withering of the marketplace, the chance of being litigated and the ignominy of being, after all, only the name in parentheses, the potential of great songwriting and its therapeutic effect on the world in which we live is impossible to exaggerate. Being a songwriter is an important job. In his acceptance speech at his induction into the Songwriters Hall of Fame, Billy Joel spoke of his experiences in the [then] Soviet Union and his encounters with citizens from many walks of life who were amazingly familiar with American songs. "I realized once again how important it is, what we do," Joel said, "and we tend to denigrate it and we make fun of it and I tend to slough it off, but the children of these songwriters, of the Doc Pomuses and the Mort Schulmans should know that the Cold War didn't end because of Nixon and Agnew, but maybe because of Schulman and Pomus, okay? They knew us through the music of Doc and Mort, Lennon and McCartney, Paul Simon and Bob Dylan, even though their graffitti artists spelled Dylan, D-i-l-l-o-n." Take notice people, 'twas rock 'n' roll that killed the beast, 'twas 'I Wanna Hold Your Hand,' and Levi 501's that brought down the Berlin Wall, not missles and anti-Communist rhetoric.

The sinking of the *Titanic* in 1912 and all its attendant drama and public outcry made stars of an Italian inventor named Marconi and "wireless" or *radio* in that order. The world was breathless with the idea that messages had been sent invisibly through the air by the stricken liner even if to little or no avail. Marconi, the self-proclaimed "discoverer" of the radio wave, was portrayed in a *New York Times* cartoon with a laurel wreath crowning his brow—a modern day Mercury. In actual fact, the first man to have demonstrated the viability of sending messages "through the ether" via radio waves had been an eccentric Croatian named Nikola Tesla. In 1893 Tesla had demonstrated the first radio transmission at the National Electric Light Association in St. Louis, Missouri. Though the message was only transmitted a distance of thirty feet it was nevertheless a proper radio broadcast incorporating all the fundamental principles of modern radio.

On December 24th, 1906, a disciple of Tesla's named Reginald Fessenden commenced the first known public radio broadcast from Brant Rock on the sea coast twenty miles southeast of Boston to an audience of ships. Fessenden played a recording of Handel's "Largo," and his own version of "Oh, Holy Night," one verse of which he sang. He then read a bible verse. By 1932 twelve million American homes—two out of every five—boasted a radio and a curious thing happened to the infant record industry's sales figures: *they accelerated.*

> Radio has forced us into a long, dark narrow hall, a corridor of people obsessed to fit us into the margins of what "makes a hit" because the "suits" have taken over and there are few record company heads like Jack Holtzman, who was interested in the music at least as much as he was the money, and proud to have and love the great artists on his label even if their records didn't sell or "go gold." Now at the top we have too many people who don't know about or even like music.
>
> —Carly Simon

If physicists and other adherents to the theories of Albert Einstein are to be believed, Fessenden's program is still floating, perfectly intact and decipherable in the black void of outer space and traveling away from this earth at the speed of light (186,000 miles per second) and will continue until possibly at some point in eternity it will curve back upon and catch up with itself. Somewhere out there the *Titanic* is still sending out the S.O.S. that was never answered. Likewise, the Glenn Miller Orchestra is playing a live concert from The Casino on Avalon Bay in wartime. Minnie Pearl is calling hogs and yellin', *"Howdeeeee!,"* from the stage of the Ryman Auditorium. Alan Freed is still on the air and the payola scandal hasn't happened yet. That means, if you will indulge this far-flung Saganesque fantasy for a few more moments, that an awful lot of music is on its way out to distant galaxies where—we have been told—someone or ones may be listening even as I write and you read. Or—all those songs—all that Hoagy Carmichael and Johnny Mercer and Hank Williams and Tommy Boyce and Bobby Hart and Marc Cohn and Sheryl Crow and Jerry Lee Lewis and Peter, Paul & Mary, and Jerry Herman—all kinds of songs from every imaginable genre—space being no respector of different sounds, and styles are cruising along in a great unending ragtag Battlestar Galactica-like fleet of songs—as yet unheard and undiscovered on their way to God Knows Where.

Meanwhile, back on Mother Earth, human ants are indefatigably and industriously engineering their own demise, busily constructing an all-carcinogenic environment, mishandling apocalyptic viruses and being remarkably nonchalant about the whereabouts of many a black market nuclear device—being careless enough in fact that some day in the not too distant future those songs—that vast moving formation of music—along with the movies, newscasts and television shows that accompany them might very well be all that remains of us.

It is *inevitable*, scientists say, that eventually a large asteroid or even a comet will impact the earth, possibly resulting in the extinction of our species and some would say no great loss, even cause for celebration among the elephants, rhinos and grizzly bears. (It is easy to imagine all the cockroaches and rats getting together for a not overly somber memorial service.) And then out there somewhere, someday, the spaceborne remains of our entire civilization will eventually be found sounding clear as a bell after its eternal journey and the equivalent of a giant intelligent butterfly will gawk in wonder and converse telepathically with its friends as they watch the *Honeymooners* and attempt to decrypt the meaning of "to the moon, Alice!" But what of our emotions, dreams and heartaches, the stuff that really made us what we were? How would a thinking butterfly begin to suspect the existence of those? By listening to our songs, of course. And after all is said and done perhaps these are the most important works we could ever leave behind us as evidence that we were at times caring beings in spite of our penchant for violence and unilateral destruction. The butterflies care not a whit for our buildings and television programs and nuclear bombs but they fall in love with our music (they are particularly fond of Joe Raposo's "It's Not Easy Being Green") and are eventually known throughout the universe as a beautiful, iridescent singing race of winged songwriters.

Respectfully dedicated to the memory of the songwriters who have left us during the writing of this book. A partial list includes:

Mae Axton	September 14, 1914–April 9, 1997
Sonny Bono	February 12, 1935–January 5, 1998
Tommy Boyce	September 29, 1944–November 23, 1994
Jeff Buckley	November 17, 1966–May 29, 1997
Irving Caesar	July 4, 1895–December 17, 1996
Sammy Cahn	June 18, 1913–January 15, 1993
Cab Calloway	December 25, 1907–November 8, 1994
Kurt Cobain	February 20, 1967–April 5, 1994
John Denver	December 31, 1943–October 12, 1997
Sims Ellison	March 10, 1967–June 6, 1995
Jerry Garcia	August 1, 1942–August 9, 1995
Morton Gould	December 10, 1913–February 21, 1996
Michael Hutchence	January 22, 1960–November 22, 1997
Burton Lane	February 12, 1912–January 5, 1997
Jonathan Larson	February 4, 1960–January 25, 1996
Nicolette Larson	July 17, 1952–December 16, 1997
Henry Mancini	April 16, 1924–June 14, 1994
Gerald Marks	October 13, 1900–January 27, 1997
Linda McCartney	September 24, 1942–April 17, 1998
Bob Merrill	May 17, 1921–February 17, 1998
Roger Miller	January 2, 1936–October 25, 1992
Harry Nilsson	June 15, 1941–January 15, 1994
Laura Nyro	October 18, 1947–April 5, 1994
Carl Perkins	April 9, 1932–January 19, 1998
Eddie Rabbitt	November 27, 1941–May 8, 1998
Charlie Rich	December 14, 1932–July 25, 1995
Tupac Shakur	June 16, 1971–September 13, 1996
Frank Sinatra	December 12, 1915–May 14, 1998
Jule Styne	December 31, 1905–September 20, 1994
Carl Wilson	December 21, 1946–February 6, 1998
Tammy Wynette	May 5, 1942–April 6, 1998

PUBLISHING CREDITS

index